LABYRINTHS OF DECEIT

Culture, Modernity and Identity in the Nineteenth Century

LIVERPOOL ENGLISH TEXTS AND STUDIES 44

LABYRINTHS OF DECEIT

Culture, Modernity and Identity in the Nineteenth Century

Richard J. Walker

LIVERPOOL UNIVERSITY PRESS

First published 2007 by
Liverpool University Press
4 Cambridge Street
Liverpool L69 7ZU

British Library Cataloguing-in-Publication data
A British Library CIP record is available

ISBN 978-0-85323-849-2 cased

Typeset by XL Publishing Services, Tiverton
Printed and bound in the European Union by Biddles Ltd, King's Lynn

Contents

Part III

Infected ecstasy: addiction and modernity in the work of Thomas De Quincey, Alfred Tennyson, Christina Rossetti and Bram Stoker

Acknowledgements

I would like to thank Professor Tony Lopez, Dr Robert Gee and Professor Geoff Ward, who supported this project in its early stages. Thanks also to all my friends at the University of Plymouth where it had its origins. I must also acknowledge the support and friendship of colleagues at the University of Central Lancashire, particularly the office staff in the Department of Cultural Studies, and Dr Daniel Lamont, Karen Adams, Dr Alizon Brunning and Dr Jason Lee. The English Literary Studies cohort of 1999–2002 had to put up with me using some of the ideas in this book in their seminars. The R. L. Stevenson conferences at Stirling and Gargnano made appreciative noises when I presented some of the work as papers. The chapter on Thomas De Quincey first appeared in an abbreviated form in S. Brewster *et al.* (eds.), *Inhuman Reflections: Thinking the Limits of the Human* (Manchester: Manchester University Press, 2000). Thanks to Robin Bloxsidge at Liverpool University Press for his patience. This book is dedicated to Tony and Celia Walker whose help, support and encouragement have been incomparable.

Introduction
Tracing the fragments of modernity

All Truth is change.[1]

All that is solid melts into air.[2]

this strange disease of modern life,
With its sick hurry, its divided aims.[3]

What is it like to be in a state of crisis? To be more specific what is it like to be in a state of crisis in the nineteenth century? The aim of this book is to explore such a condition and to ask, as a significant sub-clause: what is it like to be modern in the nineteenth century? This interaction between crisis and modernity is not a randomly chosen connection. Isobel Armstrong, in her radical rethinking of the political and subversive elements of Victorian poetry, states that 'Victorian modernism, as it emerges in its poetics, describes itself as belonging to a condition of crisis which has emerged directly from economic and cultural change.'[4]

Armstrong's positioning of Victorian culture, in particular its poetics, in direct correlation with a cultural and socio-economic topography effectively conflates the two questions posited above; nineteenth-century modernity as it appears in cultural representation is intrinsically equated with crisis. In Armstrong's definition modernism in terms of poetics doesn't get engendered by crisis or act as a response to it, it is explicitly affiliated with it; the definition therefore identifies a significant act of belonging – to engage with the strategies and devices of Victorian modernism is to be in crisis. In his study of the Gothic, *The Literature of Terror*, David Punter argues that the genre arises from a period that is affiliated with Armstrong's sense of the 'economic and cultural' changes which instigate crisis; in his investigation of the effect of these changes on culture Punter suggests that

> The period which saw the birth of the Gothic novel was that in which the early forces of industrialization were producing vast changes in the ways people lived and worked. Rural patterns of life were being broken up by enclosure of land and by the labour demands of urban-centred industry. The stability of an, at least theoretically, long-accepted social structure was being dissolved amid the pressure of new types of work and new social roles ... In the most general terms, it was of course changes of this kind that occasioned so much romantic writing.[5]

Punter refers of course to the late eighteenth and early nineteenth century, the decades conventionally associated with the main impact of the Industrial Revolution upon the British landscape and on British social structures, and also the period most closely associated with British Romanticism; indeed Armstrong defines the Victorians as 'post-Romantic' and 'post-industrial', suggesting that the changes assessed by Punter are already in operation by the time of Victorian modernism.[6] Nonetheless, certain connections can be established between the two analyses in that both identify a state of crisis emerging out of a radically reconfigured social and economic climate. At the heart of this change is urbanization. Indeed the metropolis becomes a central motif within, if not the explicit location for, the condition of crisis alluded to by Armstrong.

William Wordsworth, in a passage from *The Prelude* of 1805, also cited by Punter, compares an urban fair to the early nineteenth-century city experience:

> Oh, blank confusion! and a type not false
> Of what the mighty city is itself
> To all except a Straggler here and there –
> To the whole swarm of its inhabitants –
> An undistinguishable world to men,
> The slaves unrespited of low pursuits
> Living amid the same perpetual flow
> Of trivial objects, melted and reduced
> To one identity, by differences
> That have no law, no meaning, and no end.[7]

Punter describes the passage as 'Wordsworth's lament ... for stability, for a social system in which people knew their place'; in effect what starts out as a description rapidly turns into a critique of the urban condition and the city experience itself.[8] The poem posits the fair as a microcosmic and metonymic representation of the macrocosmic city. The experience as depicted by Wordsworth is more complex than a mere lament for past stability and social structures, however, anticipating, even literally providing a prelude, for many of the issues that will be significant in this book. The predominant feature of the urban condition is its chaotic nature, what Wordsworth refers to as its 'confusion'; this feature is intensified in the state of flux implicit in the 'perpetual flow of trivial objects' which branches out into the anarchy of 'no law, no meaning, and no end' where the city-dweller cannot read the plethora of signs in an 'undistinguishable world'. Within this topography strange things start to happen to identity and the individual: the inhabitants of the city become a 'swarm', further dehumanizing the mass, and ultimately they are 'melted and reduced / To one identity'. Again flux and change are evoked as the city induces a state of disidentity for its dwellers with Wordsworth using a vocabulary that anticipates many of the discussions of modernity in the nineteenth century.[9] At its core the experience is contradictory for the city generates a consciousness of the strange and the alien, yet also, through the creation of a dehumanized mass, induces uniformity; as Stallybrass and White put it, '[i]n the city ... differences proliferate and at the same time melt into one identity'.[10] In his reading of modernity Marshall Berman suggests that the notions of crisis and the representations of uncontrollable flux rise from a fundamental sense of division in nineteenth-century life; he argues that the

> public shares the feeling of living in a revolutionary age, an age that generates explosive upheavals in every dimension of personal, social and political life. At the same time, the nineteenth-century modern public can remember what it is like to live, materially and spiritually, in worlds that are not modern at all. From this inner dichotomy, this sense of living in two worlds simultaneously, the ideas of modernization and modernism emerge and unfold.[11]

For Berman at the root of nineteenth-century modernity there exists a basic sense of inner conflict, one that takes place between an oscillating consciousness of the old and the new. Out of these inherent conflicts and contradictions – between an apprehension of a premodern world and a modern and apparently chaotic world – emerges 'modernization and modernism'; without claiming that Wordsworth is the starting point for literary modernism, in many ways the passage cited above dramatizes the tensions and conflicts argued for by Berman.

As I have stated, many of the features in the passage from *The Prelude* prefigure the concerns of this book; and as David Punter points out, the extract is indicative of Wordsworth's anxiety regarding the chaos and confusion inherent in the industrialized city of the early nineteenth century. By the late nineteenth century, and in particular its conception of a *fin de siècle*, the urban crisis for identity as Wordsworth envisages it has transmuted into a malady. In his study of *fin de siècle* degeneration theory William Greenslade discusses this correlation between the city and sickness: 'Urban living, its diseases and pathologies, were leaving metropolitan men and women vulnerable to fatigue and debility from prolonged exposure to the pressures of the very environment which had formed them.'[12] What Greenslade argues for is a situation where urban living perpetuates its own debilitation: exposure to the territory that one lives in perversely involves exposure to 'fatigue and debility'; in short, to live in the city is to live in a climate conducive to maladies, psychosomatic or otherwise. Citing the degeneration theorist Max Nordau, Greenslade expands upon this paradoxical juxtaposition of urban life and sickness by suggesting, in a phrase that echoes Sigmund Freud's essay of the same name, that there is 'an early psychopathology of everyday life' and that 'living in a modern city was like living on the edge of nervous collapse'.[13] The extraordinary condition of 'psychopathology' is effectively translated into the ordinary environment of 'everyday life' – the life of the late nineteenth-century urban dweller. The experience of modernity is therefore one of being on the 'edge of nervous collapse'; Armstrong's invocation of a 'condition of crisis' for Victorian modernism becomes a literal mental condition, a breakdown, in Greenslade's perception of *fin de siècle* modernity. Greenslade concludes that

> the late nineteenth-century city was a territory of immanent breakdown, where the contours of that territory and the map which described it were conflated. Symptoms of the city 'condition', such as neurasthenia and hysteria, have been inherited, and so have become the determinants of the 'condition' from which they have been bred. Both symptoms are observable states of disorder and generalized symptoms of the prevailing condition.[14]

The situation is crystallized in this statement, the map of the city is the map of 'a territory of immanent breakdown' where perpetuation is the key to the malady: the city 'condition' breeds symptoms such as 'neurasthenia and hysteria' which in turn define and determine the 'condition' itself. Where Wordsworth's city is marked by 'confusion' and 'perpetual flow' and Armstrong's definition of Victorian modernism stems from the economic changes that create the nineteenth-century metropolis, Greenslade's late nineteenth-century urban environment is defined as infected, hypochondriacal and in 'observable states of disorder'. For Wordsworth, in the early decades of the century, the identity of the individual is levelled out, 'melted and reduced' to a faceless uniformity. By the close of the nineteenth-century identity in the city has become quite literally a 'condition' – to be modern in the *fin de siècle* metropolis is to be sick.

I stated above that I would be asking questions with a degree of historical specificity; in response to this it is possible to argue that the tracing of the nineteenth-century city that takes place above is too loose in terms of a sense of chronology and genre, running as it does between Victorian poetics, the Gothic novel, British Romanticism and *fin de siècle* degeneracy theory. Of course it is clearly necessary to testify that as much as there are similarities between these areas there are also significant differences, ones which I will address in due course. That said, there are traces that run through culture in the nineteenth century which can be identified and equated with the sense of crisis which has already been discussed. Isobel Armstrong establishes such traces when she refers to anxieties which

> belong to fundamental changes wrought at the end of the eighteenth century. It is the habit of marking off Victorian from Romantic which disguises the anxieties common to early and later nineteenth-century writers. But there is a difference, a difference in perception, for [the Victorians] lived with these problems in an acute and morbid form because they intensified with continued economic and political change in the nineteenth century.[15]

Armstrong provides an implicit criticism of twentieth-century literary classifications and chronologies that habitually isolate Romantic and Victorian writers. In suggesting that the anxieties inherited from changes that took place at the end of the eighteenth century are features that link writers working at the beginning and end of the nineteenth century, Armstrong effectively supports the establishment of connections between Punter's Romanticism and Greenslade's *fin de siècle* study. Nonetheless she certainly privileges the Victorians, suggesting that their experience of these problems is intensified by accelerated 'economic and political change'; as a result her argument that they manifest themselves in 'an acute and morbid form' correlates with Greenslade's definition of the psychopathology of late nineteenth-century life. If Victorian cultural life is defined by acute morbidity, everyday life eventually becomes defined by the hysteria and neurasthenia referred to by Greenslade.

The similarities yet also marked differences that exist in and create a tension between early and later nineteenth-century writing can be assessed most appropriately through the use of example. Percy Bysshe Shelley's 'Ozymandias' (1817) and Matthew Arnold's 'Dover Beach' (probably written in 1851 and published in 1867) are two of the most familiar poems of the nineteenth century; one is a central poem in the canon of British Romantic writing, the other probably Arnold's most famous lyric.[16] What links the two poems is a series of themes which revolve around fragmentation, disintegration and dislocation; ultimately it is the manner of approach to these motifs that constitutes the fundamental departure between the two writers and reveals the extent to which Armstrong's sense of the 'morbid' emerges in Victorian poetics. The location of Shelley's sonnet is the desert sands of Egypt, while Arnold's lyric opens on the shingled beach of Dover, the environment for each could hardly seem more different; nonetheless as a basic starting point both create a fragmentary and ever-shifting milieu. It is worth quoting 'Ozymandias' in full:

> I met a traveller from an antique land,
> Who said – "Two vast and trunkless legs of stone
> Stand in the desart. … Near them, on the sand,
> Half sunk a shattered visage lies, whose frown,
> And wrinkled lip, and sneer of cold command,
> Tell that its sculptor well those passions read
> Which yet survive, stamped on these lifeless things,
> The hand that mocked them, and the heart that fed;
> And on the pedestal, these words appear:
> My name is Ozymandias, King of Kings,
> Look on my Works, ye Mighty, and despair!
> Nothing beside remains. Round the decay

> Of that colossal Wreck, boundless and bare
> The lone and level sands stretch far away."[17]

The presence of fragmentation is obvious here, manifest in the 'trunkless legs of stone' and the 'shattered visage' of the 'colossal wreck' that constitute the decaying remains of the statue of Ozymandias. What we pay witness to is a symbol of collapse and disintegration in a poem that mocks the grandiose affirmation inscribed on the pedestal of the statue – 'Look on my Works, ye Mighty, and despair!' The sense of fragmentation is compounded by the environment, a desertscape symbolizing the sands of time that slowly but inexorably conceal all trace of Ozymandias. Identity is effectively translated into disidentity in the sonnet; Ozymandias' claim to history and legacy, contained in the affirmation of self – 'My name is Ozymandias, King of Kings' – is rendered meaningless through the ruin of the statue and its presence in the apocalyptic 'terminal beach' of the desert sands that 'boundless and bare ... stretch far away'.[18] Ultimately what intensifies the fragmentation represented in the poem is the way in which Shelley utilizes a distanced voice; the words of Ozymandias are conveyed to us by the poetic voice via 'a traveller from an antique land', resulting in a complex concatenation of poetic travelogue, history lesson and allegory. The result is a poem that subtly dislocates its own representation of dislocation through a systematic displacement of inscription and utterance. Shelley's achievement is to bind up all these aspects of fragmentation and dislocation in a polished sonnet and to give the conception of distance in the poem, whether historical or one of location, an unerringly contemporary message about power, history and civilization. Indeed, David Punter sees Shelley's project as an 'object-lesson in the transience of empire' with the poem arguably becoming a palimpsest inscribed 'over the decaying manuscript of the West'.[19]

Shelley's vignette of the ruined statue of an Egyptian king is therefore opened out into an ironic political and cultural allegory; Punter's suggestion that the poem is a comment on the 'transience of empire' is particularly convincing when the claims represented on the pedestal of the statue, along with their alleged permanence, are juxtaposed with the ruins and their location. Imperial claims effectively become an exercise in archaeology recounted by travellers from 'antique' lands. By contrast, Matthew Arnold's 'Dover Beach', written at the middle of the nineteenth century, initially seems unconcerned with notions of fragmentation or collapse. Indeed, what makes Arnold's lyric so unsettling is that the opening lines seem to affirm the stability and permanence of English national identity and imperial aspiration:

> The sea is calm to-night.
> The tide is full, the moon lies fair
> Upon the straits; – on the French coast the light
> Gleams and is gone; the cliffs of England stand,
> Glimmering and vast, out in the tranquil bay. (lines 1–5)[20]

The emphasis in these first five lines is upon durability, tranquility and security. The sea is 'calm', the tide is 'full', and the 'cliffs of England' – here the White Cliffs of Dover, that symbol of Englishness itself – shine in the moonlight 'vast' in the 'tranquil bay'. By this point the poem seems to be an exercise in patriotism and national cohesion, a suggestion emphasized by the juxtaposition of England with a France whose 'light / Gleams and is gone'. However, the motif of fragmentation that so marks Shelley's 'Ozymandias' immediately intrudes upon this seemingly placid scene, and the poem begins to undermine its initial sense of unity:

> Only, from the long line of spray
> Where the sea meets the moon-blanch'd land,
> Listen! You hear the grating roar
> Of pebbles which the waves draw back, and fling,
> At their return, up the high strand,
> Begin, and cease, and then again begin,
> With tremulous cadence slow, and bring
> The eternal note of sadness in. (lines 7–14)

The presence of the 'eternal note of sadness' in these lines, along with the insistent repetition of the motion of the tide in 'Begin, and cease, and then again begin', suggests a reiteration of permanence within the poem, and the 'eternal note of sadness' is certainly a concern of Arnold's at this point. However, as we move from the representation of an apparently real sea scene to a metaphoric one that ushers this theme of sadness in, Arnold's use of a landscape dominated by the 'grating roar' and the 'tremulous cadence' of pebbles flung by the tide onto Dover beach evokes a fragmented environment that can be juxtaposed with Shelley's desert sands. As the sands of time have effectively brought about the collapse of the statue of Ozymandias for Shelley, in

Arnold's lyric the fragmentary pebbles of Dover beach are gradually eroding the symbol of English national identity and permanence, the White Cliffs of Dover, and the 'tremulous cadence' of the noise that they make heralds Arnold's meditation upon and lament for cultural stability.

The dissonant noise made by the pebbles and the effect that they implicitly have upon the cliffs of Dover shifts the poem from its contemplative mode to one of dislocation; effectively Arnold's poem, in spite of the plea for permanence in 'eternal' sadness, cannot decide where to settle from line 15 onwards. As the White Cliffs of Dover seem to become decaying monuments to English national identity, broadly equatable with the statue in Shelley's poem, Arnold shifts his perspective and initially provides the reader with a history lesson in the permanence of Classical culture:

> Sophocles long ago
> Heard it on the Aegaean, and it brought
> Into his mind the turbid ebb and flow
> Of human misery; we
> Find also in the sound a thought,
> Hearing it by this distant northern sea. (lines 15–20)

Again the poem enters ambivalent territory; what Arnold seems to be suggesting is a link between the culture of ancient civilization, represented here by the reference to Sophocles, and that of the modern. He suggests that the note of sadness heard on Dover Beach was also heard by Sophocles on the shores of the Aegean, and that the insistent motion of the tide detected on the former shore is echoed in the 'turbid ebb and flow / Of human misery' traced in Sophocles' work. Arnold is certainly engaged in a poetic process of establishing connections – here between his own ruminations and Sophocles – but there is a crucial difference that problematizes these links. In the final line of this section Arnold describes the sound of 'human misery' being heard 'by this distant northern shore'; his own location is crucially 'distant', suggesting a dislocation from the permanence of Classical culture which undermines the connections that he strives to establish. In Arnold's poem the contemporary effectively becomes distant, a notion that catalyses the sense of alienation that marks the later stages of the poem. Where Shelley's use of distance and dislocation subtly undermines the claims inscribed upon the statue of Ozymandias, covering up the symbols of monarchic power and pointing to, in Punter's words, the 'transience of empire', Arnold's use of distance in relation to the contemporary indicates the transience of modern culture for the poet.

From a contemplation of the fragility of nation and culture, Arnold moves to religion:

> The Sea of Faith
> Was once, too, at the full, and round earth's shore
> Lay like the folds of a bright girdle furl'd.
> But now I only hear
> Its melancholy, long, withdrawing roar,
> Retreating, to the breath
> Of the night-wind, down the vast edges drear
> And naked shingles of the world. (lines 21–28)

The ambivalence of the earlier sections of the poem is lost; what remains is unequivocal as Arnold depicts the decline of religion. The presence of the sea is again evident, here in the figurative 'Sea of Faith'. However, where the rhythms of the tide seemed to imbue the poem with a semblance of stability that linked past and present in its earlier stages, now the tide has lost even that element of permanence, becoming just a 'melancholy, long, withdrawing roar'. What we are left with is another apocalyptic 'terminal' beach, with the world becoming 'vast edges drear / And naked shingles'; the result is an environment that is as 'boundless and bare' as the desert in Shelley's poem. Both poets utilize similar terms. Shelley's desert is 'bare' and Arnold's beach is 'naked'; however, where the sands of time in 'Ozymandias' are ultimately covering up the 'Half sunk' statue, 'Dover Beach' lays bare the vulnerable culture of the modern world. It is in the final lines of the poem that the state of crisis hinted at in its earlier stages emerges fully:

> Ah, love, let us be true
> To one another! for the world, which seems
> To lie before us like a land of dreams,
> So various, so beautiful, so new,
> Hath really neither joy, nor love, nor light,
> Nor certitude, nor peace, nor help for pain;
> And we are here as on a darkling plain

Swept with confused alarms of struggle and flight,
Where ignorant armies clash by night. (lines 29–37)

Having found nation, culture and religion all lacking, Arnold seemingly tries to find respite from despair by converting the poem into a conventional paean to the security of love, and perplexingly the lyric *seems* to become a love poem in its final stages thereby dispelling the pessimism of its earlier sections. That said, the incongruous and desperate appeal for stability contained in 'Ah, love, let us be true / To one another' proves to be illusory, for Arnold brutally undercuts this affirmation in his apocalyptic depiction of a world that, amongst all its failings and shortcomings, does not and cannot 'really' have love. It is in this final section that the unsituated nature of Arnold's perspective is established; even the apparent certitude of the 'long, withdrawing roar' of the Sea of Faith is rejected in favour of emphatic contradictions. What Arnold stresses is the insubstantial nature of the modern world which '*seems* / To lie before us like a land of *dreams*' (my emphasis), its very modernity stressed by the inclusion of the adjective 'new'. What the poetic voice finds is that this world contradicts all the promises that it offers and ultimately will not allow even an appeal for love. Where Shelley's desert is barren and empty, save for the traveller and the ruined statue, Arnold's is crammed and chaotic, 'Swept with confused alarms of struggle and flight, / Where ignorant armies clash by night'; the dignified 'ebb and flow' of 'human misery' found in Classical tragedy is parodied in the 'struggle and flight' of the shadowy armies. The lasting impression is of a vision of the world in a state of crisis, where the touchstones of nation, culture, religion and even love fail the speaker, and of a poem where the poetic voice cannot settle because the contemporary world is so dislocated from the institutions that it values. What we witness is a lucid evocation of alienation and fragmentation in a poem that systematically overthrows and undermines all the values that the poetic voice identifies with. What links Arnold and Shelley's individual poems is their use of images of fragmentation and dislocation; however, Shelley's maintains an ironic note in the undermining of the claims of Ozymandias and the location of his petrified statue in the uninhabited and desolate desert whereas Arnold's is a pessimistic lament for the contemporary which cannot maintain its connections with past culture with any credibility. Where Shelley's poem establishes a distance from the Classical past with a celebratory composure which simultaneously criticizes the aspirations of empire, Arnold's becomes an anguished, dislocated and unsettled representation of cultural alienation in the modern world which demonstrates the morbidity of Victorian poetry detected by Armstrong.

In 1856, approximately five years after the probable composition of 'Dover Beach', Karl Marx was invited to speak at the anniversary of the *People's Paper*. Referring to the European revolutions of 1848, Marx stated: 'The so-called revolutions of 1848 were but poor incidents, small fractures and fissures in the dry crust of European society. But they denounced the abyss. Beneath the apparently solid surface, they betrayed oceans of liquid matter, only needing expansion to rend into fragments continents of hard rock.'[21] As with the start of Arnold's lyric Marx's reference points are geological, and their use of this motif is deceptively gentle, encapsulated in the 'tremulous cadence' of the tide for Arnold and Marx's 'small fractures and fissures'. The result of these processes is the production of the fragments also traced in Shelley's sonnet, and the notion of the earth as a 'dry crust' which evokes the wastelands represented in both poems discussed earlier. The significant difference between Marx and Arnold's perspectives is that where these metaphoric geological processes produce the representation of cultural crisis for the latter, for Marx the process instigates a cautious tone of celebration. Like the passage from Wordsworth's *The Prelude* cited earlier, Arnold's poem is effectively a lament for stability and security; by contrast Marx identifies and, through his dynamic language, seems to revel in the illusory nature of the 'apparently solid surface' that conceals change, fragmentation and contradiction – a feature that can also be detected in the *Communist Manifesto*. It is from this climate of change, dislocation and insubstantiality that the broken, unsettled and unsettling 'Dover Beach' emerges.

Marshall Berman, in tracing the experience of modernity through the nineteenth century and into the twentieth, taking into account such seemingly disparate figures as Goethe, Marx, Baudelaire and the New York architect Robert Moses, suggests that the difference between modernity in the two centuries lies in the fact that in the twentieth century 'the modern public expands, it shatters into a multitude of fragments, speaking incommensurable private languages; the idea of modernity, conceived in numerous fragmentary ways, loses much of its vividness, resonance and depth, and loses its capacity to organize and give meaning to people's lives.'[22] Berman's argument might prove controversial with scholars of twentieth-century high modernism and modernity; however, for the purposes of the present discussion what Berman identifies is again the notion of fragmentation implicit in the discourse of modernity. Berman's understanding of modernity as 'conceived in numerous fragmentary ways' is based on his reading of the nineteenth century, hence the variety of figures that he chooses to represent the phenomenon; what he states is that in the twentieth century the culture of modernity and modernism shifts into a variety of different and cryptic modes of discourse that lose the 'resonance and depth' of the previous century. That said, elements of the poems discussed above anticipate and prefigure features and images in early twentieth-century writing in uncanny ways. Without entering into too detailed a discussion of points of comparison, two exemplary poems – W. B. Yeats's 'The Second Coming' composed in 1919 and first published in 1920 and T. S. Eliot's *The Waste Land* composed in 1921 and published in 1922 – contain cadences and echoes of Shelley and Arnold, conscious or otherwise. Yeats's poem, which deliberately alludes to Shelley's *Prometheus Unbound*, also represents a strange figure in the midst of a sandscape similar to that in Shelley's 'Ozymandias':

> a vast image out of *Spiritus Mundi*
> Troubles my sight: somewhere in sands of the desert
> A shape with lion body and the head of a man,
> A gaze blank and pitiless as the sun,
> Is moving its slow thighs. (lines 12–16)[23]

Yeats's poem is, like Arnold's and Shelley's, an examination of the decay and disintegration of contemporary civilization which, through the title itself, suggests the start of a new cycle for history. In his generating of images from what he terms the '*Spiritus Mundi*', the spirit of the universe or a vast subconscious that connects individuals and maintains past memories, a link with Shelley can be established.[24] What we have is the barren desert sand found in 'Ozymandias' and a vast sphinx figure with the 'head of a man' that evokes the ruined statue in Shelley's poem, but reanimated for a second coming; Shelley's paean to the 'transience of empire' is therefore echoed and uneasily reconfigured in Yeats's resurrecting of the desert 'shape'. Apart from this, the main difference between the two poems lies in the fact that where Shelley's sonnet, while complex in its themes and ideas, is nonetheless *readable* (particularly as the imagined inscription on the pedestal is translated and not offered in indecipherable hieroglyphics), Yeats's poem, concurring with Berman's suggestion that twentieth century writing utilizes 'incommensurable private languages', is oblique and coded in its use of a private mythology regarding history and the '*Spiritus Mundi*'. Eliot's *The Waste Land*, in its title alone, conjures up the 'boundless and bare' desert of Shelley and the faithless and belated world of Arnold. In the first section of the poem, 'The Burial of the Dead', we encounter the fragmentation which is by now a familiar motif in the poems addressed so far:

> What are the roots that clutch, what branches grow
> Out of this stony rubbish? Son of man,
> You cannot say, or guess, for you know only
> A heap of broken images, where the sun beats,
> And the dead tree gives no shelter, the cricket no relief,
> And the dry stone no sound of water. (lines 19–24)[25]

The fragments are obvious in the 'stony rubbish' and the 'heap of broken images'; so too the lack of water in this environment echoes the retreat of the 'Sea of Faith' in Arnold's 'Dover Beach' which leaves a barren and desolate world, a theme that Eliot's poem is emphatically concerned with, albeit in a circumlocutory way. Like Arnold, and in a slightly different way Shelley, Eliot's poem is about displaced and dislocated utterance. Through its adoption of a variety of ventriloquisms and cultural reference points *The Waste Land* offers a poetic topography that is displaced and fragmentary, just as Arnold's shifts between nation, culture and religion. However, where Shelley's use of dislocated utterance ironically highlights the fragility of the claims inscribed upon the statue, empowering the reader rather than the subject that makes the claims, the act of reading in Eliot results in incomprehension: we 'know only / A heap of broken images'. This lack of comprehension is reinforced by the sheer complexity of the text; its plethora of citations, languages and rapidly shifting personae render it elliptical and obtuse thus supporting Berman's views on the 'private language' of twentieth-century modernism. Ultimately what links the four poems discussed is that they all comment upon the ruins of civilization, representing this through images of fragmentation, and are involved in depicting an environment and cultural climate of flux, dissolution and collapse. Indeed, an appropriate maxim to summarize these connections can be found in Yeats's 'The Second Coming': 'Things fall apart; the centre cannot hold' (line 3).

This powerful aphorism from Yeats's poem can be applied to 'Dover Beach', for Arnold's lyric is thematically on the verge of collapse, unable to settle or establish any conception of permanence or stability. However, it is clear that there are significant differences in Arnold's poem when compared to the other three pieces of writing. The presence of fragmentation in Shelley's sonnet provides the source for a celebration of the impermanence of imperial tyranny and its grandiose claims; there is little in Arnold's lyric that can with any justification be described as celebratory. In addition where Yeats and Eliot, although not obviously comparable figures, use the coded language described by Berman, Arnold's 'Dover Beach' is an open and ingenuous representation of cultural crisis. Arguably Yeats hides behind an obscure personal mythology and Eliot conceals the poetic voice through utilizing a variety of personae and often obscure references; by contrast, Arnold's 'Dover Beach' reveals a poetic identity that is rapidly stripped away as the poem shifts between the uncertainties of patriotism, religious devotion, western cultural heritage, ultimately and fruitlessly seeking refuge in the conventions of the love lyric. The result is a poem that creates a plethora of irresolvable contradictions; shifting smoothly and lucidly as it does through its anxieties, it nonetheless reveals the stress implicit within the rapidity of these shifts by making an appeal for a possible permanence of love in a world that is represented as incapable of love. Things don't *literally* fall apart, but it is clear that for Arnold the things that he values as central cannot hold; in the face of contradiction and unremitting change what he represents is the Victorian cultural landscape as a wasteland, a 'darkling plain'.

It seems strangely appropriate that Arnold's disillusioned and self-contradicting poem should be composed in the same year that witnessed the Great International Exhibition, an event housed in the specially constructed Crystal Palace and designed to celebrate the prowess of the British and Continental industrial bourgeoisie. This appropriateness lies in the tension between the purpose of the exhibition and the building within which it was placed. The exhibition provided a celebration of the virtues of enterprise, economic endeavour and technological innovation in the marketplaces of the modern metropolis as seen by the industrial middle class. Arguably it privileged the pre-eminence of European economics, commerce, science and technology over previously held notions that religion or poetry or aesthetics were culturally central. By contrast Crystal Palace represented the avant-garde in architecture; Marshall Berman's description of it as 'the most visionary and adventurous building of the whole of the nineteenth century' hints at the ambivalence with which it was regarded by its contemporary audience.[26] Indeed Berman's analysis of Crystal Palace is telling, for he states that the builders 'far from presenting the building as final and indestructible, prided themselves on its transience'; in many ways the very 'transience' of the building chosen to house a celebration of the permanence of British industry echoes the ruins of the statue of Ozymandias in Shelley's poem, yet the shifting and transient nature of the building itself is a strangely appropriate monument when the fragility and the dislocated nature of nineteenth-century modernity is considered.[27] Naturally this uneasy juxtaposition of bourgeois aspiration and avant-garde experiment proved controversial. Berman notes that '[m]ost of the British cultural establishment condemned it' and identifies John Ruskin as a particularly virulent critic who saw the building as 'a frontal assault on civilization'; as a result Crystal Palace was rejected by both the so-called cultural establishment and the industrial bourgeoisie, whose achievements it was designed to contain.[28] Berman goes on to state tentatively that '[i]t might be argued that the unwillingness of the British bourgeoisie to accept and live with such a brilliant expression of its own modernity presaged its gradual loss of energy and imagination ... [i]n retrospect, 1851 appears as its zenith and the beginning of its gradual decline', a perspective that reinforces the contradictory and unlocated nature of the building when we consider that for the world in general it proved a 'symbol of England's world vision and leadership'.[29]

In the variance between exhibition and building, in the transient nature of Crystal Palace itself (dismantled after the exhibition and then reassembled in 1854), and in the response that it inspired amongst its critics, we can detect something of the strange and problematic relationship that existed between the nineteenth-century bourgeoisie and its own modernity. Arnold echoes, evokes and implicitly provides a critique of such a relationship in the dislocated and shifting shorelines of 'Dover Beach'. Indeed notions of change at the hands of uncontrollable forces, of points of crisis, and of the malleable nature of identity that results from such occurrences are at the heart of nineteenth-century modernity. As Tennyson states in the line from the collection *Poems, Chiefly Lyrical* of 1830, cited at the start of this introduction, 'All Truth is change'. This notion of fluidity, relentless change, even chaos being at the root of the nineteenth-century experience of modernity can be detected in the writing of many significant cultural and social commentators from the Victorian period. As editor of the Utilitarian and Unitarian journal *Monthly Repository*, William Johnson Fox, arguing that society needed a radical structural transformation of all its institutions, stated in 1832: 'According to the law of progress, both individual and social, by which God governs the world, the transition is made from one gradation of order, harmony, and beauty to a higher gradation, by the intervention of a state of apparent confusion and conflict.'[30] We are back to the 'condition of crisis' that Isobel Armstrong identified as the defining cultural environment for the emergence of Victorian modernism. However, what Fox suggests is that progress, which acts according to defined laws, paradoxically arises out of the apparent antitheses to law, 'confusion and conflict'; as a result, crisis is not necessarily a bad thing. The features which so debilitate the poetic perspective and persona for Arnold actually facilitate development and advancement in terms of 'order, harmony and beauty' for Fox. In addition, and incongruously perhaps, he invokes God as the arbitrator in this seemingly contradictory approach to the notion of progress. If for Fox the key to social and individual advancement lies *in* the chaotic processes of 'confusion and conflict', Karl Marx's slant on modernity, change and progress in the nineteenth century is more complex and teasingly equivocal than this. In the *Communist Manifesto* he states:

> Constant revolutionizing of production, uninterrupted disturbance of all social conditions, everlasting uncertainty and agitation distinguish the bourgeois epoch from all earlier ones. All fixed, fast-frozen relations, with their train of ancient and venerable prejudices and opinions are swept away, all new-formed ones become antiquated before they can ossify. All that is solid melts into air, all that is holy is profaned, and man is at last compelled to face with sober senses, his real conditions of life, and his relations with his kind.[31]

By the 'bourgeois epoch' Marx is obviously referring to the post-Industrial Revolution nineteenth century and the emergence of the new industrial middle classes. This is the period of 'economic and cultural change' that inspires Victorian modernism for Isobel

Armstrong, and when 'long-accepted social structure was being dissolved', as Punter puts it, creating a class that inhabits and makes its living from the modern urban metropolis. What defines Marx's perspective is his use of a dynamic language to represent chaotic and relentless flux. there is 'uninterrupted disturbance', 'everlasting uncertainty' (itself a curious and paradoxical conflation of permanence and irresolution), 'agitation', everything that was previously 'fixed' is 'swept away', all new opinions 'become antiquated before they can ossify'. In short, in the modern bourgeois epoch '[a]ll that is solid melts into air', indicating the incessant upheavals of the present. What we are left with is a condition where identity is in crisis, a situation where the modern individual is 'compelled', when confronted by this inexorable and escalating climate of change, 'to face with sober senses, his real conditions of life, and his relations with his kind'. The description of progress as reliant upon 'confusion and conflict' that is posited by Fox is underpinned by the authority of God, thus suggesting a sense of positivity and security at the heart of his definition of the modern world. Marx, by contrast, contradicts this theocratic position by emphatically stating that 'all that is holy is profaned', and by the 'holy' Marx means not just religion, but *all* 'ancient and venerable prejudices'. As a result, where Fox sees individual and social progress as ultimately stable, Marx states that humanity has to rethink its whole social identity fundamentally. Berman, who borrows Marx's phrase '[a]ll that is solid melts into air' for his analysis of the experience of modernity, asks rhetorically '[w]hat kinds of people does this permanent revolution produce?'. The answer that he gives is a significant one:

> In order for people, whatever their class, to survive in modern society, their personalities must take on the fluid and open form of this society. Modern men and women must learn to yearn for change: not merely to be open to changes in their personal and social lives, but positively to demand them, actively to seek them out and carry them through.[32]

Berman defines the society that Marx is depicting as 'fluid', and suggests that in some way the modern individual must take on its qualities. Moreover, he reads Marx's interpretation of the bourgeois epoch as a time when the individual, rather than passively accepting the transformations implemented by a changing social and economic climate, must *actively* change *alongside* this shifting society, indeed must 'yearn for change' in what becomes a self-conscious and almost hedonistic self-transformation for transformation's sake. Identity in the modern environment must therefore symbiotically take on the qualities of flux and fluidity that *mark* modern society in a manner that evokes Wordsworth's description of the loss of individual identity in the vast and faceless metropolis found in *The Prelude* and Greenslade's definition of the determinant interplay and interdependence between city condition and physical well-being in his study of late nineteenth-century degeneration. To conflate Marx, Berman and Greenslade: living in the modern environment, particularly the city, in the nineteenth century is to have an identity that is constantly changing, shifting and being both redefined and redefining itself. In such an environment Arnold's desire for cultural stability and his apprehension of its impossibility in the face of the dislocating and disorientating modern experience is hardly surprising.

In many ways we are back to the nineteenth-century city, which provides the location for the condition of crisis as understood by Armstrong, and to the urban condition, or 'psychopathology of everyday life', described by Greenslade. Indeed the metropolis provides one of the main locations, though not the exclusive one, for much of the writing addressed in this book, whether as a backdrop for the *fin de siècle* Gothic novel, the site for Thomas De Quincey's opium reveries and meditations, or as the environment within which James Thomson's alienated inhabitants sing their hymns of despair. The effect of the city on the individual is significant here as it conduces a strange liminality with regard to identity; identity is both clearly situated in terms of location but profoundly unsituated because the urban condition renders it an unstable entity. Such effects can be detected in many of the texts under scrutiny here; however, Charles Dickens's *Bleak House*, in spite of the variety of regions that it covers, is a significantly London-based novel and provides a useful paradigm for an introductory study of the effects of the city on identity. Identity in *Bleak House* is a fundamentally unstable quantity; on an obvious if slightly superficial level we can see this encapsulated in the variety of different names and appellations given to or appropriated by characters in the novel. For example, the main protagonist, Esther Summerson, states, after becoming the housekeeper of the eponymous house, 'This was the beginning of my being called Old Woman, and Little Old Woman, and Cobweb, and Mrs Shipton, and Mother Hubbard, and Dame Durden, and so many names of that sort, that my own name soon became quite lost among them.'[33] This use of nicknames can also be found in the cases of, amongst others, Young Smallweed, who is 'metaphorically called Small and eke Chick Weed', George Rouncewell, who is alternatively referred to as 'Governor' and 'Commander' by Phil his partner-cum-batman, and in the names 'Quebec', 'Malta' and 'Woolwich' that are used for the Bagnet children.[34] In terms of assumed identities there is Tony Jobling who adopts the 'impromptu name' of Weevle when seeking lodgings at Mr Krook's rag and bottle shop.[35] In addition, Krook's shop provides the site for another adopted identity, the significantly titled law-writer Nemo ('nobody' in Latin). Nemo is assumed by one Captain Hawdon, who, in appropriating this appellation, is effectively trying to obliterate the traces of his original identity by quite literally becoming a nobody. It is in relation to Nemo that Esther's nicknames take on a significance that transcends their apparent frippery, for, as the illegitimate daughter of Hawdon and the aristocratic Lady Dedlock, in the course of the narrative she is presented by Dickens as being involved in a process of trying to establish a stable and secure identity, and her initial lack of family history becomes encapsulated in the variety of names that are applied to her. As a result, as well as the nicknames and pseudonyms found in the text, there is a serious discussion of the place and nature of identity in the modern city and amongst its institutions. For Dickens the relationship between the two is usually negative; in *Bleak House* the Court of Chancery and the legal system itself turns Hawdon into Nemo and strips the mad Miss Flite of her sanity. The modern city also creates its own peculiar class, the *residuum* that Marx refers to as the '"dangerous class", the social scum, that passively rotting mass thrown off by the lowest layers of old society'.[36] In many ways the residuum, here represented by the illiterate crossing-sweeper Jo, embody disidentity, left behind by the progress advocated by Fox and, in Jo's case, perpetually 'a-moving and a-moving on, ever since I was born'.[37] Jo's name, in its almost anonymous brevity, signifies this vacuous identity:

> Name, Jo. Nothing else that he knows on. Don't know that everybody has two names. Never heerd of sich a think [*sic*]. Don't know that Jo is short for a longer name. Thinks it long enough for *him*. *He* don't find no fault with it. Spell it? No. *He* can't spell it. No father, no mother, no friends. Never been to school. What's home? Knows a broom's a broom.[38]

In effect all that Jo *does* have, as he is bereft of family, friends, home and even the most rudimentary education, is his own pitifully truncated name and that of the broom by which he makes his meagre living.[39] Jo's lack of a definable and defined identity is an exaggerated version of the urban condition. So too the place where he *does* live is an exaggerated version of the modern city itself:

> Jo lives – that is to say, Jo has not yet died – in a ruinous place, known to the like of him by the name of Tom-all-Alone's. It is a black dilapidated street, avoided by all decent people; where the crazy houses were seized upon, when their decay was far advanced, by some bold vagrants, who, after establishing their own possession, took to letting them out in lodgings. Now, these tumbling tenements contain, by night, a swarm of misery. As on the ruined human wretch, vermin parasites appear, so, these ruined shelters have bred a crowd of foul existence that crawls in and out of gaps in walls and boards; and coils itself to sleep, in maggot numbers, where the rain drips in; and comes and goes, fetching and carrying fever ... Twice, lately, there has been a crash and cloud of dust, like the springing of a mine, in Tom-all-Alone's; and, each time, a house has fallen ... The gaps remain, and there are not unpopular lodgings among the rubbish. As several more houses are nearly ready to go, the next crash in Tom-all-Alone's may be expected to be a good one.[40]

This representation of the living quarters for Jo and his fellow residuum seem as far as conceivably possible from Crystal Palace; yet in this fragmentary 'ruinous' and 'dilapidated' city space, left behind by the progress that inspired the Great Exhibition and which is 'avoided by all decent people', we can detect a parody of modernity. Just as Jo exaggerates the disidentity of the urban condition, Tom-all-Alone's, as stated above, exaggerates features of the modern city; for example, it has its own entrepreneurs who opportunistically seize possession of the premises and let them out for their own profit. Greenslade's definition of the hypochondriacal and nervous disorders and illness intrinsic to urban life is literalized here in the 'fever' transmitted amongst the tenements of the street. Most significantly, Tom-all-Alone's is, like Crystal Palace, a transient and impermanent spectacle – with 'a crash and a cloud of dust' houses collapse and disappear as the 'solid melts into air'.

In effect it is this sense of the transient and fluid that marks modernity in *Bleak House* and in the nineteenth-century modern city in general. Just like the identity of its inhabitants, the actual environment of the city is fluid and shifting. What typifies the topography of London for Dickens is the omnipresence of its fog and the shadowy gas lamps that illuminate it; in the second paragraph of the novel he states:

> Fog everywhere. Fog up the river, where it flows among green aits [*sic*] and meadows; fog down the river, where it rolls defiled among the tiers of shipping, and the waterside pollutions of a great (and dirty) city ... Gas looming through the fog in divers places in the streets, much as the sun may, from the spongey fields, be seen to loom by husbandman and ploughboy. Most of the shops lighted two hours before their time – as the gas seems to know, for it has a haggard and unwilling look.[41]

Referring later to fog as the 'London ivy' and to the 'innumerable gas-lamps', Dickens identifies the cityscape as fluid and insubstantial, shrouded in fog and lit by fitful lights.[42] In many ways it is such an environment that evokes the defining aesthetic of nineteenth-century modernity in cultural representation. For Marshall Berman '[f]luidity and vaporousness ... become primary qualities' in 'self-consciously modernist' culture', echoing Marx's maxim about solidity and air, the state of identity for the nineteenth-century city dweller, and the condition of the city itself.[43] In this environment the *fin de siècle* Gothic villains of Robert Louis Stevenson and Bram Stoker, like the shadowy and contradictory real life urban myth of the 1880s, Jack the Ripper, can vanish and melt into air in the fog of London.[44] Perhaps the ultimate representation for Dickens of this city condition and of city-generated disidentity lies in the demise of Krook, the 'Lord Chancellor' of the rag and bottle shop:

> There is very little fire left in the grate, but there is a smouldering suffocating vapour in the room, and a dark greasy coating on the walls and ceiling. The chairs and table, and the bottle so rarely absent from the table, all stand as usual. On one chair back, hang the old man's hairy cap and coat ... Here is a small burnt patch of flooring; here is the tinder from a little bundle of burnt paper, but not so light as usual, seeming to be steeped in something; and here

> is – is it the cinder of a small charred and broken log of wood sprinkled with white ashes, or is it coal? O Horror, he is here! and this from which we run away, striking out the light and overturning one another into the street, is all that represents him ... Call the death by any name ... it is the same death eternally – inborn, inbred, engendered in the corrupted humours of the vicious body itself, and that only – Spontaneous Combustion, and none other of all the deaths that can be died.[45]

Krook, in a room with a 'suffocating vapour', has, through the phenomenon of spontaneous combustion, quite literally melted into air, with the only trace of his identity lying in fragments of cinders and ashes.

This book considers many of the issues discussed so far. It addresses three phenomena found in literary texts that would seem to involve the collapse of a cohesive identity in nineteenth-century modernity, namely the split personality, religious crisis and addiction. The discussion of the split personality and disidentification has its origins in Cartesian dualism, but finds significant parallels in cultural criticism during the course of the century, in particular in the work of Arthur Hallam and Matthew Arnold, and in the discourse of the degeneration theorists of the *fin de siècle* such as Cesare Lombroso and Max Nordau. Underpinning the first section is a study of the Gothic novels of James Hogg, Robert Louis Stevenson and Oscar Wilde. Their work, in a supposedly popular medium, dramatizes significant and resonant aspects of the experience of modernity in the nineteenth century, in particular the rapid changes relentlessly and systematically imposed upon social and cultural constructions of the bourgeois individual during this period. The main trajectory of my argument is that such texts represent metaphorically the divided priorities of the subject in nineteenth-century modernity, the subsequent crisis for and fragmentation of identity in such a climate, and, certainly by the *fin de siècle* Gothic of Stevenson and Wilde, the so-called 'city-condition'. The Gothic *doppelgänger* novel, due to its apprehension by nineteenth-century cultural criticism as a 'low' and therefore populist literary medium, functions as a resonant commentary on and mirror for the preoccupation with disintegration and degeneration in 'high' cultural discourse and embryonic sociology. Ultimately the fragmented and vaporous Gothic villain stands as a metaphor for the instability of bourgeois identity within the institutions and ideology that it apparently celebrates and chooses to privilege. The result is a myriad of uncomfortable and potentially destructive cultural mirrorings, where central cultural and social anxieties find echoes and traces in Gothic thematics.

Part II considers one of the most prominent crises of the nineteenth century, that of religion. In a social, cultural and intellectual climate influenced by post-Enlightenment empiricism and pragmatism, the nineteenth century pays witness to the escalating instability of religion, a feature notably dramatized in texts of the period. With the advent of evolutionary theory, the emergence of a political voice for radical atheism, schisms within the established Church of England and a generally more materialistic conception of the human all taking place during this period, the effect that the decentring of religion has upon individual identity is explored. Works by Alfred Tennyson, James (B. V.) Thomson and Gerard Manley Hopkins, as well as medical analyses of insanity caused by religion, provide the focus for a section which examines the way in which affirming identity is problematized by a climate where religious meaning seems to be evaporating. Work by Tennyson oscillates between a semi-ironic critique of the prevailing cultural climate with regard to religion and an apparently genuine articulation of the crisis of faith. In the poem 'St. Simeon Stylites' the eponymous saint privileges physical mortification, with its subsequent paradox of self-assertion and self-denial, as a way to achieve spiritual renown and identification. In *In Memoriam* an elegiac tribute to Hallam instigates a meditation upon the fragility of belief in the face of scientific materialism and the seeming malice of the natural world; in such an environment poetic and personal identity is rendered unstable and can only be reaffirmed by a reversion to the conventions of elegy. In the work of Thomson and Hopkins a common theme of utter despair can be traced. However, where in Thomson this takes the form of a resolute and atheistic nihilism that can offer some stability in the chaos of the modern city, albeit with the possibility of relinquishing a defined and purposeful identity for the individual, in Hopkins's 'terrible sonnets' the whole precept, namely prayer, for poetic utterance is dissipated in poems that dramatically suggest abandonment by God.

Part III explores addiction in the nineteenth century. In many ways the history of nineteenth-century modernity is a history of addictions: from the compulsive colonial project, through the relentless accumulation of capital, to the over-production and consumption of commodities within the marketplace. There is a plethora of addictions in evidence during the period; indeed opium itself, perhaps the most notorious of nineteenth-century narcotics, would seem to be a ubiquitous intoxicant, utilized and administered in a variety of contradictory and significant ways that renders its omnipresence simultaneously unlocated. Ultimately discussions or representations of addiction in literature of the nineteenth-century mask or metaphorize a number of resonant preoccupations and anxieties in modernity. The works of Thomas De Quincey, Tennyson and Christina Rossetti proffer instances of addictions that are either literal or implicit. As much as they are concerned with altered states of consciousness and intoxication, these texts suggest that disidentity is very much tied up in the strategies and dynamics of modernity: for example, the relentless changes mentioned earlier, the emergence of the metropolis and its disorientating topography, and the centrality of a male-dominated commercial marketplace in the nineteenth century. In addition, the theme of addiction covers wide-ranging anxieties about the instability of cultural and national identity, colonization, orientalism, disease, sexuality and infection. The final chapter closes this project with a discussion of Bram Stoker's *Dracula*, which, if not a text about addiction *per se*, can be read in such a way that the vampire and the vampiric process stand in for a dynamic concatenation of addictions. Stoker's text effectively demonstrates the way in which identity is troubled by a modern environment that is vampiric and addictive in many different ways.

Part I

(De)Generating doubles: duality and the split personality in the prose writing of James Hogg, Robert Louis Stevenson and Oscar Wilde

Introduction

> [D]elusions are familiar to every medical man conversant with insanity. Two contradictory and incompatible convictions. Here is no defective government of moral or sensual propensities, but two distinct acts of the thinking powers destructive of each other. It seems to me absolutely impossible to conceive any other explanation than the possession of two distinctive minds – results of two distinct organs of thought.[1]

> Those who go beneath the surface do so at their peril.[2]

In his treatise of 1844, *The Duality of the Mind*, the physician A. L. Wigan determined to demonstrate that the human brain consisted of two distinct cerebra, each of which was manifestly capable of being in conflict with the other within the individual. Wigan subtitled his work 'A new view of insanity ... proved by the structure, functions, and diseases of the brain, and by the phenomena of mental derangement, and shown to be essential to moral responsibility', and aimed to prove that 'each cerebrum is capable of a distinct and separate volition, and that these are very often opposing volitions'.[3] What Wigan argues for is a fundamental duality within human consciousness, where the human brain is divided and capable, when 'opposing volitions' exist, of entering a state of conflict. To have a divided brain therefore is to have the potential to be at war with oneself, or, as Wigan puts it, when '[t]wo contradictory and incompatible convictions' occur, 'two distinct acts of the thinking powers destructive of each other' emerge. In a deluded or disordered state contradiction escalates to become destructive conflict within the individual. Wigan's theory, as the title of his work clearly indicates, is located in an understanding of the brain and consciousness as divided, suggesting that in the deluded individual the bilateral symmetry of the human cerebrum provides a physiological basis for psychological disturbance. For Anne

Harrington the book marks 'the climax of the pre-1860 period of thought on the double brain'.[4] If Wigan's theories proved contentious they did so largely because of his claim that they were a 'new view of insanity'; as Harrington puts it reviewers were dismissive of the book 'not so much because they disagreed with its essential premises but because they were offended by Wigan's extravagant claims to originality'.[5] John Elliotson's essay in *The Zoist* provides an interesting gloss on Wigan's work, in an apparently ironic (though when contextualized significant) aside he notes that 'if to do two things at once, a person requires two brains, he ought to require several brains when he does several things at once'.[6] This seemingly flippant comment conceals a significant idea, that in the nineteenth century conventional binary dualisms are amplified or exploded into numerous or fragmentary forms.

The notion of the individual – at least the Western individual – being divided in a modern philosophical and cultural context arguably has its origins in the work of the seventeenth-century philosopher René Descartes, particularly in the now-seminal *Discourse on Method* (1637) and *Meditations on First Philosophy* (1641). Avoiding archetypal Christian or ethical distinctions, the binary oppositions of good and evil being the most obvious, Descartes posits a vision of human consciousness as composite, consisting of varied apprehensions of what constitutes the self, and one which is based in a fundamental division between body and mind. Despite the apparent affirmation of the Perfect Being (God) in the *Discourse* and writing the *Meditations* in a theocratic context (they are after all dedicated to the Dean and Doctors of the Faculty of Theology in Paris), what Descartes effectively achieves in his radical interrogation of subjectivity is to take the notion of agency in human consciousness of the self and the external material world away from God and locate it in the human mind. The result is a problematic that haunts much of the literature of duality: what is the relationship between mind and body? are they distinct entities? and are we therefore divided or unified beings? Descartes' writing articulates this problem of self-division in interesting and significant configurations. Francis Barker in *The Culture of Violence* voices the impact of a Cartesian construction of the self and its inherent yet unavoidable contradictions succinctly; indicating the ambivalence of the emergence of a notion of 'the individual' in the early modern period, he states that a 'great deal has depended historically, in bourgeois Western modernity, on the fashioning in early modernity of the punctual autonomous self as the centre of value and "sociality", even if this was no more than a set of appearances, a "lived ideology" rather than a real historical entity.'[7] What Barker indicates is the manner in which a construction of the notion of the 'autonomous' self is central to Western modernity, and problematizes this centrality by revealing the construction to be precisely that: a 'set of appearances' rather than a tangible, material historical phenomenon. Nonetheless the construction of the notion of the unified, independent self is valuable in that it brings with it its own *doppelgänger*, one that Barker argues Descartes brings into being:

> one of the persistent and central problems with this history of identity is, of course, that as soon as the punctual and self-possessed individual appeared on the stage of history, so did his opposite, the dispersed and fragmented disidentical, alienated, critical persona whose *existenz* consisted at best in an unstable play of masks and guises. Descartes, as in so much else, emblematizes the problematic. In one sense he is the author of the self; in another sense the Cartesian subject is already deeply divided in and from itself. It is not only separated from its body, but from that self which it utters as self at every moment that it confirms its self-hood by self-pronunciation.[8]

What Barker suggests is that concurrently with the construction of the unified autonomous self we witness the emergence of its alter ego, the 'fragmented disidentical' self. Citing Descartes as its originator, he indicates the ambivalence of the Cartesian position: as much as Descartes is responsible for constructing the notion of the autonomous self found mainly in the self-affirming incantation '*cogito, ergo sum*' of the *Discourse*, this unified subject is divided.[9] This division not only manifests itself in the body-mind split, but also in the summoning, uttering and confirmation of selfhood; in short to speak the self is to objectify and split the self. The result is a cunning if fragmented hall of mirrors, where self simultaneously reflects and establishes difference with self. This convoluted and complex system of doubling and division is appropriately represented by Barker in terms of a vocabulary of appearances. If the emergence of the autonomous individual is 'no more than a set of appearances' that 'appeared on the stage of history', then its opposite, the 'fragmented disidentical' self, consists of an 'unstable play of masks and guises'.

This complicated interaction between illusion, reflection and division is crucial in the literature of duality in the nineteenth century.

Turning directly to Descartes we can find many instances of this problematic division within the subject; he states in his synopsis to the *Meditations* that

> we cannot understand a body except as being divisible, while by contrast we cannot understand a mind as being indivisible. For we cannot conceive of half of a mind, while we can always conceive of half of a body however small; and this leads us to recognize that the natures of mind and body are not only different, but in some way opposite.[10]

Alfred Wigan's position in the middle of the nineteenth century seems to contradict Descartes explicitly. However, Wigan's perspective is emphatically physiological: the mind can be divided because it consists of two separate cerebra. By contrast, Descartes identifies division lying in the difference, indeed opposition, between body and mind; for him the mind is unified, and it is the body that is capable of being fragmentary. In the sixth meditation, which concludes the project, he amplifies this tension:

> It is true that I may have (or, to anticipate, that I certainly have) a body that is very closely joined to me. But nevertheless, on the other hand I have a clear and distinct idea of myself, in so far as I am simply a thinking, non-extended thing; and on the other hand I have a distinct idea of body, in so far as this is simply an extended non-thinking thing. And accordingly, it is certain that I am really distinct from my body, and can exist without it.[11]

Here Descartes oscillates between body and mind and between distinction and unity. He is conscious of the connection between the 'I' and the body, yet at the same time establishes a clear division, for the 'I' is a 'thinking ... thing' whereas the objectified body is that 'non-thinking' thing. Ultimately he concludes that the 'I' is actually separate from the body and 'can exist without it'; however, the act of uttering the self as 'I' also divides self from self through a further instance of objectification. This conclusion raises a number of interesting propositions that are effectively dramatized in two of the most canonical Gothic novels of the nineteenth century, Mary Shelley's

Frankenstein (1818) and Robert Louis Stevenson's *The Strange Case of Dr. Jekyll and Mr Hyde* (1886). Given the creative potential of human agency, is it possible for man (for doctors in the nineteenth century are always men) to create or artificially induce an objective 'distinct idea of body', and if so will it be a 'thinking' thing (that is, be conscious of the self) or a 'non-thinking' thing (that is, capable only of sensation), or, in Barker's words, a 'punctual autonomous self' or an 'unstable play of masks and guises'? Descartes, if less than unequivocal, is still clear that the body as a distinct entity (and what does Shelley's Victor Frankenstein create if not an animated body?) is a basic automated technology:

> I might consider the body of a man as a kind of machine equipped with and made up of bones, nerves, muscles, veins, blood, and skin in such a way that, even if there were no mind in it, it would still perform all the same movements as it now does in those cases where movement is not under the control of the will or, consequently, of the mind.[12]

These issues regarding the status of the body and the nature of consciousness and identity become significant in the nineteenth century as industrialization produces an increasingly mechanized way of life and where, as David Punter has put it, the 'stability of ... social structure was being dissolved amid the pressure of new types of work and new social roles'. For Punter even a sense of time changes in industrialized society as 'living and working according to the seasons' is replaced by the 'time of the machine'.[13] We can also detect them represented in the case of Jo in Dickens's *Bleak House*, who, parentless, is the offspring of the industrial city, a 'non-thinking' thing (he 'don't know'), and ultimately becomes a basic, functional technology within the metropolis: a broom.

I do not intend to offer a definitive overview of the phenomenon of the split-personality in nineteenth-century medical thinking, nor do I intend to provide an extensive catalogue of instances of doubling and duality in nineteenth-century literature.[14] What this section of the book achieves is to explore duality in relation to the fragmentation of identity in the nineteenth century, its causes and symptoms, as suggested in the introduction. Inevitably an assessment of duality in nineteenth-century writing is a limited exercise, mainly due to the plethora of manifestations of doubling in the literature; for example, duality is a stock feature in the Gothic novel – the presence of *doppelgängers* being a staple element in the Gothic tradition – and also occurs in its hybrid offspring the sensation novel and detective fiction. In addition, apart from its presence in popular literature, doubling can also be detected in less obvious contexts, its appearance suggesting a cultural resonance that reflects its uncanny embodiment in Gothic writing. Examples of the literature of duality include Alfred Tennyson's poem 'The Two Voices' (*Poems*, 1842), which represents a dialogue between the poetic 'I' and its other self, Arthur Hugh Clough's dramatic poem *Dipsychus* (1865), which explicitly suggests a divided self, and Elizabeth Gaskell's *North and South* (1854–55), which, in a broader sense, proposes a divided national consciousness between the industrial north and the rural south, a division that Gaskell attempts to heal through the symbolic marriage between the northern middle class mill-owner John Thornton and the southern minister's daughter Margaret Hale.

However, it is in discussions *of* culture in the nineteenth century that instances of self-division emerge in significant ways. In his essay of 1831, 'On Some of the Characteristics of Modern Poetry', Arthur Henry Hallam 'analysed the cultural fracture and alienation of post-revolutionary Europe as the modern condition', as Isobel Armstrong puts it.[15] In the essay Hallam sees the modern condition as inducing a lack of harmony or disconnection in the powers of the poet; as a result the ingredients of poetry, 'Sensitive', 'Reflective' and 'Passionate' emotions, rather than being unified, as they were in earlier English poetry, are now separated and isolated. As a consequence of this Hallam regards modern poetry as a site of conflict, with these individual components fighting for supremacy within the poetic form; his conclusion is significant: ''Hence the melancholy, which so evidently characterises the spirit of modern poetry; hence that return of the mind upon itself, and the habit of seeking relief in idiosyncrasies rather than community of interest.'[16]

In many ways, through the presence of 'melancholy', we are back to the morbidity that marks the problems of the Victorians for Armstrong and which is evoked throughout Arnold's 'Dover Beach'. In addition Hallam indicates a sense of division within modern poetry in the early decades of the nineteenth century; rather than stressing a holistic 'community of interest', which would presumably eradicate the melancholy, it finds its refuge in individual 'idiosyncrasies'. Ultimately modern poetry involves what Hallam calls the 'return of the mind upon itself'; the phrase is important because, along with its solipsistic and introspective nature, it suggests an objectification of the mind and thus a sense of internal division – the mind can only return upon itself if it is divided from itself. In many ways Hallam's essay anticipates Matthew Arnold's writings on culture from the 1850s onwards; the phrase cited above in particular finds echoes in the 'Preface' to the *Poems* of 1853, an essay which Armstrong refers to as Arnold's 'brilliant but limited diagnosis of modernity and its problems'.[17] In the 'Preface' Arnold sets out to justify why he has omitted the poem 'Empedocles on Etna' from the 1853 collection, particularly as that poem had provided the title for a collection published in the previous year. His reason for the omission lies in the fact that for him the Greek philosopher Empedocles represents a figure living in a time that is changing uncontrollably, and to such an extent that the influence of these changes stamp themselves on his thinking in negative ways:

> I intended to delineate the feelings of one of the last of the Greek religious philosophers ... having survived his fellows, living on into a time when the habits of Greek thought and feeling had begun fast to change, character to dwindle, the influence of the Sophists to prevail. Into the feelings of a man so situated there entered much that we are accustomed to consider as exclusively modern; how much the fragments of Empedocles himself which remain to us are sufficient at least to indicate. What those who are familiar only with the great monuments of early Greek genius suppose to be its exclusive characteristics, have disappeared; the calm, the cheerfulness, the disinterested objectivity have disappeared; the dialogue of the mind with itself has commenced; modern problems have presented themselves; we hear already the doubts, we witness the discouragement, of Hamlet and Faust.[18]

The immediate feature to establish is that Arnold defines the problems experienced by Empedocles as 'exclusively modern' in spite of the fact that he was born some two to three thousand years prior to the writing of the essay. He applies the word with a degree of specificity and a sense of establishing a parallel between Empedocles' time and his own; Empedocles' position as experiencing 'modern' feelings is down to the effect that relentless change has upon his philosophical perspective. In effect Empedocles becomes an emblematic figure, one whose principles and values lie in a past tradition yet who lives on into a time that disrupts these values and tradition – he consequently becomes trapped between past and future. Arnold describes him as 'situated', yet this word is ironic when Empedocles' *un*situatedness is considered: he is the last of his philosophical lineage living on into a changed and changing epoch. As a result all that we are left with are his fragments, both literally in terms of the remains of his writing but also symbolically as a figure fragmented and dislocated within his own time. As with Shelley's 'Ozymandias' we are left with the fragmented monument to a past regime (here arguably the despotism of philosophy rather than dynasty); however, where Shelley's sonnet clearly locates the inscriptions that represent Ozymandias' dynasty in the past, Arnold takes the fragments of Empedocles and defines them as 'exclusively modern'. The connection between Empedocles and modernity is stressed by Arnold in a significant phrase: claiming the 'calm, the cheerfulness, the disinterested objectivity' of previous writing to be absent in Empedocles' remains, he finds that 'the dialogue of the mind with itself has commenced; modern problems have presented themselves; we hear already the doubts, we witness the discouragement, of Hamlet and of Faust'. Hallam's depiction of the inwardness and self-division that characterizes modern poetry for him is taken in a further and more explicit direction by Arnold. Where Hallam's definition involves the 'return of the mind upon itself', Arnold spells out the inner division with 'the dialogue of the mind with itself' – a formulation that is almost emphatically Cartesian in its objectification of the mind and the establishment of a dialogue with it. This diagnosis of culture is firmly defined as 'modern', and involves 'doubts' and 'discouragement' that echo Hallam's 'melancholy' and again adhere to the morbidity that Armstrong sees as defining the Victorian cultural response to modernity. In effect Arnold claims Empedocles for modernity, arguing that his mode of discourse and the themes that it takes up are modern ones – inward, divided and morbid – which can be placed alongside that of Shakespeare's Hamlet and Goethe's Faust. The citing of these characters as representative of a modern cultural malaise is not as arbitrary as it might at first seem; indeed, for Marshall Berman Goethe's *Faust* offers a significant representation of the origins of modernity for the nineteenth century. As a dramatic work it

> begins in an epoch whose thought and sensibility are modern in a way that twentieth-century readers can recognize at once, but

> whose material and social conditions are still medieval; the work ends in the midst of the spiritual and material upheavals of an industrial revolution ... [it] expresses and dramatizes the process by which, at the end of the eighteenth century and the start of the nineteenth, a distinctively modern world-system comes into being.[19]

The connection between the divided 'dialogue of the mind with itself', the character of Faust and of modernity itself is also significant with regard to the three texts under scrutiny in this chapter: James Hogg's *The Private Memoirs and Confessions of a Justified Sinner*, Robert Louis Stevenson's *The Strange Case of Dr Jekyll and Mr Hyde* and Oscar Wilde's *The Picture of Dorian Gray* all contain an updated version of the original Faustian contract.

Putting Hallam and Arnold's essays on modern poetry together we have two definitions of poetry, stemming from the early and middle stages of the nineteenth century, as involving a divided consciousness and consisting of a melancholy or morbid frame of mind. By the *fin de siècle* this morbidity and inwardness had become a pathological condition, particularly as conceived by the prominent degeneration theorists. Max Nordau, author of *Degeneration* and a cultural critic who, in William Greenslade's words, 'identified and then attacked the seminal movements of the age: philosophical relativism and the aesthetic experiment of modernism', was a particularly emphatic commentator.[20] In *Degeneration* he effectively translates the Arnoldian dialogue into a corrupt and destructive narcissism, stating that 'whoever worships his "I" ... [is] an enemy of society': where Hallam and Arnold implicitly suspect a falling away in cultural cohesion, Nordau explicitly identifies objectified self-reflection as a danger to the fabric of civilized society.[21] Cesare Lombroso, Nordau's contemporary, argues in his study of deviant genius that defining features of this condition are 'exaggerated mutism, morbid vanity, excessive originality and excessive preoccupation with self, the tendency to put mystical interpretations on the simplest facts'.[22] At the centre of this definition we once again encounter the narcissism that Nordau suggests; morbidity has become vanity and vice versa, and 'excessive preoccupation with self' again threatens social structures. As a result, by the *fin de siècle* decadence as an artistic movement is virtually synonymous with degeneration for theorists of the latter phenomenon, and the decadent artist becomes 'the carrier of a prevailing cultural sickness'.[23] In the last decade of the nineteenth century art, morbidity, and the divided inwardness of the Arnoldian dialogue become narcissistic, degenerate and the site of cultural infection.

Degeneration theory – which informs much of this chapter, particularly as two of the texts under scrutiny belong to the nineteenth-century *fin de siècle* – covers a variety of areas from criminal psychosis, through racial difference, to decadent art. What is significant about it is its reliance upon a terminology and system of categorization that leans heavily towards dualism. Indeed, it is possible to argue that degeneration marks the culmination in the nineteenth century of a medical and social conception of conditioning that is fundamentally dualistic. As Robert Nye notes, there was a tendency amongst French doctors in the 1870s to argue for a 'medical bipolarity of the normal and pathological' founded upon a commonsensical rationale of which was which.[24] These categories, as William Greenslade points out, are essentially reductive; for him degeneration 'facilitated discourses of sometimes crude differentiation: between the normal and the abnormal, the healthy and the morbid, the 'fit' and the 'unfit', the civilized and the primitive.[25] Degeneration, with its reliance upon these dualistic categories, essentially becomes an exercise in establishing a series of constraining and containing oppositional classifications – '*this*' as opposed to '*that*', or, as amplified by Nye, a series of 'binary terms that regulate the perception of social life: moral–immoral, criminal–honest, sane–insane, violent–passive'.[26] Greenslade, referring to the work of Michel Foucault on areas of discourse that constitute social and cultural beliefs and practices, notes that the discourse of psychopathology is one where such oppositional strategies are employed.[27] The affirmation of difference is dependent upon assuming that apparently quite discrete examples of 'deviancy' are in some way associated: assumptions about the human subject and institutions form a frame around discrete 'objects' of that discourse: the criminal, the 'feeble-minded', the neurotic woman, the hooligan, the artist.[28] As a result, in the discourse of psychopathology 'normality', its polar opposite, is established or at least assumed through collecting together discrete bodies of deviancy as an organized and consistent collective. For Foucault power is at the heart of these strategies; discourse which encourages acts of inclusion and exclusion results in, as Greenslade phrases it, the 'active production of categories and distinction' which regulate and govern morality and normality.[29] This correlation between discourse, categorization and power is clarified by Robert Nye. Medicine gains its ability to organize the social and the anti-social because 'experts shaped a medical discourse that spoke to all those problems in comprehensible language, which appeared to many contemporaries to be an accurate portrayal of the world'; in effect medical discourse has a special power in that its binary terms create and regulate what seems to be an 'accurate' version of the real world.[30] This 'active production' of containing categories becomes increasingly prevalent in the cultural and social malaise of the nineteenth-century *fin de siècle*; in effect degeneration theory provides a response to the symptoms of perceived cultural sickness because, as Greenslade notes, '[a]s the authority of norms falters the regulation through categories becomes more necessary'.[31] It becomes noticeable in the *fin de siècle* that as anxieties regarding cultural, social and national sickness intensify the discourse of degeneration becomes essentially contradictory and even unlocated in nature. This is apparent in the wide and incongruous groups that are embraced by the exclusive and excluding category of being degenerate; Greenslade lists them, stating that the 'referents are manifold: men of genius, anarchists, lunatics, hooligans, prostitutes are all dealt with by this expedient of attributing to them symptoms of a pathology, congenital criminality, hysteria or neurasthenia'.[32] This sense of dislocation within a supposedly distinct category is increased when we consider that these symptoms are also applied to the 'prevailing urban condition' of the supposedly ordinary bourgeois city-dweller of the *fin de siècle*. In effect, just as Francis Barker notes that the Cartesian subject is divided yet also mirrored by its disidentical self, so too the late nineteenth-century hotchpotch of degenerate types mirror the normal individual in his or her own symptoms. At this point it can be argued that the carefully constructed discourse of inclusion and exclusion collapses into a fragmentary and contradictory understanding of normality and abnormality. Greenslade sums up this contradictory element in the discourse of degeneration by stating that 'the ambiguity and instability of the term itself, [with] its twin interlocking semantic properties ... [suggests] on the one hand, generation and reproduction, on the other decline, degradation, waste'.[33] To enter this discourse, therefore, is to enter one that attempts to rationalize and regulate morality and normality, yet one that is also deeply divided and self-contradictory.

It will be apparent from the series of oppositions posited above that one of the main categories for degenerate deviancy is that of criminality; indeed criminality, like degeneracy itself, is a classification in the nineteenth century which subsumes a variety of different examples of anti-social behaviour. The perceived anti-social nature of criminality is particularly significant; as Jon Stratton notes in his essay on serial killing and the social, criminality in terms of its correlation with the discourse of insanity is tied up again with dualism, and adheres to the Foucauldian notion of discourse, power and regulation: 'In modernity a clear distinction was made between sanity and insanity. The sane were rational, which is to say that they engaged in instrumental rationality acceptable to the dominant moral order and for ends within the bounds of that moral order.'[34] If to be sane in modernity is to adhere to 'the dominant moral order', to be insane is to fail to meet this guiding principle; to be insane is to be *anti*-social, and criminality fits in with this definition. Stratton's definition and its correlation with modernity is instructive, for the distinction that he makes is one that clearly corresponds with those manifest in nineteenth-century discourse. Foucault crystallizes the manipulatively synonymous relationship between insanity and criminality in his essay on 'The Dangerous Individual', stating, 'Nineteenth-century psychiatry invented an entirely fictitious entity, a crime which is nothing but insanity, an insanity which is nothing but a crime. For more than half a century this entity was called homicidal mania.'[35] What Foucault again indicates is the loaded relationship between medical discourse and perceived notions of normality. In this case what is significant is the tautological hall of mirrors at the heart of the definition of 'homicidal mania' – the crime that is insanity, the insanity that is crime, which is which? – and the fact that it is 'invented', suggesting a Gothicized Frankensteinian narrative at the heart of nineteenth-century psychiatry's construction of the criminal. It is this notion of fictionality that is particularly important, for it is the nineteenth-century Gothic novel which dramatizes the psychopathology of modernity with all its inherent contradictions and complications, and arguably each of the three texts under scrutiny in this section represents the Foucauldian homicidal maniac. Ultimately the 'fictitious entity' created by nineteenth-century psychiatry is mirrored by its monstrous twin in the Gothic novel.

The Gothic novel haunts much of this project, and Gothic motifs can be found intruding in unlikely forms and configurations within many areas of nineteenth-century cultural discourse. However, the notions of duality and doubling, and the way in which such constructions ultimately reveal the fragility of the polarized claims that are made for them, are particularly resonant in what David Punter has labelled the 'Literature of Terror'. Judith Halberstam's assessment of the Gothic is particularly helpful in analyzing the way in which the genre dramatizes the fragility of duality; stating that 'the monsters of the nineteenth century metaphorised modern subjectivity as a balancing act between inside/outside, female/male, body/mind, native/foreign, proletariat/aristocrat', she argues that the

> tendency within the Gothic of one thing to slip into its opposite … makes mincemeat of any notion of binaries. This is one of the reasons that it becomes so difficult to pinpoint the political impetus of any given Gothic text but it also is what produces the multiple web of interpretations.[36]

Halberstam invokes the binaries of 'modern subjectivity' only to problematic them as a brittle 'balancing act' and, more emphatically, to state that the Gothic makes 'mincemeat' of them. What she indicates is the unlocated nature of the genre: like degeneration theory it is a contradictory site of discourse. Gothic narratives rely on basic dualisms, good versus evil, human versus inhuman, etc., only to blur these apparently intransigent boundaries; the result is a genre that suggests a variety of readings, a 'multiple web of interpretations', which seem to offer a limitless ability to confound expectations. As much as the Gothic serves to translate or renegotiate the self-reflexive and divided elements of 'High' cultural discourse exemplified in Hallam and Arnold's analyses of modernity and modern poetry into a popular medium, where the 'Private Memoirs' in Hogg's novel, the 'Full Statement' of Jekyll in Stevenson's and the contemplative ruminations of Dorian Gray in Wilde's either anticipate or echo the self-obsessed Arnoldian dialogue of the 'mind with itself', it also suggests through its dislocation of binary opposition that identity is becoming more fluid. Karl Miller suggests that during the nineteenth century 'duality, as a paradigm of mental behaviour, was to give the impression of turning into multiple personality, dispsychism into polypsychism'.[37] The Gothic dramatizes this shift, making 'mincemeat' of received wisdom, and therefore achieving a subtle political resonance which challenges the normalizing discourse of contemporary psychiatry with its reliance upon inclusive and exclusive categories. The monstrous creations of the nineteenth-century Gothic are ultimately unlocated, they establish polarized boundaries, the division between Jekyll and Hyde being an obvious paradigm, only to contradict and overrun them; as a 'metaphorized' response to modern subjectivity they become emblematic of the alienated and disidentical individual who nonetheless reflects and is intrinsically part of the 'punctual and self-possessed individual'. What the Gothic creations of nineteenth-century modernity do, as the contradictory discourse of degeneration so unwittingly does, is question the parameters between identity and disidentity, human and inhuman, social and anti-social. In *Skin Shows*, Judith Halberstam identifies the distinction between the origins of Gothic fiction in the late eighteenth century and its revitalized manifestation in the nineteenth century: 'Gothic ... marks a peculiarly modern preoccupation with boundaries and their collapse. Gothic monsters, furthermore, differ from the monsters that came before the nineteenth century in that the monsters of modernity are characterized by their proximity to humans.'[38] As we will see the boundary between the monstrous and the human, the social and the anti-social, cohesive identity and alienated fragmentation of the self are not as clear cut as they seem.

Although by no means the exclusive province of these writers, James Hogg's *The Private Memoirs and Confessions of a Justified Sinner* (1824), Robert Louis Stevenson's *The Strange Case of Dr Jekyll and Mr Hyde* (1886) and Oscar Wilde's *The Picture of Dorian Gray* (1891) explore and represent the contradictory possibilities of duality in complex and sophisticated ways through the use of the Gothic genre. Each novel deals with a series of interchangeable themes, and there is a certain cross-pollination between them; for example, Hogg's and Stevenson's work share a mutual sense of Scottish literary tradition. Apart from their common representation of doubling, the three texts in question are linked by a significant reliance upon inheritance and the value of capital within the framework of duality, and the fluidity of identity that obviously occurs in a literature that deals with the divided self. Just as Charles Dickens suggests in *Bleak House* that identity within modernity is a profoundly unstable quantity, so too James Hogg, for example, represents a series of familial relationships dislocated by a fragmentation of family name: in *The Private Memoirs* the family name for the eponymous Sinner oscillates with a shifting textual uncertainty between Wringhim, Colwan and Dalcastle. To paraphrase one of Oscar Wilde's maxims in the Preface to *Dorian Gray*, all three texts point out the perils of going beneath the surface;

ultimately, going beneath the surface is an enterprise that reveals things about the self that are perhaps best left concealed.

Judith Halberstam, in her discussion of *Jekyll and Hyde*, notes of the book that Stevenson rather disparagingly referred to as his 'shilling shocker', that its 'very popularity announces it as nonliterary within a Victorian context and its appeal for a mass audience suggests that it must fail to satisfy the high cultural expectations that critics like Matthew Arnold espoused'.[39] Halberstam cites *Culture and Anarchy*, published in 1869, as the text that most clearly represents Arnold's theories of culture. Without entering into too detailed an overview of this complex work, in *Culture and Anarchy* Arnold offers his famous translation of aristocrat, middle-class and working-class distinctions into 'Barbarians', 'Philistines' and 'Populace'; it is also where he posits a series of binary cultural equations, the one between culture and anarchy themselves being the most prominent.[40] To paraphrase a sophisticated and subtle work in a rather reductive manner, *Culture and Anarchy* is concerned with advocating the positive benefits of culture for the social and political life of the bourgeoisie, making them fit to govern the other echelons of the social infrastructure, and by culture Arnold means 'High' culture. If there is such a thing as 'High' culture then there must, by implication, be a 'Low' culture, one which – if we consider that the 'High' is the province of the educated, discriminating, bourgeois elite – is broadly popular in appeal. John Storey notes in his assessment of Arnold's contribution to the discourse of popular culture that it 'is never actually defined' by him but that 'it becomes clear ... that the term "anarchy" operates in part as a synonym for popular culture'.[41] 'Low' or popular culture therefore becomes an unspoken, even unspeakable, presence for the Arnoldian perspective on culture. Stevenson's *Jekyll and Hyde*, defined as popular and therefore 'nonliterary' in Victorian terms by Halberstam, can be posited as representative of this strata of culture, a crude, anarchic, uncivilized and revolutionary alter ego to the 'sweetness and light' of Arnold's privileged culture.[42] However, as indicated above the Gothic novels under scrutiny here, and Stevenson's is the most obvious example, in many ways eloquently evoke the dialogue of the mind with itself the presence of which so disillusions Arnold's perception of modernity and its 'High' culture. Again there is a sense of cultural doubling at work. In spite of Arnold's attempt to affirm a singular and partial 'culture', the implicit suggestion that an 'other' culture exists reveals the deficiency of such an enterprise, for the

Gothic can be read as shamelessly dramatizing his critical territory. Similarly we can find examples of concealed identity and the perils of going beneath the surface, resonant with Stevenson and Wilde's work, in Arnold's own self-consciously *literary* (as opposed to Stevenson's *non*-literary) oeuvre.

Arnold's poem 'The Buried Life', written roughly around the same time as 'Dover Beach' and published in 1852, is a prominent case in point and, strangely enough, provides a useful paradigm for representations of the exploration for a concealed identity. Like 'Dover Beach' the poem masquerades as a love lyric, its initial lines reading as an address by the poetic voice to its lover which is reminiscent of Keats's 'Ode on Melancholy'. However, just as 'Dover Beach' conceals its assessment of the decline of Western culture within the conventions of love poetry, so too 'The Buried Life' plays upon a juxtaposition between depths and surfaces. In the case of this poem the initial address to the externalized lover merely contains a rumination upon the notion that an authentic, internalized self exists within the self. It is in the contemplative and introspective sections of the poem that the sense of an uncanny 'other' self emerges; in effect there are, in an appropriately Gothicized manner, suggestions of the divided self buried in 'The Buried Life'. This apprehension is initially evoked by Arnold in a passage that hints at the artificiality and hypocrisy of the outer self, and which utilizes a vocabulary of disguise and deception which we have already seen Francis Barker apply to the Cartesian construction of the modern individual, and one which is particularly resonant in the Gothic literature of duality:

> I knew the mass of men conceal'd
> Their thoughts, for fear that if revealed
> They would by other men be met
> With blank indifference, or with blame reproved;
> I knew they lived and moved
> Trick'd in disguises, alien to the rest
> Of men, and alien to themselves – and yet
> The same heart beats in every human breast! (lines 16–24)[43]

What Arnold posits is the contrast between a superficial and deceptive self – one that is 'Trick'd in disguises', but one that is the social and socialized self, the public self that meets 'other men' – and the 'conceal'd' authentic self. However, this juxtaposition between external, disguised self and internal authentic self is more complex than a representation of English masculine reserve; it is closer to the 'inner dichotomies' of modernity as defined by Marshall Berman. At the heart of the depiction is the sense of an alter ego, the authentic self, which is concealed precisely because if it was revealed it would be met by 'blank indifference' or, and more tellingly, 'with blame reproved'; it is in the second response that the possibility occurs that the authentic self incorporates a shameful, and therefore submerged, secret. The solution therefore is the utilization of the theatrical masks and disguises which effectively conduce a state of disidentity; the disguised individual is not only alien to others but also unrecognizable to itself. By problematizing the boundaries between internal and external through concealing the objectified yet internalized self, the subject becomes confused with regard to authentic identity. Arnold goes on to note that

> Fate, which foresaw
> How frivolous a baby man would be –
> By what distractions he would be possess'd,
> How he would pour himself in every strife,
> And well-nigh change his own identity –
> That it might keep from his capricious play
> His genuine self, and force him to obey
> Even in his own despite his being's law,
> Bade through the deep recesses of our breast
> The unregarded river of our life
> Pursue with indiscernible flow its way (lines 30–40).

Again Arnold posits a juxtaposition between depths and surfaces, unknowing and knowing, authenticity and inauthenticity. His articulation of this interplay is complex and convoluted, and the dense syntactic structure, with hyphens and commas which result in fragmented clauses, further complicates meaning. What seems to emerge is a picture of the superficial but socialized self as 'frivolous', 'capricious', an unstable and composite being that can even be regarded as degenerate, if we consider Greenslade's definition of the contradictory qualities of degeneration, through the conjunction of adult and child in 'baby man'. This self, which is given to 'capricious' unpredictability, actively pursues and engages with a chaotic condition of 'strife' that produces a constant 'change' in 'his own identity'. The superficial self therefore, through its instability and constant and active change, reflects the 'fluid' social identity of modern men and women which, as defined by Marshall Berman, is a response to Marx's description of a permanently revolutionizing bourgeois epoch. In Arnold's poem the socialized self therefore exists in a recognizably chaotic and consequently modern environment, and responds appropriately to the permanently changing conditions of modernity by embracing these changes to a point that renders identity a flux. By contrast the 'genuine self', buried in the 'deep recesses of our breast', as opposed to the limpid representation of the fluid social identity, is confused and confusing; what can be deduced is that the so-called 'genuine self' is difficult to fathom, and that Arnold likens its presence and progress to a river that is 'unregarded' and 'indiscernible' in its circulation within the individual. It is at the start of the fifth section of the poem that Arnold's exploration of the internalized genuine self reaches a significantly ambiguous pitch; the location of the urge to detect this self is important:

> But often, in the world's most crowded streets,
> But often, in the din of strife,
> There rises an unspeakable desire
> After the knowledge of our buried life (lines 45–48).

In the 'crowded streets' and the 'din of strife', which the fluid and socialized identity revels in, we are back to the chaos of the nineteenth-century metropolis described by Wordsworth in *The Prelude*. For Arnold, however, the experience is different; where the modern city reduces identity for Wordsworth, dehumanizing man and rendering progress purposeless, for Arnold the chaotic qualities of the urban experience can induce a closed-off urge towards self-revelation. Being in the midst of the nineteenth-century city inspires a quest for the authentic self. However, in the context of this discussion the apparently epiphanic moment is undercut by the nature of this 'desire' to unearth the buried self, for Arnold describes it as 'unspeakable'. It would seem that his use of this word indicates the failure of any meaningful communication between the 'mass of men' that earlier sections of the poem alluded to; the alien and alienated nature of the 'genuine self' means that the desire to detect it, due to the 'blank indifference' or 'blame' that revealing it would inspire, quite literally cannot be uttered. Yet if we consider that there is a buried theme within 'The

Buried Life', and the notion of the 'genuine self' that exists concealed within the individual is at best equivocal, then Arnold's inclusion of the notion of 'unspeakable desire' takes on striking resonance, particularly as later in the poem he refers to the emotions equated with the buried self as 'nameless feelings' (line 62). The 'unspeakable', particularly in conjunction with 'desire', suggests taboo or forbidden territory, an idea that then explains the 'blame' which would be the response to a revelation of the genuine self. Such a conjunction is also a primary feature in Gothic fiction, and Arnold's carefully chosen words, as much as they try to convey the gravity of the exercise, render the attempt to locate the authentic self ambivalently monstrous.

The buried life of the poem can therefore be read as a secreted, guilty self, one that arouses 'unspeakable desire' and one that cannot be uttered because it *is* unspeakable. Judith Halberstam notes with regard to the idea of a buried self that '[l]ive burial is certainly a major and standard trope of Gothic ... [it] is the entanglement of self and other within monstrosity and the parasitical relationship between the two'.[44] Hogg, Stevenson and Wilde's *doppelgänger* texts all explore the construction, emergence and establishment of unspeakable or buried selves in interesting concatenations. One of the original titles for Hogg's *Private Memoirs* was 'The Suicide's Grave', and the pseudo-factual editorial narrative that frames the Sinner's memoirs recounts the disinterring of both a buried body and a buried autobiographical text, for a leather case found on Robert Wringhim's buried body 'contained a *printed pamphlet*'.[45] Similarly in Stevenson's *Jekyll and Hyde* Dr Lanyon's testimony, which describes an instance of Jekyll's transformation into Hyde, consists of a sealed document placed within another sealed document and metaphorically buried in Mr Utterson's private safe, and Jekyll's own account of his double consists of 'a considerable packet sealed in several places', just as Dorian Gray's own strange memoir of his life – the portrait that documents his moral degeneration – is 'hidden away at all costs' in an attic.[46] What we therefore have is a series of personal accounts of the shameful buried life that are themselves either literally or metaphorically buried. The purpose of each narrative is to unearth that which has been buried alive, to make public the shame-inducing private and to enter the perilous territory that lies below the surface. All three texts go further in many different ways to explore the buried life that Arnold reticently, and as a result ambiguously, examines in his poem, effectively liberalizing the hints at guilt and possible monstrosity in Arnold's shadowy terminology. That said there is still a sense, even within the sensationalist strategies enlisted by the Gothic, that the genuine, authentic and buried self of modernity remains 'unspeakable' or 'nameless'. In Stevenson's so-called 'shilling shocker' the lawyer Utterson, on first encountering Jekyll's buried self Hyde, finds the nature of Hyde's monstrosity problematic and indefinable. There 'is something more, if I could find a name for it' he notes; later in the text, in a letter to Utterson, Jekyll himself states that 'I have brought on myself a punishment and a danger that I cannot name'.[47] In the contradictory, unreliable and shifting discourse of duality it would seem that a conception of the real or the authentic self is unutterable as the boundaries between self and other blur and fragment, just as in Arnold's 'The Buried Life' 'High' cultural discourse can be read as infected by the concepts and vocabulary of the populist Gothic. In this context Stevenson's novel, which emphasizes the emergence of the buried life whilst simultaneously representing its paradoxical nature in that it is both nameless or unutterable but also has a name (Hyde), forms the obvious focal point for this chapter.

1 Speaking and answering in the character of another: James Hogg's private memoirs

> It is impossible that I can have been doing a thing, and not doing it at the same time. But indeed, honest woman, there have several incidents occurred to me in the course of my life which persuade me I have a second self; or that there is some other being who appears in my likeness.[1]

> I knew a very intelligent and amiable man, who had the power of thus placing before his eyes *himself*, and often laughed heartily at *his double*, who always seemed to laugh in turn.[2]

In the context of the issues that have been discussed so far James Hogg's *The Private Memoirs and Confessions of a Justified Sinner* may seem an unusual text to choose when the themes and ideas at stake in this project are considered. Neither the first nor the most famous representation of duality in fiction – the latter accolade must surely go to Stevenson's *Jekyll and Hyde*, a text which in its title alone has become virtually synonymous with populist accounts of schizophrenia – Hogg's strange and idiosyncratic novel initially seems very removed from the debates regarding modernity and identity alluded to earlier in this discussion. Indeed *Private Memoirs* seems to inhabit a historical and geographical territory that has little to do with the urban metropolis of the nineteenth century and the crises that it engenders. The novel is set in the late seventeenth and early eighteenth century and is unequivocally located in the Scottish lowlands; its carefully constructed historical reference points establish this and as such it would seem, regardless of its subtly ambiguous supernatural elements, to have a purely local, vividly picturesque appeal that contradicts the conventional European locations found in other Gothic novels by Hogg's predecessors and contemporaries. Indeed the possibility that Hogg's single major work of fiction may be a literary one-off is compounded by the fact that its historical and geographical specificity also incorporates and systematically alludes to the political and religious conflicts and upheavals of the period in Scottish history that it evokes, namely the conflicts between Protestant and Presbyterian Covenanters and Catholic Jacobites, and the emergence of the extreme antinomian Calvinism that the eponymous Sinner adheres to. David Punter refers to the apparent generical isolation of the text, stating that 'the material from which Hogg's *Confessions of a Justified Sinner* is forged is liable to seem a little parochial, since the particular tyranny which most exercises Hogg is the evil produced by antinomianism.'[3] However, Hogg's frequently perplexing novel is more sophisticated and resonant than such an account would suggest, for Punter goes on to state that a parochial reading is 'only the starting point … for on this basis Hogg produces a detailed and terrifying account of schizophrenia'.[4] In fact Hogg's work, distanced as it is from the popular cultural baggage thrust upon Stevenson's 'shilling shocker', articulates a nineteenth-century crisis of identity *vis-à-vis* the problematics of modernity in potentially radical ways that help to contextualize the urban writings on a similar theme by Stevenson and Wilde later in the century. In this sense Punter's interpretation of the novel as an account of schizophrenia is a bit misleading, particularly when we consider that schizophrenia as a category for mental illness is largely a twentieth-century psychiatric phenomenon. Indeed, as a starting point it is the parochialism itself manifest in Hogg's novel that is significant for the purposes of this discussion. What Hogg's *Private Memoirs* aims to represent in terms of its context and frame for the account of Robert Wringhim's life is a divided nation and national identity, a political division that effectively becomes focused and intensified in the divided capital chosen as the location for similar accounts of self-division in the work of Stevenson and Wilde, one where the haves vie with the have-nots, leisured hedonists with guilt-wracked or austere professionals. In effect Hogg's low-key, quasi-satirical novel sets a precedent for the interaction between individual and environment (and the effect that the latter has upon the former) which Greenslade detects in his analysis of the *fin de siècle* city condition. Punter neatly stakes a claim for the wider relevance of the novel by stating that it belongs to 'a particular kind of modernity, that kind of modernity which takes very seriously the problems of social and psychological conditioning, and which therefore questions the supremacy of the realm of the "moral"'.[5] In effect its parochial and located elements become a cypher for a wider discussion of division and dislocation in the nineteenth century.

We can immediately establish the manner in which the text articulates fragmentation and uncertainty through its narrative structure, where a sceptical and ironic editorial voice frames Robert Wringhim's own testimony. In addition Hogg's work appears under a variety of titles and in different manifestations from its moment of conception onwards. The novel has its origins in a letter published in the Scottish literary journal *Blackwood's Magazine* in August 1823; entitled 'A Scots Mummy' and signed by James Hogg, a frequent contributor to the magazine, it detailed the digging up and exhuming of the preserved corpse of a suicide.[6] This letter, in turn, advertised the novel that would be published in 1824 as *The Private Memoirs and Confessions of a Justified Sinner*. In this edition the letter previously published in *Blackwood's* was reproduced in the second editorial narrative in an abridged form and framed by an editorial gloss; the editor also notes that the original title for the text which had Robert Wringhim's authentic memoir as its centrepiece was 'A Self-justified Sinner', but that this was changed back to the title used by Wringhim on his document at the request of the editor's publishers.[7] This manipulation of document, letter and title is further emphasized by the fact that the novel was reprinted in 1828 as *The Suicide's Grave*, in 1837 under the title *Confessions of a Fanatic* and then again in 1895 as *The Suicide's Grave*. The result is a profoundly plastic text in terms of the bias of the title; the tensions between 'Justified Sinner', 'Self-justified Sinner' and 'Fanatic' alone indicate the multiplicity of different interpretative positions possible regarding Robert Wringhim and also the tension in the text itself between Robert's apparently deluded religious fanaticism and the detached, sceptical and cold voice of the editor which frames the confessions. This tension essentially invites two basic readings of the text: it is either a case study in psychiatric disturbance or a tale of diabolic possession. However, the scattering of titles for a text that is known as *Private Memoirs* today, but which has appeared in a variety of different manifestations during the course of the nineteenth century, initiates and generates a series of contradictions and inconsistencies with regard to structure, narrative, identity and authority that evade a single unified reading.

The instability of the eponymous Sinner's family name has already been noted; what should be added is that Robert's origins are less than unequivocal. In the first editorial narrative the births of George Colwan and Robert Wringhim are compared and consequently indicate the ambivalence of the latter's claims for legitimacy:

> our saintly and afflicted dame, in due time, was safely delivered of a fine boy, whom the laird acknowledged as his son and heir, and had him christened by his own name, and nursed in his own premises ... the boy grew up, and was a healthful and happy child; and, in the course of another year, the lady presented him with a brother. A brother he certainly was, in the eye of the law, and it is more than probable that he was the brother in reality. But the laird thought otherwise; and, though he knew and acknowledged that he was obliged to support and provide for him, he refused to acknowledge him in other respects. He neither would countenance the banquet, nor take the baptismal vows on him in the child's name; of course the poor boy had to live and remain an alien from the visible church for a year and a day; at which time, Mr Wringhim, out of pity and kindness, took the lady herself as sponsor for the boy, and baptized him by the name of Robert Wringhim, – that being the noted divine's own name ... [George] was brought up with his father ... [and] was a generous and kind-hearted youth ... Robert was brought up with Mr Wringhim ... and there the boy was early inured to all the sternness and severity of his pastor's arbitrary and unyielding creed. He was taught to pray twice every day, and seven times on Sabbath days; but he was only to pray for the elect, and, like David of old, doom all that were aliens from God to destruction. He had never, in that family into which he had been as it were adopted, heard ought but evil spoken of his reputed father and brother; consequently he held them in utter abhorrence, and prayed against them every day.[8]

There are a number of things going on in this lengthy extract: firstly a sibling rivalry is established between the acknowledged and 'kind-hearted' George Colwan and the unacknowledged and ('as it were') adopted Robert Wringhim; secondly the legitimacy of Robert remains ambiguous – he is George Colwan's brother in 'the eye of the law' yet this certainty is undercut by the ensuing reservations that it was 'more than probable that he was his brother', that 'the laird thought otherwise', and that both are apparently 'reputed' family connections. Beyond this uncertain family origin, and the subsequent rejection of young Robert Wringhim by George Colwan Lord Dalcastle, we learn that Robert is adopted by his namesake Mr Wringhim and initiated into the extreme Calvinism that is remorselessly satirized in the novel. The novel's claim for modernity is that the young Robert's 'social and psychological conditioning' (as David Punter puts it) is problematized through his antinomian indoctrination and consequent condemnation both of those who aren't of the elect and of his 'reputed' father and brother. Rejected by his possibly natural paternal parent and indoctrinated by his adopted one, the Justified Sinner clearly spells out the perils of conditioning.

The result of this familial instability is that Robert's identity is rendered uncertain, he is *apparently* a legitimate Colwan/Dalcastle yet is embraced by and embraces his Wringhim identity and his marginalized status as a Calvinist antinomian.[9] This oscillation between family connections, and the overall fragility of certainty within the structure of the text itself, contributes to the ultimate sense of displacement and contradiction manifest in Hogg's work. As Wringhim puts it in the confessions themselves, 'I was born an outcast in the world, in which I was destined to act so conspicuous a part,' thus effectively centring and decentring himself simultaneously within his own narrative.[10] Judith Halberstam has noted the Gothic novel's tendency to explode notions of binary opposition, and in Hogg's *Private Memoirs* we can see this demonstrated; as much as he relies upon a series of equations, between Robert Wringhim and George Colwan, Lord Dalcastle and Mr Wringhim, we can also detect an accelerating collapse of binaries into thematic and textual fragmentation. One of the most striking examples of this poised instability can be found in Hogg's use of the ironic editorial voice. The editor states in the final paragraph of his first narrative, by way of introducing Wringhim's confession, 'I have now the pleasure of presenting my readers with an original document of a most singular nature, and preserved for their perusal in a still more singular manner.'[11] There is a manifest irony in this testimony, particularly when we consider that a claim for authenticity is being made yet that the text as a whole – editorial narratives and Sinner's confession combined – plays upon a series of contradictions and conflicting accounts from different sources that consistently problematize any claims for authority. In this sense the supposition that this is a 'document of a most *singular* nature' (my emphasis) is especially ironic considering that the text is about the establishment and subsequent questioning of binary relations, and that the editorial frame provides an auto-critique or gloss upon the central confessions, thus effectively entering into dialogue with them. As a result the editorial voice contradicts its own text at this point, for what we are presented with is a series of fragments, tentatively united under a shifting title, consisting of '[a]utobiography, diary, confession, memoirs, chronicle, detective story, picaresque, allegory, parable, folk-tale, sermon, edited manuscript, romance, and anti-romance: the genres form, dissolve, and reform while we read'.[12]

For Fred Botting the complex repercussions of Hogg's radical splintering of narrative and genre instigate a recognizably modern nineteenth-century Gothic, one that dispenses with the genre's traditional melodramatic trappings and continental location. This updated medium begins to explore the possible instability of identity in modernity through dramatizing extraordinary states of consciousness within apparently ordinary and familiar environments, namely, the nineteenth-century metropolis. Hogg's innovatory skills lie in his ability simultaneously to maintain yet question the boundaries between apparent opposites, an aptitude that Judith Halberstam has detected in the nineteenth-century Gothic's metaphorizing of modern subjectivity as a fragile 'balancing act' between binary equations. Botting notes that the

> *Memoir*'s ironic distance manages to sustain a distinction between internal and external worlds even as it acknowledges the curious, ambivalent effects of writing's duplicity. Its fascination with delusion and psychological disturbance maintains an individual case as its object. The fascination with deranged states and uncanny experiences, uncertainly imagined or horribly real, recurs throughout later Gothic fiction in attempts to represent these conditions subjectively or objectively. The different narratives of Hogg's novel perform both strategies, one looking at mental deterioration from the inside, the other from the outside. Both these angles are explored in nineteenth-century renderings of the uncanny: they are internally presented with the attention on doubles and mirrors, and externally objectified as cases of criminal or psychological degeneration. Between the two, the status of human identity, social forms and Gothic styles underwent significant changes in location and significance.[13]

Botting's analysis draws attention to the way in which Hogg's *Private Memoirs* thematically and stylistically manage to sustain a sense of the division between internal and external whilst at the same time revelling in the ability of writing to disrupt such clarity; for Botting the effect of writing becomes uncanny in terms of its duplicity. Similarly he highlights the fact that Hogg's writing also initiates a lineage of

Gothic writing in the nineteenth century that juggles representations of consciousness subjectively and objectively. The subjective, internalized representation finds its medium through the use of doubles and mirrors and the externalized, objectified representation concentrates on case studies of criminals or degenerates, motifs which are explicitly utilized and interwoven in the *fin de siècle* Gothic fictions of Stevenson and Wilde. Significantly, what Botting finds is that between this emphasis on objectivity and subjectivity the nature and status of human identity begins to shift and change. The most startling way in which Hogg's fragmented, duplicitous and deceptive writing renegotiates and therefore calls into question the notion of a stable, autonomous and unified identity can be found in the case of Hogg himself. Hogg can be identified with the anonymous, ironic editor whose comments frame Wringhim's memoirs; yet, as noted, Hogg also appears by name as the contributor to *Blackwood's Magazine* and author of the letter previously published as 'A Scots Mummy', the authenticity of which the editor calls into question, stating that 'so often had I been hoaxed by the ingenious fancies displayed in that Magazine, that when this relation met my eye, I did not believe it'.[14] Given that Hogg also appears in character as his literary pseudonym 'The Ettrick Shepherd' in the Editor's second narrative we can deduce that identity becomes increasingly dispersed and unstable, and that the whole notion of authority is simultaneously ironized and troubled. This shifting around of authorial identity becomes particularly resonant when we consider that, through his association with the writer of 'A Scots Mummy' and the editor of the second narrative, which details a second exhuming of Wringhim's corpse, Hogg himself, in his different guises and disguises, can be identified with a Gothic creation of the early decades of the nineteenth century: the grave-robbing resurrectionist who makes profit from the corpse that he disinters. In an appropriately Frankensteinian manner, Hogg produces a literary *corpus* from the suicide's exhumed corpse, a novel stitched together from the fragments found upon Wringhim's body.

The apparent parochialism of Hogg's work is largely deceptive, particularly as a significant interaction between environment and personal identity shadows *Private Memoirs*, a feature which largely anticipates the urban Gothic of Stevenson and Wilde. In addition, what should be remembered is that, for all its use of folk idiom and dialect (the story of the town o' Auchtermuchty recounted to Wringhim is a particularly good example of Hogg's use of this), a significant portion of the novel, both in terms of the editorial frame and Wringhim's confession, is located in Edinburgh. Mark L. Schoenfield, in his essay on Hogg and identity in the magazine culture of the late eighteenth and early nineteenth century, notes that 'in the early nineteenth century ... Edinburgh attempted to establish itself as a centre of British, and European, culture and trade'; in effect Hogg's strange and idiosyncratic work is produced within the environment and institutions of the modern metropolis where, as Marshall Berman has suggested in his reading of Marx, identity is compelled to embrace fluidity.[15] It can therefore be suggested that as much as Hogg's novel has a purely local appeal, it also consciously (Hogg's fragmenting of identity into identities demonstrates this) and perhaps by implication (in its substantial use of Edinburgh as a location and frame of reference) negotiates the effects and symptoms of modernity in the identity of the individual. Schoenfield's reading of Hogg is particularly helpful here; he acknowledges the interaction between environment, its institutions and identity which mark modernity for William Greenslade and David Punter, stating that 'the boundaries producing the notion of identity [in the nineteenth century] are not personal but institutional and always entail social agendas'.[16] In Hogg's case, and in the magazine culture of the late eighteenth and early nineteenth century where the writer becomes a commodity within a literary marketplace, identity is tied up with the processes implicit in a recognizably modern mode of industrial and bourgeois capitalism; one effectively 'created within a matrix of consumption and production'.[17] The result is a sense that identity is taken out of the hands of the individual and is subsequently manufactured by the demands of the marketplace, or as Schoenfield puts it by way of a series of hypothetical questions:

> For many [R]omantic writers, identity became vexed upon entering (or imagining entering) the literary marketplace, at the moment of glimpsing a literary double. 'Who am I,' the questioning might run, 'once a publisher, a journal, a series of reviews incorporate my labour? At what risk am I from the mediating persons and institutions? Does a double confirm the self, deny it, supplant it?'[18]

Identity therefore becomes a fragile entity in this environment, something surrendered to the shadowy forces of the marketplace and something which inspires the paranoid anxiety that the commodification of writer and writing might generate a Gothic 'literary double' which, as capable as it is of confirming self, also indicates the instability of self. What we effectively have is the objectified and fragmented disidentical individual of Cartesian dualism, newly (re)created by the Frankensteinian dynamics of capital. In effect Hogg, in his repetitious use of doubling and contradiction and, most emphatically, in the disintegration of his own literary persona in *Private Memoirs*, dramatizes the crisis of identity experienced within the modern city and more specifically within the literary marketplace.

Hogg's text therefore becomes the most equivocal of representations of identity in the context of this discussion. Due to the complex narrative infrastructure and shifting variety of perspectives utilized by Hogg, the reader is never quite sure of who is who and what is what in the *Memoirs*. The retrospective arrival on the scene of the diabolic Gil-Martin in Wringhim's confession further compounds this problem, particularly as, due to the different perspectives manifest in the text, it is almost impossible to identify with any certainty the presence of the monstrous in the novel. Wringhim's account of his first encounter with Gil-Martin is proof of this; he notes:

> What was my astonishment, on perceiving that he was the same being as myself! The clothes were the same to the smallest item. the form was the same; the apparent age; the colour of the hair; the eyes; and, as far as recollection could serve me from viewing my own features in a glass, the features too were the very same.[19]

There seems to be an explicit instance of doubling taking place at this point and, as Fred Botting points out, the double is utilized in the Gothic novel as a device that 'threatens the loss of identity'.[20] The problem here though is that Wringhim, as well as having a dispersed sense of self in the context of family connections and family name, is not even quite sure of his own physical appearance: his likeness to Gil-Martin has a degree of specificity in his own eyes but it is also influenced by the fact that his own sense of physical self is founded upon how far 'recollection could serve me'. This ambivalent identification is rendered even more problematic by the suggestion that Wringhim believes the apparently satanic Gil-Martin to be his own guardian angel. Identification is made unstable by the fact that throughout the novel, both in the editor's account and Wringhim's own testimony, Gil-Martin, mirroring Hogg himself, appears in a veritably protean variety of guises.

To temper all the confusion and slippage of identification in the text, one of the main avenues explored in an attempt to stabilize identity is that of inheritance, namely Wringhim's inheritance of the Dalcastle estates after the murder of George Colwan and the subsequent death of old Lord Dalcastle. Wringhim's inheritance of the estates should arguably give him a certain degree of verification with regard to identity but inevitably the authority of authenticity, as the structures and strategies employed by Hogg have demonstrated, is itself radically unstable. Consequently, as Wringhim inherits his apparently natural father's property, his sense of individual identity collapses even further. At first the inheritance of the estates seems relatively unambiguous, as Wringhim notes, 'No sooner were the obsequies of the funeral over, than my friend and I went to Dalcastle, and took *undisputed* [my emphasis] possession of the houses, lands, and effects that had been my father's'.[21] However, upon acquiring the Dalcastle property, Wringhim's ability to differentiate between objectivity and subjectivity starts to evaporate as his whole conception of time collapses. Confronted by an angry woman who claims that he has seduced and corrupted her daughter, Wringhim asks, 'Do you consider how short a time I have been in this place? How much that time has been occupied? And how there was even a possibility that I could have accomplished such villainies?'[22] Wringhim believes that he has occupied the estates for only thirty or forty days, but this is contradicted by the woman who emphatically states that it has been four months and seven days. Faced with this contradiction, Wringhim appeals to his 'friend' Gil-Martin for confirmation of his own judgement; however Gil-Martin replies:

> You are wrong, my dear friend; you are wrong. It is indeed the space of time that the lady hath stated, to a day, since you came here, and I came with you; and I am sorry that I know for certain that you have been frequently haunting her house, and have often had private correspondence with one of the young ladies too. Of the nature of it I presume not to know.[23]

Gil-Martin further compounds Wringhim's confusion by confirming the woman's accusation that he has spent all his time at Dalcastle in an alcoholic stupor, stating that 'of late, you have been very much addicted to intemperance. I doubt if, from the first night you tasted the delights of drunkenness, that you have ever again been in your right mind.'[24] Faced with these contradiction all that Wringhim can helplessly conclude is that 'there have several incidents occurred to me in the course of my life which persuade me I have a second self'.[25] Of course it is never entirely clear whether Wringhim has performed these actions in an intoxicated state, or whether the shape-shifting Gil-Martin has performed them for him. What is clear though is that Wringhim's sense of an integrated autonomous identity is falling apart, most evidently symbolized by his loss of a sense of time. The inheritance of the estates, which should validate and authorize identity, basically produces the opposite of the required effect, a feature compounded by Wringhim's inability to recognize documents that he has apparently signed after taking control of Dalcastle.

At the core of Hogg's representation of the fragility of identity is power. In Schoenfield's assessment of identity and the magazine market, power is obviously manifest in the ability of the publisher to create a literary double, to somehow trouble the identity of writers as they surrender their labour, a power that is implicitly tied up with that of capital. It is possible to suggest that the collapse of Wringhim's identity after he inherits the Dalcastle estate is reliant upon the fact that he has no ready capital – he notes that, although he possesses the land and buildings of the estate, old Dalcastle's 'plate, and vast treasures of ready money, he had bestowed upon a voluptuous and unworthy creature, who had lived long with him as a mistress'.[26] In effect, although Wringhim has property he has no financial power in a marketplace where capital determines identity. However, the main power struggle in the text, and the one that determines the problems for individual identity, is between Wringhim himself and Gil-Martin. This power struggle is not merely an instance of basic dualism, something that is capable of confirming as well as negating self. Instead, due to Gil-Martin's apparently protean powers, it leads to a total fragmentation and disintegration of Wringhim's identity; as a result he shifts outside selfhood and is to all intents dispossessed of identity. During the course of this relationship Wringhim increasingly enters a liminal state of being, as we have seen apparently oscillating between consciousness and unconsciousness, subjectivity and objectivity, in a way that consistently and remorselessly undermines identity. Ultimately it is not the possibility that there is a satanic Gil-Martin present and manipulating events that is significant in the novel, but the effect that possibly having a second self has upon Wringhim. As Masao Miyoshi puts it:

> Whatever action performed in the name of Wringhim is carried out by the double, or by that part of himself over which he, as a whole man, has no control at all. The sense of an integral true self is gone, and Wringhim as an identifiable person is reduced to a helpless observer.[27]

In effect Wringhim becomes the alienated, extended and disidentical self of Cartesian dualism. In many ways the collapse of identity that Hogg dramatizes also anticipates nineteenth-century psychiatry's analysis of the split personality. In his confessions Wringhim notes of his relationship with Gil-Martin, 'I sometimes fumed and sometimes shed tears at being obliged to yield to proposals against which I had at first felt every reasoning power of my soul rise in opposition, but, for all that, he never failed in carrying conviction along with him in effect.'[28] Wringhim's response is essentially contradictory by nature, confusing and blurring the boundaries between faculties, and playing the empiricism of 'reasoning powers' off against an indefinable soul. It also demonstrates the effortless dominance of Gil-Martin, whose argumentative proposals 'never failed in carrying conviction'. In *The Duality of the Mind* of 1844, Alfred Wigan, as noted in one of the epigraphs for this chapter, cites the case of one of his patients – 'a very intelligent and amiable man' – who had the ability of 'placing before his eyes *himself*'. This creates an initially jocular situation where self and double laugh at each other. What interests Wigan though is that this case study 'became gradually convinced that he was haunted by himself, or ... by his self. This other self would argue with him pertinaciously, and to his great mortification sometimes refute him, which, as he was very proud of his logical powers, humiliated him exceedingly.'[29] Although Wigan's study of the divided self was published twenty years after Hogg's novel, the experience depicted is noticeably similar. Where Wringhim in *Private Memoirs* endeavours to assert his 'reasoning power' over the suggestions of his apparent double, Wigan's patient has his 'logical powers' refuted; similarly Wringhim states that he 'fumed, and sometimes shed tears at being obliged to yield', indicating his sense of humiliation, where Wigan's case study has a double that 'humiliated him exceedingly'. Just as Hogg's representation of the perils of duality echoes the literary marketplace in which he is writing, so too it anticipates the medical discourse on the fragmentation of identity in nineteenth-century modernity.

As Karl Miller has noted, during the nineteenth century 'duality, as a paradigm of mental behaviour, was to give the impression of turning into multiple personality'; this disintegration of binary equations can be explicitly detected in Hogg's representation of the collapse of Wringhim's cohesive identity. In a telling moment of illness Wringhim experiences a near-hallucinatory perception of what constitutes self in an apparently triangular relationship between himself, Gil-Martin and his own brother George Colwan. It is worth quoting the passage in some detail:

> I generally conceived myself to be two people. When I lay in bed I deemed there were two of us in it; when I sat up, I always beheld another person, and always in the same position from the place where I sat or stood, which was about two paces off me towards my left side. It mattered not how many or how few were present: this my second self was sure to be present in his place; and this occasioned a confusion in all my words and ideas that utterly astounded my friends, who all declared, that instead of being deranged in my intellect, that they had never heard my conversation manifest in so much energy or sublimity of conception; but for all that, over the singular delusion that I was two persons, my reasoning faculties had no power. The most perverse part of it was, that I rarely conceived myself to be any of the two persons. I thought for the most part that my companion was one of them, and my brother the other; and I found, that to be obliged to speak and answer in the character of another man, was a most awkward business at the long run.[30]

Again Wringhim's powers of reason are troubled by his inability to differentiate between differences that should be clear cut. In addition any attempt to present a clear sense of doubling is exploded by the presence of a consistent third figure. Any possible control that Wringhim may have over an autonomous identity is taken away from him as identity becomes both fluid and fragmented. Wringhim perceives himself to be 'two people' and that he has a 'second self' that haunts his bedside. However, the significant feature of this perception is that he fails to identify himself with either the internalized, subjective or externalized, objective self; indeed, what he finds is that his 'companion' was one of these selves and his 'brother' the other. To be 'obliged to speak and answer in the character of another' becomes a difficult business as Wringhim finds himself effectively sidelined in his own perception of self, a 'helpless observer'. Any attempt to assert and validate identity is demonstrated to be a futile exercise as Wringhim appears to be neither the internal nor external self.

The displacement of Wringhim's sense of an integrated identity is based upon a form of Faustian contract established between himself and Gil-Martin. This collapse of personal autonomy is stressed by Gil-Martin in *Memoirs* in terms that indicate the unnatural nature of their relationship. He notes, 'I am wedded to you so closely that I feel as if I were the same person. Our essences are one, our bodies and spirits being united.'[31] In a manner that echoes Wringhim's surprise at his first meeting with Gil-Martin, where he finds that 'he was the same being as myself', Gil-Martin stresses the inability to distinguish between the two. However, as Gil-Martin's own appearance is notoriously plastic, this says little about Wringhim's sense of an authentic identity; rather than confirming self, Gil-Martin's identification further disrupts self for Wringhim. Similarly the affirmation of union as an inverted marital connection reveals the perversity of the relationship. It is in the Faustian contract that the collapse of Wringhim's autonomy can be most clearly traced. Drafted entirely on Gil-Martin's terms and inverting Christian sacrament it consists of this proclamation: 'Hear me then farther: I give you my solemn assurance, and bond of blood, that no human hand shall henceforth be able to injure your life, or shed one drop of your precious blood, but it is on the condition that you walk always by my direction.[32] Presenting the contract as a 'bond of blood', Gil-Martin effectively mocks the Communion rite of Christianity. In addition Wringhim's valued sense of being one of the Calvinist 'elect' is remorselessly undermined as he becomes diabolically rather than divinely claimed, a feature that is emphasized when Gil-Martin, in a blasphemous parody of Christ's, refers to Wringhim's blood as 'precious'. However, the most significant clause of the edict for Gil-Martin is that Wringhim promises that he will 'walk always by my direction', effectively denying him free will. Through this clause in the pledge Hogg satirizes the notion of predestination in extreme Calvinism where, through the primal Fall, Adam and Eve relinquished a claim to free will. Salvation is achieved through divine election rather than the exercising of free will within the parameters of moral law; in short to choose to do good or bad in a worldly context is irrelevant as the distinction between saved and damned has already been established by God. Hogg drastically inverts this position through Gil-Martin's pledge, where a diabolical nullification of free will provides a perverse substitute for that found in

Calvinism. In either situation Wringhim is bereft of free will; however, where in the Calvinist code exercising good or bad within moral law is irrelevant with regard to salvation, thus effectively freeing the individual from the imperatives of moral law, Gil-Martin translates the theological nuances to an earthly context. If extreme Calvinism *frees* Wringhim on earth, its replacement by Gil-Martin's 'bond of blood' *imprisons* him: commanded by Gil-Martin to 'walk always by my direction' Wringhim becomes an automaton, controlled by his master. This notion is also hinted at during the first editorial narrative in an account of George Colwan's murder given by one Mrs Calvert; she suggests that the murder is committed by Wringhim acting under the guidance of a figure to whom he states '[y]ou shall instruct me in this, as in all things else'.[33] When asked if she would recognize Wringhim again, Mrs Calvert attests: 'I think I could, if I saw him walk or run: his gait was very particular: He walked as if he had been flat-soled, and his legs made of steel, without any joints in his feet or ancles [*sic*]', suggesting that, in a manner that troubles a conception of the human, Wringhim's body has become some sort of primitive mechanism or technology.[34] Again the situation reflects the one experienced within the literary marketplace of the early nineteenth century, with the subsuming of Wringhim's identity and autonomy within theological constructions, or at least parodies of them, echoing a similarly troubled manufacturing of identity for the writer within the matrix of modern industrial capital. In both situations the problem is that the individual seems to have no control over self and, as Hogg increasingly indicates in the case of his character Wringhim, is profoundly aware of this state of affairs.

This consciousness of the consumption of identity by a force beyond the power of the individual begins to manifest itself in Wringhim in an objective apprehension of the disintegration of subjectivity. At first his growing comprehension of the process is undercut by an incredulous response; alluding to his own liminal condition he notes that to 'be in a state of consciousness and unconsciousness, at the same time, in the same body and same spirit, was impossible'.[35] However, consciousness of the displacement of an authentic conception of self results in the burgeoning sense that he and Gil-Martin are becoming one and the same thing: Wringhim notes that 'we were incorporated together – identified with one another, as it were, and the power was not in me to separate myself from him', and later Gil-Martin affirms that '[o]ur beings are amalgamated, as it were'.[36] In each case the control of the latter in the respective situations is stressed. As this consciousness of displacement accelerates Wringhim begins to wish for a state whereby he can voluntarily relinquish and obliterate identity:

> My principal feeling, about this time, was an insatiable longing for something that I cannot describe or denominate properly, unless I say that it was for *utter oblivion* that I longed. I desired to sleep; but it was for a deeper and longer sleep, than that in which the senses were nightly steeped. I longed to be at rest and quiet, and close my eyes on the past and future alike, as far as this frail life was concerned.[37]

The desire presented here is a complex one in as much as it demonstrates the extent to which Wringhim has lost control over experience and language, for he cannot 'describe or denominate properly' what it is he longs for. The italicized desire for '*utter oblivion*' apparently indicates a desire to embrace the possibility that there may be no afterlife, in effect a wish to utterly obliterate all traces of self; a desire no doubt enhanced by a simultaneous consciousness of a disintegration of self and of the consequences of the Faustian contract. The most poignant feature of this 'principal feeling' for Wringhim lies in his desire to 'close my eyes on the past and future alike'; the inclusion of 'future' in this inclination reveals an awareness that his life and therefore autonomy are no longer his own. In many ways what Wringhim desires is the 'bucolic pastoral of disidentity' as described by Francis Barker, with its dislocation from the 'burden of responsibility either for the past or future'; however, as noted already, for the nineteenth-century individual the decentring of identity and its subsequent fragmentation is based upon a profound consciousness of past and future. Wringhim cannot achieve utter oblivion because he no longer belongs to himself.

What is odd in Hogg's presentation of the disintegration of Wringhim's control over his own conception and understanding of self is that when he is most distanced from self, displaced by the union with Gil-Martin, he achieves rare and unprecedented moments of insight. For example, he defines his experiences with Gil-Martin in a perceptively figurative manner: 'I felt as one round whose body a deadly snake is twisted, which continues to hold him in its fangs, without injuring him, farther than in moving its scaly infernal folds with exulting delight, to let its victim feel to whose power he has subjected himself.'[38] Strangely enough the experience of being controlled by an apparently external power leads to a surprisingly objective account of the collapse of subjectivity. Wringhim may have lost control over identity and experience but in a way he is still able to write *about* the self if he is not capable of writing the self. To be displaced at least allows some detachment and objectivity. As a consequence Wringhim is arguably able to see Gil-Martin in his real guise, as the serpent that tempted Eve in the Garden of Eden and as a result caused humanity to relinquish free will. Whatever the case – and we have to remember that Gil-Martin's material presence in the text as a whole remains equivocal – the experience itself is significant as the Faustian bond of blood is translated into something akin to sexual fantasy. What we are presented with is something that is disturbingly playful in the 'exulting delight', indeed almost sado-masochistic in tone. In a way Wringhim's acknowledgement of loss of control over identity confirms him as deviant for it invokes a response that simultaneously entertains and blurs the edges between revulsion and ecstasy.[39]

In a final attempt to extrapolate himself from his relationship with Gil-Martin, Wringhim runs away to Edinburgh where, hungry and fatigued – and in a move that appropriately enough again echoes the instability of identity in the literary marketplace – he finds himself a post as typesetter at the Queen's printing house, then conducted by the publisher James Watson. He notes of this institution that it is here 'I first conceived the idea of writing this journal'; however, as is now familiar, to enter the commercial world of printing problematizes rather than affirms the identity of the writer.[40] As a result of attempting to write, print and publish the memoirs, Wringhim's identity further fragments. Watson finds them blasphemous and orders them burnt. Gil-Martin also apparently appears on the premises, and Wringhim, in an attempt to avoid the persistent attentions of his 'friend', begins the final flight that leads to his suicide. As identity begins to collapse totally, control over narrative consistency in the memoirs themselves begins to fragment into a series of random journal extracts. Nonetheless, there is one more significant instance of self-examination to be found within them. Wringhim observes:

> I was become a terror to myself; or rather, my body and soul were become terrors to each other; and had it been possible, I felt as if

> they would have gone to war. I dared not look at my face in the glass, for I shuddered at my own image and likeness. I dreaded the dawning, and trembled at the approach of night, nor was there one thing in nature that afforded me the least delight.[41]

What is taking place is a total collapse of the integrated self, as the elements that constitute 'Robert Wringhim' mutiny and 'would have gone to war' with each other. The significance of it is that Wringhim becomes completely displaced, alienated from his self, and therefore embodies Miyoshi's 'observer'. However, in a way this displacement is strangely empowering, certainly in terms of narratorial voice, for Wringhim is able to objectify his body and soul and, through his detached analysis of their conflict, effectively becomes his own editor, providing a gloss upon his own collapse as he rewrites 'I' with 'they'. Furthermore disassociation from identity is stressed by the fact that he cannot bear to view his reflection in a mirror, particularly as physical self is equated with terror. In many ways, as Wringhim distances himself from the turmoil and conflict going on internally, he ends up alienated from and external to the uncannily Cartesian struggle going on within.

Wringhim's demise in Hogg's novel proves typically ambivalent and inconclusive. His desire for 'utter oblivion' has already been noted and one of the titles for the novel, *The Suicide's Grave*, seems to unequivocally state that this was the cause of death. Nonetheless, in the second editorial narrative the *nature* of Wringhim's demise apparently causes more problems. He is found hanging from a rope made of hay which, as the editor notes,

> was accounted a great wonder; and every one said, if the devil had not assisted him it was impossible the thing could have been done; for, in general, these ropes are so brittle, being made of green hay, that they will scarcely bear to be bound over the rick. And the more to horrify the good people of this neighbourhood, the driver said, when he first came in view, *he could almost give his oath* that he saw two people busily engaged at the hay-rick.[42]

The ambivalent possibility that Gil-Martin might have been present at the death of Wringhim and the incredulity expressed at the manner of death is compounded by the fact that the first person on the scene of Wringhim's demise can only '*almost*' swear that there were two people there. As a result, even down to the demise of its central figure, the text shifts between perspective, opinion, hearsay and authority with a stubborn and provocative refusal to be pinned down. It can be read as an account of diabolic possession and as a case study in mental disorder, yet this proves to be ultimately a reductive way of negotiating a novel that explores the role of conditioning and environment in the determining of identity, the nature of authority and authenticity, and which subtly evokes the effect of market forces and capital upon the writer. Unlike Krook's body in *Bleak House*, Wringhim's body persistently refuses to melt into air; nonetheless, the perplexing variety of perspectives within and surrounding his testimony ensure that a stable unified reading of the confession is impossible. As the editor states at the start of his second narrative: 'What can this work be? Sure, you will say, it must be an allegory; or (as the writer calls it) a religious *parable*, showing the dreadful danger of self-righteousness? I cannot tell.'[43] Ultimately the complexities of the text seem to go beyond the control of the editor. In an environment where even his own identity seems to be fragile, all that he can do is relinquish authority and state lamely, 'I cannot tell.'

2 He, I say – I cannot say, I: Robert Louis Stevenson's strange case

> Modern bourgeois society with its relations of production, of exchange and of property, a society that has conjured up such gigantic means of production and of exchange, is like the sorcerer, who is no longer able to control the powers of the nether world whom he has called up by his spells.[1]

> As I came through the desert thus it was,
> As I came through the desert: I was twain,
> Two selves distinct that cannot join again.[2]

In an attempt both to celebrate and contribute to the mythologized folk traditions of Scottish lowland life popularized by such luminaries as Walter Scott and Robert Burns, Robert Louis Stevenson, in his unfinished novel *Weir of Hermiston*, created four brothers known as the 'Black Elliotts'. Ironically, in a novel where Stevenson aimed to engage with psychology, culture and historicity with greater veracity than in his previous fiction, Hob, Gib, Dandie and Clem have a largely symbolic function: they represent the stock virtues of the lowland, agrarian worker of Scotland. In the character of Dandie, Stevenson attempted to evoke the type of untutored, rural, poetic genius epitomized by James Hogg at the start of the nineteenth century; indeed, Stevenson notes of Dandie that '[t]he Ettrick Shepherd was his sworn crony; they would meet, drink to excess, roar out their lyrics in each other's faces, and quarrel and make it up again till bedtime'.[3] This is one of the few explicit reference by Stevenson to his compatriot Hogg, nonetheless echoes of the Ettrick Shepherd, and in particular *Private Memoirs*, haunt much of his writing. Both writers are steeped in a mutual sense of a national, cultural and religious heritage that shapes their writing. More importantly the fragmented narrative strategies employed by Hogg, his preoccupation with the status of authority, and his consistent troubling of apparently located boundaries find clear traces in Stevenson's *fin de siècle* Gothic novel. Hogg's obsession with the instability of identity is largely translated into a late nineteenth–century bourgeois London setting, with the ambivalence of perspective manifest in *Private Memoirs* evoked by the fact that Stevenson's *The Strange Case of Dr Jekyll and Mr Hyde* consists of a third-person narrative, a short account by Dr Lanyon, Jekyll's full statement and the testimonies of a variety of letters and documents. In addition the title itself proves to be significant. Where Hogg's *Private Memoirs and Confessions* suggests an apparently authentic document, an idea disrupted by the editor's sceptical gloss, Stevenson's use of *Strange Case* suggests something curious and inexplicable – a text which, like Hogg's, is difficult to classify. As a result the reader encounters a piece of writing that is as difficult to interpret coherently and conclusively as Hogg's.

What is certain is that Stevenson firmly locates the novel in the late nineteenth-century metropolis, and consequently deals with the impact of this environment and its institutions upon identity. Indeed some of Stevenson's most evocative writing can be found in his descriptions of the modern city. In a lengthy passage, where the lawyer Mr Utterson takes Inspector Newcomen of Scotland Yard to Hyde's lodgings in Soho after the latter has murdered the Member of Parliament Sir Danvers Carew, Stevenson depicts morning in the metropolis:

> It was by this time about nine in the morning, and the first fog of the season. A great chocolate-coloured pall lowered over heaven, but the wind was continually charging and routing these embattled vapours; so that as the cab crawled from street to street, Mr Utterson beheld a marvellous number of degrees and hues of twilight; for here it would be dark like the back-end of evening; and there would be a glow of a rich, lurid brown, like the light of some strange conflagration; and here, for a moment, the fog would be quite broken up, and a haggard shaft of daylight would glance in between the swirling wreaths. The dismal quarter of Soho seen under these changing glimpses, with its muddy ways, and slatternly passengers, and its lamps, which had never been extinguished or had been kindled afresh to combat this mournful reinvasion of darkness, seemed, in the lawyer's eyes, like a district of some city in a nightmare. The thoughts of his mind, besides, were of the gloomiest dye; and when he glanced at the companion of his drive, he was

> conscious of some touch of that terror of the law and the law's officers which may at times assail the most honest.[4]

As with the London of Dickens' *Bleak House*, what defines the topography of the city is fog. Similarly fog, in conjunction with the gas lamps of Soho and the wind which consistently shifts and reconfigures the cityscape, gives the environment a shifting and insubstantial feel. Utterson notes the change in the colour of the fog from a 'great chocolate-coloured pall' through 'dark like the back-end of evening' to 'a rich lurid brown', but in all what marks the metropolis is the 'embattled vapours' of fog that shift and reconstitute themselves in an evocation of the defining aesthetic of nineteenth-century modernity which, for Marshall Berman, consists of 'fluidity and vapourousness'. In effect this sombre, dark and threatening environment, with its 'haggard shaft(s) of daylight', its 'dismal quarter(s)' and its 'mournful reinvasion of darkness', becomes the fitting setting for a brutal murder, and one where the murderer can disappear into the fog. The city, as Stevenson states, is like 'some city in a nightmare'. In such a disorientating and threatening location the effects upon the individual are transparent; Utterson's thoughts, clearly reflecting the sable appearance of the city itself, are of the 'gloomiest dye'. Further, the effect induces a deluded sensation of guilt as he becomes 'conscious of some touch of that terror of the law and the law's officers which may at times assail the most honest'. In many ways Utterson becomes the victim of the prevailing and morbid city sicknesses of the late nineteenth century as described by William Greenslade: neurasthenia, hypochondria and nervous paranoia. He may be innocent but he circulates in an environment that presumes and therefore induces the emergence of guilty secrets. In the labyrinthine contradictions of this fluid, indefinable and yet defining setting, the criminal Hyde thrives, quite literally able to *hide* himself from his pursuers.

What marks the difference between Hogg's novel and Stevenson's is that where the monstrous, diabolic Gil-Martin remains a marginal, uncorroborated figure within the former's work – possibly a Mephistophelean manipulator of the eponymous Sinner, possibly an hallucination experienced by a deluded and deranged consciousness – Hyde's presence in the *Strange Case* is unequivocal. A variety of testimonies, not least Jekyll's own but also those of Utterson, Dr Lanyon and Richard Enfield, point to Hyde's material manifestation in the text; as a result the monstrous in Stevenson's novel is no mere ambivalent presence that can be explained away and contained as the product of a dislocated imagination but a real, tangible entity which can be communicated with and, if need be, attract the attention of the law. Yet, as Hogg's *Private Memoirs* indicates, the Gothic also performs a metaphoric function, opening up a series of interpretative possibilities when reading the monstrous, particularly as the notion of monstrosity itself taps into anxieties that are themselves fluid, determined as they are by dominant social, cultural, political and scientific modes of thought at a particular moment. As Judith Halberstam puts it, in a succinct reading of the monstrous, '[m]onsters are meaning machines ... [t]hey can represent gender, race, nationality, class, and sexuality in one body'.[5] Hyde is one of the most resonant of these 'meaning machines'; like Frankenstein's creation he is ultimately stitched together from a variety of parts, here different critical perspectives, but at the same time largely defies, through this multiplicity of meanings, clear classification. As with Stoker's Dracula after him, Stevenson's Hyde has inspired a veritable industry of critical readings. For Fred Botting Hyde, as a *fin de siècle* monster almost *par excellence*, represents the 'ghostly returns of the past ... [which] are both fearful and exciting incursions of barbarity and, more significantly, the irruptions of primitive and archaic forces deeply rooted in the human mind'.[6] This suggestion that Hyde in some way provides both an echo of the elements of the barbarism found in early manifestations of the Gothic genre, significantly relocated in the modern city, *and* represents an emergence of primitive inclinations that are supposed to have been subdued in the hyper-civilized and genteel world of *fin de siècle* England finds a parallel in David Punter's reading. Punter suggests that 'Hyde's behaviour is an urban version of "going native"', again hinting that, particularly in the context of British imperialism, the presence of Hyde represents a reversion to savagery in an apparently unlikely location.[7] For Alan Sandison Hyde is the hitherto repressed progeny of late nineteenth-century hypocrisy, 'the product of patriarchal apprehensions, inhibitions ... self deception and self-indulgence'.[8] Halberstam is even more explicit in her reading; she claims that 'Hyde combines within his repulsive aspect the traces of nineteenth-century stereotypes of both Semitic and black physiognomies', and therefore adds a more defined racial dimension to Hyde than Punter's reference to going 'native'.[9] Whether generical trace or psychological memory of barbarism, urban savage, product of patriarchal hypocrisy, metaphor for racist stereotyping, post-evolutionary atavistic throwback *and* degenerate criminal type, or representative of the instability of gender in the *fin de siècle*, Hyde seems to function as an alter ego that reflects and disrupts the notion of the normative and respectable bourgeois individual at the end of the nineteenth century.[10] In many ways the pluralism implicit in this variety of different positions mirrors the fragile discourse of degeneration theory alluded to earlier; where degeneration theory draws together and homogenizes disparate categories of 'deviancy' to define and stabilize normal bourgeois identity, here the different readings of the monstrosity of Hyde indicate the varied anxieties of the bourgeois individual and the number of possible ways in which its apparent cohesion proves illusory.

What seems to be apparent is that Hyde speaks more about the fears and the anxieties of the *fin de siècle* bourgeoisie than monstrosity in general. Nonetheless Hyde remains, appropriately enough, a deeply contradictory figure, both evolutionary throwback or reminder of civilization's barbaric origins and a peculiarly modern monster. He is, perhaps paradoxically given his unlocated nature, evidently at home in the modern city, particularly as the modern city is itself (as Tom-all-Alone's in *Bleak House* demonstrates) deeply contradictory. Stevenson notes that Jekyll's home/laboratory, from which Hyde is seen to emerge, is found in

> a square of ancient handsome houses, now for the most part decayed from their high estate, and let in flats and chambers to all sorts and conditions of men: map-engravers, architects, shady lawyers, and the agents of obscure enterprises. One house, however, second from the corner, was still occupied entire; and … wore a great air of wealth and comfort.[11]

The area is shabby genteel, its age apparently situates it, yet it is 'for the most part decayed'; in addition it is occupied by the eminently respectable Dr Jekyll, yet decidedly unrespectable and even unspecified practices are taking place in immediate proximity to his house. Such an inconsistent environment suits and is reflected by Hyde who, as Jekyll points out with reference to the sensations that Hyde inspires in him, is 'younger, lighter, happier' and 'livelier' and yet bears 'an imprint of deformity and decay'.[12] Indeed the contradictions of Hyde largely reflect the city as a whole, a feature noted by Alan Sandison who observes of Stevenson's city that

> its 'doubleness' – the contrast between facade and interior, its capacity to sustain a complex secret life, the contrast between its day- and night-time existence, the multifariousness of its aspects which can change from being one moment concretely physical to disconcertingly surreal the next – all these dualities and ambivalences contribute to the working-out of his dominant pluralist vision.[13]

Indeed Hyde is so at home in this alternately tangible and insubstantial metropolis that David Punter identifies the fictional Hyde with the real London of late nineteenth-century England, stating that part of the appeal of Stevenson's novel lies in its 'obvious connection with *actual* late Victorian fears about similarly untraceable murders, centred on the archetype of Jack the Ripper'.[14]

Initially it is Hyde-as-criminal who appears particularly at home in the *fin de siècle* metropolis; the figure who, like Jack the Ripper, is apparently above, even untraceable by, the law and whose motives cannot be defined with any certainty. The reader's first encounter with Hyde consists of an account of an event given to the lawyer Utterson by his relative and companion Richard Enfield. The account therefore has an appropriately indirect quality to it and Hyde's first appearance becomes almost anecdotal:

> I [Enfield] was coming home from some place at the end of the world, about three o'clock of a black winter morning, and my way lay through a part of town where there was literally nothing to be seen but lamps. Street after street, and all the folks asleep – street after street, all lighted up as if for a procession, and all as empty as a church – till at last I got into that state of mind when a man listens and listens and begins to long for the sight of a policeman. All at once, I saw two figures: one a little man who was stumping along eastwards at a good walk, and the other a girl of maybe eight or ten who was running as hard as she was able down a cross-street. Well, sir, the two ran into one another naturally enough at the corner; and then came the horrible part of the thing; for the man trampled calmly over the child's body and left her screaming on the ground. It sounds nothing to hear, but it was hellish to see. It wasn't like a man; it was like some damned juggernaut. I gave a view halloa, took to my heels, collared my gentleman, and brought him back to where there was already quite a group around the screaming child. He was

> perfectly cool and made no resistance, but gave me one look, so ugly that it brought out the sweat on me like running.[15]

The scene as described by Enfield is eerie enough, it is the middle of the night yet the streets are 'lighted up as if for a procession'; however, within this environment which is designed to facilitate the passage of the crowd there is nobody to be seen. Such an atmosphere seems to be particularly effective in leading Enfield's thoughts to crime because he 'begins to long for the sight of a policeman'. The subsequent criminal act is, as a result, appropriately strange and difficult to locate; what Enfield sees is a 'little man … stumping along' and a young girl who was 'running as hard as she was able' towards him; 'naturally' they collide. It is, in itself, an understated and even inauspicious occurrence; as Enfield indicates it 'sounds nothing to hear'. Nonetheless the account transcends its initially subdued anecdotal impact; although it may sound insignificant, Enfield states that it 'was hellish to see' as the small man 'trampled calmly' over the body of the girl 'like some damned juggernaut'. The incongruous and unsettling nature of the encounter is emphasized by the fact that Enfield refers to the assailant as a 'gentleman'. What we are therefore presented with is a profoundly problematic event. Enfield is forced to justify relaying it by privileging *seeing* the collision over merely *talking* about it, and Utterson – and we as readers – have to take his word that it is sufficiently strange to recount. Its impact lies in its contradictory nature: the streets are at first completely deserted and then crowded, the small man 'stumping along' becomes an impassive 'damned juggernaut', the apparently sadistic trampling is undertaken 'calmly' by a 'cool' and composed gentleman who nonetheless offers Enfield a look 'so ugly that it brought out the sweat on me like running'. The account of the event is inconsistent enough to prevent Utterson and the reader arriving at a clear impression of its, and therefore Hyde's, nature. David Punter's reading of Enfield's story is instructive:

> He [Enfield] is right: it does sound nothing to hear, and it is not even very easy to imagine. It lingers in the memory, but only because of its strangeness, which may have been Stevenson's purpose. It is, of course, symbolic: it is designed to show the inhumanity of Hyde where a more purposive crime would not.[16]

What Punter points to is the unsatisfactory nature of the crime; understated to such a point that it is not easy to picture, it is indeed strange. The significance of Punter's reading is that it is not necessarily the act itself that demonstrates the inhumanity of Hyde but that it is apparently performed without a motive, a notion supported by the fact that it is not necessarily the trampling that Enfield objects to but Hyde himself. Stephen Heath also notes the contradictory and uncertain qualities of Enfield's report of the act, stating that '[o]n the face of it ... it would sound something to hear; the report in the text, however, has no confidence and so it can end up sounding nothing, prompting Enfield's unease'.[17] What Heath suggests is that in many ways the strangeness of the report on Hyde can be accounted for by the nature of the report itself which 'has no confidence'. Finally Karl Miller also assesses the way in which the report is capable of inducing an uncomfortable response; for him the event is unsettling because Hyde's crimes 'are acts of cruelty which look more like boorishness than sadism'.[18]

Perhaps the most unsettling feature of the account lies in Hyde's own composure during the whole affair; he tramples the girl 'calmly' and is 'perfectly cool' when apprehended by Utterson. It is this calmness which is uncanny for it betrays nothing in terms of motive or emotion; it is an act of manifest indifference. The other criminal act that is explicitly attributed to Hyde is the murder, again by trampling, of Danvers Carew; the description of this provides a marked contrast with the trampling of the girl:

> The old gentleman [Carew] took a step back, with the air of one very much surprised and a trifle hurt; and at that Mr Hyde broke out of all bounds, and clubbed him to the earth. And next moment, with ape-like fury, he was trampling his victim under foot, and hailing down a storm of blows, under which the bones were audibly shattered and the body jumped upon the roadway.[19]

These two violent acts obviously echo each other, based as they are upon parallel instances of trampling. Similarly they can be read in parallel ways, one as a misogynist sexual assault, the other an attack upon the embodiment of patriarchal respectability. For the purposes of this discussion it is the difference between the two crimes that is significant, the first being performed calmly and indifferently, the second with an 'ape-like fury' as Hyde 'broke out of all bounds'. It is the disparity between the two that problematizes attempts to define

Hyde's criminality; the first is understated and therefore unsettling, the second obviously psychotic, a full-blown murder, yet neither has an apparent motive. In many ways what Hyde embodies is the Foucauldian homicidal maniac. It is uncertain if Hyde is criminal or insane: both acts suggest both interpretations. As a result the easiest way to contain him is in that 'entirely fictitious entity' of nineteenth-century psychiatry: the 'crime which is nothing but insanity' and the 'insanity which is nothing but a crime'. What does occur though is that Hyde becomes an appropriately modern monster for the nineteenth century, representing anxieties about the effects and symptoms of modernity that can be traced back to Wordsworth's description of the loss of identity in the metropolis. Martin Tropp makes a significant observation with regard to modern urban violence which can be applied to the motiveless tramplings performed by Hyde: 'Random, purposeless violence is the ultimate horror of the city in the twentieth century, a horror made possible by urban anonymity and the loss of community.'[20] Tropp identifies this experience as a twentieth-century phenomenon, yet it is – as Hyde's activities demonstrate in Stevenson's novel – manifestly applicable to *late* nineteenth-century Britain at the least, assuming that the urban Gothic articulates its anxieties. In addition Tropp's account itself seems somewhat naively nostalgic, alluding to the threat implicit in 'urban anonymity' and lamenting 'the loss of community'. As Judith Halberstam points out, the reading 'constructs a mythical time "before" when there was a community' that is now lost.[21] As far as literary representation goes, from Wordsworth's *Prelude* onwards there is a sense that the emergence of the modern metropolis merely reconfigures community into something new – albeit something that seems to level out individualism and apparently induce uniformity – that proves bewildering for the observer. This condition accelerates in intensity in representation during the course of the nineteenth century, and the problem lies not so much in the fact that the urban criminal can disappear within the crowded metropolis, but that the identity of the individual can be lost or at least troubled within the structures, institutions and symptoms of modernity. It is this latter anxiety that Stevenson's *Strange Case* would seem to address, the fragility of identity within the nineteenth-century experience of modernity.

At the heart of the novel lies the reasoning behind Jekyll's compulsion to instigate the emergence of the ultimately monstrous and murderous Hyde. The explanation that Stevenson gives Jekyll in his testimony suggests an instance of clear-cut, if consequently illusory, dualism. Appropriating Alfred Wigan's definition of psychiatric self-division, the creation of Hyde is based upon Jekyll's consciousness of 'conflicting volitions' within himself; Jekyll states that

> the worst of my faults was a certain impatient gaiety of disposition, such as has made the happiness of many, but such as I found it hard to reconcile with my imperious desire to carry my head high, and wear a more than commonly grave countenance before the public. Hence it came about that I concealed my pleasures; and that when I reached years of reflection, and began to look round me and took stock of my progress and position in the world, I stood already committed to a profound duplicity of life. Many a man would have even blazoned such irregularities as I was guilty of; but from the high views that I had set before me, I regarded and hid them with an almost morbid sense of shame. It was thus rather the exacting nature of my aspirations, than any particular degradation in my faults, that made me what I was and, with even a deeper trench than in the majority of men, severed in me those provinces of good and ill which divide and compound man's dual nature.[22]

In many ways the stimulus for the emergence of Hyde is unspecified, the closest that we come to it being Jekyll's description of 'an almost morbid sense of shame'. What is apparent though is that his experimentation arises from an acute awareness of the oscillation between public and private – a desire to appear to have a 'grave countenance' in the sphere of the former and yet to be conscious of a certain 'gaiety of disposition' that, although he accepts it can make other men happy, contradicts the public inclination. Stevenson's depiction of this dilemma is reminiscent of Arnold's 'The Buried Life' with its contrast between internal, authentic self – which if it emerged would be 'with blame reproved' by others – and the external, disguised self, a dichotomy that is effectively mirrored in a Gothic context through Jekyll's wavering between public and private. Due to his 'high views' and 'imperious desire' to appear respectable, Jekyll takes to concealing or repressing his pleasures, regarding them as shameful. Guilt, consequently, is at the heart of his sense of self, yet guilt inspired by the nature of his 'aspirations' rather than any 'particular degradation'. It is this consistent vacillation, between public and private, external and internal, and social respectability and pleasure that leads Jekyll to arrive at the conclusion that human beings have a 'dual nature'. That said, what would really seem to define this conclusion is the nature of social expectations, albeit ones generated by Jekyll himself. Again a form of conditioning with regard to identity is in operation, and one from which Jekyll deviates in his creation of Hyde. Alfred Wigan's reading of duality is again useful as a gloss on Jekyll's perception of self and identity; in fact in many ways Wigan's understanding of the effect of conditioning crystallizes Jekyll's moral dilemma. Wigan observes:

> Millions of human beings have criminal volitions passing through their minds, which, were the means of gratification suddenly presented, accompanied by a conviction of worldly impunity, would pass into acts; but the early and continuous cultivation of self-command, fear of punishment (the social conscience), religious principle, self-respect, risk of detection, and a hundred other motives, keep them always in the path of duty.[23]

What is interesting here is that where Jekyll's description of his 'faults' lies in an apparently harmless 'gaiety of disposition', only emerging as criminality with the appearance of Hyde, Wigan pinpoints 'criminal volitions' straight away in his reading of duality. Indeed, for Wigan the idiosyncratic fictional experience of Jekyll is not that unusual in terms of his own medical practice. What links the fictional and medical accounts of self-division is Wigan's allusion to the 'social conscience'; on the whole a private inclination towards transgression (in Wigan's definition quite definitely a criminal one) is tempered by a consciousness of social boundaries and an ensuing 'cultivation of self-command'. Through the emergence of the anti-social Hyde, Jekyll loses all sense of both socially prescribed and self-imposed parameters and thus falls away from what Wigan calls 'the path of duty'.

As it is, the experiment with Hyde is designed to unshackle Jekyll's moral instinct from his propensity for pleasure. Jekyll takes the analysis of his condition further, stating:

> Though so profound a double-dealer, I was in no sense a hypocrite; both sides of me were in dead earnest; I was no more myself when I laid aside restraint and plunged in shame, than when I laboured, in the eye of day, at the furtherance of knowledge or the relief of

> sorrow and suffering. And it chanced that the direction of my scientific studies, which led wholly towards the mystic and the transcendental, reacted and shed a strong light on this consciousness of the perennial war among my members. With every day, and from both sides of my intelligence, the moral and the intellectual, I thus drew steadily nearer to that truth by whose partial discovery I have been doomed to such a dreadful shipwreck: that man is not truly one, but truly two. I say two, because the state of my own knowledge does not pass beyond that point. Others will follow, others will outstrip me on the same lines; and I hazard the guess that man will be ultimately known for a mere polity of multifarious, incongruous and independent denizens.[24]

Stevenson depicts Jekyll's dilemma in an appropriately discrepant way; Jekyll describes himself as a profound 'double-dealer' yet 'in no sense a hypocrite'. As a result the beginning of the collapse of an integrated and cohesive identity starts to take place as binaries begin to break down and, in a phrase that echoes Robert Wringhim's consciousness of disintegration, the 'perennial war' among the constituent parts of the self intensifies. This fragmentation can be detected in the comparison between the public self, who labours 'at the furtherance of knowledge or the relief of sorrow and suffering', and the private self who casts off 'restraint and plunged in shame'. Jekyll states with regard to this comparison that 'I was no more myself' in either environment; the primary reading of this point of comparison is that neither self is more authentic than the other, yet it also suggests that an integrated sense of identity is being lost: Jekyll by implication is no longer himself. Just as he becomes distanced from the two selves that he has previously described, we can also see the nature of Jekyll's study itself starting to trouble located boundaries; it is 'scientific', suggesting a material empiricism rather than abstract reasoning, yet leans wholly towards 'the mystic and the transcendental'. Similarly the apparently discrete components of Jekyll's intelligence, the 'moral and the intellectual', draw together to allow him to arrive at his conclusions. What Jekyll deduces is significant; he states that the human is not a unified entity 'but truly two', yet adds the reservation that 'I say two, because the state of my own knowledge does not pass beyond that point'. This hint at the limitations of Jekyll's study also alludes to the limitations of a dualistic interpretation of identity; dipsychism, as Karl Miller has put it, is turning into polypsychism. In this context the individual becomes a fundamentally fragmented being, consisting of 'multifarious, incongruous and independent denizens' who, as a 'polity', are presumably organized by the 'social conscience', the 'path of duty', and the 'exacting nature of ... aspirations' alluded to earlier. In spite of this apparent splintering of identity into a variety of components and properties, Jekyll's scientific predicament revolves around his desire to split the self of public duty and that of private pleasure:

> If each, I told myself, could but be housed in separate identities, life would be relieved of all that was unbearable; the unjust might go his way, delivered from the aspirations and remorse of his more upright twin; and the just could walk steadfastly and securely on his upward path, doing the good things in which he found his pleasure, and no longer exposed to disgrace and penitence by the hands of this extraneous evil. It was the curse of mankind that these incongruous faggots were thus bound together – that in the agonised womb of consciousness these polar twins should be continuously struggling.[25]

This statement reveals the extent of Jekyll's hypocrisy. Initially his intentions seem to be morally sound; he desires to create 'separate identities' for what he sees as the 'upright' and 'unjust' selves in order that the upright self can perform the 'good things' synonymous with the 'exacting ... aspirations' of the moral instinct. However, this moral intention, supported by scientific progress, merely shadows the main rationale for the experiment which is Jekyll's desire to avoid the 'disgrace and penitence' that private pleasure induces. In effect Jekyll's scientific ambition merely masks an indulgent wish to eradicate the guilt and 'morbid' shame that haunts his need to wear a 'grave countenance'. This manipulative and partial interpretation of the motives for inducing the emergence of Hyde can be clearly found in Jekyll's separation of the two selves: the external, public self that walks on the 'upward path' is compared to the self of private, furtive pleasure, yet the latter is described as an 'extraneous evil', thus effectively cast off and viewed as external to the self. Jekyll subjectively and misguidedly equates a sense of the cohesive self with the respectable 'upright twin', and desires to replace pleasure synonymous with immorality with the pleasure of doing 'good things' in an attempt to alienate guilt.

This shifting to and fro – between public and private selves, moral, intellectual and scientific paradigms, and varieties of motivation –

leads to a profound consciousness of the insubstantial qualities of selfhood and in particular those of the body. Jekyll finds:

> I began to perceive more deeply than it has ever yet been stated, the trembling immateriality, the mist-like transience, of this seemingly so solid body in which we walk attired. Certain agents I found to have the power to shake and to pluck back that fleshly vestment, even as wind might toss the curtains of a pavilion.[26]

Jekyll's perception of the 'transience' of the body indicates the fragile and insubstantial nature of the self in a way that echoes Marx's maxim that '[a]ll that is solid melts into air'. This perspective is supported by other accounts of the appearance of Hyde, the figure who renders the self fluid. Utterson, in a dream inspired by Enfield's story, pictures a face that 'baffled him and melted before his eyes', and Dr Lanyon, in an account where he witnesses the transformation of Hyde back to Jekyll, finds that 'his features seemed to melt and alter'.[27] Jekyll's discovery also initiates a correspondence between shifts in identity and the city itself, a position which consolidates the suggestion that Hyde is eminently at home in the urban metropolis. The city, in the description that Stevenson provides during the murder hunt for Hyde, is shrouded in a fog that is constantly in a state of flux, shaped and reshaped by the wind just as the body, for Jekyll, becomes 'mist-like' and can be changed 'even as wind might toss the curtains of a pavilion'. Furthermore, Jekyll notes in the early stages of his experiment that Hyde 'would pass away like the stain of breath upon a mirror'.[28] Like the interchangeability and interaction between physical body and the late nineteenth-century city 'condition' in Greenslade's account of degeneration, the body becomes like the city and the city like the body. This correlation is emphasized in another description of the urban environment by Stevenson: 'The fog still slept on the wing above the drowned city, where the lamps glimmered like carbuncles; and through the muffle and smother of these fallen clouds, the procession of the town's life was still rolling in through the great arteries with a sound as of a mighty wind.'[29]

Stevenson compares the city to a body with arteries; it is in this vast and macrocosmic body that the pleasure-seeking self of Jekyll, like Charles Baudelaire's dandy *flâneur* as described by Walter Benjamin, can find 'a refuge … among the masses of the big city', and into which Hyde enters circulation.[30] What is also significant is that Stevenson describes the city as 'drowned', an association both reminiscent of Arnold's lyrical depiction of the buried life flowing unregarded through the city like a river and Benjamin's description of Baudelaire's Paris, the nineteenth-century capital of Europe, as 'sunken city, and more submarine than subterranean'.[31] What is evident is that the shifting and shifty buried self emerges in a city submerged in fog, and flows through its arterial streets in a form that is as transient and 'mist-like' as the environment itself.

It is the consistent intrusion of the elements and symptoms of nineteenth-century modernity that renders Stevenson's Gothic vision distinctive and which points to the symbolic resonance of the relationship between Jekyll and Hyde. Arguably Jekyll's compulsion to 'create' Hyde stems from his overwhelming feelings of guilt with regard to pleasure and from a desire to appear publicly respectable; in many ways Hyde's nature and characteristics are determined by the latter predilection. Indeed the fragile egotism intrinsic to Jekyll's sense of public self and identity can be attributed to the status of the scientist in the later decades of the nineteenth century. In the *Communist Manifesto* Marx and Engels note that the 'bourgeoisie has stripped of its halo every occupation hitherto honoured and looked up to with reverent awe. It has converted the physician, the lawyer, the priest, the poet, the man of science, into its paid wage-labourers'.[32] Apart from the priest and the poet, all the categories cited above are occupations represented in Stevenson's *Strange Case*. Jekyll, as 'physician' and 'man of science', finds himself a 'paid wage-labourer' in two contexts and therefore doubly stripped of his halo. In many ways his experiment with Hyde, designed to allow him to walk on the 'upward path, doing the good things in which he found his pleasure', becomes an attempt to reclaim the lost halo of the physician that was previously regarded with 'reverent awe'. This desanctification of the scientist is a significant issue in contextualizing and attempting to arrive at a reading of the metaphoric monster in Stevenson's novel because, ironically enough, it is through the emergence of Hyde that Jekyll seems to become explicitly stripped of his halo. The process can be detected in Jekyll's own description of events: referring to his motives with regard to inducing the transformation into Hyde he notes: 'Had I approached my discovery in a more noble spirit, had I risked the experiment while under the empire of generous or pious aspirations, all must have been otherwise, and from these agonies of death and birth I had come forth an angel instead of a fiend.'[33] Jekyll, acknowledging the flaws in the reasoning behind his scientific ambition, indicates the manner in which he is stripped of his halo. This decanonization is stressed when Utterson breaks into Jekyll's laboratory after his death; among the debris of Jekyll's profession, Utterson is ''amazed to find...a copy of a pious work for which Jekyll had several times expressed a great esteem, annotated, in his own hand, with startling blasphemies'.[34] The implication is that Jekyll, in his 'boorish' (as Karl Miller puts it) guise as Hyde, has provided this blasphemous gloss upon the 'pious' text. Interestingly, Havelock Ellis – one of the positivist populists of science in the late nineteenth century – argued that science had to be realistic and pragmatic, revealing the world as it really was and, in doing so, removing 'the garment of make-believe by which pious hands have hidden its uglier features'.[35] In many ways what the hypocritical Jekyll does, in his attempts to divert his own impious inclinations, is create the transient Hyde to hide his own 'uglier features' and thus regain his halo. However, if we consider that the monstrous alter ego of Jekyll emerges in a cultural and social climate preoccupied with the notion of degeneration, Hyde represents what William Greenslade calls a 'permanent secularized "fall" from grace'.[36] The emergence of Hyde, standing in as he does for Jekyll's conceited aspirations, guilt and hypocrisy, effectively symbolizes Jekyll's irrevocable desanctification. It is no wonder then that in Enfield's anecdotal encounter with Hyde the location perversely reflects the moral vacuum in which Jekyll's halo is lost, for the streets of London are 'as empty as a church'.

In spite of his efforts to present an appropriate gravitas to the public, the loss of Jekyll's halo is of fundamental significance when the emergence of Hyde is considered. Regardless of his supposed moral intentions, Jekyll becomes a 'wage-labourer' in the complex matrix of capitalism – as much defined by market forces as the writer is in the magazine culture of the early nineteenth century. However, through the creation of Hyde the baser aspects of this process can apparently be filtered off and Jekyll assumes that he can follow the 'upward path'. Marshall Berman, in his reading of Marx, indicates the way in which modern experience in the nineteenth century is divorced from any conception of transcendental or spiritual value under capitalism: '... nothing is sacred, no one is untouchable, life becomes thoroughly desanctified ... modern men and women may well stop at nothing, with no dread to hold them back; free from fear and trembling, they are free to trample down everyone in their way if self-interest drives them to it.'[37]

In effect Hyde encapsulates this modern product of capitalism, 'thoroughly desanctified' and therefore prepared to 'trample down' everything in his way, thus allowing Jekyll the ultimately spurious pleasure of 'doing … good things'. Judith Halberstam argues that the inability of other characters in Stevenson's novel to identify and locate Hyde suggests that he 'cannot be classified, he has no place in the order and history of things'.[38] However, if we consider Berman's particularly resonant reading of the modern bourgeois individual as one 'prepared to trample down everyone in their way', Hyde is very much *inside* history. He emerges as another instance of the disidentical self in nineteenth-century modernity, arising from Jekyll's acute consciousness of the reverence reserved for the man of science in the past and his own present desanctification. Indeed, as Jekyll's control over a cohesive identity erodes, Hyde emerges as bourgeois 'self-interest' incarnate, rather than the dark and savage Other or atavistic throwback suggested by Punter, Greenslade and others. This is evident when Marx and Engels' reading of identity within modernity is reflected upon; as noted already what distinguishes the 'bourgeois epoch' from prior historical moments is 'uninterrupted disturbance of all social relations, everlasting uncertainty and agitation'. For Berman this environment dictates that identity must 'take on the fluid and open form of this society', and that the modern individual 'must learn to yearn for change', to 'demand [it], actively to seek [it] out and carry [it] through'. Compulsive transformation of identity is at the core of the bourgeois experience for Marx as far as Berman is concerned, a notion that can be detected in Jekyll's apprehension of the 'mist-like transience' of the human body and in Stevenson's representation of Hyde. Identity becomes fluid in such a context as Hyde begins to epitomize an uncontrollable lust for transformation. Given his scientific leanings towards the 'mystic and transcendental', Jekyll effectively becomes the Faustian/Frankensteinian bourgeois sorcerer-scientist of Marx and Engels who 'is no longer able to control the powers of the nether world whom he has called up by his spells'. What Jekyll has basically summoned up is the dark alter ego of bourgeois individualism, the self-interested, ruthless, destructive and protean Hyde. It is a creation that Jekyll is ultimately unable to control, for he notes of his hold over a cohesive identity that

> in the beginning, the difficulty had been to throw off the body of Jekyll, it had of late gradually but decidedly transferred itself to the

other side. All things therefore seem to point to this: that I was slowly losing hold of my original and better self, and becoming slowly incorporated with my second and worst.[39]

Transformation of identity becomes a relentless, uncontrolled and compulsively addictive process for Jekyll, reflecting the fluidity of identity that Berman detects at the root of the modern experience. In addition, just as Jekyll becomes the bourgeois conjurer, caught through the loss of his halo in the 'gigantic means of production and of exchange' created by industrial capital and unable to control the powers that he has summoned up, Hyde embodies the diligent bourgeois individual's *doppelgänger*, the dandy. This identification again significantly locates Hyde as the epitome of bourgeois self-interest; Richard Dellamora notes that the dandy 'as a popular phenomenon is middle-class ... Dandyism was associated with middle-class uppityism ... dandyism also reflects a loss of balance between the dual imperatives of leisure and work incumbent upon Victorian gentlemen. The dandy is too relaxed, too visible, consumes to excess while producing little or nothing.'[40]

In spite of the many associations that are established between Hyde and the bestial which can be read as emphatically opposed to this 'relaxed' archetype, his 'ape-like' fury being just one instance, Hyde can manifestly be read as middle-class dandy. With the transformation from Jekyll to Hyde becoming increasingly biased towards the latter, the pleasurable and indulgent 'gaiety' that Jekyll attempts to conceal in Hyde becomes more and more evident, suggesting the imbalance in imperatives that the dandy encapsulates for Dellamora. Hyde can consequently be read as the unbalanced, uncontrollable and parasitic opposite of Jekyll's 'paid wage-labourer'; he 'consumes to excess while producing little or nothing' and, considering his propensity for self-gratification, he anticipates the morbid and narcissistic preoccupation with self criticized by Nordau and Lombroso. This reading of Hyde as the dark side of bourgeois progress does not necessarily need to contradict other interpretations of Stevenson's representation of monstrosity.[41] Nonetheless, as Judith Halberstam points out, there is a clear affinity between the nineteenth-century Gothic text and its immediate socio-economic climate, and it is this affiliation which allows the multiplicity of meanings to emerge:

the ability of the Gothic story to take the imprint of any number of

> interpretations makes it a hideous offspring of capitalism itself. The Gothic novel of the nineteenth century ... [is] obsessed with multiple modes of consumption and production, with dangerous consumptions and excessive productivity, and with economies of meaning.[42]

In effect what we have is another series of interpretative mirrors; just as Jekyll reflects Marx and Engels's bourgeois sorcerer whose spell has gone out of control due to the excessive demands of 'gigantic means of production and of exchange', the multiple possible readings of Hyde evoke the 'multiple modes of consumption and production', with their 'dangerous consumptions and excessive productivity', of capitalism, and in turn Hyde represents a microcosmic and metonymic version of the nineteenth-century Gothic novel, a 'hideous offspring of capitalism itself'. Just as Hyde can be equated with the modern metropolis in a variety of different concatenations, and the city (as capital) can be equated with capitalism, ultimately Hyde himself ends up evoking aspects of bourgeois capitalism.

Like Hogg's *Private Memoirs*, money and inheritance are at the heart of Stevenson's troubling of identity. Indeed, the relationship between Jekyll and Hyde becomes one that is based upon money; Jekyll notes in his testimony that, after achieving success with his transformation into Hyde, 'I next drew up [a] will ... so that if anything befell me in the person of Dr Jekyll, I could enter on that of Edward Hyde without pecuniary loss.'[43] It is this will that perplexes Jekyll's friends and colleagues; they suspect, unsurprisingly, that Hyde is blackmailing him and, in a phrase that conflates both social status and capital, Utterson's main concern is to 'save his (Jekyll's) credit'.[44] However, Hyde's relationship with Jekyll's money is far more complex than a mere hint of parasitic blackmail; Jekyll takes a house for Hyde in Soho, the house to which the police are led after the murder of Danvers Carew. This property, when discovered by Utterson and Inspector Newcomen, proves significant:

> Mr Hyde had only used a couple of rooms; but these were furnished with luxury and good taste. A closet was filled with wine; the plate was of silver, the napery elegant ... At this moment, however, the rooms bore every mark of having been recently and hurriedly ransacked ... on the hearth there lay a pile of grey ashes, as though many papers had been burned. From these embers the inspector

> disinterred the butt end of a green cheque book, which had resisted the action of the fire ... A visit to the bank, where several thousand pounds were found to be lying to the murderer's credit, completed his gratification.[45]

There is another strange contradiction here: the boorish, philistine Hyde, whose other noteworthy crime apart from trampling is blasphemy, occupies an apartment that is furnished with 'good taste' and yet is located in Soho – 'like a district of some city in a nightmare'. As with Jekyll's own house, the effect is again one of inconsistency; Hyde inhabits the disreputable part of London, yet his apartment is tastefully furnished. The suggestion is that if Hyde embodies Jekyll's 'gaiety of disposition', then that disposition, as coded as it is, is not quite as innocent as Jekyll suggests and is eminently worthy of inducing the 'morbid sense of shame'. If Hyde stands in for the unbalanced middle-class dandy who 'consumes to excess', then the apartment is an appropriate location for his adventures, indicating visible opulence and yet offering no evidence of work or diligence. However, what is most significant is the relationship between Hyde and capital itself. Newcomen, upon finding the bank funds lying to Hyde's credit, claims that he can now catch Carew's murderer because 'money's life to the man'.[46] A complex relationship between Hyde, identity, capital, and the city is established. What Newcomen suggests is that Hyde's self-interest is motivated by material greed; after all, as sole beneficiary to Jekyll's will, he is 'heir to a quarter of a million sterling'.[47] However, there is also the suggestion that Hyde is symbolically made of money, that identity and money are interchangeable things for him; indeed, as Terry Eagleton puts it, money is 'a realm of chimerical fantasy in which all identity is ephemeral and any object may be transmuted at a stroke to any other'.[48] In this sense Hyde, like capital itself, circulates through the arteries of the metropolis in strange and indefinable ways. Similarly, the fragmented ashes and the butt of the cheque book found in the hearth of the Soho apartment, like the cinders and ashes of the spontaneously combusted Krook in *Bleak House*, have melted into air. If Hyde, as the epitome of bourgeois self-interest, is symbolically made up of capital then, as well as circulating in the bloodstream of the city, he is, like the ashes found in his hearth, capable of melting into air. What we return to is the incident of the trampling of the young girl that introduces the reader to Hyde. As noted already, Marshall Berman's reading of Marx suggests that in a desanctified mode of existence the modern individual is 'free to trample down everyone in their way if self-interest drives them to it'. However, the trampling itself possesses an interesting financial dimension which suggests that the freedom of 'self-interest' can prove to be a spurious quality; everything has its price. Hyde, when apprehended after the trampling of the girl, states: 'If you choose to make capital out of this accident ... I am naturally helpless. No gentleman but wishes to avoid a scene ... Name your figure.'[49] For Hyde the trampling is tied up with financial interest, something that involves the making of a profit, and he therefore establishes himself as 'gentleman' in a fiscal marketplace of competing cash interests. There is a particular irony in this moment from the most celebrated fictional examination of doubling; just as the Gothic elements of Hogg's *Private Memoirs* echo the dynamics of the literary market, in effect Stevenson's own 'shilling shocker' allows *him* to make capital out of Hyde's 'accident'.

Duality in Stevenson's *Strange Case* does not result in a series of clear binaries, confirm the original self, or ultimately liberate the 'upright' public self as Jekyll hoped it would. Instead what we witness is the ultimate fragmentation of identity, or as Jekyll puts it in a startling moment of self-negation, referring to Hyde, '[h]e, I say – I cannot say, I'. Like Hogg's *Private Memoirs* this collapse of identity is tied up with inheritance and notions of family troubles. In one of his final moments of insight into the nature of his relationship with Hyde, Jekyll, using the third person to indicate his sense of distance from self, states:

> He had now seen the full deformity of that creature that shared with him some of the phenomena of consciousness, and was co-heir with him to death: and beyond these links of community, which in themselves made the most poignant part of his distress, he thought of Hyde, for all his energy of life, as of something not only hellish but inorganic. This was the shocking thing; that the slime of the pit seemed to utter cries and voices; that the amorphous dust gesticulated and sinned; that what was dead, and had no shape, should usurp the offices of life. And this again, that the insurgent horror was knit to him closer than a wife, closer than an eye; lay caged in his flesh, where he heard it mutter and felt it struggle to be born; and at every hour of weakness, and in the confidences of slumber, prevailed against him, and deposed him out of life.[50]

This description of a network of relationships is extraordinarily complex. Jekyll renders Hyde even more uncanny by referring to himself in the third person and therefore to Hyde as the objectified and apparently externalized 'it' and 'that creature'. In addition, the equation between Hyde and capital becomes more resonant through the depiction of the former as 'inorganic'; like blood both circulate through the metaphoric arteries of the city, yet both are ultimately inorganic and inhuman (quite literally *in*-human in Hyde's case). The result is an uncertain and disorientating oscillation between human and inhuman, living and dead, dominant and subordinate. However, it is in the familial relations established by Stevenson that Jekyll's disintegration and Hyde's polymorphous subversion are most explicit. Hyde, as the 'unjust' twin of Jekyll's original scientific experiment, the beneficiary of his will, and as his rival for consciousness is described, in terms reminiscent of sibling rivalry, as the 'co-heir' to death who seeks to 'usurp the offices of life'. The intimacy of their association is stressed – in a manner reminiscent of Gil-Martin's claim to Wringhim in Hogg's novel that 'I am wedded to you so closely that I feel as if I were the same person' – with Hyde regarded as 'closer than a wife' to Jekyll. Most disturbingly Jekyll perceives Hyde as 'caged in his flesh, where he heard it mutter and felt it struggle to be born'. The relationship has already been described in parent–child terms; as Jekyll puts it he 'had more than a father's interest; Hyde had more than a son's indifference'.[51] However, here Hyde becomes a monstrous embryo locked in Jekyll's body in a representation that blurs gender boundaries; the 'mist-like transience' of the human body apparently extends to rendering Jekyll maternal. As much as Jekyll tries to objectify Hyde, keeping him extended and at arm's length, he also appears as an internalized 'non-extended' thing that ultimately troubles the Cartesian equation between mind and body, for this suggests that Hyde is the authentic 'thinking' self, a problem compounded by the fact that Jekyll cannot decide if Hyde is physical or non-physical. In addition, the relationship represented by Jekyll between himself and the internalized Hyde, who utters 'cries and voices', also echoes the dialogue of the mind with itself which Arnold argues is the defining (and disillusioning) feature of modern culture. The description, as disturbing as it is, is ultimately an apposite one. As noted already, Judith Halberstam describes the Gothic novel as the 'hideous offspring of capitalism itself'. Similarly David Punter, reading the Industrial Revolution as 'some kind of birth trauma', views the bourgeoisie as 'the child of a curious miscegenation of class' that stems from this birth.[52] In this context the simultaneous emergence of the Gothic novel and of the industrial bourgeoisie provides an explicit instance of doubling. If Hyde can be read as metaphorising bourgeois self-interest to such a point that capital is literally 'life' for him, then, as Gothic monster, he also effectively dramatizes this interaction between literary genre and social class. Where James Hogg's elliptical and idiosyncratic novel troubles identity and authority in a playful and ultimately ambivalent manner, in Stevenson's *Strange Case* the tone is sombre and understated. Nonetheless, in Hyde Stevenson creates a monster who, at home as he is in the city, is unlocatable in such a way that he eminently lends himself to the variety of meanings that monstrosity generates. However, it is his interaction with capital, his unseen circulation through the city, and his indulgent self-interest that suggests traces of the bourgeois individual of the nineteenth century. If Stevenson's doubling and troubling of identity is understated, Oscar Wilde's proves wordy and ultimately results in an excess of meaning.

3 The psychopathology of everyday narcissism: Oscar Wilde's picture

> '*Fin de siècle*,' murmured Lord Henry.
> '*Fin du globe*,' answered his hostess.
> 'I wish it were *fin du globe*,' said Dorian, with a sigh. 'Life is a great disappointment.'[1]

> It is in ... excess that madness lies – in the exaggerated development of natural passions of human nature not in the appearance of new passions in it.[2]

> The dandy is a creation of the English who were leaders in world trade.[3]

In *The Picture of Dorian Gray*, the final seminal representation of duality in nineteenth-century fiction, Oscar Wilde, like Robert Louis Stevenson before him, offers a Gothic vision of London from the perspective of an outsider. Wilde, as an anglicized Irishman, can be regarded as a figure shaped by a radically different social, cultural and religious sensibility to that of Hogg and Stevenson, who at least share a conception of the world informed by avid and inflexible Calvinism. Nonetheless, Wilde's perspective in *Dorian Gray* provides instructive points of comparison with the tales of duality offered by the two Scottish writers. As indicated, an initial convergence, at least for Wilde and Stevenson, lies in their representation of London. At a significant point in the narrative, Dorian, after rejecting his actress sweetheart Sibyl Vane, is represented as wandering through the metropolis in such a way that both east and west -end are brought into a juxtaposition that evokes the sharply dualistic nature of the city. Wilde notes of Dorian's perambulation:

> Where he went to he hardly knew. He remembered wandering through dimly-lit streets, past gaunt black-shadowed archways and

> evil-looking houses. Women with hoarse voices and harsh laughter had called after him. Drunkards had reeled by cursing, and chattering to themselves like monstrous apes. He had seen grotesque children huddled upon doorsteps, and heard shrieks and oaths from gloomy courts.
>
> As the dawn was just breaking he found himself close to Covent Garden. The darkness lifted, and, flushed with faint fires, the sky hollowed itself into a perfect pearl. Huge carts filled with heavy lilies rumbled slowly down the polished empty street. The air was heavy with the perfume of the flowers, and their beauty seemed to bring him an anodyne for his pain. He followed into the market, and watched the men unloading their wagons. A white-smocked carter offered him some cherries. He thanked him, and wondered why he refused to accept any money for them, and began to eat them listlessly.[4]

The divisions intrinsic to the city are encapsulated in Dorian's peripatetic travels. The east of London is a Gothic creation with its 'dimly-lit streets', and 'evil-looking houses', a feature echoed by its inhabitants who are '[w]omen with hoarse voices', drunkards that curse and chatter 'like monstrous apes', and 'grotesque children'. By contrast the west-end of Covent Garden is a place of subtle refinement and heady sensations, for Dorian finds its flower sellers to be the purveyors of a beauty that, like the opiates alluded to later in this project, 'bring him an anodyne for his pain' and offer an intoxicating fruit.[5] This vision of the topography of the modern metropolis embodies the gulf between rich and poor in a way that intensifies previous representations. Here there is an explicit and emphatic differentiation between east and west, two environments that offer points of contrast: Dorian's wanderings take him from the simian drunkards and 'grotesque children' to the idealized 'line of boys carrying crates of striped tulips' and the '[i]ris necked and pink-footed' pigeons that populate the west-end.[6] Images of sterility and degeneration give way to ones of fruitfulness and health. This distinction between west and east within the city is one consistently maintained by Wilde through the way in which he posits a contrast between the squalor and deprivation of Whitechapel and Limehouse and the fashionable clubs and balls of Mayfair and Pall Mall. Wilde's understanding of the city is clearly a dualistic one that simultaneously echoes and emphasizes the division between Dorian and his portrait. Similarly the contrasting environments that Dorian inhabits during the course of the novel embody a microcosmic vision of the city and metaphorize the difference between public appearance and concealed reality. The locations are succinctly contained in a single description by Wilde of Dorian's infrequent pangs of self-pity:

> There were moments, indeed, at night, when, lying sleepless in his own delicately-scented chamber, or in the sordid room of the little ill-famed tavern near the Docks, which, under an assumed name, and in disguise, it was his habit to frequent, he would think of the ruin he had brought upon his soul, with a pity that was all the more poignant because it was purely selfish. But moments such as these were rare.[7]

The passage encapsulates the contrast between affluent west (Dorian's 'own delicately-scented chamber') and degraded and corrupted east-end ('the sordid room of the little ill-famed tavern near the Docks'). In addition it problematizes an attempt to apprehend who or what the 'real' Dorian is – is it the figure that spends sleepless nights in his 'own' chamber or the one that inhabits sordid rooms under a false identity 'and in disguise'? Such questions are necessary when reading the text; however, they cannot always be answered. The main reason for this is that Wilde's novel is one that revels in paradox, contradiction, the contrast between surface and depth, art and reality. It is one where identity is profoundly fluid because it seems to be so superficial, and one where Wilde's own often excessive verbosity leads to a plethora of inconsistencies and an apparently chaotic perspective.

Unlike the previous two fictions of duality, in Wilde's novel there is no problem with names or naming; indeed, the certainty of Dorian's nominal identity seems to be one of the stable features within the text. Where Hogg's Justified Sinner adopts the surname Wringhim, yet could also be a Colwan or a Dalcastle, and, more fundamentally, where named identity oscillates between Jekyll and Hyde in Stevenson's novel, in Wilde's work Dorian Gray would seem to remain unequivocally the Dorian Gray encountered in the opening pages of the novel. Of course the apparent stability of a given name is not quite as secure as it might be, particularly in a novel where the fact that Dorian *does* seem to remain the Dorian Gray encountered at the start of the novel problematises and further tests the boundaries between appearance and reality. Is the ever-youthful Dorian Gray who appears in public the real Dorian Gray, whatever or whoever that might be? What does link Dorian to the other two subjects of doubling in this study is a certain ambivalence with regard to family background and, once again, the significance of family inheritance. Lord Henry Wotton, the *dilettante* dandy who apparently exerts a Mephistophelean hold over Dorian, asks his uncle Lord Fermor about Dorian's background soon after first meeting him. Fermor's response is instructive, particularly as it carries the whiff of social scandal; after being prompted that Dorian is the last Lord Kelso's grandson, Fermor notes:

> Kelso's grandson! ... Of course ... I knew his mother intimately. I believe I was at her christening. She was an extraordinarily beautiful girl, Margaret Devereux; and made all the men frantic by running away with a penniless young fellow; a mere nobody, sir, a subaltern in a foot regiment, or something of that kind. Certainly. I remember the whole thing as if it happened yesterday. The poor chap was killed in a duel at Spa, a few months after the marriage. There was an ugly story about it. They said Kelso got some rascally adventurer, some Belgian brute, to insult his son-in-law in public; paid him sir, to do it, paid him; and that the fellow spitted his man as if he had been a pigeon. The thing was hushed up, but, egad, Kelso ate his chop alone at the club for some time afterwards. He brought his daughter back with him, I was told, and she never spoke to him again. Oh, yes; it was a bad business. The girl died too; died within a year. So she left a son, did she? I had forgotten. What sort of boy is he? If he is like his mother he must be a good-looking chap.[8]

There are a number of issues in this testimony that are significant with regard to Dorian's identity. Dorian's father was a junior officer in the infantry, 'a penniless fellow'; in a manner reminiscent of Dickens's treatment of Esther Summerson, who stabilizes personal identity through the emergence of family origins in *Bleak House* in spite of the fact that her natural father assumed the name 'Nemo', Dorian's father was a 'mere nobody'. As a result, and particularly as his father is not given the dignity of a proper name, like Robert Wringhim's birth in Hogg's *Private Memoirs*, the scandal attached to Dorian's background perhaps hints at illegitimacy and certainly at family disapproval. However, what is most significant is the division in Dorian's background; his mother is Margaret Devereux, his father 'a mere nobody', the division is between rich and poor: his father is 'a penniless young fellow', his mother's family a wealthy and titled one that can financially determine the assassination of a 'mere nobody'. In effect the social scandal and the division between rich and poor that define Dorian's family origins continue to haunt him throughout the text and contribute to many of the features of his transgressions. The artist Basil Hallward alludes to the scandals that follow Dorian stating to him, 'I think it right that you should know that the most dreadful things are being said against you in London,' and then proceeds to catalogue some of them:

> You used to be a friend of Lord Staveley. I met him at dinner last week ... Staveley curled his lip, and said that you had might have the most artistic tastes, but that you were a man whom no pure-minded girl should be allowed to know, and whom no chaste woman should sit in the same room with. I reminded him that I was a friend of yours, and asked him what he meant. He told me. He told me right out before everybody. It was horrible! Why is your friendship so fatal to young men? There was that wretched boy in the Guards who committed suicide. You were his great friend. There was Sir Henry Ashton, who had to leave England, with a tarnished name. You and he were inseparable. What about Adrian Singleton, and his dreadful end? What about Lord Kent's only son and his career? I met his father yesterday in St James's Street. He seemed broken with shame and sorrow. What about the young Duke of Perth? What sort of life has he got now? What gentleman would associate with him?[9]

Hallward's catalogue of scandals and indiscretions is impressively specific with regard to the identities of the participants and the results of the misdemeanours – suicide, failed careers, exile, tarnished names and broken families – yet also significantly vague in terms of the causes for these social scandals; he can only note that what Staveley revealed to him 'was horrible!' What is clear is that where Hyde's sins in Stevenson's novel are relatively low-key and isolated incidents – the trampling of the young girl 'sounds nothing to hear' in Enfield's words – Dorian's are excessive and puzzlingly contradictory, both visible to society yet vague in nature. Their visibility and excess mark Dorian as Dellamora's middle-class dandy and, although their lack of specificity can be roughly equated with the indeterminate 'pleasures' that provoke Jekyll's attempt to alleviate his feelings of guilt, unlike Jekyll Dorian's hedonistic misdemeanours are evidently public property. In addition, the excessive quality of Dorian's activities extends not only to the number of scandals that his name evokes but also to the suggestion that they involve an apparently polymorphous sexual appetite – no 'pure minded girl' should be allowed to 'know' him or 'chaste woman ... sit in the same room' as him, yet also his 'friendship' proves fatal 'to young men'. As significantly this emphasis upon an excessive appetite also involves the disparity between rich and poor in his family background and the notion of inheritance. In spite of the fact that Hallward insists of Dorian that '[y]ou are not jealous of material things are you – you who are finer than any of them', this perspective proves to be a misconception; indeed, Lord Fermor notes that '[h]e should have a pot of money waiting for him if Kelso did the right thing by him'.[10] Like Wringhim and Hyde, Dorian's financial status in the nineteenth century is founded upon an inheritance, and like Hyde's in Stevenson's novel his identity can again be established as that of the parasitic middle-class dandy whose possession of capital demonstrates the 'loss of balance between the dual imperatives of leisure and work incumbent upon Victorian gentlemen', as Dellamora puts it. Dorian's financial security, which apparently separates him from the matrix of production and consumption in the Victorian marketplace, is troubled by some of the more bizarre of his petty crimes. One of the rumours that circulates around him is that 'he consorted with thieves and coiners and knew the mysteries of their trades'.[11] Despite Hallward's protestation that Dorian is not materialist, Dorian's familiarity with theft and coining suggests an excessive accumulation of capital, one that produces nothing in compensation and, in an inversion of the principles of work and diligence, one where the trades that he learns free him from the constraints of being a 'wage-labourer'. In many ways this relentless if *dilettante* appetite for capital compensates for the lack of balance in his family background manifest in his 'penniless' father. Dorian's inheritance, which allows for a life of leisured hedonism, and his consorting with thieves and coiners would suggest that he can be simultaneously associated with the decadent middle-class dandies and with the degenerate criminal types of the *fin de siècle*.

As with the work of Hogg and Stevenson, the theme of doubling and the effect that this has upon autonomous and individual identity lies at the centre of Wilde's novel. The portrait of Dorian itself is the obvious site to turn to for the most prominent instance of doubling in the text; after all it is the picture that ages for the apparently perpetually youthful Dorian and which takes on the visible burden and effects of his transgressions. In the first instance the portrait as a double, compared to the diabolic Gil-Martin and the monstrous Hyde, seems to possess little of the Gothic trappings appropriated and manipulated by Hogg and Stevenson. Similarly, it seems to be a fairly transparent metaphor, in short, a visible sign of Dorian's guilt. What is interesting, however, is that the picture is established as emphatically modern, indeed the status of the portrait as a superlative example of modern art is stressed by Lord Henry; he describes it as 'the finest portrait of modern times' and 'one of the greatest things in modern art'.[12] The praise offered by Lord Henry is undermined to some extent by Dorian himself who claims later in the text that 'Basil is the best of fellows, but he seems to me to be just a bit of a Philistine'.[13] Dorian's observation is of course both dismissive and subjective, nonetheless through identifying Basil as Philistine (and apparently Dorian does have 'the most artistic tastes') Dorian associates him with the materialism that Hallward mistakenly identifies as absent in the former. The status of the artist is subsequently relegated to that of the wage-labourer suggested by Marx and Engels, and the work of art therefore becomes a material rather than aesthetic thing with a material purpose – here to represent Dorian's own transgressive and hedonistic materialism. Wilde's deploying of contradiction is again exemplified as the portrait is both the superlative example of modern art and a thing stripped of its halo. The use of the picture as a central motif in the text proves to embody many of Wilde's paradoxes, yet it is only one of many instances of doubling utilized by the author. As with Hogg's text, where instances of doubling proliferate, not only in the case of Gil-Martin, who variously appears as Wringhim and as George Colwan and troubles Wringhim's identity to such an extent that he cannot recognize himself, but also with the author himself who appears in different guises throughout the novel, duality proves to be a problem in *The Picture of Dorian Gray*. As stated, the obvious example of doubling lies in the relationship between Dorian and his portrait; similarly Dorian doubles himself, passing himself off in the Docklands under an assumed identity and in disguise. However, instances of doubling also exist between Dorian and the two other main characters in the novel. Dorian's identity is very much tied up with that of Lord Henry Wotton, who provides the Mephistophelean role in the Faustian compact he makes with the portrait and who influences many of his judgements with regard to aesthetics and social poise, the most notorious being his provision of the 'poisonous book' that so influences Dorian.[14] Similarly Basil Hallward, as the painter of the portrait, arguably inhabits the role of a Frankensteinian creator who, by virtue of creating the idealized image of Dorian, initiates Dorian's obsessive identification of outward identity with beauty and longevity. In many ways art therefore functions as the fulcrum for doubling and identification in the novel; if Dorian, Basil and Lord Henry can all be said to overlap and interact in their various reflections of each other then, as Karl Miller states, 'art is successively said to mirror the artist, the sitter and the spectator'.[15] Miller's equation successfully identifies the triangular relationship between Basil, Dorian and Lord Henry – artist, sitter and spectator respectively – which Wilde establishes at the start of the novel; the irony is that such a relationship, which opens duality out in a manner similar to that evoked in Hogg's *Private Memoirs*, is ultimately collapsed by Wilde as Basil and Lord Henry move away from the centre of the novel after the first few chapters. Relationships, potential doubles and reflections are all proffered by Wilde and then apparently discarded before their significance can be established.

Wilde's most consistent use of duality in the novel is that found in the relationship between Dorian and the portrait that Basil Hallward paints of him. As stated above, and in common with the two novels discussed previously, the relationship between Dorian and the picture, with its ensuing sense of a linked fate, is established via a quasi-Faustian pact. The commitment that Dorian makes is itself fairly innocuous:

> 'How sad it is!' murmured Dorian Gray, with his eyes still fixed upon his own portrait. 'How sad it is! I shall grow old, and horrible, and dreadful. But this picture will remain always young ... If it were only the other way! If it were I who was to be always young, and the picture that was to grow old! For that – for that – I would give everything! Yes, there is nothing in the whole world I would not give! I would give my soul for that!'[16]

As straightforward, indeed as flippant as it might appear, Dorian's offering of his soul in exchange for the permanent beauty represented in the painting involves more complex repercussions than it would at first seem to do. It can be observed initially that the painting of the picture itself draws Basil Hallward into his own Faustian compact, for he states, 'I am afraid that I have shown in it the secret of my own soul,' effectively putting too much of himself into it.[17] Indeed, Basil's own fate is significantly very much tied up with that of the portrait that he has painted. In addition Lord Henry is also drawn into Dorian's statement as a Mephistophelean influence; Basil suggests this characterization when he notes, after the utterance cited above, that '[t]his is your doing, Harry'.[18] The association between Lord Henry and the Faustian Mephistopheles is given an added resonance with regard to his relationship with Dorian when he notes later in the novel: 'To a large extent the lad was his own creation. He had made him premature. That was something. Ordinary people waited till life disclose to them its secrets, but to the few, to the elect, the mysteries of life were revealed before the veil was drawn away.'[19] This statement is a significant one, for it effectively determines Lord Henry's apparent position as Mephistopheles to Dorian's Faust and also conflates a Frankensteinian motif with Hogg's critique of extreme Calvinism. Dorian appears to be both Lord Henry's 'own creation', just as the creature is Frankenstein's in Mary Shelley's novel, and also one of his 'elect', just as the Calvinist Robert Wringhim assumes himself to be, little knowing that he is of the devil's party. If this is the case then Dorian, like Wringhim in Hogg's *Private Memoirs*, who is forced by Gil-Martin to accept a 'bond of blood … on the condition that you walk always by my directions', effectively relinquishes personal autonomy and functions as Lord Henry's automaton. Wilde posits this possibility later in his novel when he states:

> There are moments, psychologists tell us, when the passion for sin, or for what the world calls sin, so dominates a nature, that every fibre of the body, as every cell of the brain, seems to be instinct with fearful impulses. Men and women at such moments lose the freedom of their will. They move to their terrible end as automatons move, Choice is taken from them, and conscience is either killed, or if it lives at all, lives but to give rebellion its fascination and disobedience its charm. For all sins, as theologians weary not of reminding us, are sins of disobedience. When that high spirit, that morning-star of evil, fell from heaven, it was as a rebel that he fell.[20]

Wilde's perspective here is resolutely non-committal. He couches the possible application of the statement to Dorian in a wider reference to '[m]en and women' rather than directly referring to the main protagonist of his novel. Similarly there is a proviso contained in the discussion of sin, manifest in 'or what the world calls sin'. Wilde's ambivalence is such that the apprehension of the prime influence upon rebellion and sin, the devil, is portrayed sympathetically and even heroically as 'that high spirit, that morning-star of evil'.[21] Nonetheless, in spite of Wilde's apparent moral ambiguity, there seems to be the suggestion that Dorian is an automaton whose movements and identity are not his own. If Dorian is Lord Henry's 'own creation' then it would seem that the latter is the diabolic manipulator that turns Dorian into an automaton. However, Wilde's perspective is not as unequivocal as this, for if Lord Henry is a Mephistophelean influence, his is a rather ineffectual and tired *fin du globe* one, stripped of his cloven hooves and reek of sulphur in an increasingly secular and materialist world, just as the priest, physician, poet and man of science is stripped of his halo. Compared to Dorian, by the close of the text Lord Henry is 'wrinkled, and worn, and yellow'.[22]

Despite Wilde's equivocality with regard to Lord Henry as Mephistopheles to Dorian's Faust, the suggestion that the latter is in some way an automaton remains a resonant one. In another striking example of his ability to distance himself from the various perspectives offered in the novel, Wilde posits an instance of Dorian's ruminations upon identity, integrity and integration. Asking '[i]s insincerity such a terrible thing?', he evades answering the question which has at its core the issues regarding authenticity and disguise, identity and disidentity that lie at the heart of Arnold's 'The Buried Life'. The question is answered via a sample of Dorian's subjectivity:

> Such, at any rate, was Dorian Gray's opinion. He used to wonder at the shallow psychology of those who conceive the Ego in man as a thing simple, permanent, reliable, and of one essence. To him, man was a being with myriad lives and myriad sensations, a complex multiform creature that bore within itself strange legacies of thought and passion, and whose very flesh was tainted with the monstrous maladies of the dead.[23]

Wilde's narratorial voice distances itself from the perspective offered by suggesting that it is 'Dorian Gray's opinion', thus detaching the author from an apparently authoritative statement. The result is a slant upon identity that uncannily evokes the Cartesian equation between the integrated, punctual and autonomous self and its disidentical, fragmented other – the 'unstable play of masks and guises' suggested by Francis Barker. The echo can be found in Dorian's differentiation between the 'simple, permanent, reliable' self and the 'complex multiform creature' that he advocates as the authentic self; the interaction between authenticity and inauthenticity is bewildering and essentially paradoxical. Similarly, Dorian's critique of the 'shallow psychology' of those who believe in an integrated self and his advocating of 'insincerity' further blurs the boundaries between performance and integrity, surface and depth, appearance and reality in a way that perhaps troubles Barker's reading of Descartes and certainly Arnold's search for a coherent self in 'The Buried Life'. The emphasis upon multiformity and multiplicity by Dorian explodes Stevenson's duality and at the same time expands upon Jekyll's acknowledgement that there is potentially a polypsyche at the core of identity. In addition, Dorian's contention that human identity 'bore within itself strange legacies of thought and passion, and whose very flesh was tainted with the monstrous maladies of the dead' suggests an equation between the fragmentation of the modern individual and malady that echoes both Arnold's depiction of 'the strange disease of modern life' and the correlation between urban identity and sickness in the city 'condition' of the *fin de siècle* as discussed by William Greenslade. Furthermore, Dorian's suggestion that identity contains 'legacies' from the past supports David Punter's understanding of the nineteenth-century Gothic as a genre that evokes 'that kind of modernity which takes very seriously the problems of social and psychological conditioning'. If Dorian is in thrall to anything, then arguably it is to the past and the 'monstrous maladies of the dead'; Wilde's turn of phrase is suitably Gothic and perhaps alludes to the manner in which his text is informed by the conventions and traditions of that genre. More significantly Dorian's consciousness of the legacies of the past concurs with Berman's discussion of the experience of modernity in the nineteenth century with its 'inner dichotomy' between past and present, its sense of 'living in two worlds simultaneously'.

The conditioning alluded to above is significant with regard to the nature of (or lack of) autonomy and freedom of will available to the individual in Wilde's novel, and again iterates the possibility that Dorian, as a quasi-Faust, does not belong to himself. Again it is Lord Henry, in his vaguely Mephistophelean role, who offers a perspective upon action and will:

> The mutilation of the savage has its tragic survival in the self-denial that mars our lives. We are punished for our refusals. Every impulse that we strive to strangle broods in the mind and poisons us ... The only way to get rid of temptation is to yield to it. Resist it, and your soul grows sick with longing for the things it has forbidden to itself, with desire for what its monstrous laws have made monstrous and unlawful.[24]

In many ways the words that Wilde gives Lord Henry rewrite and offer an antidote to the repression of Jekyll and the ensuing need to create Hyde as found in Stevenson's novel. The statement also provides a subtle gloss upon that 'kind of modernity' concerned with and taking seriously the role of social and psychological conditioning. However, where Stevenson's work evokes the problematic imperative of self-repression and the ensuing destructive hypocrisy of the outwardly respectable Jekyll from whom issues forth the monstrous Hyde, for Lord Henry in *The Picture of Dorian Gray* monstrosity is produced by 'monstrous laws'. The laws of self-control that balance the individual, the moral codes discussed by Alfred Wigan in *The Duality of the Mind*, are ultimately negative; self-denial is destructive and, as Lord Henry puts it, 'The only way to get rid of temptation is to yield to it.' However, Lord Henry's words, once again, prove to be paradoxical and contradictory – he speaks but doesn't act upon his own maxims; as Basil Hallward puts it, 'You mustn't believe a word that he says,' and Lord Henry himself admits, 'I am quite content with philosophic contemplation.'[25] In many ways Wilde's novel offers an appropriate mirror image to Stevenson's perspective in *Jekyll and Hyde*; in Stevenson's work repression proves to be destructive yet Dorian's indulgence and embracing of transgression is similarly destructive – in short there is no happy medium.

In many ways the flux of perspectives offered by Lord Henry, coupled with the implication that he utters but does not act upon his own words, opens up the chaotic readings of duality and identity found in the novel. Lord Henry's opinions take the fragmentation of duality, the collapse of definable boundaries discussed in the course of this project, to such a point that they seem almost meaningless:

> Soul and body, body and soul – how mysterious they were! There was animalism in the soul, and the body had its moments of spirituality. The senses could refine, and the intellect could degrade.

> Who could say where the fleshy impulse ceased, or the physical impulse began? How shallow were the arbitrary definitions of ordinary psychologists! And yet how difficult to decide between the claims of the various schools! Was the soul a shadow seated in the house of sin? Or was the body really in the soul ... The separation of spirit from matter was a mystery, and the union of spirit with matter was a mystery also.[26]

Much of this rumination echoes the principles pondered by Descartes in his *Meditations*; however, many of the ideas overlap and become repetitive. Again, as with Dorian's discussion of the multiform identity and the critique of 'shallow psychology', there is an emphasis upon the limitations of the theories of selfhood contained in the description of the 'shallow' and 'arbitrary definitions of ordinary psychologists'. Nonetheless, Lord Henry's words prove largely tautological and ultimately fail to resolve the issues at stake as they lapse into a series of vague questions and observations. All that we are left with is a series of unanswered mysteries. It would seem then that Wilde's novel revolves arguably around the respective failures of autonomy and ability to act upon initiative.

If this is the case, then Wilde arrives at the negation of free will within the individual in a very circumlocutory manner and via the appropriation of a number of paradoxical themes. The idea that Dorian might be bereft of will can be ascribed to Wilde's description of him as Lord Henry Wotton's 'creation'. The suggestion can therefore be made that Dorian is an automaton – a possibility alluded to by Wilde in his discussion of the 'passion for sin' that strips the individual of 'the freedom of their will'. However, to balance this there is Lord Henry's rumination upon the 'mutilation of the savage' in modern society, and on the perils of resisting temptation which turn the soul 'sick with longing for the things it has forbidden itself'. In many respects Lord Henry's words advocate, even celebrate, the loss of will implicit in succumbing to sin. Wilde's narratorial position is ambiguous for he seems to criticize simultaneously the loss of will that turns the individual into an automaton yet also acknowledges the attraction of sin and rebellion. Similarly, Lord Henry recommends indulgence in sin, transgression and impulse, yet is himself unable to act upon his own words. To indulge in pleasure is to lose will by losing oneself in the sensations stimulated by the activity, yet Lord Henry cannot practise this fall into hedonism because he has not the will to do so. This dizzying vacillation between sites that identify and either celebrate or criticize will, autonomy, identity, integrity and morality are all further troubled by Dorian's contemplation of 'the Ego'. Here insincerity is privileged over sincerity, the disintegration of identity into 'myriad lives and myriad sensations' over cohesion, transience over permanence. The 'complex multiform creature' that constitutes the individual for Dorian seems to amplify and fragment Stevenson's basic duality in *Jekyll and Hyde*; the description also suggests, through the presence of 'complex', a depth to the individual that evokes Arnold's notion of a buried life in the poem of that name. Similarly, the possibility of having 'myriad lives and myriad sensations' suggests a multitude of choices, opportunities and activities that can be acted upon – in short an integrated life that cohesively covers all avenues of experience. Nonetheless, it must be remembered that Dorian is positing an interpretation of identity that is the opposite of something 'permanent and reliable'; it is insincere, superficial, an 'unstable play of masks and guises', as Francis Barker puts it, of the disidentical Cartesian self. Masao Miyoshi attempts to unravel this labyrinthine interaction between agency, will, experience and identity; the task is almost impossible such is the ambivalence of Wilde's perspective. Nonetheless Miyoshi's reading consolidates many of the problems discussed above:

> If the Wildean insincerity implies multiplicity, sincerity must imply self-integrity. To experience all possible experiences, spiritual and sensual, religious and secular, moral and amoral, man must be a 'complex multiple [*sic*] creature'. However to 'experience' at all, one must *be*, first of all. And this is what he is unable, or unwilling, to do, since for that he would have to *choose* what he wants to see, what he wants to do, and what he would like to be. And he cannot choose.[27]

Many aspects of Miyoshi's interpretation are helpful. He identifies with clarity the contrast between insincerity and sincerity and the way in which if the former suggests multiplicity then the latter indicates integrity. What is most significant is the manner through which Dorian's identity is taken away from him via his inability to '*choose*'; this inability to make choices suggests an absence of will and is most evident in his lack of discretion when it comes to experience. Miyoshi's reading is perhaps more tenuous when it comes to suggesting that Dorian cannot experience because he cannot choose the things that he experiences. Dorian does of course experience many things, from the variety of hedonistic and intoxicating activities depicted in Chapter 11 of the novel to the degradation of opium addiction represented in Chapter 16. Where Dorian's inability to choose does manifest itself is in his failure to discriminate between experience and identity; doing and being are the same thing for him, and it is this correlation that determines him as an automaton. It is possible to suggest that if Dorian is anyone's 'creation' in the course of the narrative, he is his own. He creates and recreates himself consistently and compulsively – from artist's model, to dandy, to aesthete, to Catholic convert via hedonist, and on to homicidal criminal and opium addict – in a manner that evokes Berman's diagnosis of the nature of modern identity in the flux of nineteenth century modernity and hints at the lack of an integrated, autonomous self. Similarly, through this constant reinvention of the visible, apparently socialized self, Dorian transforms and transmutes the portrait of himself hidden in his attic. If anything, Dorian *becomes* the Faustian pact, both in his visible self, which is described as 'the devil's bargain', and in his hidden self, for when Basil Hallward views the changed portrait he claims that it 'has the eyes of the devil'.[28]

In many ways the portrait, as part of the basic dualistic premise in the novel and also the thing that contributes to destabilizing duality, embodies the contradictions, paradoxes and knowing inconsistencies of Wilde's work. The portrait represents what should naturally occur to Dorian's sense of an external, physical self: it ages for him. At the same time it stands in for what happens to a more internalized, invisible, moral self: it visibly degenerates as Dorian's activities become increasingly transgressive and insalubrious. As a result the picture, itself a one-dimensional work of art, becomes the authentic self, metaphorizing Dorian's integrated sense of internal and external selves and also highlighting the inability to apply such terms to Dorian himself. As this 'authentic' self remains hidden, Dorian becomes the performative and disidentical self – the thing of 'masks and guises' discussed by Barker and the self 'Trick'd in disguises' represented in Arnold's 'The Buried Life'. Paradoxically to look inwards for Dorian is therefore to also look outwards, at the external and visible portrait, yet this outward sign of internal as well as external decay is buried in an attic, remaining hidden and invisible. Self-consciousness therefore becomes a furtive and secretive activity that demonstrates the superficiality of the apparent similar self-consciousness of the 'visible' dandy; an inverted and largely morbid narcissism. Dorian's response to the portrait is ambiguous; he returns to his attic to 'sit in front of the picture, sometimes loathing it and himself, but filled, at other times, with that pride of individualism that is half the fascination of sin, and smiling with secret pleasure at the misshapen shadow that had to bear the burden that should have been his own'.[29] The response incorporates an element of revulsion. Dorian finds himself 'loathing it and himself', yet the dominant sensation is one of pleasure demonstrated in the sense of the 'pride of individualism' and Dorian's 'smiling with secret pleasure'. The picture therefore effectively problematizes Cartesian duality discussed earlier in this project; it is an 'extended' thing that is both separate from Dorian *and* stands in for a body which is ravaged by time and excess, yet it also represents that authentic, albeit corrupted, 'non-extended' self. In short it troubles the boundaries between private and public, internal and external, identity and disidentity evoked in the descriptions of location addressed at the start of this discussion of Wilde's text.

Perhaps the key to the novel lies in the shifts between public and private, inauthentic and authentic selves; shifts that Wilde often blurs and questions. As much as Wilde's perspective is a difficult one to locate, there is nonetheless a consistency in his appropriation of themes of masking and mirroring that provide some assistance in stabilizing a text which frequently disrupts the reader's sense of interpretative equilibrium. Again Miyoshi's reading of *Dorian Gray* is instructive. Miyoshi suggests that the novel evokes a common *fin de siècle* literary thread, that of the interplay between masks and mirrors alluded to above. In an analysis of this theme which also resonates with conceptual material represented by Arnold and Stevenson, Miyoshi suggests that the

> mask hides a no-man's face, and although everyone fears exposure of his nothingness, to other's one's mask is one's face. The mirror, on the other hand, reflects not only the mask but, hopefully, the hidden truth of the face ... for the writers of the nineties ... introspection, mirror-gazing, is a sanctioned activity. For the world wear your mask; for a true glimpse of yourself, consult your mirror. The mask is for others' inspection, the mirror for one's private introspection.[30]

Miyoshi's argument contextualizes Wilde's novel within a cultural climate that is concerned with the difference between public and private and with the act of introspection itself, a climate where the degeneration theorists Nordau and Lombroso provide a critique of morbid self-obsession as a sign of cultural sickness. In addition Miyoshi's mirror, which hopefully reveals 'the hidden truth of the face', echoes Arnold's evocation of the buried, authentic self. The significant difference is that, where Arnold's 'The Buried Life' is an attempt to convey a quest for an identity that possesses integrity and depth within the fabric and machinations of modernity, Miyoshi's differentiation between masks and mirrors seems largely to deal with a superficial sense of self – the mask disguises the self, but the mirror, as much as it licenses introspection, can only reveal the truth of the face. Again Miyoshi falls a little way short in his analysis, for the mirror – the portrait of Dorian in Wilde's text – reveals both external and internal self. Compared to Stevenson's *Jekyll and Hyde*, where public appearance involves a manipulative attempt to appear hyper-respectable, a mask in itself, in Wilde's *Dorian Gray* the mask, made up of Dorian's varied disguises and *dilettante* incarnations, is decorative, the posturing of the dandy. The significance in the difference between public and private, mask and mirror, for Wilde's Dorian seems then to lie in the fact that the private self, the portrait, is the buried self, whereas the public self, the dandy, is clearly visible.

Dorian's public self, the mask that appears in a variety of different guises, is explicitly affiliated with the late-nineteenth-century dandy. Wilde, citing the French writer Théophile Gautier, notes of Dorian that 'he was one for whom "the visible world existed"'.[31] For Dellamora visibility is one of the distinguishing features of the nineteenth-century middle-class dandy, and Wilde does define Dorian as dandy, stating that

> to him Life itself was the first, the greatest, of the arts, and for it all the other arts seemed to be but preparation. Fashion, by which what is really fantastic becomes for a moment universal, and Dandyism, which, in its own way, is an attempt to assert the absolute modernity of beauty, had, of course their fascination for him.[32]

I do not wish to dwell upon Wilde's complex and fluid theories of art and aesthetics which manifest themselves, albeit in a relatively displaced manner, in this extract. For the purposes of this discussion what is significant is that depths and surfaces are again juxtaposed and incorporated with each other through the correlation between life and art. In addition there is a correspondence between the visibility of the dandy and 'absolute modernity'. If Stevenson's Hyde can be read as the middle-class dandy of nineteenth-century modernity described by Dellamora, then he is a strange one who seems capable of disappearing into the underbelly of the metropolis at will. Nonetheless there is a certain visibility to him manifest in the fact that, if witnesses are seemingly unable to describe him precisely, at least his presence in the text, unlike Gil-Martin's in Hogg's *Private Memoirs*, is unequivocal. By contrast Dorian is visible and public, to such a point that his indiscretions and transgressions, if only really alluded to rather than defined, are common knowledge. Yet, like Hyde, there is the suggestion that he too is difficult to pin down, a feature found in his constant reinvention of self, his endless chain of interests and his peripatetic travels across the two distinct and contained sections of London. Again it is possible to read Wilde's novel as providing a mirror image to Stevenson's – if Hyde is vaporous yet also distinctly visible, then Dorian is emphatically visible yet also capable of his own fluidity. In addition, another link between Dorian and Hyde with regard to the dandy is the notion that both consume 'to excess while producing little or nothing'. Dorian's propensity for the accumulation of capital has already been noted, as has his apparently voracious and excessive sexual appetite. His narcissism, which reaches such a pitch that through the Faustian pact he effectively *becomes* the portrait, is also excessive; in Nordau and Lombroso's terms he worships the 'I' and has an 'excessive preoccupation with self'. Narcissism might hypothetically prove the ultimate confirmation of identity through a complete preoccupation with and consciousness of self; however, it iterates again the superficiality of the public and external Dorian. Narcissism in Dorian's case is tied up with physical appearance and, as the portrait clearly demonstrates, looks prove deceptive.

Excess and over-consumption take many other forms in Wilde's novel, indicating the privileging of leisure and indulgence in Dorian's life that his financial independence and the pact with the portrait allow. As Miyoshi has pointed out, it is an attempt to 'experience all possible experiences'; as a result Dorian's excesses manifest themselves in a myriad of different ways. Amongst other indulgences he immerses himself in the study and appreciation of fashion, religion, mysticism, perfumes, music, jewellery, and embroideries.[33] Two other instances of overindulgence stand out in particular, and demonstrate the way in which excessive consumption correlates with many of the issues already discussed. As noted, Dorian receives a book from Lord Henry that informs many of his attitudes towards life and art. Wilde's heady description of the book is instructive:

> One hardly knew at times whether one was reading the spiritual ecstasies of some medieval saint or the morbid confessions of a modern sinner. It was a poisonous book. The heavy odour of incense seemed to cling about its pages and to trouble the brain. The mere cadence of the sentences, the subtle monotony of their music, so full as it was of complex refrains and movements elaborately repeated, produced in the mind of the lad, as he passed from chapter to chapter, a form of reverie, a malady of dreaming, that made him unconscious of the falling day and creeping shadows.[34]

The book is effectively one that cannot be located; it appears sometimes to be 'the spiritual ecstasies of some medieval saint' and at others – in a phrase that seems to explicitly evoke Hogg's novel – 'the morbid confessions of a modern sinner'. The most notable feature that it possesses is the manner in which it disorientates Dorian's senses; its repetitive, even monotonous, nature induces a soporific effect, 'a form of reverie, a malady of dreaming, that made him unconscious'. In effect the 'poisonous' book becomes an addictive narcotic, something that he returns to '[o]ver and over again' and which has 'poisoned' him.[35] This aesthetic intoxication through excessive consumption has its parallel in the alternative world that Dorian inhabits within London. As well as being addicted to the 'poisonous book', Dorian experiences other addictions, namely, a 'mad craving' which signifies the 'hideous hunger for opium'; it is this appetite that takes him to the sordid opium dens of the Docklands.[36] In effect what we are presented with is two instances of addiction that take very different forms: the book helps him 'realize his conception of the beautiful', and his opium addiction suggests that '[u]gliness was the one reality'.[37] In both instances the familiar conception of Dorian as automaton is reiterated, in the fashionable and artistic social world of the west-end he is guided by the 'poisonous' book and in the degraded and degenerate east-end he compulsively seeks oblivion in opium dens.

Dorian's interaction with the degraded areas of the east of London, his presence in its opium dens and his association with thieves and coiners, establish his criminal credentials. However, the issue of monstrosity in this Gothic text is a problematic one and one that cannot necessarily be resolved. In spite of its ambivalent treatment of the theme, Hogg's *Private Memoirs* always carries with it the possibility that Gil-Martin is the devil and that the novel is a tale of diabolic possession. More emphatically, Stevenson's Hyde, as open to a plethora of interpretations as he is, is also a demonic presence, 'not only hellish but inorganic'. In Wilde's novel it is far more difficult to locate strands of monstrosity, if there are any at all. The motif of the portrait bearing the burden of Dorian's sins and physical ageing provides a supernatural dimension to the text. Similarly the quasi-Faustian pact, along with Dorian's loose correlation with the devil, at least allows a hint of the diabolic elements that pervade the other two texts. Indeed, the very fact that Dorian remains youthful and exploits this position throughout the bulk of Wilde's novel can be regarded as monstrous in itself, at least in as much as it troubles the reader's basic conception of what constitutes human longevity. Yet even if we consider that monstrosity can be equated with crime in the three texts under scrutiny, then most of Dorian's transgressions appear to be relatively minor. In Stevenson's *Jekyll and Hyde*, Hyde's crimes initially appear to be 'nothing to hear', nonetheless they are 'hellish to see' and culminate in a psychopathic murder. By contrast, in the fashionable world of the west-end, Dorian's misdemeanours carry unspecified scandal with them. His less public activities involve inhabiting opium dens, consorting with the aforementioned thieves and coiners and, most bizarrely, being 'seen brawling with foreign sailors in a low den in the distant parts of Whitechapel'.[38] His actions are arguably even more boorish and philistine than Hyde's, arising from a mixture of ennui and the self-interest of the middle-class dandy. As David Punter succinctly and damningly puts it, his 'crimes and his feelings are alike petty and *dilettante*, and his doom evokes neither compassion nor the more elevated sympathies of tragedy'.[39] Indeed many of Dorian's pursuits demonstrate this *dilettante* world-weariness; his flirtation with Roman Catholicism for example is a temporary one that demonstrates his boredom and supports his statement, 'I wish it were *fin du globe* … [l]ife is a great disappointment.' Perversely enough, in spite of Wilde's heady prose and his character's hedonistic excesses, in many ways Dorian Gray is the most trivial, subdued and low-key member of the triumvirate under discussion. If Wilde damns Dorian in any way other than in the closing pages of the novel, then it lies in the fact that the only thing which Dorian *does* seem to commit himself to is the portrait; he remains as beautiful as the initial impact of the picture, but not much more than that.

Regardless of the possibility that Dorian is a petty and trivial figure, the murder of Basil Hallward, his most significant and explicitly represented criminal act, remains an important one in terms of this discussion. It is initiated within the now familiar territory of the nineteenth-century metropolis. Dorian encounters the artist in an environment where, when asked by Basil if he recognizes him, he can state, 'In this fog my dear Basil? Why, I can't even recognize Grosvenor Square. I believe my house is somewhere about here, but I don't feel at all certain about it.'[40] In effect Dorian can murder Basil and dispose of his body because no-one can see him do so in the fog. The murder takes place after Dorian has allowed Basil to see the transformed painting that represents his authentic self. Although it occurs in the concealed space of an attic rather than in the open, it possesses similar psychopathic qualities to Hyde's bludgeoning of Danvers Carew. Wilde writes: 'He [Dorian] rushed at him, and dug the knife into the great vein that is behind the ear, crushing the man's head down on the table, and stabbing again and again.'[41] Like Hyde's trampling of Carew, with its 'ape-like fury', Dorian's assault upon Basil is sadistic, crushing his head upon the table. In addition it is compulsively and excessively repetitive; where Hyde brings down a 'storm of blows', Dorian stabs Basil 'again and again'. The aftermath of the murder is perhaps as significant as the murder itself. Dorian, in an attempt to dispose of Basil's body, summons Alan Campbell, a scientist who has had some prior association with Dorian which has resulted in a scandal whereby when they 'met in society now, it was only Dorian Gray who smiled'.[42] Dorian effectively blackmails Campbell into getting rid of the body:

> Alan, you are scientific. You know about chemistry, and things of that kind. You have made experiments. What you have got to do is destroy the thing that is upstairs – to destroy it so that not a vestige of it will be left. Nobody saw this person come into the house … He will not be missed for months. When he is missed, there must be no trace of him found here. You, Alan, you must change him, and everything that belongs to him, into a handful of ashes that I may scatter in the air.[43]

Basil's dead body becomes for Dorian a symbol of his real nature, albeit a misguided interpretation as the portrait in the attic represents his authentic self. Like the demise of Krook in *Bleak House* and the ashes of the money that stand as a metaphor for Hyde in Stevenson's novel, Dorian wants Basil's body to melt into air, 'into a handful of ashes' that he can 'scatter' so that there is no trace left of him in order that Dorian's own guilt can evaporate. This desire to eradicate the telltale signs of his crime reveals the extent of Dorian's narcissism; he does not want to disappear himself, nor does he want the portrait that ensures his youthful longevity and apparent lack of moral corruption to vanish. Rather he desires to rid himself both of the symbol of his criminal act and of the creator of the now-blighted portrait. The action is simultaneously a way of evading responsibility and of thrusting it upon Basil – Basil's body effectively, if again misguidedly, should carry the burden of his sins. In this context it is significant that Wilde should represent Dorian objectifying Basil's body as 'the thing that is upstairs', thus blurring the boundaries between the body, the portrait, its creator, and the sitter himself. In disposing of Basil's body it is unclear as to what Dorian wants to eradicate. This emphasis upon vaporousness and insubstantiality – manifest in the foggy environment, in Dorian's instructions to Campbell, and supported by a possible ambivalence in 'the thing that is upstairs' which Dorian wants to rid himself of – reaches an interesting climax in Dorian's visit to the opium dens mentioned above. The journey takes place through an appropriately Gothic environment that corresponds with Dorian's other nocturnal perambulations in the east of London. The 'moon hung low in the sky like a yellow skull' and, in surroundings that echo the fog found in *Bleak House* and *Jekyll and Hyde*, a 'cold rain began to fall, and the blurred street-lamps looked ghastly in the dripping mist'.[44] In this setting Dorian seeks to 'buy oblivion … where the memory of old sins could be destroyed by the madness of sins that were new', in effect to obliterate temporarily traces of the self in a location that is itself defined by vapour and fluidity.[45] It is here that Dorian is confronted by James Vane, brother of Sibyl Vane who committed suicide after being rejected by Dorian eighteen years ago. Dorian's apparent youth saves him from Vane's vengeance, but when it is pointed out that Dorian looks no older than he did eighteen years ago, Vane finds that 'Dorian Gray had disappeared'.[46] In effect Dorian, like Krook in *Bleak House*, Hyde in Stevenson's novel and Basil Hallward's body, which symbolizes both Dorian's criminality and the guilty secret of his authentic self, can melt into air himself. In keeping with many of the themes that run through this project, Dorian's disappearance into the night evokes the fluidity that defines identity in nineteenth century modernity.

The novel concludes with what is apparently an attempt by Dorian to exercise free will, assert an autonomous identity and renounce narcissism, all of which result in his destruction. Perversely his death stems from what seems to be the intention to perform an act of self-denial, for Dorian determines not to seduce Hetty Merton. However, this sense of restraint involves a fundamentally narcissistic desire to restore the portrait, that symbol of his authentic self, to its original state of beauty. His inclination to 'never again tempt innocence', as much as it refers to Hetty Merton and, implicitly, the other conquests that have caused the decay of the portrait, is also applicable to Dorian himself.[47] The suggestion is that he wants to revert the image found in the picture back to what is manifest in his externalized, superficial and public self; to superimpose appearance over reality, surface over depth, mask over mirror. It would appear that it is the basic ugliness of the authentic, concealed self that so offends Dorian and inspires his hypocritical assumption of guilt and remorse; as Wilde suggests '[p]erhaps if his [Dorian's] life became pure, he would be able to expel every sign of evil passion from the face'.[48] In the penultimate moments of confronting the portrait Dorian effectively becomes aware of his inability to be anything other than the series of experiences that have defined identity, the confusing of doing with being:

> The death of Basil Hallward seemed very little to him. He was thinking of Hetty Merton. For it was an unjust mirror, this mirror of the soul that he was looking at. Vanity? Curiosity? Hypocrisy? Had there been nothing more in his renunciation than that? There had been nothing more. At least he thought so. But who could tell? ... No. There had been nothing more. Through vanity he had spared her. In hypocrisy he had worn the mask of goodness. For curiosity's sake he had tried the denial of self. He recognized that now.[49]

The words evoke the superficial and *dilettante* approach to all activities that Dorian has pursued. As with Lord Henry's analysis of soul and body, which climaxes in a series of imponderable questions, the statement seems to evoke a lack of commitment manifest in the phrase 'who could tell' which follows the questions about sincerity generated by Dorian. However, he apparently arrives at some form of self-realization in his assessment that there 'had been nothing more' in his life than a series of masks and postures. In spite of the dismissive response to the murder of Basil Hallward, the apprehension that vanity, curiosity and hypocrisy lie behind his act of self-denial suggest a new-found self-awareness. The implication seems to be that Dorian detects a certain inevitability, that he cannot change the relationship between public and private selves, and that any attempt to do good involves a purely hypocritical intention to return the portrait to its former glory. However, where consciousness of the complete fragmentation of self in Hogg's *Private Memoirs* allows Wringhim to embrace oblivion and Stevenson's Jekyll accepts that the only way to resolve his own disintegration is to destroy Hyde, Dorian's awareness of his own inability to render the self cohesive results in an act of rebellion. He turns against the portrait that represents his authentic self, resenting its influence over him, and, through Wilde's deft use of disembodied utterance, claims: 'It had been like conscience to him. Yes, it had been conscience. He would destroy it.'[50] Unlike Wringhim or Jekyll's acts of self-destruction, Dorian's fatal attack upon the portrait, appropriately enough with the knife used to kill Basil Hallward, is fundamentally narcissistic, for Dorian cannot bear the ugliness of the picture and what it embodies with regard to the self that lies beneath the surface.

The guiding principle behind this section has been an exploration of duality in three Gothic texts which posit instances of doubling. However, as should be clear by now, any attempt to offer clear binary equations is one fraught with problems. Identity within nineteenth-century modernity is itself, in many different manifestations, unstable and fragmentary in nature. The polarities that are initiated between Wringhim and Gil-Martin, Jekyll and Hyde, Dorian and his portrait in Hogg, Stevenson and Wilde's novels respectively only serve to further trouble the notion of what it is to have an integrated and autonomous sense of self. As much as each apparent double exists to provide a counterpoint to the individual, they also indicate the fragility of identity itself. If identity is as fluid and protean as Marx and Marshall Berman suggest, then in many ways these texts emphatically dramatize the crisis of modernity that faces the individual in the nineteenth century. Each novel overlaps and indicates instances of thematic cross-pollination, yet at the same time offers its own perspective on the possible repercussions of the disintegration of cohesive identity. Hogg's *Private Memoirs* evokes the instability of selfhood in the literary marketplace as well as warning of the perils of deluded fanaticism, Stevenson's *Jekyll and Hyde* proffers a monstrous vision of bourgeois self-interest run wild, and Wilde's *Dorian Gray* probes the contradictory and paradoxical terrain between surfaces and depths as well as exploring *fin de siècle* narcissism. Each writer, despite a similar use of motif and theme, explores his conceptual territory in different ways, from Hogg's dry wit, through Stevenson's grasp of understatement, to Wilde's heady and intoxicating prose. Where all converge, as Matthew Arnold does in perhaps a less lurid manner, is in pointing out the perils of going beneath the surface.

Part II

The stripping of the halo: religion and identity in the poetry of Alfred Tennyson, James 'B. V.' Thomson and Gerard Manley Hopkins

Introduction

> The bourgeoisie, wherever it has got the upper hand … has drowned the most heavenly ecstasies of religious fervour, of chivalrous enthusiasm, of philistine sentimentalism, in the icy water of egotistical calculation.[1]

> Between the buildings assigned to each sex was a third row of buildings, containing the administration, accommodation for the superintendent and staff, and that critical part of every well-wrought Victorian asylum, the chapel, in which the inmates could be brought the consolations of organized religion.[2]

In 1810 William Black, London physician and author of *Dissertation on Insanity* published in the same year, tabulated the causes of admission for approximately one third of the patients entered at Bethlem public madhouse. Bethlem, or Bedlam – the popular nomenclature used by Black and a term synonymous with insanity – had originally been founded by the Order of St Mary of Bethlehem in 1247; used for the habilitation of lunatics from 1377 onwards, the hospital had stood at Moorfields in London from 1676. In his table Black listed 'Religion and Methodism' as the most popular cause of insanity after 'Disappointments, Grief', 'Family and Heredity' and 'Fevers'. Ninety patients were diagnosed as apparently demonstrating the symptoms of religious mania, accounting for just under a tenth of those studied.[3] Black's identification of religion as constituting a significant cause for insanity or derangement is hardly surprising; madness and Christianity seem to have been intertwined from the latter's earliest days. In St Mark's Gospel it is reported that, as Christ is casting out devils from the sick, 'when his friends heard of it, they went out to lay hold on him: for they said, He is beside himself' (Mk 3:20). In addition St Paul, in his two letters to the Corinthians, advocates a condition of rapture or madness when communicating with God, and Erasmus, editor of the first Greek New Testament to be printed and placed on sale, saw Christianity as a form of madness in his *Praise of Folly* published in 1511.[4] Obversely extreme religious fanaticism or devotion could be seen to lead to deluded states of consciousness; in the final sections of his *Anatomy of Melancholy* (1621) Robert Burton saw religious melancholy as an aspect of man's fall; John Wesley, on the other hand, in his *Primitive Physick* of 1747, proved himself a staunch disciple of the influence of divine madness. Indeed, the satirical elements of Hogg's *Private Memoirs* suggest that the Calvinist supposition of being one of God's Elect can lead to maniacal disorder. By the late eighteenth century and with the development of the empirical thinking associated with the Enlightenment, religious madness was being interpreted as organic or pathological in origin rather than perceived as supernatural possession.[5]

During the nineteenth century religious madness becomes more prominent as a label determining or defining the instability of identity commonly associated with insanity. The objectification and pathologizing of a condition or state of consciousness that was previously the province of priests, theologians and philosophers becomes, as William Black's table suggests, a clear delineation for mental aberration. In fact it is a little surprising that religion should occur as the fourth highest cause for admission to Bethlem in Black's table, considering the extent to which religion is identified as a cause of insanity in the medical literature of the early nineteenth century. In the second, revised edition of his *Observations on the Nature, Kinds, Causes and Prevention of Insanity* (1806), Thomas Arnold refers to the individual 'harassed and tormented, with religious fear, the gloom of despondency and the horrors of despair'.[6] By 1828 George Man Burrows emphatically links religious fervour with insanity:

> Enthusiasm and insanity bear such close affinity that the shades are often too indistinct to define which is one and which the other. Exuberance of zeal on any subject, in some constitutions, soon ripens into madness: but excess of religious enthusiasm, unless tempered by an habitual command over the affective passions, usually and readily degenerates into fanaticism.[7]

By 1837 W. A. F. Browne, in *What Asylums Were, Are, and Ought to Be*, links religion and insanity to the significance of religion within the British social and cultural identity:

> the number of religious maniacs is greater in Britain than elsewhere. The explanation is obvious. Religion has here its due exercise and awful importance; the mind is trained, thinks and feels under its influence; and when from misfortune or ambition, or physical injury, the place of reason is usurped, it may always be predicated, first that the delusions which succeed will correspond to the natural disposition, and secondly to those impressions which have been most powerful and permanent.[8]

What Browne identifies possesses a familiar resonance. Burrows indicates that 'habitual command' is the key to the prevention of 'enthusiasm' being translated into 'fanaticism'. By contrast, for Browne religious mania, and the fragmentation of identity implicit in such a condition, is greater in Britain 'than elsewhere' due to the social and cultural conditioning that David Punter has identified as a feature of post-eighteenth-century modernity and which, in so many ways, contributes to the collapse of cohesive identities explored in the previous section of this project. Here this conditioning can be detected in the morbid 'exercise and awful importance' of religion in Britain, and the way in which 'the mind is trained, thinks and feels under its influence'. In many ways both Burrows's and Browne's definitions correspond with Wigan's description of the guiding social and moral principles that prevent the individual with 'criminal volitions' acting upon them. However, where for Wigan and Burrows such restraining influences prove a positive and necessary influence upon both the potential criminal and religious fanatic, for Browne conditioning based upon religious principles can prove to be a significant contributory factor in the emergence of mania and the collapse of identity. Indeed, as evoked in Hogg's *Private Memoirs*, religion can efficiently nullify the autonomy of the individual, effectively divesting them of an identifiable sense of self.

I do not intend to present a definitive history of the monumental significance of religious crisis and its fall-out in nineteenth-century Britain in this section. However, much of the significance of Burrows's analysis lies in the fact that by 1837 religion constituted, as William Black indicated, a major condition determining the causes of insanity, and that it, in the words of Browne, has an 'awful importance' within the social and cultural infrastructure of British life. That religion should have such a profound effect upon instances of insanity, and should so problematize the idea of a cohesive identity can be attributed to the shifting status of religion in the nineteenth century. It practically goes without saying that the nineteenth century was one that witnessed immense religious upheaval and redefinition. The scientific discoveries of Charles Lyell's *Principles of Geology* in 1830, and Charles Darwin's *The Origin of Species* in 1859, arguably shattered the grounds for believing in the Bible as a literal and authentic historical record. In 1833 John Keble's Assize Sermon instigated the Oxford Movement, creating a theological and political schism within the established Church of England. Studies of the Bible as a historical document or anthropological curiosity, influenced by the scepticism of Enlightenment thought, gained increasing credibility and can be seen in Marian (George Eliot) Evans's translation of the 1843 edition of Ludwig Feuerbach's *The Essence of Christianity*. The National Secular Society, founded in 1846, its official organ the *National Reformer* edited by Charles Bradlaugh, and Bradlaugh's own election as a Member of Parliament in 1886 all provided a platform and relative respectability for avowed atheistic thought and discourse and radical republican sentiments.[9] Marx and Engels take this destabilizing of the traditional certainties of orthodox religion even further. In the *Communist Manifesto* they indicate that as well as metaphorically stripping the halo from priests amongst other previously revered vocations, the bourgeoisie, that hegemonic social force of the nineteenth century, has 'drowned the most heavenly ecstasies of religious fervour' in the 'icy water' of self-interest' and direct exploitation. Marx and Engels's statement is particularly significant when the correlation between bourgeois social and cultural hegemony and the values of orthodox Christianity are considered.

My intention in this section is to discuss and address key poetic texts of the nineteenth century which illustrate symptoms of the disrupted religious climate of the period and its subsequent effect upon identity. The texts under discussion present the individual in the throes of doubt or despair, in states of consciousness which ultimately trouble a clear and defined sense of self, and represent states of mind influenced by religious turmoil that are close to manifestations of insanity discussed in the medical discourse of the nineteenth century. The statement by Andrew Scull that provides an epigraph for this section establishes the chapel as 'that critical part of every well-wrought Victorian asylum' where 'the inmates could be brought the consolations of organized religion'. There is an implicit irony in this assessment, that in an epoch when the foundations and consequent centrality of religion are under threat, the chapel should remain central within an environment that houses the marginalized and excluded 'other' members of the society of that time. In addition, although this comment evidently refers to the presence of established religious practice as a stabilizing force within the asylum, 'organized' religion obviously suggests the possibility of its mirror image 'disorganized' religion. It is with disorganized religion that this chapter is concerned.

In many ways the poems addressed here echo the processes of mirroring and doubling assessed in the previous chapter, and consequently dramatize the way in which such motifs trouble a defined and cohesive sense of identity. Similarly the works themselves, primarily because they do deal with religion in a destabilizing and unsituated climate, evoke the nuances of the Arnoldian 'dialogue of the mind with itself' in that prayer, the traditional medium for expressions of religious devotion, turns inward to address internalized doubt and anxiety rather than outward to address a God who might not even be there. Tennyson's dramatic monologue 'St Simeon Stylites', in terms of poetic structure, suggests a single voice, nonetheless Tennyson problematizes the suggestion of unified utterance by having Simeon talk to an audience who cannot hear his words and address a God who cannot or will not respond to his words. The assumption of discursive or argumentative voices that mark Tennyson's *In Memoriam* and James Thomson's 'The City of Dreadful Night' indicate the sense of a dialogue between aspects of a fragmented self. Finally, in Gerard Manley Hopkins's 'Terrible Sonnets' or 'Sonnets of Desolation' there is the suggestion of a breakdown of communication with God resulting in an acute and uncomfortable solipsism for Hopkins's poetic persona; the prayers of a devout Jesuit priest turn inwards and morbidly address the self in a way that suggests the absence of the divine.

4 A life of death: Alfred Tennyson's 'St Simeon Stylites'

> The ruling idea of the ascetic was the salvation of self, the means which he adopted being directed exclusively to the sure attainment of that supreme end. The inevitable effect of such a method of minute self-observation and self-tending, when carried to excess, is to produce an exaggerated sensibility and unwholesome growth of self – an extreme or actually morbid egoism issuing naturally in the ascetic and his fanatical extravagances.[1]

On initial scrutiny Tennyson's poem 'St Simeon Stylites', written in 1833 and published in the second volume of *Poems* of 1842, functions as an example of religious madness made up from self-delusion and an obsessive belief by Simeon in the importance of his own existence.[2] The poet's use of a first person monologue seems to present Simeon as an individual who fails to achieve insight into the limited perceptions that constitute his reason for existence; his vision remains destructively self-conscious and self-obsessed. If this is taken into account the poem stands as an examination of fanatical religious zeal, and Simeon, as an anchorite, exists in a paradoxical position of glorifying and centralizing masochistic self-denial. There is an evident irony in Simeon's coupling of an aspiration to erase the self and its material needs with an overwhelming and arrogant ambition to achieve sainthood. The poem can therefore be seen as the study of a man denying his self in an explicit attempt to achieve something *for* the self. This interpretation is supported by Leigh Hunt's review of the poem in the *Church of England Quarterly Review* also published in 1842. Hunt states that the poem is 'a powerfully graphic, and in some respects appalling satire on the pseudo-aspirations of egotistical asceticism and superstition ... We do not recollect to have met with a more startling picture of the sordid and the aspiring – the selfish and the self-sacrificing.'[3] The review neatly stresses the disorientating polarity manifest in the content of the poem, 'the sordid and the aspiring – the selfish and the self-sacrificing'; for

Hunt it is a 'startling picture'. By the latter part of the century Henry Maudsley is even more unequivocal about the saint's practice. For him the practice of the anchorite/ascetic results in an 'exaggerated sensibility and unwholesome growth of self' that corresponds with the excessive and morbid narcissism and preoccupation with self depicted by the *fin de siècle* degeneration theorists Nordau and Lombroso. Referring explicitly to the catalogue of actions performed by Simeon that are contained in Tennyson's poem, he states:

> The last thirty years of the life of St. Simon [*sic*], commonly called Stylites, were passed on the top of a column sixty feet high on a mountain some thirty or forty miles east of Antioch ... Such the lofty pedestal chosen for the display of such humility; such the solitude of place and spirit into which he withdrew in order to practise self-mortification; such his full-fed vanity aping humility, and all the more odious for that reason, as an ape looks the more deformed because of its being the caricature of man.[4]

Maudsley's tone is more condemnatory than Hunt's; for him the actions of Simeon are a 'full-fed vanity' that is 'odious'.[5] What Maudsley does, drawing upon a late nineteenth-century medical ethos of restraint, is interpret the historical anchorite as both narcissistic and parodic. Indeed Maudsley's conception of history is strangely inverted, he reads the historical Simeon from a Victorian perspective and regards the primate ancestors of humanity as a 'caricature of man' rather than as atavistic point of origins.

Both Hunt's reading of the poem as satire and Maudsley's vehement critique of the aspirations of the ascetic can certainly be detected in 'St Simeon Stylites'; for example, the pathetic image of an aggressive Simeon 'Battering the gates of heaven with storms of prayer' (line 7) is indicative of Tennyson's use of a biting and discomfiting sense of irony yet also points to the unqualified assumptiveness of the character. In fact the possible oscillation between interpretative perspectives regarding the poem can be ascribed to the fact that it veers between a projection or assertion of identity and a lament for a sense of cohesive self. One way to pin down the content of the poem, as Ann C. Colley points out in *Tennyson and Madness*, is to locate it within its contemporary cultural context:

> Tennyson's concern for false religious visions was topical as well as

> personal. In the nineteenth century not only were there numerous investigations into the physical and emotional sources of apparitions, but there was also a clinical interest in religious enthusiasm and hysteria. With few exceptions physicians easily linked these apparitions or 'delusions' with insanity.[6]

In this sense Tennyson's poem can be established as both a general critique of extreme religious practice and an individual case study of a crazed ascetic who admits that he is 'mad with blasphemy' (line 4), who claims to be 'Simeon, whose brain the sunshine bakes' (line 161) and who confuses self-delusion with self-denial, both of which explicitly trouble an attempt to define an integrated sense of self. However, to define the poem solely in these terms is to deny the complexity that Tennyson gives to his dramatic monologue. 'St Simeon Stylites' is certainly both critique and parody; nonetheless it also stands as a poem that only slightly amplifies aspects of Christian culture and its processes of conditioning in the early to mid nineteenth century, and which demonstrates that even in the 1830s religion and religious structures could stimulate the disintegration of a defined and definable identity.

James R. Kincaid, directly addressing Hunt's review, indicates the extent to which the subtlety of Tennyson's writing invites a reassessment of the poem. In *Tennyson's Major Poems: The Comic and Ironic Patterns*, Kincaid suggests that:

> the tendency of commentators, from Leigh Hunt on, to treat it as a satiric poem, acting in one way or another to condemn its speaker, is expressive of the strength of the ironic tension in the poem ... For the poem deals with a monstrous parody of Christianity, a parody that is both ludicrous and profound. 'St. Simeon Stylites' may present a blatant self-advertisement, but it is also a lament or confession, depending upon our angle of vision ... to view the poem as satiric twists it into a petty attack on a target that is trivial and far too easy. It also over-simplifies by responding to the pride, the confidence, and the monstrous in St. Simeon and ignoring the humility, the painful doubt, and the voice of simple humanity. The whole poem is a tortured utterance as well as a smug one.[7]

What Kincaid identifies is the fundamental capacity for interpretative vacillation manifest within the text. Hunt has already detected this in his perception of the 'sordid and the aspiring'; however, where Hunt resolutely interprets the poem as an 'appalling satire' (rendering Simeon into something of a caricature, something close to the 'ape ... being the caricature of man' depicted by Maudsley) Kincaid's reading of Simeon suggests a character that exemplifies such basic human characteristics as 'pride', 'confidence', 'humility' and 'painful doubt'. For Kincaid, therefore, Simeon is paradoxically 'not only bizarre but typical', implicitly decentred but also centred and therefore eminently locatable: the religious 'type' of the nineteenth century.[8] This suggestion of a typical but deranged humanity can easily be detected in Tennyson's text, particularly during the climactic struggle with what is apparently an angel carrying a crown:

> My brows are ready. What! deny it now?
> Nay, draw, draw, draw nigh. So I clutch it. Christ!
> 'Tis gone: 'tis here again; the crown! the crown! (lines 203–05).

Tennyson invests the episode with a grim comedy, his protagonist is deliberately taunted with the to and fro of 'tis gone: 'tis here again' and his dignity is reduced even further through the half-appeal, half-expletive 'Christ!' However, beneath this dominant sense of authorial satire there exists a pathos, the doubt, the 'voice of simple humanity' referred to by Kincaid.

It is Kincaid's identification of the polarity within Simeon's nature that locates the character within a context of extreme religious practice and allows us to examine him as an example of an excessive and deluded sense of self. The balance between the 'pride' and 'confidence' and 'humility' and 'painful doubt' defined by Kincaid frames an analysis of Simeon and his actions; this balance fundamentally manifests itself in the possibility that all his perversely superhuman acts of penance and abstinence will ultimately go unrewarded. Tennyson defines this fear explicitly and identifies the tension between arrogant self-assertion and cosmological doubt when Simeon demands:

> O Jesus, if thou wilt not save my soul,
> Who may be saved? who is it may be saved?
> Who may be made a saint, if I fail here?
> Show me the man hath suffered more than I. (lines 45–48)

The absurd lengths that Simeon goes to demonstrate how much he has suffered ('Show me the man hath suffered more than I') are, as Kincaid points out, symptomatic of the faith to which he belongs. Kincaid states that 'Simeon is isolating and exposing to view a central tendency of Christianity, the exaltation of pain'.[9] In this sense Simeon's actions are theologically consistent rather than the 'pseudo-aspirations of egotistical asceticism and superstition' described by Leigh Hunt. Roger Platizky elaborates upon the point made by Kincaid, locating St Simeon more specifically within a religio-cultural context:

> Simeon ... has been a victim of following patterns and examples that his culture has glorified: he emulates the tortured lives of Christ and the saints and models his behaviour on theirs ... in part because he wants to exceed their glory as a paragon of suffering, but more importantly because his martyrdom of the self is influenced or inspired to pathological extremes by the expectations and even the imagery ... of his Christian culture. This culture made suffering an object of worship and art; it made denial of the flesh a saintly aspiration.[10]

If Platizky's words are taken into account then Simeon, rather than functioning as a parodic figure, clearly becomes an extended reflection of the culture from which such religious practices stem. There is no doubt that the actions represented by Tennyson are of extreme, even horrific proportions; Simeon defines them as follows:

> In hungers and in thirsts, fevers and cold,
> In coughs, aches, stitches, ulcerous throes and cramps,
> A sign betwixt the meadow and the cloud,
> Patient on this tall pillar I have borne
> Rain, wind, frost, heat, hail, damp, and sleet, and snow.
> (lines 12–16)

This catalogue of suffering is an assertion of what Simeon has voluntarily endured, indicating the absurd extremity of his commitment to the religion that he symbolically embodies. It also acts as a reflection of the stipulations and aesthetics of Christianity, albeit taken to perverse excess; as Platizky states, Simeon is 'influenced or inspired to pathological extremes by the expectations and even the imagery ... of his Christian culture'. Simeon can therefore be interpreted as simultaneously an individual of 'pathological extremes' and as representative of the ethics and culture of Christianity. Tennyson defines these functions specifically when Simeon states himself to be both inheritor and agent of the legacy of the early martyrs, though again the idea is taken to an extreme:

> For did not all thy martyrs die one death?
> For either they were stoned, or crucified,
> Or burned in fire, or boiled in oil, or sawn
> In twain beneath the ribs; but I die here
> Today, and whole years long, a life of death. (lines 49–53)

What Simeon represents is a kind of *hyper*-martyrdom, where suffering is perpetuated, even becoming the very reason for existence to the anchorite, quite literally a life of death. He also passes his own legacy on to the people who flock at the base of his pillar:

> Mortify
> Your flesh, like me, with scourges and with thorns;
> Smite, shrink not, spare not. (lines 176–78)

If it is possible that Simeon represents a mirror for perverse interpretations of Christian culture, W. A. F. Browne's words – that there are more religious maniacs in Britain than elsewhere because 'religion has here its due exercise and awful importance' – take on a new significance. If Tennyson's poem is a satire upon the 'egotistical asceticism and superstition' of the early generations of Christianity, it is simultaneously a comment on the early nineteenth century where Christianity still has its 'awful importance' with regard to social and cultural conditioning. Browne also cites the case of a Venetian shoemaker who, in actions that parallel the excesses of Simeon,

> conceived that he was destined to be a sacrifice for the human race. He prepared and planted a cross, procured a sponge, nails, spear, and in fact imitated the representations of the death of our saviour ... He wounded his side, transfixed his feet and hands, and then raised himself up to the cross by some mechanical contrivance, and hung impaled for upwards of twenty-four hours before he was discovered.[11]

The significance of Browne's case study lies in his terminology – the Venetian shoemaker 'imitated the representations of the death of our saviour'. Like Platizky's interpretation of Tennyson's poem, the act itself is based upon a misguided conception of imitation. Platizky identifies the influences upon Simeon as the cultural and aesthetic 'imagery' of Christianity where suffering becomes 'an object of … art', and Browne states that the shoemaker was inspired by 'representations' of the crucifixion. A greater degree of significance lies in the implications of identification through imitation, because both Simeon and the shoemaker, through similar extremes of self-mortification, extend the precepts of Thomas à Kempis's fifteenth-century mystical text the *Imitatio de Christi* to pathological excess. Not content with adopting the philosophy and creed behind Christian thought, they strive to emulate the suffering of Christ. In effect Maudsley's simile of 1887, that Simeon's behaviour is as akin to Christianity 'as an ape looks the more deformed because of its being the caricature of man', is undermined when we consider Simeon's aspiration to be that of imitating and even surpassing the suffering of Christ. Platizky clarifies this ironic tension and also identifies the attempts at justification within Simeon's monologue:

> Simeon is driven not only by his own ambition, but also by cultural expectations and a religion of suffering prescribed by his God. In this dramatic monologue, the pillar saint searches frantically in the last moments of his life for a stabilizing identity that, for all his bravado, is dependent on the approval of his two silent audiences: the 'brethren' at the column's base and the godhead above.[12]

The statement that Simeon's identity is founded upon the dictates of a 'religion of suffering prescribed by his God' defies Maudsley's indignant simile. It is also invested with an added dimension when we consider the nature of the dramatic monologue itself; the monologue implies that the speaker has an identifiable audience, defined by Platizky as 'the "brethren" at the column's base and the godhead above'. It is to these two audiences that the pillar-saint appeals in an attempt to assert and stabilize identity. However, although Simeon does enter into direct discourse with 'the people [who] hum / About the column's base' (lines 37–38), for example, his offering of advice in lines 176–78 cited earlier, his position on the pillar 'betwixt the meadow and the cloud' (line 14) essentially distances him from interaction with this audience. Similarly, the 'godhead above' remains silent and intangible; we have no proof of its presence or existence within the poem other than through the appearance of its agents the angels, which Tennyson renders intentionally ambiguous – perhaps the hallucinations of 'Simeon, whose brain the sunshine bakes'. Consequently, although Simeon seeks to justify his actions in the face of these two audiences they remain 'silent'. As a result any attempt to stabilize and impose a definable identity proves to be illusory, particularly as Simeon's name is so much tied up with what he does and vice versa; he is after all Simeon Stylites – Simeon of the Pillar. What therefore emerges is another Arnoldian dialogue, wherein Tennyson's character asserts both his own sense of self-importance and gives voice to agonized doubts that all his self-sacrifice is for nothing.

In this sense it is Simeon's doubt that is significant in determining the degree of extremity and abnormality in consciousness of self. If his presumptive assertion that 'I think you know that I have some power with Heaven / From my long penance' (lines 141–42) is considered, then it would be simple to dismiss the poem's content and its protagonist as the 'pseudo-aspirations of egotistical asceticism'. However, it is Simeon's expression of fear and doubt that puts anxieties about faith, meaning, identity and the penultimate moments of the poem into perspective. A certain solipsism manifests itself in a repetitive use of the personal pronoun in the poem; however, this does not automatically suggest self-definition, as Platizky notes:

> Simeon's use of the pronoun *I* eighty times in this poem of 220 lines (or approximately once every three lines) attests to egoism, but Simeon's subjective exhibitionism is at the same time a defense against the terrible fear of cosmic insignificance; the repeated *I* a manic attempt to stabilize identity beyond the threats of isolation.[13]

This 'manic attempt to stabilize identity' against the fear of 'cosmic insignificance' can be found in lines 45–48 quoted earlier. The question, 'Who may be made a saint, if I fail here?' (line 47), suggests the tension between self-definition and doubt; Simeon's words are half demand, half plea. They also serve to reflect the liminal status of a protagonist who exists between heaven and earth ('betwixt the meadow and the cloud'), between life and death ('but I die here / Today and whole years long, a life of death') and faith and doubt ('Can I work miracles and not be saved', line 148). In many ways the attempt to locate and fix identity becomes of paramount importance, particularly to an individual marooned in a world that is composed of polar opposites. This sense of a vacillating dislocation is configured in

Tennyson's repetitive use of the personal pronoun to signify Simeon's claims towards self-assertion. Attempts to define and stabilize identity by Simeon also possess a more basic manifestation:

> I, Simeon of the pillar, by surname
> Stylites. (lines 178–89)

Simeon's identity becomes fundamentally and intrinsically identified with the pillar upon which he stands. His surname 'Stylites', stemming from the Greek word *stylos* for pillar, is as much associated with *what* he does and *where* he is as it is with *who* he is. In many ways the negotiation of identity is similar to that of Jo's, the crossing-sweeper in Dickens's *Bleak House*, who knows that a broom is a broom but nothing more and consequently indicates the way in which a conception and understanding of identity is tied up with what he does. In this context Simeon is both detached with regard to the crowd who flock to his *stylos*, through the literally distant position that he occupies, and yet remains the spectacular focal point of this silent audience. It also means that Simeon's identity is fundamentally indivisible from the suffering that he endures.

It is in Tennyson's representation of the relationship between Simeon's physical self and the silent, intangible God which constitutes the other aspect of the monologue's 'audience' that the dislocated nature of Simeon's state of consciousness can be detected. Platizky suggests that Simeon is 'tortured by the silence of the gods', and it is this apparent inscrutability that results in the obsessions and fears that become manifest in a preoccupation with the body. As Platizky puts it: 'Tennyson's St. Simeon, at the same time that he is falsely pious, proud, and self-righteous, is also a man who has driven himself mad with doubts that all his abstinence and all his severe penances may go unnoticed, unblest, and unrewarded, leaving him an empty shell.'[14] His doubts become focused in an inconsistent apprehension of self that is again defined through a tension between opposites. For example, Simeon offers an apologia to God, referring to the fact that his physical exertions have not apparently resulted in the intended spiritual dividends; he states that 'I do not breathe, / Not whisper, any murmur of complaint' (lines 21–22), but balances this with an attempt to assert his own importance, claiming, 'Yet cease I not to clamour and to cry' (line 41). His attempt to become like his own silent, divine audience by uttering no 'whisper' or 'murmur' is undermined by the 'clamour' and the 'cry'; as a result Simeon, both in terms of the structure of the dramatic monologue itself and the testimony by the anchorite contained therein, is torn between utterance and silence – inhabiting a space that is neither and yet paradoxically is fundamentally tied up with the former. Ultimately the lack of a tangible reward for self-mortification results in Simeon's increasing awareness of his own physicality. He celebrates his 'lead-like tons of sin' (line 25), refers to 'this home / Of sin, my flesh, which I despise and hate' (lines 56–57) and catalogues an acute sense of physical decay where 'both my thighs are rotted with the dew' (line 40). In effect he becomes engrossed in and obsessed by the acts that he commits against himself, as though he is unwilling to relinquish his perverse indulgence of the body that is supposed to provide him with access to heaven. His outer decay is therefore paradoxically both a sign of his temporal sin and representative of the lengths that he will go to prove his commitment towards achieving sainthood. As much as it is an attempt to qualify his spiritual integrity, the manipulation and modification of the body practised by Simeon also demonstrates a certain anxiety about the agent of qualification *and* functions in such a way that it prevents him from questioning his own doubts in a rational manner. In this sense his self-mortification simultaneously acts as a symbol that reflects his striving towards sanctity, his doubts and his self-obsession. The absence of an answering God that will justify his suffering results in a morbid introspection and self-consciousness. As Platizky states:

> in Simeon's case, the ascetic has been sensualized. The celibate pillar saint actually takes masochistic pleasure in his 'super-human pangs' because it is the only way that he can find to glorify the body while maintaining the illusion that he is glorifying the spirit. But because these feelings are subconscious and forbidden, they mask themselves in nightmares and pathogenically in hypochondria.[15]

Simeon's pathogenic hypochondria is emphatically clarified in the catalogue of suffering, the 'coughs, aches, stitches, ulcerous throes and cramps' that he provides. The nightmares manifest themselves in the form of diabolic visitations:

> Abbadon and Asmodeus caught at me.
> I smote them with the cross; they swarmed again
> In bed like monstrous apes they crushed my chest. (lines 169–71)

The presence of the devils conforms to traditional religious imagery – for example, in medieval paintings of St Anthony's temptation in the desert – however, what is disturbing in the imagery is its sheer *physicality*. In the depiction of the pillar-saint who is assailed by devils 'like monstrous apes' that 'crushed my chest' there is again an uncomfortable sense of Simeon's preoccupation with his own body.

This obsession with body results in a loss of perspective in terms of elements intrinsic to the aspirations of the self and identity as a spiritual thing. As Simeon states:

> and oft I fall,
> Maybe for months, in such blind lethargies
> That Heaven, and Earth, and Time are choked. (lines 100–02)

This ironic disembodiment, considering how much the poem is tied up *with* the body, is reminiscent of the temporal and experiential amnesia evoked in Francis Barker's discussion of disidentity in 'Nietzsche's Cattle'. The mixture of obsession and the results of obsession – that is, the results of an unnatural mortification and subjugation of the physical self – leads to Simeon's apparent dislocation. The sense of confusion is such that Simeon loses his perception of three of the essential components of his world, the 'Earth' that he strives to reject, the 'Heaven' that he aspires towards, and the 'Time' that constitutes the medium by which he can gauge the extent of his exertions. Henry Maudsley again offers his own critique of the ascetic, his judgement simultaneously coinciding with the effects of the practice depicted by Tennyson:

> The long fastings, the scourgings, the exposure, and the other mortifications of the body practised by the religious ascetic, who, withdrawing from the society of men to some desert solitude ... brought his monotonous and specially exercised brain to such a degree of separation from the ordinary and wholesome impressions of sense, and such a state of irritable weakness, that he frequently saw visions which, according his moods of feeling, were visions of angels who consoled his sufferings, or visions of devils who tempted and tormented him.[16]

Again Maudsley's tone is condemnatory; devils that tempt and torment are present in both Simeon's vision and Maudsley's account, but where Tennyson depicts Simeon's internal dislocation as 'blind lethargies' that negate his perception of Heaven, Earth and Time, Maudsley's account of self-induced disorientation results in a more specifically secularized 'separation from the ordinary and wholesome impressions of sense'. In terms of a comparison, Tennyson's mystic paradoxically both transcends sense and is distanced from the transcendental, whereas Maudsley's commentary states that such a case is merely divorced from 'ordinary and wholesome impressions of sense'. The most significant aspect of Maudsley's statement when compared to Tennyson's poem is the 'visions of angels who consoled him (the religious ascetic) in his sufferings'. As stated earlier in this discussion, the penultimate moments of the poem involve the apparent visitation of an angel bearing a crown which symbolizes the arrival at a cohesive sense of identity for Simeon. Tennyson renders the supernatural appearance typically ambiguous, again the suggestion being that the angel is merely the hallucinatory figment of an already disordered mind:

> What's here? a shape, a shade,
> A flash of light. Is that the angel there
> That holds a crown? (lines 199–201)

What we are presented with are four stages of recognition, the apparition is first 'a shape', then an insubstantial and vaporous 'shade', then 'A flash of light', and finally we encounter the question 'Is that the angel there?' The stages imply uncertainty; the deluded aspect to Simeon's consciousness is suggested and the use of the definite article in 'the angel' further emphasizes the reader's scepticism, suggesting as it does that Simeon already believes that it is the angel that he has been waiting for to reward his penance. However, it is the crown itself which the angel apparently bears that is important here. The crown has its origins as one of the rewards offered to the righteous in the Book of Revelation, where it is stated, 'To him that overcometh will I give to eat of the tree of life … and I will give thee a crown of life' (Rev. 2:7–10). In terms of locating Tennyson's poem within the religio-cultural context of the nineteenth century, the crown motif is notable in the work of one Dr Hawdon, who, in his essay of 1873 entitled 'The Religious Sentiment in Epileptics', states of a patient in the Montrose Lunatic Asylum that 'she has seen her heavenly Father, and that to-morrow she is to receive the crown of glory'.[17] Simeon, in Tennyson's poem, is not granted the ultimate saintly accolade of a visitation by his 'heavenly Father', but the reward offered, which is ultimately tied up with his sense of self, is much the same. In terms of comparisons such as that between the poem and Dr. Hawdon's notes, we can establish Tennyson's 'St Simeon Stylites' as a satire upon the more bizarre and extreme practices demonstrating religious fervour in the early Christian Church, as a study of a mind rendered deluded by excessive suffering and self-denial, and, in spite of the comments of Leigh Hunt and Henry Maudsley, as a reflection of aspects of Christian culture in the nineteenth century taken to an ironic, morbid and self-deluded extreme.

5 But what am I? Alfred Tennyson's *In Memoriam*

> It brings us face to face with atheistic science; the faith in God and Immortality, which we have been struggling to clear from superstition, suddenly seems to be *in the air*: and in seeking for a firm basis for this faith we find ourselves in the midst of the 'fight for death' which *In Memoriam* so powerfully presents.[1]

William Black, in the table of causes of admission to Bethlem madhouse documented in *Dissertation on Insanity* cited at the start of this discussion, notes that the most prominent factor instigating mental illness is 'Disappointments, Grief'. *In Memoriam*, a collection of lyrics written between 1833 and 1850 and published anonymously at the end of May in the latter year, is an elegaic response to the death of Tennyson's closest friend during his Cambridge days, Arthur Henry Hallam, who died on 15 September 1833 in Vienna.[2] Where 'St Simeon Stylites' represents religious turmoil and inner dislocation stemming from a possibility that there is no meaning behind the excesses of self-mortification, similar expressions of self-doubt and religious disorientation in *In Memoriam* are a result of the fact that the poem is comprehensively overshadowed by grief and the personal disruption that this emotion involves. Bernard Reardon describes the poem as

> the utterance of a mind torn by doubt of whether life has any moral meaning whatsoever; a doubt made all the heavier by the sorrow of a desolating bereavement. Any death could raise the same question, but the death at the pathetically early age of twenty-two of a man of great promise whom Tennyson loved with a rare intensity rendered it inescapable.[3]

In spite of the slightly reductive biographical elements in his reading of a complex and densely textured poem, what is interesting in Reardon's account is his use of the word 'inescapable', for there is certainly a strong sense of inevitability in terms of the issues, moral and theological, raised as a response to Hallam's death. When considering *In Memoriam* in comparison to 'St Simeon Stylites', what is significant is the topicality of both poems with regard to an expression of religious turmoil. We can read 'Simeon' as a commentary upon the ethics and aesthetics of religious culture in the nineteenth century, or as a satire upon the mysticism and ceremony advocated by the Oxford Movement's desire to revert to the institutions of the medieval Roman Church initiated in the early 1830s.[4] Similarly *In Memoriam* presents religious doubt as a response to Hallam's death, giving it a subjective topicality, and to moral dilemmas inspired by the schism between conventional Christian interpretations of the earth's history, contemporary scientific evidence and philosophical enquiry, thus giving the poem a wider cultural relevance. Both facets are interdependent, provoking each other, and are capable of generating disillusionment, whether expressed from the subjective angle of grief or a more wide-ranging perspective of doubting despair. What therefore links *In Memoriam* and 'St Simeon Stylites' is an attempt to define, or at least believe, in a divine force that has no physical manifestation and as a consequence requires unquestioning faith. In the case of 'Simeon' the doubts are dramatized in the words of the character of the semi-sane monologist. In *In Memoriam*, as Reardon points out, the death of Hallam throws the moral code of this unseen power into question. It is this ability to allow the possibility of doubt to emerge through a personal matter that opens up the more wide-reaching and topical aspects of the poem. It is certain that Tennyson was familiar with elements of evolutionary theory circulated prior to the publication of the poem in 1850, specifically with Charles Lyell's *Principles of Geology*, which appeared in 1830. This familiarity with what Henry Sidgwick terms 'atheistic science', and the attempt to confront both poetic voice and, by association, reader with the moral implications of the new discoveries, gives Tennyson's poem its dramatic if dislocated intensity.[5]

In Memoriam, in common with most elegies, functions both as an articulation of the poet's subjective grief and loss, and as a philosophical contemplation upon issues that are catalyzed by an individual death. We are thus presented with a disparate variety of possible interpretative responses by which we can assess the poem. Do we read *In Memoriam* as a poetical inner history of Tennyson, a process of reflection upon the nature of death, a personal expression and projection of grief, or a quest for the grounds of unequivocal faith? What is striking about the structure of *In Memoriam* is that it is this very disparity which lends itself to reading it as a poem of reconciliation; by compromising and coming to terms with Hallam's death Tennyson is able to resolve his philosophical and theological dilemmas.[6] The concern in this discussion is with the expression and poetic symptoms of doubt in Tennyson's poem. The collection of lyrics that constitute *In Memoriam* is wide-ranging in content, documenting a progression from confusion and despair to belief and self-affirmation, in effect plotting a poetic trajectory which is the opposite of Arnold's in 'Dover Beach'. This manifests itself in the way by which the poem shifts from the use of a vocabulary deliberately intended to represent physical and emotional impotence to one that represents serenity. In terms of the dislocation caused by doubt and the possible moral vacuum that it instigates, the earlier sections of the poem are of significant importance. Personal and cultural disorientation can be found in three forms in Tennyson's poem: in his relationship with the dead Hallam and with human mortality itself, in the poetic assumption of voice and persona that alternately indicates and masks the Arnoldian 'dialogue of the mind with itself', and in the tension between the polarity of orthodox religious assurance and doubts induced by 'atheistic science'. The medium for these expressions of inner-turmoil and consciousness of the self's relation to religion, death and doubt emerges in a language that represents the personal insecurity and impotence mentioned above.

The oscillation that takes place between faith and doubt in *In Memoriam*, and which ultimately develops into the transitional process of reconciliation, is reflected in a use of opposition that is sustained throughout the poem. This opposition manifests itself in the conceptual language used by the poet, in the consistent mirroring in the ABBA rhyme scheme found in each lyric, and in the fundamental differentiation between the living Tennyson and dead Hallam. It is through an acceptance or resolving of such differences that the aforementioned reconciliation can take place. Tennyson's use of opposition in the early stages of the poem initiates the sense of loss and disorientation experienced by the poet; in response to an initial expression of grief at Hallam's death and waiting for the body to arrive in Britain for burial, the poetic voice asks:

> What words are these have fallen from me?
> Can calm despair and wild unrest

Be tenants of a single breast,
Or sorrow such a changeling be?[7]

and later in the same lyric asks whether it is grief that has

stunned me from my power to think
And all my knowledge of myself;

And made me that delirious man
Whose fancy fuses old and new,
And flashes into false and true,
And mingles all without a plan? (XVI: lines 15–20)

What we are presented with is the sense of a disintegration of cohesive and coherent self. The result is a paradoxical juxtaposition of the chaos of extreme grief placed within the context of an inflexible ABBA rhyme scheme. In the lyric the poetic persona becomes both distanced from a sense of self and identity in line 16 and yet at the same time is able to demonstrate a profound consciousness of time schemes in line 18; this suggests the 'sense of living in two worlds simultaneously' found in Berman's evocation of the modern experience in the nineteenth century. As noted in section one, Henry Maudsley argued in 1895 that '[i]t is in … excess that madness lies – in the exaggerated development of natural passions of human nature, not in the appearance of new passions in it'; he also observed that 'the various biases of prejudice, passion, temper, interest and the like, which turn the mind from the straight path of truth … are just the causes which, when carried to excess tend towards madness.[8] For Maudsley madness lies in an exaggeration, emphasis or overindulgence in natural instincts or feelings. Taking William Black's identification of grief as one of the primary causes of admission to Bedlam into consideration, in Tennyson's account of the effects of grief upon the self we encounter an experience that seems close to Maudsley's definition of madness; for example, the adjectival exaggeration of certain aspects of temperament indicates the excesses suggested by the physician. Tennyson presents an emotional polarization that darts between 'despair' and 'unrest', emotions that are emphasized by the use of 'calm' and 'wild'; other opposites represented by the poet are 'old and new' and 'false and true'. The significance of this lyric lies in the manner in which Tennyson balances a sense of unity with one of inner chaos, thereby rendering the effects of disorientation more potent; for example, the opposites that the poet perceives within his experience of grief exist in a 'single breast' and, because his 'fancy fuses' them, a unified self is suggested, this possibility being diffused by an apprehension that everything 'mingles ... without a plan'. Tennyson, again suggesting the Arnoldian dialogue, asks himself whether he is 'that delirious man', indicating the loss of a cohesive self and pointing to an inner turbulence that is compounded by the use of a question mark. The result is that Tennyson, through the influence of exaggerated grief, becomes distanced from a previously established and consolidated identity. In lyric XVI he has lost, through the dramatic chaos of emotional and mental responses, 'all my knowledge of myself'. The effects of this inner disorientation are heightened by a cumulative repetition of the word 'And', a repetition which evokes a manic questioning of self and identity. Tennyson pinpoints this fracturing of the self by establishing three possible poetic identities: the voice that is attempting to *articulate* the experience of grief, the voice that is *experiencing* the grief and which, through the opposing sensations inspired by that experience, detects a division within the self and therefore, by implication, generates a third objectified identity in 'that delirious man'. As with many of the texts discussed in this book the boundaries and parameters between subjectivity and objectivity, internal and external, are being blurred and disrupted.

The subtle use of voice and commitment to the ABBA stanza problematizes the expression of experience in the poem in many ways. The systematic and self-conscious nature of the rhyme scheme calls into question its suitability as a frame for a discourse designed to represent inner chaos.[9] By contrast Elizabeth Jay suggests that the pattern of the stanzas mirrors the vacillation and opposition manifest within *In Memoriam*: 'Tennyson's verse conveys the sense of the ground failing beneath his feet as one world picture dissolves. The ABBA stanza form of the entire poem ... effectively mirrors the wavering graph of Tennyson's emotions and the circling process of thought which found logic inadequate.'[10] In this sense the ABBA rhyme scheme provides a suitable frame for a poem which dramatizes the fluctuation between one thing and another, between 'old and new', 'false and true'. Similarly the controlled and subtle use of voice representing a fractured and chaotic sense of self also brings to fruition Tennyson's intention to dramatize his grief. Eric Griffiths, in *The Printed Voice of Victorian Poetry*, points to Tennyson's two-fold ability: 'This double aptitude –

for vocal skill and for artistic realization of the breaking-points of voice – helped him imagine throughout his career the drama of speaking, the times of successful utterance and those other occasions on which words fail us, or we fail them.'[11]

These occasions when 'words fail us' will become more resonant later in this discussion. For the moment what is significant in Griffith's words is that 'vocal skill' is one of the ways by which we can control and define the self; when Tennyson claims that he has lost all 'power to think' and all 'knowledge of myself' he achieves Griffith's 'artistic realization of the breaking-points of voice', resulting in a mantric repetition of the word 'and' and the question about voice itself: 'What words are these have fallen from me?' In this sense Tennyson's technique reflects Maudsley's statement that '[i]t is in … excess that madness lies'; his exaggerated use of opposition (between 'calm despair' and 'wild unrest') and his sturdy rhyme-representation of inner chaos and the collapse of the self presents a mind veering towards madness, one that has lost its sense of meaning and 'power to think'. Ann C. Colley points out the poet's familiarity with the scientific thinking of his own time and his desire to maintain a psychiatric accuracy within his writing; in doing so she raises an interesting point about the relationship between literary and scientific definitions of insanity:

> For Tennyson the wish to be accurate and the desire to keep in touch with the literary conventions were not impossible goals because scientific and literary depictions of madness often reinforced one another … the two worlds complement one another, for both share the assumptions that madness comes from excessive grief, jealousy, and lust, and that madness involves distortion and error and the loss of self.[12]

The shared assumption that madness can stem from 'excessive grief' is qualified by Black in *Dissertation on Insanity* and by Tennyson in lyric XVI, and Colley's 'loss of self' echoes Tennyson's loss of 'all knowledge of myself'. The significance of these three aspects of Tennyson's poem – rhyme scheme, voice and accuracy – is contained in the way in which they present a dangerously fluctuating view of the self and the world that surrounds it. As Tennyson himself noted 'the whole truth is that assurance and doubt must alternate in the moral world in which we at present live'.[13]

Hallam's death provides the stimulus for the subject matter of a poem where 'assurance and doubt ... alternate'. The crisis of faith for Tennyson lies in a struggle to extract meaning from a world-view that is faced with the possibility that it exists in a vacuum and that its previously revered institutions, codes and practices have all been stripped of their halos. The death of Hallam provokes an individual response expressing personal bereavement that in turn leads to a broader response that ruminates upon the possibility that conventional faith may no longer be tenable in the face of new scientific discoveries. The poem is inspired by and commemorative of Arthur Hallam but, before the poet can reconcile himself to his sense of loss, issues have to be addressed that transcend a lament for one man. As Henry Sidgwick stated, much of the power of the poem lies in the fact that it 'brings us face to face with atheistic science', and that in seeking 'a firm basis for ... faith' the poet is found in the 'midst of the "fight for death"'. In *The Power of the Soul over the Body* published five years prior to *In Memoriam*, George Moore tried to provide an antidote to the issues that Sidgwick later saw as the significant aspects of Tennyson's poem. Moore, a Member of the Royal College of Physicians in London, stated that

> man is impelled by a belief, which seems essential to his rational existence, that this beautiful world is not altogether a delusive show; for he cannot think that the wondrous facts of creation teach him to look for the end of truth only in death; but he feels that, in proportion as the intellect expands and expatiates in knowledge, does it aspire to immortality, and when most intimate with the realities of time, his reason finds stability, satisfaction, and rest, only in communication with the Eternal.[14]

Moore, as is evident in the title of his text, establishes a fundamental and orthodox dichotomy behind his philosophy: that 'belief' is equated with a 'rational existence' and that 'reason finds stability' in the knowledge of its own 'immortality'. Moore, in asserting the power of the soul over the body, suggests that to doubt, that is, to see the world as a 'delusive show' and find 'the end of truth only in death', is unreasonable or irrational and therefore, by implication, insane. The other defence that Moore supplies against encroaching 'atheistic science' is his belief in a 'beautiful world' and the 'wondrous facts of creation'; this orthodoxy is rendered apparently obsolete when evolutionary theories reveal an overall moral void within natural processes, an issue that torments Tennyson in *In Memoriam*. In many respects Tennyson's point of view in the poem supports the comments made by Moore, at least in as much as the action of doubting or questioning traditional responses to nature and existence is capable of driving one to the brink of irrationality and unreason. However, Tennyson essentially defies Moore's conservative stance, largely by addressing and attempting to transcend or incorporate the facts that Moore ignores into his own poetic perspective. Whether he is ultimately successful in reconciling his poetic vision and doubts with science or not, the articulation of doubt inspired by the evidence that science shows him (further emphasized in a personal aspect by the loss of Hallam) possesses a moral complexity absent in Moore's writing. Tennyson complicates the problem of belief and the function of his own identity within the spaces created by moral doubt through a strategy of manipulating voice and personae, and by employing parallel images of chaos and inarticulacy.

In lyric XXXIV Tennyson expresses the conflict between explicit doubt and the need for an emotional anchor in blind faith within a context that is essentially pessimistic. The poetic voice represents uncertainty, fluctuating between blank despair and the emotional urgency to find moral security. In the light of Hallam's death, this predicament hinges upon a meditation on human immortality:

> My own dim life should teach me this,
> That life shall live for evermore
> Else earth is darkness at the core,
> And dust and ashes all that is. (XXXIV, lines 1–4)

This would seem to be predominantly an expression of the rift between conventional Christian teaching, what Tennyson's 'dim life should teach' him, and the possibility that life will not continue after physical death. If the latter is the case then the earth and any moral purpose that might define a reason for its existence are rendered meaningless; the earth therefore has 'darkness at the core' and consists of sterile 'dust and ashes'. However Tennyson complicates this dichotomy, firstly by making the division between faith and doubt equivocal; he achieves this effect by inserting the word 'dim' in front of 'life' and stating that his beliefs 'should' teach him that individual life is immortal. Through this the teachings of conventional religious faith are disempowered, ironically thrusting the balance of certainty towards doubt. Secondly there is an semantic slippage between Tennyson's 'life' and human 'life', the first is personal and experiential, the second collective and elemental. The suggestion is that it is the second collective 'life' that 'shall live for evermore'. If this is taken into account then Tennyson, again pushing the balance of his argument towards the factors that constitute doubt, replaces individual and theological immortality with a perpetuation of collective species in a synopsis for existence that is proto-Darwinian. There is a disillusionment and finality in this stanza that almost excludes the possibility of the Arnoldian dialogue.

This expression of pessimism is expanded into an image of the earth and existence as random and purposeless:

> This round of green, this orb of flame,
> Fantastic beauty; such as lurks
> In some wild Poet, when he works
> Without a conscience or an aim. (XXXIV, lines 5–8)

It is notable that the images employed by Tennyson mirror the positivism of Moore regarding nature and creation; Moore's 'beautiful world' and 'wondrous facts of creation' are echoed by Tennyson's 'Fantastic beauty' and 'round of green'. However, where Moore's vision remains resolutely locked within a celebratory Christian context, overshadowed by the 'divine Eternal', Tennyson's maintains and expands upon the ambiguous and pessimistic doubts of the previous stanza. Certainly his image of the earth as void, stale with 'dust and ashes', is reassessed in that the earth regains its elemental aspects of 'flame' and 'beauty'. Nonetheless, this revitalized interpretation is possibly more terrible for the poet, for it raises a problem as to whether a thing of beauty can exist if its beauty and existence is fundamentally purposeless and its creator ultimately irresponsible. This dilemma provokes a suitably double-edged simile; the creator, supposing that there is one, has worked like a 'wild Poet' 'Without a conscience or an aim' if the earth itself exists without an aim. The simile also doubles back upon itself mirroring Tennyson as the self-conscious artist. If God the 'wild Poet' works 'Without a conscience or an aim', then Tennyson, an aspect of creation and himself a 'wild Poet', also works without an aim. The aim of the poem is to commemorate Hallam, yet if life is both purposeless and final, there is no point in celebrating a dead man. In many ways the dilemma in theory nullifies the poem itself. What is significant is that Tennyson personifies himself within the poem in the context of a chaotic image. The poet 'should' believe that life continues 'for evermore' but there is the possibility that existence is meaningless; thus orthodox belief hangs upon the tentative 'should' whereas the pessimistic possibility is contained in the direct statement that it would be better

> To drop head-foremost in the jaws
> Of vacant darkness and to cease. (XXXIV, lines 15–16)

Tennyson's indirect representation of himself as a 'wild Poet' whose view is chaotic is followed in lyric XXXV by a similar though more startling representation. This takes the form of an appeal by the poet to the afterlife, asking for a voice to provide an answer or solution to the present state of traditional Christian belief:

> Yet if some voice that man could trust
> Should murmur from the narrow house,
> 'The cheeks drop in; the body bows;
> Man dies: nor is there hope in dust.' (XXXV lines 1–4)

The poetic voice asks for an answer to resolve a further moral dilemma: if there is no life after physical death then life is meaningless, and if life is meaningless then love – an idealized and metaphysical emotion – has no meaning in a purely functional existence. By briefly resurrecting a voice from beyond the grave Tennyson seeks to define a moral and emotional reason for existence by challenging the voice himself. If 'Death were seen / At first as Death' (XXXV, lines 18–19) and therefore final, then love would be 'Mere fellowship of sluggish moods' (XXXV, line 21), why then its idealized existence within the world? Again we witness Tennyson fracturing the poetic self to summon up a voice that the 'I' can argue with, a voice which summarizes the doubts of the 'I' to great effect. This necromantic ventriloquism is shadowed by a further personification when we consider that Tennyson is appealing for the dead voice of someone 'man could trust'. The implication is that the appeal is made to Hallam, yet the words effectively undermine this second personification, putting them into a context that is as potentially chaotic as Tennyson's own representation of himself as the 'wild Poet'. If the voice that states 'Man dies: nor is there hope in dust' is identified with Hallam, then the purpose of the poem is again problematized. If individual life is not eternal and therefore purposeless, then the dilemma becomes extended from a metaphysical one to a poetic one. What lyrics XXXIV and XXXV depict is a division between a belief in an unseen and unknown entity (what the poet 'should' believe) and the visible evidence of the earth (the 'round of green' that has no 'aim'). The inability to compromise the two invokes a dramatic point where the internal dialogue that marks modern poetry for Arnold is masked by personification and where, as Griffiths states, 'words fail us' and definition and meaning are lost.

Tennyson's 'artistic realization of the breaking-points of voice' builds up cumulatively within the poem. In lyric XXXVI he turns to the Gospels in an attempt to provide himself with an anchor that will reinvest his life with a meaning, but finds that the words within them are 'More strong than all poetic thought' (XXXVI, line 12). Consequently the poet's persona attempts to define truth, however, in both his own writing and any writing that tries to redress logically the balance of faith against doubt, this intention 'in closest words shall fail' (XXXVI, line 6). It is ironic that only by depreciating his own poetic purpose can he dispel the doubts that are inspired by it. In lyric XXXVII the dialogue of the mind with itself is again externalized, this time personified in a confrontation between the two muses Urania and Melpomene. Urania, the Muse of astronomy and therefore in the context of metaphysical speculation the Muse of heaven, states to the lyrical voice, 'This faith has many a purer priest, / And many an abler voice than thou' (XXXVII, lines 3–4). Melpomene, the Muse of elegy and appropriated by the voice as 'my Melpomene', replies, 'I am not worthy even to speak / Of thy prevailing mysteries' (XXXVII, lines 11–12). Here not only do the words fail us but also, as Griffiths states, 'we fail them'. In effect we are not 'worthy' or, by implication, knowledgeable enough to address the issue of finding a meaning in life. Finally Tennyson's representation of himself as inarticulate culminates in a contemplation of the limitations in his ability to express adequately his love for Hallam. He states, 'My words are only words, and moved / Upon the topmost froth of thought' (LII, lines 3–4), and describes himself as 'An infant crying for the light: / ... with no language but a cry' (LIV, lines 19–20). This second assessment of self, where language becomes nothing but an incoherent 'cry', is a virtuoso performance of subtlety on the part of the poet; the utterance represents an experience that is chaotic, meaningless, *speechless*, yet conversely the etymological derivation of the identity applied to the self, 'infant', is *infans* meaning 'unable to speak'.

The doubts expressed and agonized over by Tennyson climax in the celebrated evolutionary lyrics, in a consistent generation of images of chaos, and in an ambiguous and solipsistic perception of self by the poet. The latter steadily emerges in lyric L, where Tennyson makes an appeal to Hallam using a voice that fluctuates between despair and tentative hope:

> Be near when my light is low,
> When the blood creeps, and the nerves prick
> And tingle; and the heart is sick,
> And all the wheels of Being slow.
>
> Be near me when the sensuous frame
> Is racked with pangs that conquer trust;
> And Time, a maniac scattering dust,
> And life, a Fury slinging flame. (L, lines 1–8)

There is a marked consciousness of the body in these two stanzas and one that stands as a parallel to the catalogue of mortifying acts in 'St Simeon Stylites'. Tennyson depicts a body that seems to be gradually coming to a halt, one where the blood creeps', the 'nerves prick', the 'heart is sick', in fact one where 'all the wheels of Being slow'. As with Simeon, Tennyson depicts a self that is in the liminal state between life and death with a body that can be read as a basic Cartesian technology. In Simeon's case this is one designed to facilitate his saintly aspirations, and for the voice in *In Memoriam* designed to mark physically the effects of doubt. We also encounter a form of hypochondria; however, where Simeon's is the result of self-inflicted assaults upon the physical self, the voice in *In Memoriam* acquires its morbid sense of physical self from an internalization of both grief and personal anxiety. Picking up upon Arnold's anxiety about the doubts and discouragement in modern poetry, Eric Griffiths, taking us back to the nervous illnesses identified in the introduction to this volume, identifies such inward-looking self-examination as morbid:

> By the middle of the nineteenth century, awareness of the circumstances which form the self was not only a key to unlimited human

> self-improvement but also a possible cause of mental unease, perhaps even disease; the 'analysis' of mind which was to combat morbidity and other failings then came to be suspected of promoting what it was supposed to remove ... the power of man over his mind turned out to be self-thwarting, and left its possessors impotently knowledgeable – morbid, in fact.[15]

Tennyson's self-analysis takes the form of an almost clinical examination of his body, one that is focused in a perception of the slowing down or decay of physical attributes; the morbidity and impotence takes the form of hypochondria. It is ironic therefore that such a self-conscious apprehension of physical, material self should be found in an appeal to the dead, intangible, invisible Hallam. It is, however, also appropriate in that the appeal is made when 'my faith is dry' (L, line 9) and when all that mankind's purpose seems to be is to 'lay their eggs, and sting and sing / And weave their petty cells and die' (L, lines 11–12). In the light of this display of startling pessimism, where to be human is to be as insignificant as a fly; the appeal of the metaphorically decaying Tennyson is made to a literally decaying Hallam. In this penultimate stanza of lyric L we again encounter images of random chaos. 'Time' has already been likened to 'a maniac' and 'life' to 'a Fury'; now, in an embodiment of human existence that heralds the amorality of evolution, Tennyson envisages man's purpose as purely sensual, to 'sting', 'sing', 'weave' and 'die', images that effectively render a conception of human existence as morally significant void. In doing this Tennyson, although not necessarily adopting a position that he believes in, indicates the possible nihilistic responses of the believer whose faith has been fundamentally undermined by science.

The factors contributing to Tennyson's expression of doubt and moral insecurity culminate in lyrics LV and LVI. Here we encounter irreconcilable opposition, inarticulacy, images of chaos, a language representing impotency and an excessive consciousness of self. The poetic voice's doubts are projected into a vision of conflict between faith and science:

> Are God and Nature then at strife,
> That Nature lends such evil dreams?
> So careful of the type she seems,
> So careless of the single life (LV, lines 5–8)

Again the internal dialogue is present and again it is externalized by Tennyson; his faith and doubt are personified in very simple and elemental terms as God and Nature. Ultimately what is established is a conflict between the rational and irrational poetic selves. The irrational self (which George Moore, ironically, had asserted to be rational) wants to believe what it 'should' believe; the rational self by contrast can perceive Nature and what its functions are. The problem for Tennyson arises when we consider that morality is actually on the side of the irrational self, the one that 'trust(s) that somehow good / Will be the final goal of ill' (LIV, lines 1–2), whereas the rational self can only apprehend Nature with dread in the light of her carelessness and indifference to the individual self ('So careful of the type she seems, / So careless of the single life'). The result is a maddening, circular conundrum that Nature's indifference, because it is clearly visible, is capable of forcing the self to abandon its hope that 'good' will be the ultimate result of 'ill'.

In the face of this conundrum, Tennyson subtly represents an inarticulate and incapacitated plea to the unknown:

> I falter where I firmly trod
> And falling with my weight of cares
> Upon the great world's altar-stairs
> That slope through darkness up to God,
>
> I stretch lame hands of faith, and grope,
> And gather dust and chaff, and call
> To what I feel is Lord of all (LV, lines 13–19)

Again the body is emphasized, and in such a way that what it marks out embodies the metaphysical doubts. However, compared to the grinding down and sense of collapse found in lyric L, here we have an oscillation between positive and negative attributes; the previously firm step of faith is replaced by faltering, the 'hands of faith' that 'stretch' are 'lame' and can only 'grope', and though they try to 'gather' all they retain is 'dust and chaff'. Similarly in lines 15 and 16 the poetic voice stretches 'through darkness up to God', but by line 19 this apparent knowledge of God's presence is replaced by the doubtful and tentative 'what I *feel* is Lord of all' (my emphasis). Through the preoccupation with the body, touch and tangibility are all that Tennyson trusts to erase doubt and negate his sense of personal powerlessness; 'feel' is therefore as much a sensory word in this context as it is emotional. In these lines Tennyson represents a sense of failure or at least limitation, his 'hands of faith' are 'lame', he cannot reach 'through the darkness' towards the security of belief, and therefore the world of faith becomes one of 'dust and chaff', as barren as the faithless world of 'dust and ashes' in lyric XXXIV. The disorientation of doubt is rendered more dramatic through the dynamic and monstrous personification of 'Nature' as 'red in tooth and claw' (LVI, line 15). Again there is a subtle and conscious disparity between form and meaning in terms of voice: Nature 'shriek[s] against his [man's] creed' (LVI, line 16), invoking a chaotic image of inarticulacy, irrationality and insane rage. However this can be compared with the words that Tennyson gives to Nature:

> From scarped cliff and quarried stone
> She cries, 'A thousand types are gone:
> I care for nothing, all shall go.
>
> 'Thou makest thine appeal to me:
> I bring to life, I bring to death:
> The spirit does but mean the breath (LVI, lines 2–7)

There is little of the primeval, shrieking, mad entity here. The words applied to the personification of Nature stand in direct contrast to the shriek and to the tentative, morbidly impotent words that Tennyson apportions to himself. They are authoritative, cold and logically measured ('I bring to life, I bring to death'). They are also qualified, when compared to the 'world's great altar-stairs / That slope through darkness up to God', by the visible testimony of 'scarped cliff and quarried stone'.

The vocal testimony given by Nature and the geological testimony that qualifies her words provoke the poetic voice into a series of reflections that are histrionic, highly dramatized and again chaotic. The words that he ascribed to Nature seem to force him into an articulation of fears that he cannot bear, that man 'Who loved, who suffered countless ills' (LVI, line 17) should be rewarded by being 'blown about the desert dust, / Or sealed within the iron hills' (LVI, lines 19–20). The possibility that human existence as transitory, even vaporous, might be the only possible moral view of the world results in Tennyson's most anguished utterance, where existence and an apparently illusory faith becomes 'A monster then, a dream, / A discord' (LVI, lines 21–22). Here the final word epitomizes the chaotic images that the poet has been accumulating. Tennyson's response in the face of self-inspired and conscious despair is to orchestrate an evasive poetic escape, a vanishing for the persona concerned with faith and doubt. Once again it takes the form of an appeal:

> O life as futile, then, as frail!
> O for thy voice to soothe and bless!
> What hope of answer or redress?
> Behind the veil, behind the veil. (LVI, lines 25–28)

Doubt and loss are effectively contained in the words 'futile' and 'frail', catalyzing the appeal for reassurance. The focus of this appeal is ambiguous; the explicitly religious word 'bless' suggests that it is God, the non-capitalized 'thy' suggests Hallam. The effect is to blend the two, the longed-for presence of the deceased Hallam and the longed for presence of the deity; the combining of the two, initiating love for God through love for Hallam, suggests a conventional religious reconversion. However, this ambiguity complicates the appeal, especially when the word 'redress' is conceptualized. 'Redress' functions on a literal level of representing the poet's desire to have his grievances against Nature resolved to a positive degree; however, if God is taken as the focus of the appeal, then this desire for redress is directed towards the core of the dilemma that constitutes his previous doubts, An intangible God has inspired the irresolvable conflict between the objectively material (Nature) and subjectively unseen (God), and therefore initiated the whole of Tennyson's spiritual crisis. Because there is still no tangible evidence of either Hallam or God's presence beyond physical death, the response is the obscure and insubstantial 'Behind the veil, behind the veil'. The 'veil' image is tantalizing and provocative, taking on its real significance when compared to James Thomson's use of the same image in 'The City of Dreadful Night'. For the moment the initial question of the evolutionary debate – 'Are God and Nature then at strife' – can only engender more questions; Tennyson's solution is to attempt to embrace and find solace in the irrational. The veil image is therefore climactic in terms of agonized questioning, and offers no real answers. The repetition of the phrasing offers a fluid and shifting multiplicity of meanings: it suggests a separation between life and death, it functions as an obscuring device that inhibits vision or conviction, it implies that reality may be beyond visual appearances or life itself, and the repetition also suggests that there are a plethora of veils that have to be passed through. Because the veil offers no tangible answers, Tennyson's response, in lyric LVII, is:

> Peace; come away: the song of woe
> Is after all an earthly song (LVII, lines 1–2)

This is an effective rejection of spiritual confusion. Tennyson relocates himself in the hypothetical present and within the familiar confines of the elegy where poetic identity is at least a secure thing; after existing in a primal geological and metaphysical battleground the poetic persona returns to the 'earthly song' that eulogizes Hallam and defines him as elegist. It seems that the only way for the poet to reconcile the 'discord' of morbid contemplation is to urge himself to 'come away' and reject not the core of the dilemma but the dilemma itself. Tennyson's poetic voice therefore fractures and subsequently resolves itself; 'What hope of answer or redress?' is answered by 'Peace; come away'; it is not God or Hallam's voice that soothes but the poet's own. Identity and meaning can only be secured by one's own initiative.

In this context Tennyson's 'Peace; come away' paves the way for a return to the more orthodox Christian thinking that shapes the later lyrics of the poem. Masao Miyoshi suggests that the 'I' of *In Memoriam* does not 'ever really try to reconcile science and faith', and that the embracing of conventional faith, what Miyoshi terms 'conversion', is 'one of mood and emotion'.[16] Certainly 'Peace; come away' indicates a calmer, more objective poetic voice that replaces the self-destructive identity which is concerned with the irresolvable conflict between traditional faith and new science. However, the poem, up to this point, is not really concerned with a reconciliation between science and religion; as Henry Sidgwick indicated, its power lies in bringing us 'face to face with atheistic science' and with locating us in the 'midst of "the battle for death"'. In this sense, as the use of opposition, contradiction and chaotic imagery suggests, the poem represents a site of conflict and tension, a struggle to make possible sense of the nihilistic responses potentially inspired by science's assault upon belief and their subsequent effect upon a sense of cohesive self. Matthew Arnold, in his preface to the second edition of the *Poems* of 1853, expands upon his differentiation between classical writers and modern poetry, claiming: 'They [the classical writers] can help to cure us of what is, it seems to me, the great vice of our intellect, manifesting itself in our incredible vagaries in literature, in art, in religion, in morals: namely that it is *fantastic*, and wants *sanity*.'[17] However, in spite of its dislocation, its images of chaos and its representation of the failure of voice and words, the process of examining the madness of doubt in *In Memoriam* achieves the quality that Arnold finds lacking in poetry – sanity. Ann Colley points out that

> *In Memoriam* is a poem in which Tennyson tries to combine the material and non-material worlds so that he will not be crushed by materialism. The poem is a fight for survival, a fight to revive his faith in a world that is now defined by physiologists and geologists. He is searching for a world in which he can acknowledge scientists' truths without risking the loss of the spiritual dimensions of life and, of course, without surrendering the power of the will.[18]

Sidgwick's apprehension of conflict within the poem is incorporated in Colley's perception that *In Memoriam* is a 'fight for survival'. More significantly, by metaphorically surrendering his voice at key points in the poem Tennyson surrenders his sense of a cohesive self and poetic identity; by extracting himself from the conflict between faith and science through 'Peace; come away' he reclaims a sense of self, poetic purpose and the possibility of autonomy. It is in James Thomson's 'The City of Dreadful Night' that the negativity and loss of will approached by Tennyson manifests itself in a voice of unified and uncompromising despair.

6 All is vanity and nothingness: James 'B. V.' Thomson's haunted city

> There may or may not be beings superior to us. But I cannot think so ill of any possible supreme being as to accuse him of the guilt and folly of the voluntary creation of such a world and such lives as ours. I cannot accuse a possible Devil of this, much less a possible God.[1]

Where Alfred Tennyson's *In Memoriam* involves a return to orthodox faith and the apparently conventional elegaic utterance, thus reclaiming will, sanity and identity in the face of overwhelming doubts, James Thomson's 'The City of Dreadful Night' addresses the loss of faith and will in man, manifest in a poetic voice of thematic and ideological unity which suggests that life is ultimately meaningless and repetitive. Thomson's poem was first published in four installments in Charles Bradlaugh's *National Reformer*, between 22 March and 17 May of 1874.[2] This weekly newspaper, first emerging in the April of 1860, had made clear its manifesto *vis-à-vis* religion in an advertisement released in February of the same year: 'The present platform, of theological advocacy, will be that of antagonism to every known religious system, and especially to the various phases of Christianity taught and preached in Britain.'[3]

It was within this avowedly radical atheistic and egalitarian context that 'The City of Dreadful Night' emerged. The editions of the paper in which the poem appeared were soon out of print, and Thomson's opus remained in a similar state until it was republished in the collected edition *The City of Dreadful Night and Other Poems* in 1880.

The poem consists of a 'Proem' of six stanzas, and twenty- one sections that alternate between even-numbered cantos in the past tense and odd-numbered cantos in the present tense.[4] The cantos written in the present tense provide the reader with a detached and objective voice, a Victorian Dante's Virgil who guides the reader through an urban Inferno; the sections in the past tense of the poem present the observational voice of an individual wandering the city, encountering its inhabitants and locations, and therefore function as a nightmarish inversion of the Wordsworthian excursion. More significantly the poem metaphorizes the modern city of the nineteenth century in a way that echoes many of the representations of the metropolis found in the texts under scrutiny in this project. Thomson's description is particularly reminiscent of those found in the *fin de siècle* Gothic novel; indeed the poet's nightmare city has much the same atmosphere as the one into which the criminals of Stevenson and Wilde's writing disappear. For Thomson:

> The city is not ruinous, although
> Great ruins of an unremembered past,
> With others of a few short years ago
> More sad, are found within its precincts vast.
> The street-lamps always burn; but scarce a casement
> In house or palace front from roof to basement
> Doth glow or gleam athwart the mirk air cast.[5]

Like the street inhabited by Jekyll in Stevenson's novel, Thomson's city juxtaposes past and present in its architecture. Nonetheless it is recognizably modern, with its precincts, its street-lamps and the 'mirk air' that suggests the fog of London found in Dickens, Stevenson, Wilde and Bram Stoker. In such an environment the poetic voice can be equated with Baudelaire's *flâneur*, the stroller of the modern city, who, as Walter Benjamin puts it, 'goes botanizing on the asphalt' – observing, writing, describing, collecting fragments of the city'.[6] It is noticeable that many of the details that Benjamin ascribes to the *flâneur*, in his analysis of Baudelaire and modernity, can be detected in Thomson's poem. The *flâneur* is in many ways a contradictory figure for Benjamin, part of and yet distanced from the nineteenth-century crowd, disappearing into the crowd yet prominent and visible, ambling through the arcades and boulevards of the metropolis and yet threading his way along the pavements with apparent purpose. Thomson's poem often evokes this sense of contradiction and possible instability in that the poetic voice is clinically observational, distancing himself from the masses who 'With weary tread, / Each wrapt in his own doom ... wander, wander, / Or sit foredone and desolately ponder (I, lines 53–55), and amongst whom he himself wanders. Nonetheless we also encounter the apparently purposeful peripatetic, who Baudelaire, assessing Edgar Allan Poe's short story 'The Man of the Crowd', describes as the archetype for the *flâneur*.[7] In Canto II the speaker comes upon a man who 'seemed to walk with an intent / I followed him; who shadowlike and frail, / Unswerving though slowly onward went, / Regardless, wrapt in thought as in a veil' (II, lines 1–4). In different ways, therefore, Thomson offers images and characteristics of the modern city that concur with the contradictory elements defined in other writings – the nightmarish city juxtaposes old and new, glaring artificial lights and fog-enshrouded mirk, prominence and invisibility.

Thomson, as a poet, had little time for Tennyson's apparent pre-eminence within that vocation. In an essay on William Blake, published in the *National Reformer* in January and February of 1866, he noted:

> Scarcely any other artist in verse of the same rank has ever lived on such scanty revenues of thought ... as Tennyson ... His meditation at the best is that of a good leading article; he is a pensioner on the thought of his age ... Nothing gives one a keener insight into the want of robustness in the educated English intellect of the age than the fact that nine-tenths of our best known literary men look upon him as a profound philosopher.[8]

There is something in this disparaging remark that is akin to Matthew Arnold's criticism of modern poetry. Where Arnold's perspective finds fault in the inward-looking emphasis on the 'doubts' and 'discouragement' traceable in contemporary verse (a feature that his own poetic practice can be accused of), Thomson's complaint is directed towards the 'want of robustness'. Both prosecute and express disenchantment with a poetry of doubt, indecision and dilemma. However, in spite of his dismissal of Tennyson's 'scanty revenues of thought', in 'The City of Dreadful Night' Thomson approaches a system of ideas that, although expressed in a very different way, is conceptually similar to significant aspects of *In Memoriam*. Both poems address the nature of belief, possible responses that would result from its absence, and the way in which its presence or absence would provide a basis for individual identity or a meaning for the existence of the collective species. As discussed in the previous section, Tennyson's poem offers a voice of reconversion and personal survival in the face of agonizing doubts and overwhelming scientific evidence; by contrast 'The City of Dreadful Night' systematically negates the possibility of faith. In this sense Thomson's poem works as a mirror to *In Memoriam*: where Tennyson uses a sequence of histrionic crescendos and crisis points to instigate a relinquishment of doubt and a poetic reclamation of sanity, identity and will, Thomson utilizes a pessimistically consistent unity to encapsulate a negative world view.

The parallel aspects of the two poems can be detected in Thomson's use of opposition in 'The City of Dreadful Night'. In Canto XI, using the detached voice of the present tense, the poet asks with reference to the inhabitants of the city:

> What men are they who haunt these fatal glooms,
> And fill their living mouths with dust of death,
> And make their habitations in the tombs,
> And breathe eternal sighs with mortal breath,
> And pierce life's pleasant veil of various error
> To reach that void of darkness and old terror
> Wherein expire the lamps of hope and faith? (lines 1–7)

The opposition is manifest in a juxtaposition of life and death. This is particularly evident in lines 2–4 where Thomson builds the opposites – 'living' and 'death', 'habitations' and 'tombs', 'eternal' and 'mortal' – into the structure of the verse lines. The elaborate scheme, that alternates interlaced and couplet rhymes, is therefore enhanced by an equally elaborate system of internal opposition within the lines themselves. Thomson answers his own question, and again incorporates a vocabulary of opposition:

> They are most rational and yet insane:
> An outward madness not to be controlled;
> A perfect reason in the central brain,
> Which has no power, but sitteth wan and cold,
> And sees the madness, and foresees as plainly
> The ruin in its path, and trieth vainly
> To cheat itself refusing to behold (XI, lines 15–21)

The presence of thematic division is manifold here, 'rational' against 'insane', 'outward' against 'central', 'madness' against 'reason'. The conceptual language utilized is similar to that of Tennyson's in lyric

XVI of *In Memoriam*; the capacity to be 'rational' and 'insane' simultaneously reflects the conflicting emotions in 'a single breast', the 'eternal sighs' of Thomson echo the 'calm despair' of Tennyson, and the fusing of 'false and true' by the latter is similar to the ability to see 'madness' whilst also 'refusing to behold'. In addition there is a mantric repetition of the word 'And' in verse 1 of Canto XI that reminds us of a similar use of the word by Tennyson in the fourth and fifth stanzas of lyric XVI of *In Memoriam*. Similarly there is the presence of the word 'veil' that has been used by Tennyson in lyric LVI of his poem and which will become more significant in the course of this discussion. The important difference between the perspective of each poet lies in the context and standpoint of their respective utterances. Thomson's positioning of the poetic self is apparently objective and detached, Tennyson's internalized, subjective and indicative of a division within the self. Tennyson initiates his questioning in the context of the self-conscious statement 'What words are these have fall'n from me?', suggesting a self-analysis that perceives but cannot comprehend the split within the self, whereas Thomson's words are directed outwards to the 'men' of the city. Similarly the use of the word 'And' by Tennyson indicates a personal and experiential cumulating of sensation whereas Thomson's is used to emphasize and reinforce an objective opinion. As a result, where Tennyson's inward examination of self leads to a private (albeit in the public forum of a published poem) identification with Hallam, Thomson's detached method of identifying opposition, unified within the structure of the verse, has a political effect on the poem. In describing the inhabitants of the city, Thomson, by implication, metonymically describes the condition of the city itself.

It is also worth noting that through explicitly combining the two polar aspects of conceived insanity in 'They are most rational and yet insane', Thomson identifies one of the characteristics of the study of the insane in nineteenth century. In his preface to *Observations on the Nature, Kinds, Causes and Prevention on Insanity* Thomas Arnold notes: 'No person, indeed, can be more cunning, more consistent, more acute, or more connected, than maniacs, not only according to my definition, but according to the definitions, and acknowledgements of others, are not only sometimes, but often, found to be.'[9] Henry Maudsley, in 1887, makes the point more emphatically: '… it is a fact not to be lost sight of … that the sincerest person to self, and at the same time the insincerest to nature all round, is the lunatic.[10]

What Arnold suggests is that to the observer the insane individual can seem 'consistent' and 'connected' and that their actions are capable of having these qualities to a more pronounced degree than the supposedly sane individual. Maudsley internalizes this detached perspective; stating that the insane individual is fundamentally true to self suggests an integral integrity, what defines them as insane is their inability to be sincere to aspects of their existence peripheral to the self; subjectivity is privileged over objectivity. Thomson's words reflect something of both these points of view and help to conceptualize the poet's own perspective within the poem. The basic dichotomy of being rational and also insane reflects Thomas Arnold's definition of the insane as 'consistent' and 'connected', and the internal 'perfect reason of the central brain' that sees 'madness' and 'ruin' yet tries to 'cheat itself refusing to behold' is echoed by Maudsley's differentiation between sincerity to self and insincerity to things external to the self. Thomson's words therefore go beyond the simple differentiation between appearance and reality, subjectivity and objectivity; if we conceptualize Canto XI as a metaphor for the effects of the religious climate of the latter decades of the nineteenth, century then Thomson, using a detached and observational voice and manipulating psychiatric concepts, indicates that the men of faith who try to 'pierce life's pleasant veil' will only find a snuffing of 'the lamps of hope and faith'. In effect the attempt to find a rational moral basis for existence through probing the 'veil' between life and death is fundamentally insane.

Thomson's question in Canto XI is therefore rhetorical; he answers 'What men are they?' with his own response 'They are'. This technique is emphasized by a resolutely bleak world-view constructed from irony and paradox. The sterility of existence is manifest in the words 'haunt', 'dust' and 'eternal' to create a vision of the 'death-in-Life' (V, line 10), and the bleakness of this is contained in a 'void' perversely *filled* with 'darkness' and 'terror'. This pessimistic perspective is also inherent in the power struggle established in this Canto, which takes the form of a conflict between an 'outward madness' that cannot be 'controlled' and a 'perfect reason' that 'has no power'. The horror that Thomson creates for the inhabitants of the city is all the more effective for its irony; the only option for reason in the face of chaotic madness is to adopt an unreasonable response. The sole way to combat its chaotic antithesis is for reason to embrace a self-defensive deception, trying 'vainly / To cheat itself refusing to behold', thereby becoming a travesty of itself.

Thomson establishes his poetic identity and the tone of rhetoric and examination inherent in much of 'The City of Dreadful Night' in the Proem that prefigures the poem. The initial question:

> Why disinter dead faith from mouldering hidden?
> Why break the seals of mute despair unbidden,
> And wail life's discords into careless ears? (Proem, lines 5–7)

is again answered by the poet:

> Because a cold rage seizes one at whiles
> To show the bitter old and wrinkled truth (Proem, lines 8–9)

The question is therefore, as in Canto XI, rhetorical; it also establishes itself as inward-looking, coming close to the Arnoldian dialogue. However, this is dispelled in the main body of the poem when Thomson externalizes dialogue in dramatic voices. Where Tennyson's use of personification masks the dialogue of the mind with itself and therefore the expression of doubt inherent in that dialogue, Thomson's use of the dramatic voice, demonstrated later in this discussion, is revelatory, exhibiting the poet's personal perspective. The Proem involves not so much a revealing of poetic intention as a defence, a limitation of responsibility. Thomson establishes both his own poetic identity, the 'I' that is seized by 'cold rage', and sanctions a sympathetic, elite audience:

> If any cares for the weak words here written,
> It must be some one desolate, Fate-smitten,
> Whose faith and hope are dead, and who would die.
> (Proem, lines 26–28)

He emphasizes this exclusiveness by implying that there is a code for understanding the poem:

> None uninitiate by many a presage
> Will comprehend the language of the message.
> (Proem, lines 40–41)

What Thomson suggests is that the poem is exclusively designed for those 'desolate' and 'Fate-smitten', whose 'faith and hope are dead'. If those individuals reading the poem are not subject to such pessimistic experiences, then they will not 'comprehend the language' of 'The City of Dreadful Night'. This initiation into the code of the poem is of course metaphorical; Thomson is specifying a reciprocal audience that is 'Fate-smitten' for a poem where 'faith and hope are dead'. In addition, by suggesting that the only audience that will be able to 'comprehend' the poem is one that is 'desolate', he limits the responsibility for the atheistic and negative content contained therein. What is really disturbing in Thomson's words is that the other requirement of being one who 'cares' for the poem is to be one 'who would die'; by being able to read Thomson's 'weak words' the reader is implicated with an audience of would-be suicides. It is significant however that to be a member of this 'sad Fraternity' (Proem: line 9) is, in Thomson's terminology, an act of assertion, will and integrity. In a manner similar to the conceptual shifts between sanity and madness in Canto XI, Thomson, representing the audience of his choice, suggests that to despair in some way empowers an impotent perspective on the world; for example, despair urges the desire to 'show the bitter old and wrinkled truth', and:

> It gives some sense of power and passion
> In helpless impotence to try to fashion
> Our woe in words howe'er uncouth (Proem, lines 12–14)

Addressing 'dead faith' and articulating 'mute despair' gives a 'sense of power and passion'; it also, in a 'Death-in-Life' world, involves an attempt to reclaim '*living* words' (my emphasis) from within a sterile environment. Henry Maudsley's philosophy throughout his medical writing involves a fundamental determinism; this view, that the biological and social world is dictated by inflexible laws, coincides to a great extent with Thomson's vision of existence in 'The City of Dreadful Night'.[11] However, in spite of his resolutely bleak depiction of the world and its inhabitants, Thomson's perspective is, in many ways, more discretionary that Maudsley's; Maudsley believed that madness was unavoidable, the result of genetic determinism. In *Responsibility in Mental Disease* he states:

> Suicide or madness is the natural end of a morbidly sensitive nature, with a feeble will, unable to contend with the hard experience of life. You might as well, in truth, preach moderation to the hurricane as

> talk philosophy to one whose antecedent life has conducted him to the edge of madness.[12]

For Thomson, in the dramatic context of the Proem of 'The City of Dreadful Night', suicide is not the result of a 'feeble will' or associated with the individual 'unable to contend with the hard experience of life'. Instead Thomson, speaking for the 'sad Fraternity' 'who would die', faces the world without the illusion of a reassuring religion, perceives it for what it is ('False dreams, false hopes, false masks and modes of youth', Proem, line 11), and also attempts to assert his will over both despair and illusion by 'try[ing] to fashion / Our woe in living words'. In this sense Thomson manipulates both the Proem and his potential audience to suggest that the responses of despair and suicide are fundamentally sane in a world that has never had a moral purpose behind it.

It is in the main body of the poem that Thomson defines his perspective regarding a world that no longer possesses the Christian virtues of faith and hope. Where Tennyson temporarily neutralizes the personal expression of doubt by using personified voices in *In Memoriam*, Thomson, also focusing the poetic voice through externalized dramatic voices, uses personification to articulate his philosophy. As we have seen in Canto XI, Thomson deals with a split in the self amongst the inhabitants of the city. In Canto IV, one of the perambulatory Cantos of the poem, this sense of division is clarified by one of the inhabitants of the city who claims 'I was twain, / Two selves distinct that cannot join again' (IV, lines 71–72), suggesting the collapse of a sense of cohesive self and identity. This irresolvable division in the dramatic voice is epitomized in Canto VIII where Thomson splits his poetic persona, in much the same way as Tennyson adopting the voices of the muses Urania and Melpomene, into two distinct identities. What is significant is that, instead of using strictly contradictory voices, Thomson uses dramatic identities that are symptomatic of the environment that he has created. The first voice is that of a blasphemer who criticizes the relevance of the orthodox Christian mythos within the city; its tone is one of anger, resentment and self-pity:

> 'Who is most wretched in this dolorous place?
> I think myself; yet I would rather be
> My miserable self than He, than He

Who formed such creatures to His own disgrace.

The vilest thing must be less vile than Thou
From whom it had its being, God and Lord!
Creator of all woe and sin! abhorred,
Malignant and implacable!' (VIII, lines 21–28)

The language used by Thomson is emotive, the speaker is 'wretched' and 'miserable' and God, in a shower of blasphemous accusations, is 'vile', 'abhorred', 'malignant' and 'implacable'. God is shifted from 'Creator of all' to 'Creator of all woe and sin' in an argument that possesses convincing logic. If God the Creator has brought 'woe and sin' into being then, by implication, God's creation of vile creatures suggests that these entities 'must be less vile than Thou / From whom it had its being'. The blasphemous voice exists in a theological vacuum where God has no place except as a focus for hatred and contempt. If God *has* created the city ('this dolorous place') then He is either mad or evil. By contrast the second voice of the argument is that of an atheist who, rejecting the emotive vocabulary of the first voice, finds even less meaning in existence:

'As if a being, God or Fiend, could reign,
At once so wicked, foolish, and insane,
As to produce men when He might refrain!

The world rolls round for ever like a mill;
It grinds out death and life and good and ill;
It has no purpose, heart or mind or will.' (VIII, lines 33–38)

The tone, in contrast to the bitterness of the first voice, is pragmatic and rational, and the subject matter reveals a reductive reading of life; man's existence is not determined by a vile Creator but simply by the perpetual motion of the earth. There is a telling irony in this rational voice depicting an irrational precept for existence; it rejects the moral, intellectual and psychological judgements ('wicked, foolish, and insane') advocated by the first voice, and also suggests that the world has no moral reasoning either – like the Cartesian automaton Jo in *Bleak House* it is a basic technology, a mill merely grinding out 'good and ill'. Because the world has 'no purpose, heart or mind or will', the traditional ethical understanding of existence is negated; the second voice is therefore not only atheistic but nihilistic. The significance of the atheistic statement lies in the fact that no sentient entity would be 'wicked, foolish, and insane' (note that it is not just one but all three of these characteristics that would have to qualify the 'God or Fiend' for responsibility) enough to create man. This effectively dramatizes Thomson's statement, made in the year before the appearance of 'The City of Dreadful Night' and cited as the epigraph for this section, where he claims, 'I cannot think so ill of any possible supreme being as to accuse him of the guilt and folly of the voluntary creation of such a world and such lives as ours.' It can therefore be assumed that in terms of content and conviction the second voice is representative of Thomson's personal perspective. All that the indifferent world offers the inhabitants of the city is the prospect of 'eternal death' (VIII, line 17); this becomes established as the only consolation for living in the city.

Compared with what he presents as the inadequacy and futility of metaphysical speculation, Thomson offers the perpetual and cyclical motion of the earth depicted in lines 36–38 of Canto VIII as the only basis for existence in a world that is futile enough already. Tennyson, in lyric XXXIV of *In Memoriam* has presented such motion as purposeless; his perception of this, however, manifests itself in chaotic and random imagery, the 'Fantastic beauty' of the world being likened to the work of a 'wild Poet' who writes 'Without a conscience or an aim'. By contrast Thomson, through thematic repetition, offers a uniformly pessimistic interpretation of the earth's motion. In Canto II of 'The City of Dreadful Night' time is used as a metaphor for the effects of this motion within the city:

> Take a watch, erase
> The signs and figures of the circling hours,
> Detach the hands, remove the dial-face;
> The works proceed until run down; although
> Bereft of purpose, void of use, still go. (II, lines 32–36)

Where Tennyson's conception of the earth's motion crystallizes the agitated expression of doubt within his poem, Thomson's is laborious in nature. Motion is equated with Time and vice versa; they are likened to a watch which, without figures, hands or dial-face, no longer has a purpose. An emphatically negative vocabulary of 'erase', 'detach', 'remove', 'Bereft' and 'void' nullifies any purpose in the sense of relentless, meaningless, but perpetual motion. The effect, compared to

Tennyson's use of a similar concept, *severs* 'the knot of doubt' (II, line 43) and stimulates enlightenment; existence is composed solely of 'Perpetual recurrence' (II, line 47). As stated above, Henry Maudsley's determinist interpretation of the biological and social world comes close to Thomson's vision in 'The City of Dreadful Night'. In *Natural Causes and Supernatural Seemings* he argues that man, whether supposedly sane or insane, '[s]till imagines himself to be the supreme aim of the universe of things, and the end for which the whole of creation has groaned and travailed through countless ages, and groans and travails still'.[13] The perpetual motion of Thomson is reflected in Maudsley's use of 'groaned and travailed through countless ages, and groans and travails still'. Both writers, the poet and the physician, denigrate man's presumption that he should have pre-eminence within the natural world. However, Maudsley is more sympathetic in terms of purpose than Thomson; he disparages man's delusion in seeing himself as 'above nature ... instead of, as he is actually, a part of it that develops from and in and for it, and commands only by obeying.[14] This vision, holistic as it is, still awards man a function in 'command[ing] ... by obeying'. By contrast, Thomson condenses and reinforces his perception of existence in Canto XIII, describing:

> This Time which crawleth like a monstrous snake,
> Wounded and slow and very venemous [*sic*];
> Which creeps blindwormlike round the earth and ocean,
> Distilling poison at each painful motion,
> And seems condemned to circle ever thus. (XIII, lines 15–21)

Again there is a sense of eternal but stagnant motion contained in this simile of a snake that is 'condemned to circle ever thus'. Here however the image is actively dangerous; the snake is 'very venemous', 'Distilling poison'. Time and motion are represented as fundamentally purposeless except, as here, to distill poison as they move. There is something reciprocal in the action; Time is 'venemous' but it is also 'wounded' itself, its motion is 'painful' and it is 'condemned' to move in this way. Again there is a unity in terms of a vision of existence; as a clock the world, though 'Bereft of purpose', still engages itself in motion, and, as a snake, is 'condemned to circle ever thus'. Motion, though meaningless, is constantly cyclical. Thomson indicates that there is only one fruitful purpose in the motion of the earth for the inhabitants of the city, contained in the assertive statement:

We yearn for speedy death in full fruition,
    Dateless oblivion and divine repose. (XIII, lines 41–2)

Such a longing echoes Robert Wringhim's yearning in Hogg's *Private Memoirs*, whilst also suggesting the condition of disidentity defined by Francis Barker, with its emphasis upon relinquishing responsibility for past and future; it is paradoxically appropriate that this desire for Barker's 'bucolic pastoral' should take place within the confines of the modern metropolis. Thomson uses an ironic vocabulary; in the face of a fruitless existence 'full fruition' suggests completion and fulfilment. All that Time offers to the inhabitants of his city is the possibility of personal oblivion, where Time itself is nullified by becoming 'Dateless'.

In his tract of 1845, *The Power of the Soul over the Body*, George Moore offered a positivist interpretation of existence that was as committed as Thomson's pessimistic vision. His words present a critique of new science and assert metaphysical conviction, claiming that spiritual well-being dictates mental and physical health. His perspective stands in stark contrast to Thomson's scepticism and Tennyson's articulation of doubt: 'All who have looked below the surface of things, must account that science despicable, and that philosophy pitifully meagre, which afford no higher object of pursuit than a little sensuality; no brighter prospect than a phantom life, no better end than an endless death.'[15] Moore's voice is robust and contemptuous, dismissing the theological aspects of science and philosophy as respectively 'despicable' and 'pitifully meagre'. Thomson's analytical poetic vision is, however, as concerned with the perilous activity of looking 'below the surface of things' as Moore's, and is in many ways more convincing. This is most apparent in what is perhaps the definitive statement of Thomson's intent; Canto XIV of 'The City of Dreadful Night' both dramatizes and confirms his inflexible and relentless comprehension of the mechanics of existence. Adopting the persona of a prophet whose eyes 'burned as never eyes burned yet' (XIV, line 18), Thomson invests his character with the authority and eloquence of its Old Testament counterparts:

And now at last authentic word I bring,
Witnessed by every dead and living thing;
    Good tidings of great joy for you; for all:
There is no God; no fiend with names divine

Made us and tortures us; if we must pine,
It is to satiate no Being's gall. (XIV, lines 37–42)

The words are as authoritative as Moore's; the latter's probing 'below the surface of things' is matched by the 'authentic word' of Thomson's prophet. What gives Thomson's vision greater credibility is his subtle inversion of the role of the biblical prophet and his parody of scriptural text. His prophet's announcement of 'Good tidings of great joy for all' echoes the acclamation of the angel of the Lord in St Luke's Gospel, who proclaims the birth of Christ to the shepherds of Bethlehem with the words 'Good tidings of great joy' (Lk. 2:10). However, where the utterance of the angel delivers a message of hope, Thomson's prophet denies such a possibility; the poet uses an inversion of a Christian vocabulary to consolidate his atheistic platform. A language of qualified insight, contained in 'authentic' and 'witnessed', in the universal 'by every' and 'for all', and in the pronounced utilization of negatives, gives credence to the words of the prophet. In addition the negation of Old Testament prophecies, filtered through 'There is no God', echoes the words of the second voice in Canto VIII and Thomson's own words that prelude this discussion of the poem, rendering the pattern of thought behind 'The City of Dreadful Night' more comprehensive and cohesive. The words of Thomson's prophet reinforce the content of Canto VIII; although the inhabitants of the city may feel tortured to the point of insanity or suicide, there is no external, omnipotent force that induces their suffering; any collapse of identity is their own responsibility.

Canto XIV can therefore be read as the culmination of Thomson's philosophy. Counterbalancing Moore's critique of the science and philosophy that teaches 'no brighter prospect than a phantom life, no better end than an endless death', the prophet reasserts the bleak facts of existence with its solitary hope lying in the security of death:

This little life is all we must endure,
The grave's most holy peace is ever sure,
We fall asleep and never wake again;
Nothing is of us but the mouldering flesh,
Whose elements dissolve and merge afresh
In earth, air, water, plants, and other men. (XIV, lines 49–54)

Moore's denigration of the 'phantom life' and 'endless death', two features perhaps traceable in the experience of Simeon Stylites as dramatized by Tennyson, are recontextualized by Thomson as a 'little life' where 'The grave's most holy peace' is permanent. Death for Thomson allows a cyclical blending where man's 'elements dissolve' and 'merge afresh' to contribute to the further existence of 'earth, air, water, plants, and other men'. Through these words the poet looks steadily at the reality of physical decay, proffering a consciousness of the transience of the body as opposed to a metaphysical interpretation of the profits of existence. The death of the individual contributes to essential elements of existence, thereby perpetuating both life in general and the continued survival of mankind. This celebration of the function of decay also involves another inversion of Christianity. The sacrament of Communion, Christ's body manifest in the form of bread, symbolically involves death, resurrection and consumption of the physical body; Thomson, using similar themes, transforms the symbolic thinking at the heart of Christian communion into, at the least, part of a food chain, or, at the worst, cannibalism.

Moore's perspective upon the nature of existence is again different, his concern being with the moral implications of life which, for him, transcend physicality:

> We find ... that our minds are governed by laws that have nothing to do with material organization: for our sense of right and wrong, truth and falsehood, virtue and vice, has no relation to bodily structure, but as the vehicle and instrument of mind ... Above all, we retain amidst the changes of our bodies and the shifting variety of decay around us, a distinct consciousness of our own identity, and an intuitive conviction, as far as reason is awakened, that we hold our faculties and endowments not from the fortuitous action of nature, as a blind power, but from the purpose of God as an informing spirit, in whom we live, and move, and have our being for ever.[16]

Almost paradoxically, what Moore attempts to lay claim to is an authoritative, autonomous, cohesive human identity that is nonetheless shaped by a divine 'informing spirit'. This manifests itself in a belief in a metaphysical and moral shaping of life that defies the 'variety of decay' surrounding mankind. Any such claim for consciousness is effectively denied in Thomson's poetic negation of individual or collective identity – 'Nothing is of us' but the 'elements' that 'dissolve and merge afresh'. For Thomson depersonalization, the extinction of the self and self-conscious identity, is indeed the key to the perpetuation of the human species. Similarly, Moore urges a vision of life 'governed by laws' that have 'no relation to bodily structure', and where 'our faculties and endowments' come from God, therefore giving existence the moral framework of 'right and wrong', 'truth and falsehood' and 'vice and virtue'. Thomson also suggests that we are 'governed by laws', these however are the laws of natural existence that are intrinsic to our 'material organization'; for him it is not relevant to talk of laws in terms of ethics:

> We bow down to the universal laws,
> Which never had for man a special clause
>   Of cruelty or kindness, love or hate. (XIV, lines 61–63)

Humanity, from Thomson's perspective, is subject to neither 'cruelty or kindness, love or hate' merely the indifference of nature. He emphasizes this sense of inhabiting a moral vacuum by stating, through his prophet:

> I find no hint throughout the universe
> Of good or ill, of blessing or of curse;
>   I find alone Necessity Supreme (XIV, lines 73–75)

The vision is reinforced by thematic repetition in lines 73 and 74, consolidating the active amorality of existence. What is significant here is the determining element of 'Necessity Supreme' which determines the experience of being human in this nightmare metropolis. His perception finds significant parallels in Henry Maudsley's perspective. Moore has stated that the laws which govern man and his mind have nothing to do with 'material organization'. However, Maudsley, in *Body and Mind* of 1873 denies this; using the same key word 'organization', he states: 'No one can escape the tyranny of his organization; no one can elude the destiny that is innate in him, and which unconsciously and irresistibly shapes his ends, even when he believes that he is determining them with consummate foresight and skill.'[17] For Moore life is determined by the laws of God filtered through the human mind by moral conviction and consciousness of a cohesive and defined identity, Maudsley indicates that we are at the mercy of our own physical and mental constitutions

– the 'tyranny of ... [our] organization'. He emphasizes the inflexibility of his perception in *Responsibility in Mental Disease*:

> It was a pregnant saying that the history of a man is his character; to which one might add that whatsoever would transform a character must undo a life history. The fixed and unchanging laws by which events come to pass hold sway in the mind as in every other domain of nature.[18]

Again Maudsley indicates that an individual life is fundamentally shaped by the elements that constitute it. His use of 'fixed and unchanging laws' echoes Thomson's 'universal laws', and, like Thomson's, contrasts with George Moore's apprehension of the laws that affect what the latter would no doubt perceive as a common human condition. Thomson and Maudsley both establish inflexible visions of existence where self-consciousness and identity are determined by laws over which the individual has either no control or is provided with no 'special clause'.

Thomson presents two main conclusions, one defining and reinforcing the nature of existence, the other interpreting its effect upon humanity. The first conclusion is tendered through the dramatic voice of the prophet, again in Canto XIV:

> We finish thus; and all our wretched race
> Shall finish with its cycle, and give place
> To other beings, with their own time-doom
> Infinite aeons ere our kind began;
> Infinite aeons after the last man
> Has joined the mammoth in earth's tomb and womb.
> (XIV, lines 55–60)

In many ways this stanza reiterates much of what the prophet has said already, pointing to the inflexibility of life's laws, the insignificance of humanity within the broad historical spectrum of existence, and the endless cycles of birth and death. There are, however, subtle shifts that render the vision even more remorseless. Regardless of natural progression, Thomson's prophet suggests that each species has its own 'time-doom'; there is a constant cycle of death and regeneration, but because it is essentially meaningless there is no real difference between man and mammoth. The association between man and prehistoric beast and the time-scheme of 'Infinite aeons' expands Thomson's perspective, enhanced by the grandiloquent poetic mantle of the prophet, into one of grand and fatalistic pessimism. Human significance, with this expansion of historical perspective, is therefore reduced even further; the dismissive erasure of the 'mouldering flesh' of an individual 'little life' is replaced by a judgement of the species as 'our wretched race'. Similarly, where the prophet claimed 'we fall asleep and never wake again', now the function of death is demoted to 'We finish thus'; it is as though human insignificance is such that the fatal word 'never' is superfluous. Finally, where before the use of 'We fall asleep' is followed by a revival of the physical self through 'merg[ing] afresh' with other elements of life, in this conclusion the balance is weighted more emphatically towards death. Man according to the biological code of 'time-doom' must return to the 'earth's tomb and womb'; the phrasing is carefully dichotomous, man returns to 'earth's tomb' as 'mouldering flesh', the earth engenders 'other beings', and is therefore also a 'womb', an object of fecundity. However, because the perspective of this conclusion is that of the prophet addressing the inhabitants of the city and therefore addressing the issue of position of humanity within the infrastructure of existence, the death aspect of the earth becomes explicitly important, basically because mankind must 'finish with its cycle'. As a result, through the repetition of 'Infinite aeons' (which reminds us of Maudsley's 'countless ages' of creation) a huge time-span is evoked that is fundamentally sterile; human presence within it as the 'little life' of a 'wretched race' renders the productivity of the earth into an indifferent function rather than a celebratory force.

The second conclusion of the poem is climactic in terms of denying any possible meaning or purpose within existence. However, although poetically powerful in providing a cohesive culmination of the poem's philosophical structure, in the context of Thomson's use of repetition the third from the last stanza of the whole poem (found in Canto XXI) is appropriately anticlimactic and pessimistic in tone. Thomson defines the profit of life within the city as:

> The sense that every struggle brings defeat
>   Because Fate holds no prize to crown success;
> That all the oracles are dumb or cheat
>   Because they have no secret to express;
> That none can pierce the vast black veil uncertain

Because there is no light beyond the curtain;
That all is vanity and nothingness. (XXI, lines 64–70)

Thomson's nihilistic point of view is paraphrased in this stanza; the meaningless quality of life in his city is contained in the fact that 'every struggle brings defeat', summing up the 'helpless impotence' of trying to write the poem in the first place. The word 'every' is indicative of the remorseless finality of trying to find a reason for existence, and is therefore allied to the word 'never' – as in 'never wake again' and 'never had for man a special clause' – encountered before in the poem. The inevitability of Thomson's philosophy is such that every 'struggle' against the established mechanism of existence is preordained to meet with 'defeat'. Similarly, any reliance upon external sources of comfort or hope is futile because all oracles are 'dumb or cheat' and, as the prophet of Canto XIV has pointed out, 'there is no God'. The fatalism of Thomson's vision is manifest in the words 'dumb', 'cheat', 'defeat', 'nothingness' and 'no prize'. This cumulation of pessimism functions on two levels; with the denial of God's existence and the exposure of false oracles Thomson invests humanity with a lack of meaning that corresponds to the indifference of the earth that has engendered it.

Like Tennyson in *In Memoriam*, Thomson, in Canto XXI of 'The City of Dreadful Night', uses the image of the veil to articulate a sense of the beyond in existence. However, where Tennyson's veil is tantalizing and provocative, Thomson's use of the image suggests that the veil might not even exist. It is 'uncertain' and there is 'no light beyond it', rendering it obscure. The veil for Thomson inspires dread and a sense of being overwhelmed because it is 'vast' and 'black'. Therefore, where Tennyson has the conventions of the 'earthly song' of Hallam's death as a focus for progression beyond the veil, Thomson's vision is pitilessly blank because there is no light to lead him on. In effect the absence of light suggests deadness, numbness to the possibility of anything existing behind the metaphysical veil, or that nothing ever was 'beyond the curtain'. Thomson's conclusion is therefore articulated in a fundamentally disturbing way; his statement 'all is vanity and nothingness' is simultaneously succinct and empty. The juxtaposition of the expansive 'all' and the negative 'nothingness' is devastatingly powerful, propelling a profound conception of the pointlessness of attempting to assert a unified identity in such a nihilistic context. His words parody the Book of Ecclesiastes to great effect; the Preacher of that text states 'vanity of vanities; all *is* vanity' (Eccl. 2:2). Many of Thomson's previous articulations of the cyclical nature of existence echo Ecclesiastes; for example, the Preacher of Ecclesiastes continues: '*One* generation passeth away, and *another* generation cometh: but the earth abideth for ever' (Eccl. 1:4). This concept of existence has obvious parallels in Thomson's writing; his statement that mankind finishes' with its cycle and give[s] place / To other beings' reflects '[*o*]*ne* generation' dying and '*another* generation' coming into being. The cycle of birth and death is evident in both. Thomson's words, however, invert the words of the Preacher of Ecclesiastes; where the fact that 'the earth abideth for ever' can be seen as comforting because it offers permanence in relation to the fleeting life-span of man, Thomson's vision is one where 'The world rolls round for ever like a mill', rendering its motion mechanical and impartial. By subverting the notion of the earth as a constant force and simultaneously allying himself with a critique of man's existence as 'vanity', Thomson suggests that the idea of permanence, a facet of God's creation for the preacher of Ecclesiastes, is disturbing and dreadful. What is significant in Thomson's depiction of human experience in the city is his inversion of orthodox Christian belief; As Tom Leonard states, 'The City of Dreadful Night'

> Would tell of a city in one aspect like a reverse picture of the New Jerusalem of Revelation: where that Biblical city had eternal light, a River of Life, and ever-present God ... this city would always be in darkness, would be crossed by a river of Suicides, and its citizens would have for inner knowledge, that God does not exist.[19]

7 Dead letters: Gerard Manley Hopkins's 'Terrible Sonnets'

> I shall shortly have some sonnets to send to you, five or more. Four of these came like inspirations unbidden and against my will. And in the life I lead now which is one of a continually jaded and harassed mind, if in any leisure I try to do anything I make no way – nor with my work alas! but so it must be.[1]

Tennyson's dramatic monologue, 'St Simeon Stylites', implies an identifiable audience to whom the eponymous anchorite periodically appeals; in Simeon's case the dramatically involved but emphatically silent addressee for the monologist can be defined at various stages as the divine (God) or human (the crowd that flocks at the base of the pillar). In each case the silence of the audience has a dramatic logic: God's silence is symptomatic of the division between natural and supernatural and of the traditional inscrutability of the divine, whereas the audience's is the result of the more conventional distancing device of height, Simeon's physical elevation on his pillar prohibits communicative interaction with the crowd. However, poetically what remains is the 'dialogue of the mind with itself' voicing the 'doubts' and 'discouragement' discussed by Matthew Arnold. The result is a colloquy that is defined by Roger Platizky as 'the tension between individual trust and social expectations' and in the 'psychological dynamic between the nonconforming self (the hyper-vigilant, mad speaker) and ... the silent auditor[s]' to whom it speaks.[2] In addition to the colloquies that exist within the text – between persona and silent audience(s) and between aspects of the fragmented persona – there is also the extra-textual colloquy. This further colloquy takes place between the poet's public voice and its, again silent, reading audience. That 'St Simeon Stylites' was published well within Tennyson's lifetime suggests his consciousness of a defined contemporary audience. The Arnoldian dialogue that the reader witnesses is made public. In *In Memoriam* and 'The City of Dreadful

Night' the dialogue suggested by Arnold is simultaneously expanded upon and detached from the personal voice through its manifestation in Tennyson and Thomson's respective utilization of dramatic personae: for example, in the colloquy that takes place between the two voices in Canto VIII of 'The City of Dreadful Night'. Furthermore Thomson, in the Proem that preludes his work, explicitly establishes an audience for whom his poem is intended and with whom he is prepared to enter hypothetical discourse. In each of these cases dialogue is of both an introspective and subjective Arnoldian nature, the mind debating issues with itself, and an expansive, outward-looking nature where either an audience is established or poetic personae are created to objectify or isolate discussions of experience or opinion.

The four sonnets mentioned by Gerard Manley Hopkins in his letter to Robert Bridges of the 1 September 1885, the sonnets that came to the poet 'like inspirations unbidden', are generally accepted to be the poems 'To Seem the Stranger', 'I Wake and Feel', 'Patience' and 'My Own Heart', found amongst Hopkins's papers after his death in 1889. Two further poems can be added to this list, 'Carrion Comfort' and 'No Worst, There Is None', also frequently accepted to have been written in 1885. The six poems can constitute a body of work that I will refer to as the 'terrible sonnets'.[3] If these poems are taken together as a group their content reveals the most profound point of introspection in terms of the Arnoldian dialogue. If this is the case then the self-consciousness of St Simeon and the personal voice in the two poems by Tennyson and Thomson are outweighed in terms of self-examination by the extraordinary solipsism manifest within these six sonnets by Hopkins. However, what reinforces this acute consciousness of self and marks out the poems in terms of the overall subject matter of this chapter is the pronounced absence of a colloquy with God, that should technically define their nature.[4] The sonnets are a pointed and occasionally overwhelming poetic articulation of desolation and abandonment. As J. Hillis Miller suggests: 'Hopkins has, beyond all his contemporaries, the most shattering experience of the disappearance of God.'[5] In many ways religious poetry illuminates belief via the establishment of a relationship between the human and the divine, the temporal and the eternal. Bernard Richards states that 'it might be claimed that the religious habit of mind, of seeing the invisible via the visible, the holy via the secular, the universal via the particular, the eternal via the historical, and the significant via the apparently contingent are directly analogous to poetic practices'.[6] In Hopkins's 'terrible sonnets' this interactive, mutual reliance deteriorates into the poetic solipsism indicated above.

A standard critical reception of the 'terrible sonnets' is to see them, through Bridges's use of Hopkins' thirty-fifth folio (which orders the four sonnets drafted there as 'To Seem the Stranger', 'I Wake and Feel', 'Patience' and 'My Own Heart'), as a sequence that describes a progression from despair to personal redemption.[7] Daniel A. Harris, in *Inspirations Unbidden: The 'Terrible Sonnets' of Gerard Manley Hopkins*, suggests that viewing the sonnets as sequential or as providing a positive spiritual biography of Hopkins is 'suspect as the basis for any interpretation'.[8] Harris goes on to state that orthodox criticism has 'freely superimposed upon the poems a doctrinaire Christian narrative or spiritual autobiography whose teleology is fulfilled by God's extension of consolation and Hopkins' intact survival of extreme trial.[9] Tennyson's *In Memoriam*, though not necessarily originally intended to be a lyrical cycle, has a clear and self-conscious sequential structure behind it where the poet posits a spiritual progression that involves resilience, reclamation and reconversion; indeed a procession of themes that allows the poetic voice to affirm a stable and cohesive identity. As a point of contrast Hopkins's 'terrible sonnets' arguably do not provide as sequentially homogenous a group as previous criticism has indicated. Such a reading impedes a study of the content of the poems, therefore their association will be based upon what Harris defines as a unity 'derived primarily from a common emotive pressure'.[10]

The real significance of Hopkins's 'terrible sonnets', compared to the spiritual progression favoured by his apologists, lies in their theologically heterodoxical nature and in the apparently overwhelming subjective anguish portrayed by Hopkins within the poems. Harris succinctly paraphrases this reassessment of the significance of these sonnets:

> Catholic and non-Catholic commentators alike have persistently hesitated to acknowledge the phenomenon of an impeccably devout Jesuit priest who gives witness to God's brutality ('Carrion Comfort'), courts nihilism and suicide ('No Worst'), puns with ferocious sarcasm on the idea of Christian 'comfort' ('No Worst', 'My Own Heart'), and insinuates through ambiguous syntax that his own disaster is 'worse' than that of 'the lost' ('I Wake and Feel').[11]

What is significant in Harris's analysis is his use of the words 'persistently hesitated'; the fact that Harris avoids the condemnatory 'failed to see' and instead opts for a phrasing that in itself suggests denial indicates the undeniable bleakness of a group of sonnets that include lines such as:

> I see
> The lost are like this, and their scourge to be
> As I am mine, their sweating selves; but worse.[12]

Compared to his earlier poetry the natural imagery that renders Hopkins's writing distinctive is all but abandoned; it is this imagery which established a relationship between the poet and external reality, and therefore recognized the incarnation of God within the natural world, a way of seeing the 'invisible via the visible' that Bernard Richards refers to.[13] In the 'terrible sonnets' imagery relating to and recognizing the external world is lost, replaced by an inward-looking and private solipsism; what Hopkins creates is an internal landscape. W. David Shaw objectifies Hopkins's obsessive self-consciousness in the 'terrible sonnets' and adds an interesting comparison: 'Hopkins is so totally obsessed by each exquisite and refined torture he thinks peculiar to himself that he loses sight of what connects him with Orestes and King Lear.'[14] Shaw identifies the solipsism of self-obsession with tortures that Hopkins thought 'peculiar to himself'; what marks this statement is the observation that Hopkins fails to see his association with Orestes and King Lear. These icons of tragic drama echo Matthew Arnold's appropriation of Hamlet and Faust; however, there is a difference in interpretation here. Arnold's disillusionment with modern poetry stemmed from its giving voice to the doubts that typify these iconic characters whereas Shaw argues that Hopkins's poetry, by the 1880s, has 'lost sight' of its association with a possible thematic uniformity of doubt and dilemma, and transformed itself into a state where the anguish caused by such experiences becomes obsessively 'exquisite and refined'. In many ways what Shaw seems to be describing is a *decadent* and indulgent celebration of the senses, defined through cruelty, pain and masochism; indeed, there is a possibly psychopathological solipsism in some of the sonnets, validated when the sado-masochistic potential of some of the phrasing is considered. Nonetheless, Hopkins's verse suggests elements of some of the constituent symptoms of religious anguish, and in particular the fragmentation of the poetic identity. Harris notes that 'Hopkins found himself assailed by self-division only as his brief career neared its close. Nor could he then find energy, time, or spiritual strength either to recover the wholeness he had lost or to achieve a new integration'.[15] We have seen how Tennyson resolved his crisis of disidentified self-division within *In Memoriam* through a rejection of spiritual confusion in lyric LVII ('Peace come away'), and Matthew Arnold resolved his via a near-complete rejection of poetry and therefore of 'doubts and discouragement'. By comparison the fact that Hopkins was to die four years after writing the 'terrible sonnets' suggests that, in terms of his poetic writing, there was little opportunity for him to resolve the self-division that Harris refers to.

Much has been made of the tension in Hopkins's life between the calling of his ministry as a Jesuit priest and his vocation as a poet.[16] To read Hopkins's writing on the basis of biographical material is not necessarily a fruitful interpretative avenue to pursue, though aspects of his life and his extra-poetical writing do serve to illuminate traits within the 'terrible sonnets'. For the purposes of this discussion, the division experienced by Hopkins that is noted by Harris is significant in that it is echoed by the division within the form of the sonnets themselves; octaves and sestets break into quatrains and tercets, suggesting a fragmentation within the poems.[17] This division can also be detected, from a theological perspective, within the poetic identity and its artistic consciousness. Howard W. Fulweiler notes that the personal anguish that marks Hopkins's later years involved a sense of inner conflict:

> Not only was the struggle between God and Hopkins; it was also between two separated personalities of Hopkins: Hopkins as Christ, immanent and creative in man and nature; Hopkins as Lucifer ... alienated from God by pride in himself and in his art ... In the continuing war between these apparently irreconcilable versions of the self lie the causes of Hopkins's personal agony.[18]

By the time of the 'terrible sonnets' it seems as though Christ is no longer 'immanent and creative' in Hopkins; in fact what marks them is the absence of a specific religious focal point. For example, Christ is referred to as 'dearest him that lives alas! away' ('I Wake and Feel': line 8), or actively identified as the source of the poet's anguish: 'Comforter, where, where is your comforting' ('No Worst': line 3).

The result is the feeling of alienation depicted by Fulweiler as the Luciferian aspect of Hopkins's poetic self, and which is epitomized in 'To Seem the Stranger' ('lies my lot, my life / Among strangers'). If a main theme can be isolated within the 'terrible sonnets' it is the absence of a vocative address directed emphatically towards God, and therefore a demise of the colloquy with the divine presence that forms an important aspect of *The Spiritual Exercises* of St Ignatius Loyola which Hopkins, as a Jesuit, would have used as his staple form of religious meditation.[19] It is this failure of the colloquy with the divine that causes and is caused by the feeling of alienation from and abandonment by God. This experience is familiar already from the medical writing of the nineteenth century. Thomas Arnold, in 1805, has already defined the effect of religious joy on the insane individual thus: '... a state of intoxication will sometimes be succeeded by languor and depression of spirits; and, in its stead, [they] are harassed and tormented, with religious fear, the gloom of despondency and the horrors of despair.'[20] And Henry Maudsley, in 1887, refers to the afflicted person as 'apathetic, inert, despairing, and sure that he is, or is about to be, overwhelmed by some unspeakable calamity – perhaps that he is forsaken by God and given over to eternal damnation'.[21]

Apart from the obvious association of offering poetic representations of crisis points, we can also establish other important links between the 'terrible sonnets' and the three poems analyzed prior to this discussion of Hopkins. An initial association that can be made is that the three poets all refer to the Book of Job in some form. For example, in 'St Simeon Stylites' Simeon is described as 'From scalp to sole one slough and crust of sin', echoing the afflictions of Job whom Satan 'smote ... with sore boils from the sole of his foot unto his crown' (Job 2:7).[22] In *In Memoriam*, in one of the poem's graveyard lyrics, Tennyson addresses the archetypal 'Old Yew' of the cemetery thus: 'Thy roots are wrapt around the bones'; similarly Bildad the Shuhite, speaking in the Book of Job of the godless man, claims that 'his roots are wrapped about the heap, / He beholdeth the place of stones' (Job 8:17).[23] James Thomson's 'The City of Dreadful Night' offers more distinctive parallels with Job, both in terms of language and thematic resonance. In the first canto of the poem Thomson describes the location of his work thus:

> The City is of Night; perchance of Death,
> But certainly of Night.[24]

In the Book of Job, Job describes the Hebrew underworld of Sheol as follows:

> A land of thick darkness, as darkness *itself*;
> A *land* of the shadow of death, without any order,
> And where the light is as darkness. (Job 10:22).

The two landscapes envisaged in each work are defined as consisting of darkness (literal darkness or the darkness of night); they also present locations where there is no order or where order has become meaningless, and this itself can be represented by the suggestion that even the light is dark in both the City and the land of Sheol.[25] In Hopkins's 'terrible sonnets' three of the few nature images in the poems can also be found in the Book of Job. In 'No Worst' God is likened to a 'whirlwind', similarly 'Carrion Comfort' obliquely refers to God as possessing the qualities of a 'tempest', in addition in the latter poem the poet tries to justify the apparently relentless cruelty of God as an attempt to ensure that 'my chaff might fly; my grain lie, sheer and clear' ('Carrion Comfort'); the images of the whirlwind and of chaff and grain can all be detected in Job.[26] The association seems somewhat tenuous given the comparisons provided here; however, it is significant that in 'St Simeon Stylites', *In Memoriam* and 'The City of Dreadful Night' there is the sense of an ability to transcend personal anguish. In 'St Simeon Stylites' this takes the form of an explicit dedication to self-mortification, deluded as this may be, in *In Memoriam* the phrasing of 'Peace; come away' allows the poetic voice to distance itself from its previous crisis of belief and reaffirm purpose and identity within the poem and , and in 'The City of Dreadful Night' the sheer unrelenting negativity of the tone and subject affords the poetic voice some comfort, resilience or satisfaction.[27] In the Old Testament, Job's family, wealth and dignity are all reinstated by God as the reward for his patience; it is this virtue, in the face of intense physical and mental suffering that allows Job to transcend personal adversity. Patience is also advocated by St Ignatius in his *Spiritual Exercises*, particularly when utilized in the face of spiritual desolation: 'In this state (the exercitant) should also strive to abide in patience, which is the antidote to the trials that beset him. He should also reflect that he will soon be comforted, and should put forth all his efforts against this distress.'[28] Patience is also the theme of one of the 'terrible sonnets'. Defined as both severe and serene, the function of patience is also somewhat ambiguous, for it 'masks / Our ruins of wrecked past purpose' ('Patience', lines 6–7), suggesting that all it does as a virtue is hide previous failures. For the moment what is significant within the poem is the demand made by Hopkins:

> And where is he who more and more distils
> Delicious kindness? – He is patient. (lines 12–13)

The question suggests an appeal to a fictive, communal and reading audience; however, because the poet answers his own question, it becomes more indicative of a divided self indulging in a private and inward colloquy. What the question and answer also indicates is that while the poet is patient so too is God ('He is patient'), suggesting that God is neither immanent nor involved in the poetic meditation upon patience, and therefore postponing St Ignatius's confident belief that those in a state of spiritual desolation 'will *soon* be comforted'. In this sense there is much in the 'terrible sonnets' that runs parallel to the Book of Job and yet also contrary. Patience, for example, holds no tangible promise of dividends, no Jobean reward for waiting. As a result the transcendence of anguish discussed above does not seem to be offered to or by Hopkins. The Book of Job is a justification of God's inscrutable ways revealed through dramatic dialogue; however, the God, who appears at the end of the Book of Job, and enters into direct speech with Job, seems to be singularly absent in the 'terrible sonnets'. If we scrutinize 'Patience' Hopkins is compelled to refer to Him in the third person and diminutive 'he', indicating the distance between appeal and appealant. Nonetheless, when God *is* referred to or manifest in the 'terrible sonnets', as I will demonstrate later in this discussion, He is more like the Hebraic Jehovah than the Comforter of Ignatian meditation.

What also links Hopkins with the poems of Tennyson and Thomson are hints in works other than the 'terrible sonnets' of negativity and a consciousness of the cyclical nature of mortality which provides an alternative world-view to that anticipated in theologically orthodox interpretations of existence. We encounter negative undercurrents and a perception of the routine of physical decay in 'The Leaden Echo and the Golden Echo' (1882), 'Spelt from Sibyl's Leaves' (1884–85) and in 'That Nature is a Heraclitean Fire and of the Comfort of the Resurrection' (1888). Taking lines from these poems, regardless of their meaning as completed works, we can detect nihilism in the repetitive use of negatives in 'The Leaden Echo':

O there's none; no no no there's none:
Be beginning to despair, to despair,
Despair, despair, despair, despair.[29]

which anticipates the remorselessness of 'No Worst, there is None'. In the same poem Hopkins indicates his consciousness of physical decay in terms of the fact that natural beauty signifies nothing more than

Ruck and wrinkle, drooping, dying, death's worst, winding sheets
tombs and worms and tumbling decay. (line 11)

This repetition of images of mortality ('winding sheets', 'tombs', 'worms', 'decay') echoes similar preoccupations exhibited by Tennyson in *In Memoriam*, who described the state as one where 'The cheeks drop in; the body bows; / Man dies: nor is there hope in dust', and Thomson in 'The City of Dreadful Night' who defines the dividend of man's existence as 'Nothing is of us but the mouldering flesh, / Whose elements dissolve'.[30] There is a similar fixation with mortality and transience in 'Spelt from Sibyl's Leaves', where

Evening strains to be time's vast, | womb-of-all, home-of-all,
hearse-of-all night.[31]

As with Tennyson's dramatic proclamation by Nature that 'I bring to life, I bring to death' and Thomson's combination of 'earth's tomb and womb' there is a cyclical interdependence between life and death in Hopkins's manifestation of Evening as both 'womb-of-all' and 'hearse-of-all'. There is also an overwhelming sense of dissolution in 'Spelt from Sibyl's Leaves' ('Let life, waned, / ah let life wind / Off her once skeined stained variety', lines 10–11) and of inner division ('thoughts against thoughts in groans grind', line 14) which anticipate the 'terrible sonnets'. Finally, in the apocalyptic 'That Nature is a Heraclitean Fire' there is further evidence of the routine of decay:

Flesh fade, and mortal trash
Fall to the residuary worm; world's wildfire, leave but ash.[32]

This echoes Tennyson's suggestion in *In Memoriam*:

My own dim life should teach me this,

That life shall live forevermore,
Else earth is darkness at the core,
And dust and ashes all that is.[33]

and his description of the world as 'this orb of flame' (XXXIV, line 5). There is a similar emphasis upon fire ('wildfire' and 'Flame') and its residue ('trash', 'ash' and 'dust and ashes'). However, where Tennyson's words are, as defined earlier in this discussion, an articulation of doubt and despair, Hopkins's, in 'That Nature is a Heraclitean Fire', anticipate the spiritual resurrection predicted in the Revelations of St John in the New Testament:

In a flash, at a trumpet crash,
I am all at once what Christ is, since he was what I am.
('That Nature is', lines 18–19)

Hopkins's interpretation of physical decay in this poem functions within a conventionally orthodox Christian context compared to that of Tennyson and Thomson. Decay for Tennyson offers the possibility of a meaningless existence, Thomson's 'worm' indicates a sterile perpetuation of existence yet also an ambivalent celebration of the biological food chain (we 'merge afresh / In earth, air, water, plants, and other men') inherent within it; for Hopkins, in 'That Nature is a Heraclitean Fire', physical mortality is explicitly indicative of the imminent resurrection of the Christian soul.

The apocalyptic vision of 'That Nature is a Heraclitean Fire' offers the poet, as its full title indicates, 'the Comfort of the Resurrection'. In the 'terrible sonnets' the absence of natural imagery shifts the perspective of this vision; nature represents the inward solipsistic aspect of Hopkins's writing rather than a proleptic symbol of the collective resurrection. In this context God, intrinsically incarnate in the latter, can again be said to be absent within the six sonnets, further indicating the failure of a colloquy with the divine and the consequent collapse of a reliable and cohesive poetic identity.

The overall emotion that is obviously manifest in the poems is grief, grief caused by a perception of being abandoned, resulting in a feeling of desolation.[34] Desolation itself is a sensation that can be emphatically traced within religious writing; Job experiences it in the Old Testament, as do Simeon in 'St Simeon Stylites' ('I had hoped that ere this period closed / Thou wouldst have caught me up into thy rest', lines

17–18), the Tennysonian I in *In Memoriam* ('To drop head-foremost in the jaws / Of vacant darkness and to cease', XXXIV, lines 15–16) and, obversely, the implied atheist reader of 'The City of Dreadful Night' ('If any cares for the weak words here written, / It must be some one desolate). The ultimate vindication of religious desolation lies in the last words of Christ as he dies on the cross – '*E-li, E-li, la-ma sa-bach-tha-ni?* that is to say, My God, My, God, why hast thou forsaken me?' (Mk 15:34).[35] Grief, however, seems to be a more secular, personal experience, linked to human bereavement. Tennyson naturally explores this emotion in *In Memoriam*, providing a further link between his collection of lyrics and Hopkins's 'terrible sonnets'. However Tennyson's debate upon the possible absence of the divine and the effect of this absence is filtered through an articulation of grief at the death of Hallam, therefore locating speculation upon the possibility of a meaningless existence within conventional poetic practice. In the 'terrible sonnets' there is no filter for an articulation of desolation; grief is explicitly directed towards the divine and its absence ('Comforter, where, where is your comforting?', 'No Worst', line 3). The experience of desolation is therefore, particularly in 'To Seem the Stranger', represented via a conception of dislocation:

> To seem the stranger lies my lot, my life
> Among strangers. Father and mother dear,
> Brothers and sisters are in Christ not near.
>
> ('To Seem the Stranger', lines 1–3)

In the chiastic first sentence of this poem Hopkins defines his own self-division, to be a stranger amongst strangers. There is also a familial alienation inspired by religion, where his parents and siblings, who were not Roman Catholic, 'are in Christ not near'. This second dislocation leads to a sense of national alienation that perhaps echoes Matthew Arnold's representation of national dislocation in 'Dover Beach':

> I am in Ireland now; now I am at a third
> Remove (lines 9–10)

The desolation of grief therefore takes the form of three distinct forms of dislocation – from self, family and nation, and all the varied identities these involve; hence 'now I am at the third remove'.

The articulation of grief experienced through the failure of the colloquy with God is contained in a language that represents the loss of language, the loss of the ability to communicate with anything external to the self. In 'My Own Heart' language becomes repetitive and self-fixated, and the linguistic structure of the poem becomes fragmented:

> My own heart let me more have pity on; let
> Me live to my sad self hereafter kind
> Charitable, not live this tormented mind
> With this tormented mind tormenting yet.
>
> ('My Own Heart', lines 1–4)

The self-consciously reflexive nature of this chiastic structure, with its repetition of the notion of 'torment' and indecisive apprehensions of quality of life yet also self-obsession, suggests both a confused mind and a confused linguistic aptitude. There is a sense of the inadequacy of language to represent the cataclysmic experience that is supposedly taking place in the 'terrible sonnets', and also that the speaker is becoming increasingly unable to use human language in a rational and cogent manner. In 'I Wake and Feel' the mode of communication seems initially to be non-verbal:

> my lament
> Is cries countless, cries like dead letters sent
> To dearest him that lives alas! Away.
>
> ('I Wake and Feel', lines 6–8)

However, the 'dead letters' are balanced by the chaotic 'cries countless'; written communication with God is futile as the letters are dead before even being sent, and the vocal communication that would constitute the colloquy is random and chaotic. Language is therefore either moribund or fragmented beyond coherence. In 'No Worst' language is represented as having failed even further, the speaker stating that 'My cries heave, herds-long' and the personification of Fury within the poem 'had shrieked'. The comparison with Tennyson's representation of impotent articulation is obvious; the personified Fury's shriek matches that of Nature's in *In Memoriam*, and the cries of the speaker in Hopkins's poem match the Tennyson's speaker's 'with no language but a cry'. What occurs therefore is the representation of a devolution of the self in the face of chaotic inarticulation: Hopkins's speaker's cries are beast-like as they 'heave, herds-long'. The equation of the human voice with the animalistic is, in the context of Hopkins's beliefs, symptomatic of an existence within which Christ is absent; man becomes the 'monster' and the 'discord' that Tennyson suggested he might be.

'No Worst' is in many ways the most desolate of the 'terrible sonnets', depicting a state where the pangs of abandonment by God are 'Pitched past pitch of grief', and man starts to devolve into something no better than a beast. As Daniel Harris puts it:

> The dramatic failure of [an] effort to achieve colloquy drives the speaker back into renewed, and now exaggerated, self-definition as beast and thing; Hopkins's structuring insists that humankind deprived of Christ has no humanity. In place of the desired answer from Christ or God, the speaker hears only a terrific pagan voice, void of redemptive power or concern.[36]

What Harris identifies is the dehumanizing and disidentifying process represented by Hopkins, which, through the absence of God, renders the world meaningless. The 'pagan voice' is of course the 'Fury', which can be equated with Tennyson's Nature through the similar use of the shriek. However, what is interesting here is that, where in Tennyson's poem God and Nature are antagonistic characters, for Harris 'Fury' in 'No Worst' is the voice of God, albeit a degenerate version of the Judaic, vengeful God. In Hopkins's poem God has arguably become akin to the indifferent Nature of Tennyson's *In Memoriam*; in Harris's words 'void of redemptive power'. The world for Hopkins therefore becomes increasingly solipsistic in this poem, and in the final sestet the imagery becomes self-consciously physical, revolving around sensory perception and an apprehension of the pathetic nature of being human. The result of this is that Hopkins creates a fantasy landscape within the mind, internalizing and subjectifying the creation that he has striven to celebrate in an objective manner in much of his earlier poetry. Nature in 'No Worst' becomes emblematic of private religious anguish:

> O the mind, mind has mountains; cliffs of fall
> Frightful, sheer, no-man-fathomed. ('No Worst', lines 9–10)[37]

The ultimate effect of this feeling of religious desolation is that, in the sonnet 'I Wake and Feel', Hopkins defines himself as the yardstick by which the damned are to be measured:

> I see
> The lost are like this, and their scourge to be
> As I am mine, their sweating selves; but worse
> ('I Wake and Feel', lines 12-14).

Like Thomas Arnold's definition of the 'Effect of Religious Joy on Insanity', where the patient is 'harassed and tormented, with religious fear, the gloom of despondency, and the horrors of despair', cited at the start of this chapter, and Henry Maudsley's description of the religious maniac who feels 'that he is forsaken by God and given over to eternal damnation', Hopkins defines himself in this poem as 'worse' than the 'lost'.[38] There is a four-fold fear in this quotation, a fear of the lost, a fear of damnation (represented by 'sweating' in hell), a fear of the self (contained in 'to be'), and a fear that ultimately one might actually be worse than the lost. Balanced against this there is a bizarre affirmation of self and identity; the speaker claims 'I am gall, I am heartburn' (line 9) effectively shifting the Cartesian equation that confirms self identification from *Cogito Ergo Sum* ('I think therefore I am') to *Aegroto Ergo Sum* ('I am sick therefore I am'). At this stage in the poem it would appear that self-assertion can only be traced through being *in* the body.

In addition to exploring the effect of religious dislocation on the self and identity, my concern in this section of the book has been with the Arnoldian notion of the 'dialogue of the mind with itself'. As demonstrated this idea is maintained and manipulated in the work of Tennyson and Thomson. In 'St Simeon Stylites' the nature of the dramatic monologue demands the suggested presence of an audience with which the monologist enters into debate; in *In Memoriam* the 'doubts' and 'discouragements' defined by Arnold are manifest in the colloquy with the self, one which allows the poetic voice to distance itself from doubt through demanding 'Peace; come away'. In 'The City of Dreadful Night' dialogue with the self also allows the poetic voice to express doubts and fears while, at the same time, through the assumption of voices of authority (for example, the persona of the prophet) investing responses to a meaningless existence with some form of gravitas. The dialogue with the self therefore both demonstrates Arnold's fears about the nature of poetry and allows the poetic voice to slip away from representations of complete despair. By contrast, in 'To Seem the Stranger' Hopkins describes an experience that completes his engagement with the most introspective form of Arnold's dialogue, and which, ironically, represents a moment at which speaking, listening and therefore communication of any kind are utterly absent:

> Only what word
> Wisest my heart breeds dark heaven's baffling ban
> Bars or hell's spell thwarts. This to hoard unheard,
> Heard unheeded, leaves me a lonely began.
>
> ('To Seem the Stranger', lines 11–14)

The language is evocative of prohibition ('heaven's ... ban') and disorientation ('baffling'), and once again the concern is with the inadequacy of the self, where the apparent silence of heaven leaves the speaker 'a lonely began'. In the final two words the speaker stresses both his isolation and his failure in terms of potential; the word 'began' is a noun defining the self and also automatically in the past tense. As stated the absence here is one of communication; the inadequacy of the speaker, his isolation and therefore the experience of despair are all attributable to the fact that the words that would bring him presumably into contact with God are 'hoard[ed] unheard' or 'heard unheeded'. The prayer is therefore unuttered or if uttered unheard. Harris, contextualizing the poem in terms of Hopkins's position as a member of a religious order, states that the poem 'chronicles the devastating breakdown of all coherences in Hopkins' life'.[39] The poem, considering the 'coherences' suggested by Harris, therefore documents Hopkins's feeling of distance from self, family and nation, and distance from God that is defined by his inability to speak or be heard. For Tennyson and Thomson the presence of an Arnoldian dialogue within their respective poems allows them some relief from despair and the ability to escape poetically from the possibility of religious madness. For Hopkins, the 'dialogue of the mind with itself' represents the extent to which he feels abandoned by a God who should give meaning to his existence, his inability to communicate with this God, the subsequent dislocation of identity that this involves, and the feelings of anguish and despair that stem from this experience.

Part III

Infected ecstasy: addiction and modernity in the work of Thomas De Quincey, Alfred Tennyson, Christina Rossetti and Bram Stoker

Introduction

> Amongst the circumstances that more immediately determine those forms of cerebral disorder which manifest themselves in insanity, is a vitiated state of the blood ... when the blood has adventitious ingredients of several kinds mingled with it, the function of various organs becomes perverted, and especially those of the brain and nervous system ... Alcohol, opium, cannabis, indica, and chloroform, amongst other ingredients, act upon the brain and nervous system.[1]

> The *flâneur* is someone abandoned in the crowd. In this he shares the situation of the commodity. He is not aware of this special situation, but this does not diminish its effect on him and it permeates him blissfully like a narcotic that can compensate him for many humiliations. The intoxication to which the *flâneur* surrenders is the intoxication of the commodity around which surges the stream of customers.[2]

Addiction manifests itself in a variety of forms in social, cultural and medical conceptions of deviancy or antisocial behaviour during the nineteenth century: drug addiction, alcoholism, compulsive criminal behaviour, addictive sexual masturbation, even cannibalism, can all be cited as examples.[3] According to William Black's assessment of the most frequent causes of admission to Bedlam the category 'Drink and Intoxication' constitutes the seventh (out of sixteen classifications) highest catalyst for insanity, represented by fifty-eight cases in the hospital.[4] Intoxication is, obviously, a reference to the results of excessive indulgence in alcohol and drugs, suggesting in both cases overconsumption or addiction.[5] Curiously Black's tabulations, although drawing explicit attention to the role of alcohol, do not include the clear identification of clinically addictive or consciousness-altering narcotics, significant in that such drugs as opium and its alcoholic tincture laudanum were as easily available, if not more available, than alcohol. The result is that the consumption of such drugs perhaps goes without saying. Victoria Berridge and Griffith Edwards, in *Opium and the People: Opiate Use in Nineteenth Century England*, note of the drug:

> The opium preparations on sale and stocked by chemists' shops were numerous. There were opium pills ... opiate lozenges, compound powder of opium, opiate confection, opiate plaster, opium enema, opium liniment, vinegar of opium and wine of opium. There was the famous tincture of opium ... known as laudanum, which had wide spread popular sale ... The dried capsules of the poppy were used, as were poppy fomentation, syrup of white poppies and extract of poppy.[6]

Noting that '[o]pium was an everyday part of the drug trade', Berridge and Edwards also indicate the correlation between opium and a *laissez-faire* market economy prior to the 1868 Pharmacy Act, when the sale of drugs was limited to professional pharmacists:

> Opium ... passed through a mechanism of wholesaling and retailing which finally brought it within reach of the ordinary consumer of the drug. Until 1868, there were no bars on the process at all (and even after 1868 restrictions were quite minimal) ... opium was used not just medically but for non-medical reasons as well at all levels of society.[7]

What Berridge and Edwards imply is both the relative ubiquity of opium as a form of medication and the fact that as well as having a medicinal value it was utilized for recreational purposes. In fact opium and laudanum had an almost universal currency as medication during the early and mid-nineteenth century; this fact is easily demonstrated by the presence of opium as a pacifier in cordials – such as 'Godfrey's Cordial', 'Dalbey's Caminative', 'McMunn's Elixir', 'Batley's Sedative Solution' and 'Mother Bailey's Quieting Syrup' – given to children in the nineteenth century.[8] Similarly there is evidence that opium was used as a mild stimulant or sedative in the higher echelons of society; William Wilberforce and Gladstone were known to take opium and laudanum respectively prior to making speeches in Parliament.[9]

Nonetheless addiction, or at least overindulgence, was significant enough an issue to warrant an assessment of the forms that it took by doctors and surgeons writing during the nineteenth century. It is also a significant issue that with the emergence of a psychiatric exploration of the physiological and mental dangers involved in addiction, medical writers also felt obliged to foreground warnings about the moral perils implicit in such activities. George Man Burrows, in his *Commentaries on ... Insanity* published in 1828, restricts his judgement of addiction to material substances to alcohol; however, he suggests an interesting correlation between alcohol abuse and 'moral vice':

> Habitual drunkenness is a moral lesion, productive among the common people of the larger number of the insane. Excessive venery is another fruitful source. So, in fact, in peculiar constitutions, is indulgence to excess in any sensual pleasure. A certain solitary vice, which youth are so apt to contract through bad example, is a wide-spreading cause of insanity.[10]

Burrows smoothly shifts his argument, through association, from alcoholism to masturbation (the 'moral vice') via 'excessive venery', in fact 'excess in any sensual pleasure'. In Burrows's context addiction to alcohol can be equated not only with sexual overindulgence but also with deviant sexual overindulgence. Alcoholism is prevalent among 'the larger number of the insane' and masturbation is a 'wide-spreading cause of insanity' – both are linked by the stress on an abundance of cases – however, it is the spread of masturbation that Burrows likens to an infection. Ten years later William Willis Moseley, in *Eleven Chapters on Nervous and Mental Complaints*, expands the slender categorization of alcohol, and approaches the notion of addiction and its relationship with insanity from a more physiological perspective:

> [that] the liquids which have an immediate influence on the organ of the brain, should produce disease in it, can create no surprise. Man is so constituted, that all liquids which contain *alcohol* act immediately on the brain, through nerves which it meets with in the *mouth* and in the *throat*, and in its passage to as well as when it arrives in the stomach.[11]

What Moseley indicates is the physical correlation, primarily an oral one, between the consumption, circulation and effect of alcohol in relation to the brain. Nonetheless, he also stresses the moral debilitation involved in overconsumption and indulgence:

> Inebriation is temporary madness. If often repeated it may become permanent madness ... They [intoxicating liquids] may brighten the eye for the moment, but they will inflict deadly wounds in the head and the heart by and by.[12]

Moseley's vision of the results of alcoholic excess is a hyperbolically deterrent one; overconsumption leads to 'permanent madness', and the effects are 'deadly wounds'. These effects are manifest in the physical and mental harms done to the 'head' and the emotional and moral harms on the 'heart'. The definitions of inebriation and intoxication presented by Moseley are still restricted to the effects of drunkenness and 'all liquids which contain *alcohol*'. It is not until 1853, with Daniel Noble's *Elements of Psychological Medicine*, that the list of 'adventitious ingredients' that are capable of 'vitiat[ing] ... the blood' is increased to include 'opium, cannabis, indica, and chloroform'. In Noble's statement, cited at the start of this section, the emphasis on the debilitating, addictive qualities of these substances is one firmly rooted in their effect on the body itself – what we are presented with are narcotics that determine insanity through infection of the blood and perversion of the organs. Where Burrows refers to masturbation as the contaminating addiction, the one that is 'wide-spreading' and therefore a moral threat to the populace, Noble shifts addiction into a physical context and relocates infection and contamination in the bloodstream.

Nonetheless, it seems ironically significant that opium was used to counteract the effects of too much drinking; as Berridge and Edwards point out, opium 'appears to have been a widespread popular means of controlling and counteracting excessive drinking. The number of cases where overdoses of opium were accidentally taken in these circumstances is some indication of this'.[13] Berridge and Edwards indicate the use of opium as self-medication, its utilization as a hangover cure, and also the correlation between the moral vice of excessive drink and opium as its cure. What is also significant is that Berridge and Edwards note that it is eminently possible to overdose (to overconsume) when taking opium. The overdose suggests one of two things: either a lack of familiarity with the drug or addiction to it resulting in increasing tolerance of its effects and therefore the necessity of taking increasing doses thereby risking an overdose.[14] Opium, at the same time as being circulated as medication, is acknowledged as potentially fatal; the consequences of addiction are death by overdose or the madness explored by Moseley and Noble. It is therefore similarly ironic that opium was used in significant proportions in the treatment of the insane. Roy Porter, in *Mind Forg'd Manacles*, notes that at Manchester Lunatics Hospital, instituted in 1767, treatment of patients involved mechanical restraint, blood-letting, purges and drugs – '[o]pium was to be given in "large doses" for maniacs'.[15] Porter also notes that applications of opium treatments were popular for nervous conditions, small doses were given to stimulate the nerves in depressives and large doses as sedatives for maniacs. By the end of the eighteenth and at the start of the nineteenth century Porter states that '[p]hysicians such as Erasmus Darwin prescribed opium in quite heroic doses'.[16]

However, the condition of addiction to drugs, certainly as a medical classification, is in broad terms a twentieth-century definition. In fact in the early to mid nineteenth century the *notion* of being addicted to opium was largely unknown; its popularity as medication and its use in counteracting the effects of that other addictive stimulant alcohol reflects this. As Berridge and Edwards state:

> Generally, dependence on opium went largely unrecognised, either by the consumers themselves or by those who sold opium to them. Doctors could be quite unaware of the drugs the patients they saw briefly were using in self-medication. The only occasion on which the situation was made clear to both user and the medical profession was when supplies were for some reason cut off.[17]

In effect the problems of addiction in the nineteenth century existed in a social rather than medical context; for example, the opium addict could build up a dosage sufficiently strong enough to prove financially crippling or noticeably harm work capacity. Again Berridge and Edwards indicate the often unlocated nature of drug addiction in the nineteenth century:

> the fact that addiction itself was not sharply conceptualised for the larger part of the century, in many of the relevant debates and social movements, meant that the addict did not suffer the sort of secondary social damage which comes from labelling and stigma,

> and which has been so much part of the present-day reaction of the Western world to drug-taking and the drug-taker.[18]

What is clear is that there is a relative inconsistency in the apprehension and utilization of narcotics like opium during the nineteenth century; it is simultaneously a prescribed and self-medicated drug, overindulgence in it can cause insanity yet lunatics are given huge doses of it, it is equated with alcohol as an addictive stimulant and is popularly used as a 'cure' for inebriation. As much as its effects are capable of disorientating consciousness and destabilizing individual identity, there is something unsituated about opium and opium addiction itself during the Regency and Victorian periods. My concern in this section of the book is with the unlocated nature – by which I mean the manner in which narcotic intoxication in medical, social and cultural representation, transcends, transgresses and evades strict definition – of both opium and the varied manifestations of addiction in the nineteenth century, with opium as an imported commodity, with its status as both remedy and infection, with its ability to stimulate insanity, and with the oscillation of its effects between ecstasy and insanity.

The process of addiction, to opium and other stimulative or narcotic substances, can be explicitly detected in texts of the period. However, it is useful to note that in general references to opium use are presented in a negative light; the medicinal purposes of the drug are rarely alluded to other than in an oblique manner, and its possible recreational values are presented as indulgent or depraved. Just as the nineteenth-century physician represents overindulgence as a moral malady, so too the nineteenth-century writer highlights the negative connotations of indulgence in narcotics or alcohol. On the whole, there is little sense of an attempt to evaluate addiction, address its causes, or indicate the widespread consumption of opium. As in society, opium in nineteenth-century culture is represented as having an unlocated status oscillating between medication and leisure and therefore indicative of its paradoxical qualities; it is a staple hunger suppressant for the impoverished industrial labouring classes and also a recreational but degenerate substance for the upper middle classes. In Elizabeth Gaskell's Industrial Novel *Mary Barton*, the heroine's father John Barton turns to opium use mainly as a result of the rejection of the Chartist petition represented in a text concerned with industrialization in the 1840s. Gaskell presents Barton's addiction in a significantly moral context, roughly equatable with the moral vigour of Burrows, Moseley and Noble. Of Barton's thoughts Gaskell states:

> It is true, much of their morbid power might be ascribed to the use of opium. But before you blame too harshly this use, or rather abuse, try a hopeless life, with daily cravings of the body for food. Try, not alone being without hope yourself, but seeing all around you reduced to the same despair, arising from the same circumstances ... Would you not be glad to forget life, and its burdens? And opium gives forgetfulness for a time.
>
> It is true they who thus purchase it pay dearly for their oblivion; but can you expect the uneducated to count the cost of their whistle? Poor wretches! They pay a heavy price. Days of oppressive weariness and languor, whose realities have the feeble sickliness of dreams; nights whose dreams are fierce realities of agony; sinking health, tottering frames, incipient madness, and worse, the *consciousness* of incipient madness; this is the price of their whistle.[19]

Barton's addiction (for Gaskell's reference to 'abuse' suggests an inappropriate consumption of the drug) acts as a prelude to the murder of young Harry Carson, a mill-owner's son. It also provides a reason for the violent actions undertaken by Barton; Gaskell suggests that it is not only social injustice that is responsible for uncontained and homicidal action but anti-social habits as well. As a result Barton is represented later in the text as both guilt-racked murderer and degraded addict:

> No haunting ghost could have had less of the energy of life in its involuntary motions than he, who, nevertheless, went on with the same measured clock-work tread, until the door of his own house was reached. And then he disappeared, and the latch fell feebly to, and made a faint and wavering sound breaking the solemn silence of the night. Then all again was still.[20]

There is something strange emerging in Gaskell's text in terms of her representation of addiction and addicts. In the first section quoted from the book, a somewhat conventional depiction and discussion of the moral anxieties implicit for the middle class writer is offered; addiction is not only a disease, but also one that is explicitly associated with madness as well as ailing physical health. Gaskell strives to avoid apportioning blame, urging the reader to resist making emphatic judgements unless they have experienced the lot of the impoverished and starving working man; nonetheless, opium is still demonized as open to abuse. What is significant is the association between opium and cost; Gaskell mentions that the users who 'purchase' the drug must 'pay dearly for their oblivion', that they 'pay a heavy price' and have to 'count the cost' of their dependency, that in the end addiction has a 'price'. The emphasis on this cost is both moral and financial – that overindulgence bears with it its own moral cost and that, as stated above, addiction can prove financially crippling and noticeably impede the ability to work. However, Gaskell is emphatic in her repetition of notions of cost, and as a result opium becomes a market commodity in the text, the product of a matrix of production and consumption. In the second quotation Gaskell implies something even stranger about the addict. Addict and murderer are both anti-social enough categories, yet here Gaskell turns Barton into a spectre – someone who has less energy than a 'haunting ghost' and who 'disappeared' rather than enters his own home. Reading the text literally Barton passes through the doorway, yet, in striving for an unsettling effect in her depiction of a man who will soon be dead, there is a textual gap between the disappearance of Barton and the mechanical motion of the door – like a spectre he just vanishes. Gaskell gives her addict a Gothic resonance. He becomes an undead presence in the text, a ghost and yet not quite a ghost; at the same time she likens him to an automaton who walks with 'the same clock-work tread'. In *Mary Barton* opium and addiction become associated with homicidal inclinations, money and, ultimately, the Gothic when John Barton slides into the closing stages of the novel as a ghostly hybrid of Dracula and Frankenstein's creature.[21] In a text that exists in a transitional and dislocating historical moment – depicting this in its oscillation between rural idyll and urban realism, industrial labour and the skilled artisan, city poor and suburban *nouveaux riche*, and ultimately which cannot determine its own status as either 'industrial' novel or romance – opium, also of an indeterminate nature, inhabits the text as a Gothic, spectral presence.

In this section my main concern is with the nature of addiction in nineteenth century texts and the effect that this condition has upon identity and consciousness. Apart from Thomas De Quincey's *Confessions of an English Opium Eater*, first published in 1821, the texts that I will be addressing do not explicitly refer to that most prominently abused of nineteenth-century pharmaceuticals. That said, the process of addiction and the correlative issues that stem from or are associated with the condition can be equated with important factors implicit in the sale and consumption of opium – for example, madness, criminality, capital, imperialism and decentred, unstable states of consciousness. These issues, as I have just demonstrated, can be detected in the hints at the subversive potential possessed by opium addiction posited by Gaskell in *Mary Barton*. In Alfred Tennyson's 'The Lotos Eaters' addiction and altered consciousness are associated with the overconsumption of the mysterious lotos flower; however, if the poem is read in conjunction with other poems written in the 1830s and published in 1842, certain issues about imperialism, colonial expansion (implicitly associated with the market force of opium as I will demonstrate later in this argument) and the dominant ideology of the Victorian bourgeois hegemony become evident. Such issues can also be detected in the dreams, nightmares and fears of the Orient, Egypt and China manifest in the hallucinations represented in De Quincey's *Confessions*. In Christina Rossetti's poem 'Goblin Market' (from *Goblin Market and Other Poems*, published in 1862) addiction involves the consumption of forbidden goblin fruit, bought at a market, and sold by strange and exotic semi-human creatures. The text is located in a world that oscillates between a centralized domestic world and a marginal, mysterious world represented by the alien economic locus of the market. Rossetti's poem is not a literal depiction of addiction; nonetheless, the ramifications of the fruit offered by the goblins in terms of economic status, addictive properties and the creation of and tension between centralized and marginalized worlds present a cogent metaphor for the processes, symptoms and cultural connotations of addiction. In addition 'Goblin Market' for a number of reasons that I will explore with greater detail later in this section, can be read as a vampiric text. The vampire, both as a cultural motif and through its presence in Bram Stoker's *Dracula* (1897), becomes an ideal metaphor for the addict in the nineteenth century. The vampire's parasitic and infectious properties can be equated with both narcotic and addict, for example, the vampire draws life from the overconsumption of blood and simultaneously infects its victim's blood. However, there are a multitude of features manifest in vampirism and Stoker's novel that resonate with addiction and in particular the opium trade in the nineteenth century. *Dracula* implicitly involves a fear of the infection of the individual *and* of late nineteenth-century

London society as a whole by a poisonous foreign source imported from the mysterious east. In addition much of the vampire's ability to infiltrate even the most sacrosanct of institutions in Victorian society (the home or the female body) is dependent upon its economic capacity. It has to be remembered that Marx compares capitalism, in *Capital* (volume 1 was first published 1867), to a vampire that lives parasitically by exploiting living labour, and frequently uses other Gothic similes and tropes to indicate the negative aspects of capital and capitalism.[22] Consequently, although this section begins with an exploration of the correlation between addiction and madness in the nineteenth century, there are a number of other issues that have to be addressed in the course of this discussion. Prominent amongst these are the commodity status of addictive substances, the Gothic tropes manifest in cultural representation of addiction, and anxiety with regard to those areas from which these substances are imported, and therefore the possible instability and fragility of national as well as individual identity in nineteenth-century modernity. Ultimately addiction and madness are but features of a broader narrative of disintegration, disidentity and haunting.

8 A change in physical economy: Thomas De Quincey's confession

> Whether desperate or not, however, the issue of the struggle in 1813 was what I have mentioned; and from this date, the reader is to consider me as a regular and confirmed opium-eater, of whom to ask whether on any particular day he had or had not taken opium, would be to ask whether his lungs had performed respiration, or the heart fulfilled its functions.[1]

In his singular account of addiction, *Confessions of an English Opium Eater*, Thomas De Quincey – journalist, essayist, contributor to *Blackwood's Magazine*, budding political economist, friend of the Lake Poets, and opium user *par excellence* – indicates that 1813 is the year that marks his descent into opium addiction, and the ensuing physical change that takes place within his body.[2] The condition suggested is one wherein opium consumption seems to become as essential, even as natural, to him as respiration and circulation. Apart from the fact that it heralds De Quincey's daily dependence on the drug and the hallucinatory mania that dominates the final sections of the text, 1813 seems to be a rather strange year to choose to announce his addiction; in fact De Quincey suggests that it was his 'happiest year'.[3] Nonetheless, as the writer indicates, this year provides the basis for an apprehension of physical transformation, where opium becomes apparently as intrinsic to the user's sense of self as bodily functions. This state of being is later defined by De Quincey as a change in 'physical economy', the main symptom of which is 'the re-awakening of a state of eye generally incident to childhood or exalted states of irritability'.[4] The condition that De Quincey refers to here is the initial onset of the visions that become more detailed in the course of the narrative, culminating in the waking dreams symptomatic of acute opium addiction. What is significant here, however, is the phrasing used by De Quincey to define his physiological transformation; it is significant that he alludes to his body as a 'physical economy' in a text so dominated by economics and economies.

The title chosen by De Quincey for his opium narrative invites comparisons with Rousseau's posthumous *Confessions* of 1781–88. However De Quincey, at the start of his work, refutes any connection between his and Rousseau's writing:

> Nothing, indeed, is more revolting to English feelings, than the spectacle of a human being obtruding on our notice his moral ulcers or scars, and tearing away that 'decent drapery', which time, or indulgence to human frailty, may have drawn over them ... for any such acts of gratuitous self-humiliation from those who can be supposed in sympathy with the decent and self-respecting part of society, we must look to French literature, or to that part of the German, which is tainted with the spurious and defective sensibility of the French.[5]

There is both distrust and disparagement of the foreign at work here in the presentation of the 'spurious and defective sensibility of the French', together with an implicit confidence in the moral superiority of the English, an issue that can be detected in De Quincey's identification of himself as an '*English* Opium Eater' (my emphasis) and which I will return to later in this discussion regarding De Quincey's apprehension of the Orient. Rather than taking its inspiration from the Rousseauian confession, De Quincey's account of his opium experience perhaps owes more to the conversion narratives of the evangelical and dissenting sects, and indeed religion and religious metaphor appear in a variety of significant manifestations in the *Confessions*.[6] Indeed, rather than being purely an account of addiction or even an autobiography, De Quincey's *Confessions* cover a wide variety of subjects including the nature of dreams, the influences of childhood and De Quincey's reading interests. In terms of the latter, as De Quincey's addiction starts to reach its height he turns to reading political economy and in particular David Ricardo's *Principles of Political Economy and Taxation* of 1817. He notes that he takes to this as his opium consumption impedes his capacity to study mathematics and read philosophy, stating:

> In this state of imbecility, I had, for amusement, turned my attention to political economy; my understanding, which formerly had been as active and restless as a hyena, could not, I suppose ... sink

> into utter lethargy; and political economy offers this advantage to a person in my state, that though it is eminently an organic science (no part, that is to say, but what acts on the whole, as the whole again reacts on each part), yet the several parts may be detached and contemplated singly.[7]

In fact De Quincey, through reading Ricardo, eventually turns to writing his own work, *Prolegomena to All Future Systems of Political Economy*, drolly noting that 'I hope it will not be found redolent of opium; though indeed, to most people, the subject itself is a sufficient opiate'.[8] What is significant here is that De Quincey gives political economy an 'organic' status, drawing attention to the fact that, like an organism, the parts that constitute its main principles are interrelated. Ultimately it is his study of political economy that leads to a contemplation of the change in his body and the definition of it as a physical economy; indeed, it seems as though economic systems, the body and opium are all connected. However, in spite of the fact that De Quincey identifies 1813 as the year that initiates his change in 'physical economy', in fact the change – which brings the body, economics and opium into conjunction – takes place much earlier in the narrative chronology of the text, and even prior to De Quincey's induction into opium consumption. This ambivalence regarding dates, events and processes of cause and effect is typical of De Quincey's account of his addiction and its rather elusive status; one need only refer to the title of the *Confessions*, which identifies De Quincey as an 'Opium *Eater*' (my emphasis), to see this demonstrated. In reality he took opium in its liquid form as laudanum; De Quincey was effectively an opium *drinker*, identifying himself as such when he first enters a druggists and purchases 'the tincture of opium'.[9]

The real change in De Quincey's 'physical economy', and the one that instigates his addiction to opium, takes place during his account of the early poverty-stricken years that he spent in Wales and on the streets of London. De Quincey notes, after leaving his lodgings in Bangor, that

> In a fortnight I was reduced to short allowance; that is, I could allow myself only one meal a day. From the keen appetite produced by constant exercise, and mountain air, acting on a youthful stomach, I soon began to suffer greatly on this slender regimen; for the single meal, which I could venture to order, was coffee or tea.[10]

Soon after this, mentioning his move to London, he states:

> I now suffered, for upwards of sixteen weeks, the physical anguish of hunger in various degrees of intensity; but as bitter, perhaps, as ever human being can has suffered who has survived it ... a few fragments of bread from the breakfast-table of one individual (who supposed me to be ill, but did not know of my being in utter want), and these at uncertain intervals, constituted my whole support.[11]

Here De Quincey's own finances and his physical economy are intrinsically linked – his fiscal condition is such that it has a direct effect upon his body, causing a stomach ailment that later in life inspires him to turn to opium consumption. Indeed, his changed physical state, and the deprivation of hunger, provoke dreams 'which were only not so awful as those which I shall have to describe hereafter as produced by opium'.[12] Consequently a correlation between financial capacity, changed physical states and opium and the dreams that stem from its use is clearly established by De Quincey prior to his representation of the effects of opium taking. V .A. De Luca, in his analysis of De Quincey's imaginative writings, argues that he 'offers the narrative of incidents in Wales and London following his flight from school, not for its own sake, but to "furnish the key" to some of his opium dreams'.[13] Although De Luca does acknowledge that De Quincey 'becomes addicted from an increased dosage designed to relieve a stomach ailment', his interpretation of the account of the Wales and London experiences are rather reductive.[14] He refers to 'the sometimes tedious accounts of his financial preoccupations', when in fact De Quincey's financial status and preoccupations, whether consciously intended to be so or not, are crucial to his account of addiction and the changes, physical and mental, that are involved in it.[15] In effect the passages that deal with De Quincey's financial privations in London provide an important stimulus for an analysis of the problems of identity, and all that these entail, manifest in the discourse of addiction.

The crucial passage that ties all these issues together takes place when De Quincey provides an account of going to a Jewish money-lender, as a last desperate measure, to borrow money using his father's will and his own expectations as a guarantee. It is worth quoting the observations at length:

> To this Jew, and to other advertising money-lenders (some of

> whom were, I believe, also Jews), I had introduced myself with an account of my expectations; which account, on examining my father's will at Doctor's Commons, they had ascertained to be correct. The person there mentioned as the second son of ——, was found to have all the claims (or more than all) that I had stated: but one question still remained, which the faces of the Jews pretty significantly suggested, – was *I* that person? This doubt had never occurred to me as a possible one ... It was strange to me to find my own self, *materialiter* considered (so I expressed it, for I doted on logical accuracy of distinctions), accused, or at least suspected of counterfeiting my own self, *formaliter* considered.[16]

There is a complex debate regarding inheritance, capital and identity taking place at this point in De Quincey's text, one that is particularly significant when the similarity with issues of inheritance in the Gothic texts of Part I of this book is considered. For the purposes of the present argument, and in terms of the notion of a physical economy, the body becomes a site which demonstrates financial deprivation; that is De Quincey's physical state transparently reveals his poverty. His body indicates a negative change in economy. More importantly this changed physical state, the one that causes his opium addiction *and* his compulsion to seek out the moneylender, involves an appearance that provokes the Jewish moneylender to doubt that De Quincey is actually who he claims to be. In short, this exchange initiates the crisis of identity that gains momentum in De Quincey's text; this initial change in physical economy instigates the possibility that De Quincey is capable of 'counterfeiting my own self'. A fixed sense of identity is disrupted through economic limitations, and as a result it is hinted that De Quincey is his own double, his own *doppelgänger*. In spite of his claim to dote 'on logical accuracy of distinctions' and his employment of a formal legal vocabulary, he hints at a Gothic narrative that will become increasingly significant in the discourse of addiction. As De Quincey's *Confessions* progress it becomes more and more evident that this is a text which revolves around notions of doubling and repetition; just as the disturbed dreams of hunger predict the opium hallucinations so too the stomach ailment inspires the opium reliance ten years later, providing a link between two changes in physical economies.

This hint at the possibility of an unstable identity seems strange given that the identity of the Opium Eater seems so assured and stable.

As stated, De Quincey has clearly established himself, both in the title of his *Confessions* and in the disparaging treatment of the French, amongst others, as an Englishman. The *Confessions*, certainly if we read them as autobiographical, seem to be trying to affirm the national identity of the speaker. This affirmation and insistence upon a stable identity can also be detected in De Quincey's representation of himself as an opium taker. During the height of his experiences of opium consumption as pleasurable, De Quincey insistently portrays himself as a bourgeois gentleman of leisure wandering through the streets of London at the weekend. In his account of these perambulations a tension emerges between the educated, comfortable opium eater (De Quincey) and the poor, with the former conveniently forgetting that these streets were the location for his own economic privation. The result is a casual and voyeuristic gaze into the street life of the capital provided by a detached voice which explicitly states that the wandering takes place under the influence of opium:

> Now Saturday night is the season for the chief, regular, and periodic rest to the poor ... I feel always, on a Saturday night, as though I also were released from some yoke labour, had some wages to receive, and some luxury of repose to enjoy. For the sake, therefore, of witnessing, upon as large a scale as possible, a spectacle with which my sympathy was so entire, I used often, on Saturday nights, after I had taken opium, to wander forth, without much regarding the direction or the distance, to all the markets, and other parts of London, to which the poor resort on a Saturday night, for laying out their wages. Many a family party, consisting of a man, his wife, and sometimes one or two of his children, have I listened to, as they stood consulting on their ways and means or the strength of their exchequer, or the price of household articles. Gradually I became familiar with their wishes, their difficulties, and their opinions ... And, taken generally, I must say, that, in this point at least, the poor are far more philosophic than the rich – that they show a more ready and cheerful submission to what they consider irremediable evils, or irreparable losses. Whenever I saw occasion, or could do it without appearing to be intrusive, I joined their parties; and gave my opinion upon the matter in discussion, which, if not always judicious, was always received indulgently. If wages were a little higher, or expected to be so, or the quartern loaf a little lower, or it was reported that onions and butter were expected to fall, I was

> glad: yet, if the contrary were, I drew from opium some means of consoling myself ... Some of these rambles led me to great distances: for an opium-eater is too happy to observe the motion of time. And sometimes in my attempts to steer homewards, upon nautical principles, by fixing my eye on the pole-star, and seeking ambitiously for a north-west passage, instead of circumnavigating all the capes and headlands I had doubled in my outward voyage, I came suddenly upon such knotty problems of alleys, such enigmatical entries, and such sphinx's riddles of streets ... I could almost have believed, at times, that I must be the first discoverer of some of these *terrae incognitae*, and doubted, whether they had yet been laid down in the modern charts of London ... Thus I have shown that opium does not, of necessity, produce inactivity or torpor; but that on the contrary, it often led me into markets and theatres.[17]

A series of issues emerge from this lengthy extract. Firstly, that the experience of walking the streets of London is presented as taking place under the influence of the narcotic. In addition to this the passage is very much concerned with a discussion about capital: De Quincey provides a comparison between rich and poor, actively representing himself as sympathizing with the poor, becoming 'familiar with their wishes, their difficulties, and their opinions'. What is significant in this is that where De Quincey, in his guise as street walker, sympathizes with the poor he nonetheless remains distanced from them, establishing them as existing in family units debating 'the strength of their exchequer, or the price of household articles' where by contrast he is isolated, individual, overhearing and observing their conversations. In addition, even though De Quincey establishes himself later in the text as having a propensity for political economy, on a street level his knowledge counts for little; he contributes to the debates on the domestic exchequer, but his contributions are 'not always judicious'. Most importantly, if the wages of the poor fall and the price of food rises, then De Quincey, although unhappy for them, 'drew from opium some means of consoling myself'. We can therefore see two functions that opium has; on one level, as is the case with John Barton in Elizabeth Gaskell's novel, opium is used as an appetite suppressant, on another level, as in De Quincey's case at this point in the *Confessions*, opium is used for recreational purposes by the bourgeois perambulator. It is ironic that De Quincey should use the drug, his consumption of which stems directly from his own poverty on the streets of London, to evade the privations of the families that he views as he carelessly wanders through the city. Nonetheless, there is something in drug consumption and addiction that correlates both with poverty and with the cosmopolitan world of the market and the theatre. However, De Quincey, who has stressed that his identity is firmly tied up with being English, who has pointed out his integrity on the first page of his *Confessions* compared to that of his French contemporaries, and who has suggested that his own experiences of hunger were 'as bitter, perhaps, as ever any human being can have suffered who has survived it', comes across as *dilettante* in his treatment of the poor during this episode. It would seem that the speaker in the *Confessions* does not have as clearly defined an identity as suggested, and that part of the process of addiction in this text involves a fragmentation of identity in spite of the intentions of the addict. However, in this extract De Quincey does seem to have a clearly *recognizable* identity; in effect the experience that he depicts is uncannily reminiscent of the dandy *flâneur* of Walter Benjamin.

It is significant that Benjamin's assessment of the *flâneur* should be found in his work on the French poet Baudelaire. Benjamin describes the dandy *flâneur* at home in the streets and the arcades of mid-nineteenth-century Paris; quoting an illustrated guide to Paris of 1852, he states:

> 'The arcades, a rather recent invention of industrial luxury ... are glass-covered, marble-panelled passageways, which are lighted from above, are lined with the most elegant shops so that such an arcade is a city, even a world, in miniature.' It is in this world that the *flâneur* is at home; he provides 'the favourite sojourn of the strollers and the smokers, the stamping ground of all sorts of little *metiers*', with its chronicler and its philosopher ... The street becomes a dwelling for the *flâneur*; he is as much at home among the facades of houses as a citizen in his four walls ... The walls are the desk against which he presses his notebook; news-stands are his libraries and the terraces of cafés are the balconies from which he looks down on his household after his work is done.[18]

Like De Quincey, the *flâneur* is a street walker, as at home on the streets as 'a citizen in his four walls'; like De Quincey the dandy *flâneur* is therefore also outside the domestic unit. In addition, just as Benjamin describes the *flâneur*'s environment as a 'world', so too De

Quincey, in his night-time opium wanderings, describes the streets of London in terms of an uncharted world with its own 'capes and headlands' that have to be circumnavigated , in fact as a '*terrae incognitae*'. What Benjamin also draws attention to is the leisure of the *flâneur*, who is, like De Quincey, a reader and a writer. Just as De Quincey's attempt to give his opinion on the domestic economy is 'not always judicious' because he is outside the domestic, so too the *flâneur* is incapable of participating in work in the conventional sense; his workplace is not the mercantile office, the shop, the study, the university or the factory, but the street and that product of 'industrial luxury', the arcade. The comparison between the two is itself reminiscent of Richard Dellamora's description of the dandy as middle class, who, in a phrase resonant with De Quincey's intoxication, 'consumes to excess while producing little or nothing'. The objection can be made that De Quincey's *Confessions* predate the *flâneur*, who in Benjamin's definition, taking into consideration the dates when Baudelaire was writing (from the late 1840s onwards), is a mid-nineteenth-century phenomenon.[19] Nonetheless, the three decades that separate the two are sufficiently close – particularly when the relative consistency of social and economic conditions in the nineteenth century as presented by Isobel Armstrong, David Punter and Marshall Berman in the introduction to this project are considered – to suggest that the conditions for the street walking De Quincey and the *flâneur* were not radically dissimilar, although Benjamin does stress that the *flâneur* exists in an environment that emphatically benefits from industrialization. The correlation between the two becomes increasingly resonant when the statement by Benjamin that provides an epigraph for this chapter is taken into consideration:

> The crowd is not only the newest asylum of outlaws; it is also the latest narcotic for those abandoned. The *flâneur* is someone abandoned in the crowd. In this he shares the situation of the commodity. He is not aware of his special situation, but this does not diminish its effect on him and it permeates him blissfully like a narcotic that can compensate him for many humiliations. The intoxication to which the *flâneur* surrenders is the intoxication of the commodity around which surges the stream of customers.[20]

Just as De Quincey represents himself as lost in the crowds of the London streets in a narcotically altered state of consciousness, so too

Benjamin's *flâneur* surrenders to the crowd as to a narcotic; the *flâneur* allows it to permeate him 'blissfully'. De Quincey draws attention to the opium eater being 'too happy' to be aware of the passage of time; there is an obviously similar ecstatic experience shared by the two as they walk the streets. In addition when Benjamin draws attention to the association between *flâneur* and commodity, we can also see that De Quincey has already established a bond between the peregrinating self and economic systems, structures and discourse. It would seem as though it is possible to establish a stable identity for the intoxicated De Quincey that uncannily predicts the Baudelarian *flâneur*. Where De Quincey's peripatetic identity sympathizes and engages in discussions with the poor, thereby evading a clear identification as bourgeois, the *flâneur*, through irregular habits and avoiding the domestic environment, is as inscrutable but as easily identifiable.

However, despite the clear similarities in habits and classification – the unconventional lifestyle, the equation with narcotics – De Quincey ultimately fails to present a convincing case for his identification as a proto-*flâneur*, the main reason being that he swiftly follows the representation of himself as intoxicated street walker by stating:

> Yet, in candour, I will admit that markets and theatres are not the appropriate haunts of the opium-eater, when in the divinest state incident to his enjoyment. In that state, crowds become an oppression to him ... He naturally seeks solitude and silence, as indispensable conditions of those trances, or profoundest reveries, which are the crown and consummation of what opium can do for human nature.[21]

The criterion that Benjamin presents for the *flâneur* is that it is the crowd itself that intoxicates him, whereas De Quincey admits that the natural state for the opium eater is isolation and solitude; in fact 'crowds become an oppression to him'. Another reason that prevents identifying De Quincey as the progenitor for the *flâneur* is that he attests that the opium eater is 'too happy to observe the motion of time'. The issue of De Quincey's problems regarding time will become more significant later in this discussion as, rather than being symptomatic of happiness and ecstasy, it becomes associated with the anxieties of addiction and the fragmenting identity of the addict. Regarding the *flâneur*, De Quincey's lack of consciousness of time is significant in that Baudelaire is possibly, as Marshall Berman suggests, the writer 'who did more than anyone in the nineteenth century to make the men and women of his century aware of themselves as modern'.[22] By contrast De Quincey, certainly in the *Confessions*, both presents himself as increasingly more and more outside time schemes, and frequently invokes the past and classical traditions to describe his life and validate his literary aspirations.[23]

However, just as the change in physical economy that De Quincey identifies as symptomatic of addiction is prefigured by the changed physical self that ultimately initiates the addiction, and the opium dreams themselves echo the dreams that were experienced when De Quincey is starving in London, so too the identification of the writer as a street walker also has a parallel in the first London passages. Here the nomenclature is explicitly given: 'Being myself at this time of necessity a peripatetic, or a walker of the streets, I naturally fell in more frequently with those female peripatetics who are technically called street-walkers.'[24] Again there is a process of doubling taking place in the text, as though De Quincey's account of his life and addiction is involved in a constant act of retrospective repetition. This account of his activities in London introduces one of the more celebrated sections of the *Confessions*, that of De Quincey's relationship with the young prostitute Ann, who he claims to have saved his life 'with a glass of port wine and spices'.[25] I do not intend to enter into a discussion of the dynamics of this relationship, nor to raise the issues implicit in the gender differences between male and female street walkers. Suffice to say that Deborah Epstein Nord observes that

> [t]hose who have theorised about the nature of public experience in the nineteenth-century city have always assumed that the walker of the streets ... was a man ... women – that is, educated middle-class women who might have constructed and articulated an urban consciousness – did not enjoy the freedom to be anonymous or even to be alone out of doors in the metropolis.[26]

Nord explores the position of the prostitute and the *flâneuse* in a series of nineteenth-century texts; regarding De Quincey's *Confessions* she offers two significant observations. Firstly that, during the episodes with Ann, '[t]o the as-yet-unaddicted and uninitiated opium eater London is ... as surreal and as hallucinatory as an opium dream', giving further validation to the idea that the *Confessions* consist of a series of repetitive moments; secondly, that the fallen woman can stand 'as a projection of or analogue to the male stroller's alienated self', and that Ann is De Quincey's 'alter ego' and 'his projection'.[27] Through such processes of repetition and doubling, De Quincey's text starts to haunt itself; that is to say, as the consumption of opium escalates and the identity of the eater becomes increasingly fragile, memories and experiences begin to re-emerge in increasingly spectral manifestations, and the Gothic tropes mentioned earlier start to crystallize. In addition the possibility that De Quincey could 'counterfeit' himself gains increasing resonance, as a variety of alter egos, projections and apparitions start to seep into the text. The consequence of addiction in De Quincey's account is that a seemingly established identity crumbles allowing all sorts of visitations.

An immediate example of this process can be detected in a statement made by De Quincey directly after he presents himself as a stroller in the passage quoted above. He has described himself navigating the uncharted streets of London in a state of opium ecstasy, but adds the following reservation: 'For all this, however, I paid a heavy price in distant years ... the perplexities of my steps in London came back and haunted my sleep, with the feeling of perplexities moral or intellectual, that brought confusion to the reason, or anguish and remorse to the conscience.'[28] The significant point here is that De Quincey is 'haunted' by his memories of London, by the capital in which he had previously both suffered privation and wandered at intoxicated leisure. Again a further repetition takes place; the city that seemed 'hallucinatory' to the pre-addicted De Quincey becomes, not inappropriately, part of his later hallucinations. A point of comparison with the artist Piranesi can be made, whose '*Carceri d'Invenzione*' (Imaginary Prisons) are represented by De Quincey, apparently paraphrasing a comment by Coleridge, as '[r]ecord(ing) the scenery of his own visions during the delirium of a fever'.[29] Describing both Piranesi's imaginary prisons and his own opium dreams, De Quincey writes:

> Creeping along the sides of the walls, you perceived a staircase; and upon it, groping his way upwards, was Piranesi himself: follow the stairs a little further, and you perceive it come to a sudden abrupt termination ... allowing no step onwards to him who had reached the extremity, except into the depths below. Whatever is to become of poor Piranesi, you suppose, at least, that his labours must in some way terminate here. But raise your eyes, and behold a second flight

> of stairs still higher: on which again Piranesi is perceived ... Again elevate your eye, and a still more aerial flight of stairs is beheld: and again is poor Piranesi busy on his aspiring labours: and so on, until the unfinished stairs and Piranesi both are lost in the upper gloom of the hall. – With the same power of endless growth and self-reproduction did my architecture proceed in dreams.[30]

This description tells us more about De Quincey than it does about Piranesi; the labyrinthine nature of the prisons reflects the tortuous routes and alleyways taken by the opium eater in his *flâneur*-style perambulations around London, and which now haunt his dreams. Similarly the observation about 'self-reproduction' can be applied to the variety of ways in which De Quincey represents himself in his text and to the repetition of experiences that consistently occur. As a result, just as De Quincey represents Piranesi as haunting his own engravings, so too he haunts his own text, doomed to wander the streets of the tortuous London that provides a major location and stimulus for both his art and his dreams. Indeed, he has already affirmed his own spectral nature by suggesting that 'markets and theatres are not the appropriate haunts of the opium eater'.

Ultimately De Quincey's opium narrative is one about ghosts and haunting, again evoking the strange Gothic moment in Gaskell's *Mary Barton*.[31] Evidence of this can be detected throughout the opium experience, not just in its later stages, for, as the introduction to Part III suggests, opium, as well as the opium eater, holds a spectral position in its refusal to be located. This can be clearly detected in De Quincey's account of opium; for example, De Quincey ascribes his first encounter with opium to the year 1804 when he visits a druggist on Oxford Street to purchase laudanum and then offers this curious observation:

> he [the druggist] has ever since existed in my mind as the beatific vision of an immortal druggist, sent down to earth on a special mission to myself. And it confirms me in this way of considering him, that, when I next came up to London, I ... found him not: and thus to me, who knew not his name (if indeed he had one) he seemed rather to have vanished from Oxford-street than to have removed in any bodily fashion. The reader may choose to think of him as, possibly, no more than a sublunary druggist: it may be so: but my faith is better: I believe him to have evanesced, or evaporated.[32]

De Quincey gives a quasi-mystical, even divine quality to the druggist who first provides him with opium. Nonetheless, the event seems more ghostly than anything; the individual vanishes in a manner that De Quincey acknowledges is not of any 'bodily fashion', and he goes on to suggest that he has 'evaporated' rather than disappeared in any explicable way.[33] Again the equation between opium, addiction and the supernatural is being affirmed. In fact De Quincey makes the connection more explicit when he defines, in the early stages of addiction, the intoxicated state as one where 'the hopes which blossom in the paths of life, [are] reconciled with the peace which is in the grave', again positing the addict in a liminal site between life and death.[34]

The main experience of being haunted takes place in the text with the introduction of the character known as the Malay. De Quincey's suspicion of the foreign has been well established in the *Confessions* through his disparaging view of French writing; however, his enthusiastically vehement Englishness is particularly reserved for the Orient. Initially this vehemence is focused upon Turks; for example, he states of the pleasures offered by opium:

> I question whether any Turk, of all that ever entered the paradise of opium-eaters, can have had half the pleasure I had. But, indeed, I honour the barbarians too much by supposing them capable of any pleasures approaching to the intellectual ones of an Englishman.[35]

De Quincey's sense of cultural superiority is evident here; he rejects the sensitivity of the Turks to opium intoxication compared to his own as an Englishman. The Turks and Turkey are, however, an important aspect in any debate about opium consumption in the nineteenth century – a factor that will be explored in greater detail when assessing Bram Stoker's *Dracula* – particularly as Turkey was the main source of opium for Britain.[36] However, De Quincey's main anxiety manifests itself in the section about the Malay, a passage as celebrated as that about the prostitute Ann. The encounter with this individual is obviously significant, for De Quincey claims of the incident that 'trifling as it was, the reader will soon meet it again in my dreams, which it influenced more fearfully than could be imagined'.[37] The Malay arrives at the door of De Quincey's cottage in the Lake District, and his presence is immediately perplexing. De Quincey claims that his servant has never had contact with anyone of Oriental extract before, therefore 'recollecting the reputed learning of her master', she seeks out De Quincey 'and gave me to understand that there was a sort of demon below, whom she clearly imagined that my art could exorcise'.[38] The Malay therefore is immediately invested with supernatural qualities, albeit with ones reported by De Quincey, and the demonization of the character is carried through into a comparison between the Malay and the English serving girl:

> a more striking picture there could not be imagined, than the beautiful English face of the girl, and its exquisite fairness, together with her erect and independent attitude contrasted with the sallow and bilious skin of the Malay, enamelled or veneered with mahogany, by marine air, his small, fierce, restless eyes, thin lips, slavish gestures and adorations.[39]

There is a crude racial stereotyping at work here in the contrast between the 'erect and independent' English girl and the 'slavish' Malay which serves to further alienate the Malay, emphasizing how much he is out of place. De Quincey's solution to the barriers in communication is to address him 'in some lines from the *Iliad*; considering that, of such languages as I possessed, Greek, in point of longitude came geographically nearest to an oriental one'.[40] In effect De Quincey uses the symbol of Western culture and learning to combat the unknown and inscrutable East and to demonstrate, to his servant as much as the Malay, his cultural superiority. It would seem that again we are being presented with a secure identity, and one that incorporates both nation and learning. However, this stability is threatened when De Quincey offers the Malay, upon his departure, a piece of opium:

> To him, as an Orientalist, I concluded that opium must be familiar: and the expression of his face convinced me that it was. Nevertheless, I was struck with some little consternation when I saw him suddenly raise his hand to his mouth, and ... bolt the whole, divided into three pieces, at one mouthful. The quantity was enough to kill three dragoons and their horses.[41]

We can either read this as an act of monumental irresponsibility by De Quincey, or suggest that there is something more significant in the action; for example, it must be remembered that De Quincey has already presented himself as consuming opium in heroic proportions, thereby establishing a correlation between himself and the Malay.

The result of this alarmingly generous action is that De Quincey fears that the Malay will be found dead, then convinces himself that he is used to opium, and finally admits that 'this Malay fastened afterwards upon my dreams, and brought other Malays with him worse than himself, that ... led me into a world of troubles'.[42] The Malay, seemingly an addict like De Quincey himself, therefore initiates a series of dreams that repetitively increase. It is this experience with the Malay, innocuous as it seems, that leads to the fragmentation of De Quincey's identity, and inspires the Gothic nightmares that dominate the final sections of the opium narrative. From this point De Quincey represents himself as being dislocated from time, space, history and nation – all the things that have seemed to provide him with a stable identity. In the preliminary stages of his assessment of the pains of opium he states of his observations:

> Some of them point to their own date; some I have dated; and some are undated. Whenever it could answer my purpose to transplant them from the natural or chronological order, I have not scrupled to do so. Sometimes I speak in the present, sometimes in the past tense, Few of the notes, perhaps, were written exactly at the period of time to which they relate; but this can little affect their accuracy; as the impressions were such that they can never fade from my mind.[43]

Despite the fact that De Quincey draws attention to the accuracy of his recollections of the later stages of his opium addiction, we get a sense that he is starting to move outside chronology, and that time-schemes in the narrative are being disrupted. However, as we have already noticed, the past in De Quincey's narrative frequently overshadows the hypothetical present. The notion is further consolidated as concepts of time and space are exploded by overconsumption:

> The sense of space, and in the end, the sense of time, were both powerfully affected. Buildings, landscapes, &c. were exhibited in proportions so vast as the bodily eye is not fitted to receive. Space swelled, and was amplified to an extent of unutterable infinity. This, however, did not disturb me so much as the vast expansion of time; I sometimes seemed to have lived for 70 or 100 years in one night; nay, sometimes had feelings representative of a millennium passed

> in that time, or, however, of a duration far beyond the limits of any human experience.[44]

This sense of dislocation manifests itself in an acceleration in instances of being haunted; when discussing the change in his 'physical economy', the 're-awakening of [the] state of eye' involves seeing 'phantoms' and 'apparitions', and, after the discussion of the art of Piranesi, dreams of architecture are replaced by dreams of lakes that De Quincey claims 'haunted me'.[45] The shift outside temporality and the experience of being haunted reaches its culmination in the return of the Malay, whose spectral quality brings into conjunction a series of issues regarding identity, nation, chronology, sanity and addiction.[46]

In spite of the fact that the return of the Malay marks the culminating point of De Quincey's addiction, his reappearance explicitly provides the catalyst for a debate about nation and Orientalism; the curious and disturbing dreams are shadowed by a discussion of the East. National identity reflects the personal anxieties of the English Opium Eater, manifesting itself in a sense of being haunted by the East. De Quincey notes:

> The Malay has been a fearful enemy for months. I have been every night, through his means, transported into Asiatic scenes. I know not whether others share in my feelings on this point; but I have often thought that if I were compelled to forego England, and to live in China, and among Chinese manners and modes of life and scenery, I should go mad. The causes of my horror lie deep; and some of them must be common to others. Southern Asia, in general, is the seat of awful images and associations.[47]

The Malay is, of course, an apparition; the significance of this statement lies in De Quincey choosing to present his feelings about Asia rather than describing the dreams and scenes. The national anxiety is revealed when he suggests that he 'should go mad' if he was compelled to live in China – it seems as though it is national dislocation that is capable of causing insanity rather than overconsumption of the intoxicating opium. However, De Quincey's reading of the Orient is curiously ambiguous: rather than demonstrating cultural superiority, as in the first encounter with the Malay, there is a clear feeling of awe in place:

> The mere antiquity of Asiatic things, of their institutions, histories, modes of faith, &c. is so impressive, that to me the vast age of the race and name overpowers the sense of youth in the individual. A young Chinese seems to me an antediluvian man renewed. Even Englishmen, though not bred in any knowledge of such institutions, cannot but shudder at the mystic sublimity of *castes* that have flowed apart, and refused to mix, through such immemorial tracts of time; nor can any man fail to be awed by the names of the Ganges, or the Euphrates. It contributes much to these feelings, that Southern Asia is, and has been for thousands of years, the part of the earth most swarming with human life; the great *officina gentium*.[48]

There is something odd taking place in this statement as De Quincey represents himself being overpowered by the antiquity of Asiatic culture, history and institutions.[49] There is an evident sense of admiration in the language used, the antiquity of the East is 'impressive', the age of the races 'overpowers' the individual, there is a 'sublimity' in the *caste* system, and one cannot 'fail to be awed' by the names Ganges and Euphrates. De Quincey even goes so far as to suggest that the Englishman is ignorant when stating that he is 'not bred in any knowledge of such institutions'. However, the significance of this passage lies in the rather coded empathy that we can detect if we place it in the context of other statements made by De Quincey. It is the antiquity of the Asiatic institutions that so impresses him, the 'thousands of years' that they have been established; yet De Quincey has himself claimed that in his opium reveries he feels as though 'a millennium passed ... or ... a duration far beyond the limits of any human experience', thereby suggesting a correlation between the East and his own opium experiences. In addition he describes Southern Asia as the '*officina gentium*', the manufactory of nations; in effect De Quincey is suggesting that even the English have their roots in the East, again bringing that seemingly sure national identity under threat.[50]

The correlation between the Orient and the Occidental opium eater is consolidated when we consider the relationship between De Quincey and the Malay. De Quincey claims, in the closing stages of the *Confessions*:

> Not the opium-eater, but the opium, is the true hero of the tale; and the legitimate centre on which the interest revolves. The object was

> to display the marvellous agency of opium, whether for pleasure or for pain: if that is done, the action of the piece has closed.[51]

This claim is typically misleading; the hero of these *Confessions* is De Quincey and the documentation of the crisis of identity as an addict, as a writer (the text is one written about not writing – all of his projects are abandoned) and as an Englishman. As the rational, rationalizing self fragments, moving outside time, history and nation, the fearful, mysterious Orient starts to seep into the gaps. De Quincey, in his elaboration upon the first change in his physical economy, has already entertained the possibility that the self can be 'counterfeit' or copied. In addition, as Deborah Epstein Nord has indicated, the prostitute Ann can be read as a projection of De Quincey's alienated self, his street walking alter ego; indeed De Quincey even copies himself by appearing in two guises, as a street walker and proto-*flâneur*. As a result the Malay, who haunts De Quincey at the height of his opium consumption, can also be read as his double, as a projection of his addicted self. Again we are dealing with otherness, with the demonized; the alter egos of De Quincey in poverty and addiction are a prostitute and an Oriental. The doubling of De Quincey and the Malay rests upon the fact that, as well as both seeming to be addicted to opium *and* capable of consuming unlikely quantities of the drug, both are spectral; the Malay haunts De Quincey's dreams, but De Quincey has already established that, as an addict, he haunts London. The anxieties about the East therefore represent the anxieties about the alienated self.

The main symptom of this fragmentation is a parallel representation of fears of insanity and the most bizarre visions encountered so far, dictated by anxieties regarding the East in spite of the fact that De Quincey never travelled outside England. The opium eater maintains the suspicion of the Orient:

> In China, over and above what it has in common with the rest of Southern Asia, I am terrified by the modes of life, by the manners, and the barrier of utter abhorrence, and want of sympathy, placed between us by feelings deeper than I can analyse. I could sooner live with lunatics, or brute animals.[52]

The anxiety about the Orient reaches a point of 'utter abhorrence' here, and De Quincey starts to identify himself with the insane, claiming, 'I could sooner live with lunatics.' The dreams reach their pitch with the following hysterical description:

> Under the connecting feeling of tropical heat and vertical sun-lights, I brought together all creatures, birds, beasts, reptiles, all trees and plants, usages and appearances, that are found in all tropical regions, and assembled them together in China or Indostan. From kindred feelings, I soon brought Egypt and all her gods under the same law. I was stared at, hooted at, grinned at chattered at, by monkeys, by paroquets, by cockatoos. I ran into pagodas: and was fixed for centuries, at the summit, or in secret rooms; I was the idol; I was the priest; I was worshipped; I was sacrificed. I fled from the wrath of Brama through all the forests of Asia: Vishnu hated me: Seeva laid wait for me. I came suddenly upon Isis and Osiris: I had done a deed, they said, which the ibis and the crocodile trembled at. I was buried, for a thousand years, in stone coffins with mummies and sphinxes, in narrow chambers at the heart of eternal pyramids. I was kissed with cancerous kisses by crocodiles; and laid, confounded with all unutterable slimy things amongst reeds and Nilotic mud.[53]

What we have here is a chaotic representation of all sorts of aspects of the Orient, a jumble of nation, location, history and religion. De Quincey becomes a spectacle mocked by the creatures of the 'tropical regions', and he is secured in the pagodas of China, the temples of India and the pyramids of Egypt. More bizarrely he is established as a god or priest in India, earning the enmity of the Hindu deities; and, in Egypt, he encounters Isis and Osiris, who inform him that he has performed some unspeakable act for which he is incarcerated in a pyramid 'for a thousand years'. Any sense of perspective has evaporated as De Quincey shifts through time, space, culture and identity, presenting himself as a god at one moment, the next as a debased thing lying 'with all unutterable slimy things' in the Nile. This fragmentation through dream ultimately undermines and disrupts the Romantic project with its emphasis on the mind's ability to present a coherent vision of the world. In the end it is the crocodile that De Quincey obsessively represents as haunting the dreams, claiming '[t]he cursed crocodile became to me the object of more horror than almost all the rest. I was compelled to live with him; and ... for centuries', also stating 'this hideous reptile haunt[ed] my dreams'.[54] In response to these experiences, De Quincey offers this observation:

> I thus give the reader some slight abstraction of my Oriental dreams, which always filled me with such amazement at the monstrous scenery, that horror seemed absorbed, for a while, in sheer astonishment. Sooner or later, came a reflux of feeling that swallowed up the astonishment, and left me, not so much in terror, as in hatred and abomination of what I saw. Over every form, and threat, and punishment, and dim sightless incarceration, brooded a sense of eternity and infinity that drove me into an oppression as of madness.[55]

The initial response to the dreams is 'horror' and 'terror', the traditional responses to Gothic texts and the supernatural, but again the ultimate sense is of being lost within the timeless states of 'eternity and infinity'; the experience, as De Quincey puts it, drives him 'into an oppression as of madness'.

The only way that this disoriented, completely fragmentary identity can be reassembled is by turning towards the reassurance of traditional order. In the spirit of the conversion narratives that inspire the structure of the *Confessions*, De Quincey experiences something very like a religious vision:

> The scene was an Oriental one; and there also it was Easter Sunday, and very early in the morning. And at a vast distance were visible, as a stain upon the horizon, the domes and cupolas of a great city – an image or faint abstraction, caught perhaps in childhood from some picture of Jerusalem. And not a bow-shot from me, upon a stone, and shaded by Judean palms, there sat a woman; and I looked; and it was – Ann! She fixed her eyes upon me earnestly; and I said to her at length: 'So then I have found you at last'.[56]

Ann – the saviour of De Quincey's life in London – is, like the Malay, an apparition, but at this stage a benign one, more angelic than demonic. Separated from her during his youth on the streets of the capital and unable to find her again, what we have here is a symbolic resolution in the words: '[s]o then I have found you at last'. The utterance dispels one anxiety of De Quincey's, his inability to find Ann, and simultaneously reunites the self with its alter ego; the projected, alienated self is restored, seemingly piecing together the fragmented self. More importantly, this vision takes place in an 'Oriental' scene, but involves the presence of the city of Jerusalem. The fragmentation of the self and the condition of opium mania are healed via the agency of traditional order, that is, by orthodox religion and the city of Jerusalem, symbolic centre for Western civilization. Moreover the city itself stands against the 'Oriental' scene, dispelling the fears that have assailed De Quincey at the height of his addiction.[57] De Luca has claimed that '[t]hroughout his work ... De Quincey asserts with forceful and sometimes tiresome iteration his adherence to orthodox Christian doctrine', and here we are presented with a conversion to orthodox Christianity, for De Quincey has previously claimed '[t]his is the doctrine of the true church on the subject of opium: of which church I acknowledge myself to be the only member'.[58] The suggestion is that by reversion to ordered religious belief addiction can be cured and sanity restored. In the *Communist Manifesto* Marx and Engels, under the category of 'Socialist and Communist Literature', note, speaking of 'Conservative, or Bourgeois, Socialism', that the Socialist bourgeoisie

> want all the advantages of modern social conditions without the struggles and dangers necessarily resulting therefrom. They desire the existing state of society minus its revolutionary and disintegrating elements. They wish for a bourgeoisie without the proletariat. The bourgeoisie naturally conceives the world in which it is supreme to be the best; and bourgeois Socialism develops this comfortable conception into variously more or less complete systems. In requiring the proletariat to carry out such a system, and thereby march straightway into the social New Jerusalem, it but requires in reality, that the proletariat should remain within the bounds of existing society, but should cast away all its hateful ideas concerning the bourgeoisie.[59]

De Quincey is clearly not a bourgeois socialist; nonetheless, there is a similarity between the definition of Marx and Engels and the process of reconfiguring the self as described by De Quincey, not least in that both use the image of Jerusalem as a touchstone for a potentially retrogressive step. For Marx and Engels what bourgeois socialism fundamentally wants is a world without disruptive 'disintegrating elements', and one where the bourgeoisie is supreme – this being the 'best' kind of world for them. By comparison, what the disturbed De Quincey desires is a return to a stable world, without the disruptive elements of opium or Orientals; the solution is to turn to the

Jerusalem of orthodox Christianity and to Ann, the friend of his pre-opium past. As Marx and Engels phrase it, this is a 'comfortable conception', and although one point of view is forward looking (the bourgeois socialist's) and the other backward (De Quincey's) both are similarly involved in a process of idealizing *and* securing their own position, and dispersing the threat of the demonized other (the proletariat and the Oriental). Certainly De Quincey's text deals with the fluidity and vaporousness that Marshall Berman suggests defines the art of modernity; nonetheless, despite his ambivalent response to the shifts in identity, nation and time, De Quincey chooses to reaffirm the self through a reversion to the stability of the symbols of traditional Christianity and Western culture. If we are looking for a text that deals with addiction and modernity, we will have to look elsewhere than De Quincey's *Confessions*.

9 Coming like ghosts to trouble joy: Alfred Tennyson's 'The Lotos Eaters'

> We hear it reported of Dryden, and of Fuseli in modern times, that they thought proper to eat raw meat for the sake of obtaining splendid dreams: how much better for such a purpose to have eaten opium, which yet I do not remember that any poet is recorded to have done, except the dramatist Shadwell: and in ancient days, Homer is, I think, rightly reputed to have known the virtues of opium.[1]

Alfred Tennyson's 'The Lotos Eaters' is, given its limitations in terms of length, apparently a less fruitful source for representations of addiction – if indeed it can be read as such – than De Quincey's *Confessions*.[2] Nonetheless, despite being a poem inspired by Homer's *Odyssey* (a text which actually plays a significant if not explicit role, certainly in terms of cultural location, in this work), it raises a series of issues that place the previous analysis of De Quincey into perspective, and which contribute significantly to a debate about addiction and the networks that circulate around it in the context of nineteenth-century literature, culture and modernity. The most immediately noteworthy issue is, once again, the spectral qualities possessed by drug and by addict, characteristics that possess a cumulative significance in this discussion. However, other important features re-emerge in the poem, with notions of nation and class again playing important parts in a consideration of addiction and intoxication.

By using an episode from Homer's *Odyssey* as a source, and a fantastic island visited by Odysseus and his exiled Ithacan crew for the location of a poem set in an unspecified mythical time, it would seem that Tennyson is capable of isolating his poetry and poetic from the immediate concerns of the early decades of the nineteenth century. Indeed by doing so he seems to adhere to the principles set forth by Hallam in his review of Tennyson's *Poems, Chiefly Lyrical* of 1830, where Hallam claims that 'modern poetry, in proportion to its depth and truth, is likely to have little immediate authority over public opinion', suggesting that poetry by the time of Tennyson's early publications is a marginalized and even aloof practice; Hallam goes on to celebrate the fact that Tennyson 'comes before the public unconnected with any political party, or peculiar system of opinions', further emphasizing Tennyson's isolation and imperviousness regarding his own immediate social condition.[3] These comments by Hallam suggest that poetic practice is one that exists outside the parameters of contemporary social milieus. The poet, much like De Quincey's raving Opium Eater, is self-consciously outside society, history and culture, and his art has little bearing upon the mass populace and the experience of modernity. Certainly Tennyson's 'The Lotos Eaters' represents both an episode inspired by the stories of an ancient and distant culture and a condition of being that isolates the individual from its native and familiar territory, suggesting a two-fold distancing from English culture of the 1830s and 40s. However, contesting the issues raised by Hallam, this is not to say that the poem and its projection of an intoxicated state of consciousness is utterly alien to the early Victorian period, for many of the anxieties manifest in the experience of addiction as presented by De Quincey can also be detected in Tennyson's poem. An immediate, if rather oblique, example of this lies in the stimulus for the poem; as stated the poem takes its cue from the Greek classics, that bastion of Western culture used by De Quincey in the *Confessions* to combat the Oriental Malay. The Greek classics do in many ways represent a sense of traditional cultural stability for the English in the nineteenth century, but in addition in the discourse of addiction there is a consistent tension between Greece and the Orient (in particular Turkey) – a conflict manifest in the representation of the Isle of the Lotos Eaters as exotic and Other in the poem. Such debates about national and cultural superiority underpin this discussion of addiction. For the present Hallam's interpretation of the poet's position and Tennyson's writing has been challenged in recent years. Alan Sinfield, in his study of Tennyson, convincingly identifies the position of the poet, and by implication Tennyson, within a social order where notions of culture are dependent upon utilitarian perspectives dictated by a bourgeois hegemony.[4] He argues that poetry in the early parts of the Victorian period is dominated by notions of centres and margins, with the centre representing utilitarian notions of culture and society and which exiles poetry to the margins; as Sinfield states: '... poetry is a valued part of the utilitarian world so long as it does not intrude on the real conditions of life. It is *marginalized*.'[5] The marginalized position of the poet suggests a peripheral, unlocated status, intensified by the fact that, as a poet, Tennyson's own position as Laureate problematizes this; Terry Eagleton, in his preface to Sinfield's work, draws attention to this apparent contradiction, identifying Tennyson as 'on the one hand poet laureate, spokesman for conservative values and Victorian patriarch; on the other hand a radically alienated, deeply subjective refugee from the march of bourgeois progress'.[6] Furthermore, Sinfield, after indicating the marginalized position of the poet, demonstrates how, nonetheless, the poet becomes an agent of dominant bourgeois ideology.[7] This perspective is significant when applied to 'The Lotos Eaters', particularly as the poem can be read (and Sinfield does so) as concerned with marginalization and the remote; however, it seems that there is something disruptive in this poem that challenges both comfortable notions of nation and home, and which Sinfield does not quite allow for, namely, that the poem reaffirms the spectral nature of the addict in nineteenth-century culture and, even, Tennyson's own unlocated position – oscillating between centres and margins – as poet.

Significantly, Sinfield argues that the poem is one that involves the 'destruction of purpose, personality and culture', suggesting that it has an association with the opium traumas represented by De Quincey in the *Confessions*.[8] What is immediately striking about 'The Lotos Eaters' is, in the context of the previous discussion of De Quincey's text, the representation of such dislocation. This experience is not just reserved for 'The Lotos Eaters'; in fact representation of fractured and fragmentary culture and the self is a project that we can see Tennyson embarking upon in many of the poems written in the 1830s and published in the collections of 1833 and 1842, and it is also epitomized in Arnold's 'Dover Beach' as discussed in the introduction to this book. Before engaging upon a detailed analysis of 'The Lotos Eaters' it is worth examining this procedure in 'The Palace of Art', a poem which is traditionally read as documenting the shift from an aesthetic to a moral life. In the poem the speaker builds a dwelling place for his soul which he fills with artistic artefacts and portraits of celebrated cultural figures. The first significant point is that the speaker represents himself as divided – into speaking self and soul – a division further emphasized when, assuming that the speaker is masculine, the soul is presented as feminine. In addition to this, the insubstantial, ephemeral nature of the soul suggests that the palace is haunted, a feature that becomes clearer towards the end of the poem. Certainly dislocation via isolation is emphasized, the soul 'sing[s] her songs alone' (line 160) and speaks of 'God-like isolation' (line 197), a feature that is compounded by the inwardness of the soul who delights in her own song as it echoes back to her.[9] Against this we seem to have a fixed cultural identity established for the works of art that are found in the palace, Tennyson referring to them as stemming from the 'supreme Caucasian mind' (line 126). However, in spite of this seeming security, national and cultural fragmentation is consistently represented within the palace as exhibits range between Christian, Classical and Oriental sources: we are presented with St Cecily (line 99), 'a group of Houris' (line 102), 'mythic Uther's ... son' (line 105), Ganymede (line 121), and Milton, Shakespeare and Dante (lines 133–35) amongst others; cultural fragmentation echoes that of the poetic self. Isobel Armstrong notes that the soul who wanders through the palace

> passes through a series of discrete, enclosed rooms which are a museum or, rather, mausoleum to the whole culture and knowledge of the civilised world, occidental and oriental. Her environment is at once fragmented and overdetermined – not one picture but many, not one religion, but many – so that no myth is privileged above another. Arthurian legend ... the origin of Roman polity, India, home of Sanskrit ... and Greece ... all coexist. These legends of the Caucasian or Indo-European mind are jumbled together, just as portraits of the great philosophers and poets are hung in no historical order. All is contemporary, simultaneous, available, and thus all is estranged.[10]

In Armstrong's account of the poem, national and cultural identities become jumbled in a way that accelerates the Oriental melting pot of religion and nations in the *Confessions* of De Quincey. Here the blurring of territory, history and culture expands out from the East to take on Western myth, literature and religion, dissolving any clear sense of differentiation in a seemingly random and compulsive accumulation of cultural articles. As Armstrong points out historicity is nullified, 'everything is contemporary', resulting in a self-conscious sense of alienation and estrangement. The soul in Tennyson's 'Palace of Art', like De Quincey's Opium Eater, is thus faced with a shift outside time, history and culture. The cultural artefact becomes a 'luxury commodity', something that can be dipped into and out of; in addition, like the capitalist and the colonialist, the Palace of Art 'plunders indiscriminately' in its choice and exhibition of representations.[11] The ultimate result of this dizzying accumulation of cultural effluence, which rather than affirming the superiority of the Caucasian mind indicates a random bombardment by various territories, not all of them European, is that the soul becomes increasingly dislocated. The celebration of isolation within the parameters of an enclosed 'mausoleum to the whole culture and knowledge of the civilised world' becomes solipsistic avarice:

> Communing with herself: 'All these are mine,
> And let the world have peace or wars,
> 'Tis one to me.' (lines 181–83)

Like Hallam's conception of the marginalized artist who has no bearing upon everyday experiences and public opinion, indulging in a practice that is ultimately aloof from 'reality', the soul in Tennyson's poem becomes – willingly – detached from a world outside the palace and careless of what state it might be in.

This accumulation of dislocations and disorientations, involving the divided self, the inability to affirm the Caucasian mind in the face of a barrage of Eastern and Western cultural motifs and talismans, and this isolated divorce from the social and political world, results in the soul becoming what its incorporeal state hints at: spectral. Just as De Quincey's psychic collapse at the peak of opium addiction involves the experience of being haunted, so too the soul in 'The Palace of Art' enters a state of paranoid isolation that allows for an equatable sensation:

> But in dark corners of her palace stood
> Uncertain shapes; and unawares
> On white-eyed phantasms weeping tears of blood,
> And horrible nightmares,
>
> And hollow shades enclosing hearts of flame,
> And, with dim fretted foreheads all,
> On corpses three-months-old at noon she came,
> That stood against the wall (lines 237–44)

Haunting is again symptomatic of disintegration; just as the songs of the soul provided echoes of themselves, now the fractured self is indicated by omnipresent 'shades' or echoes of the self. In addition the 'phantoms', 'shapes', 'nightmares' and 'shades', as well as possessing a Gothic resonance that I have suggested is intrinsic to the cultural discourse of addiction, also evoke, through their insubstantiality, the vaporous aesthetic of modernity as defined by Marshall Berman. In spite of the soul's distance from the real world and modernity within a palace which hoards the artefacts of the past, it is possible that modernity itself intrudes into the palace in the form of vaporous spectral presences. The palace therefore oscillates between past and present; the collection of artistic products from the past, through its random nature, becomes, as Armstrong has suggested, contemporary in its lack of historical perspective, and the attempt by the soul to evade the modern is nonetheless haunted by the aesthetic symbol of modernity: the spectre. The result is that the soul becomes spectral herself:

> She, mouldering with the dull earth's mouldering sod,
> Inwrapt tenfold in slothful shame,
> Lay there exiled from eternal God,
> Lost to her place and name;
>
> And death and life she hated equally,
> And nothing saw, for her despair,
> But dreadful time, dreadful eternity,
> No comfort anywhere. (lines 261–68)

Alienation for the soul is from location and identity, but also from God, reintroducing the orthodox totem of Christianity as the sanctum for the cohesive self; just as the disintegrating De Quincey is isolated from God as the only member of the 'true church' of opium, so too the fragmented soul is alienated from God. More significantly the result of this alienation is the inability to choose between death and life, thus dislocating the condition of being more fundamentally than the oscillation between past and present, and, in such a limbo situation, anticipating a time-span that is outside conceptions of time, namely 'eternity'.

In the end, as with De Quincey in the *Confessions*, a form of conversion takes place, with the soul rejecting the solipsistic aesthetic world, abdicating her position as monarch of the Palace of Art (much as De Quincey refutes his status as High Priest of the Church of

Opium), and seeming to turn to God and the 'real' world that exists outside art:

> What is it that will take away my sin,
> and save me lest I die?
>
> So when four years were wholly finished,
> She threw her royal robes away.
> 'Make me a cottage in the vale,' she said,
> 'Where I may mourn and pray.
>
> 'Yet pull not down my palace towers, that are
> So lightly, beautifully built:
> Perchance I may return with others there
> When I have purged my guilt.' (lines 287–96)

The emphasis upon a religious vocabulary involving sin, prayer and guilt indicates the process of conversion taking place. In addition the desire to dwell in a 'cottage in the vale' suggests a rejection of the affluence and privilege associated with the Palace of Art and an entry into the world of work and community, an idea compounded by the hint that if the soul should return to the Palace it will be with 'others'. The soul, which has been situated outside the boundaries that seem to secure the Victorian English identity – namely religion, family and home – seems to be reaffirmed in terms of an identifiable self by subscribing to another Victorian notion, that of submission; duty is prioritized over pleasure in a way that leads to Henry Jekyll's dilemma in Stevenson's Gothic novel. It would seem as though the identity fractured through a rejection of this world, and through an obsession with isolation and art has been restored in unequivocally submitting to duty. Significantly the choice of the cottage echoes one of the images on the tapestries in the Palace which pictures an

> English home – gray twilight poured
> On dewy pastures, dewy trees,
> softer than sleep – all things in order stored,
> A haunt of ancient Peace. (lines 85–88)

The correlation between the cottage chosen by the soul and the 'English home' suggests that the cultural chaos represented in the

Palace is replaced by a stable national identity, reintegrating self and location through a sense of 'order'. However, at the same time a mirroring is established between the Palace and the cottage, and it is possible that this environment is as illusory and ephemeral as that inside the palace, for the outside world has been established as a place of peace and war whereas the 'English home' only knows 'ancient peace' and exists in that vaporous time of 'grey twilight'. Although 'The Palace of Art' depicts a world that has art at its margins and the English home at its centre, an aesthetic world versus a 'real' world, and indicates that a transition takes place from one location to the other, it appears that in terms of representation the real, modern world is not as secure as it seems.

In 'The Lotos Eaters', Tennyson's poem that most clearly involves a defined representation of the dangers of intoxication, there is no such resolution. Nonetheless, many of the issues raised in 'The Palace of Art' are applicable to a poem that once again affirms the spectral as a potent facet of addiction, and which also explores fragmented and marginalized states of being. The description of the topography of the island immediately alerts the reader to its contradictory and consequently insubstantial nature:

> In the afternoon they came unto a land
> In which it seemed always afternoon.
> All around the coast the languid air did swoon,
> Breathing like one that hath a weary dream.
> Full-faced above the valley stood the moon;
> And like a downward smoke, the slender stream
> Along the cliff to fall and pause and fall did seem.
>
> A land of streams! some like a downward smoke,
> Slow-dropping veils of thinnest lawn, did go;
> And some through wavering lights and shadows broke,
> Rolling a slumbrous sheet of foam below. (lines 3–13)

Many of the features of a stereotypical representation of intoxication are present here: the languid atmosphere of an environment that 'seemed' (immediately drawing attention to the illusory nature of the location) 'always afternoon' obviously anticipates the soporific effects of the consumption of the Lotos flower; indeed motion is almost completely suspended in the extract quoted above. However, in spite of the obvious hints of intoxication that prefigure the 'Choric Song' of the drugged sailors, the description of the island contains significant details that establishes it as a liminal area. Although seeming to be constantly afternoon, this fixity is somewhat problematized by the presence of the 'full-faced' moon, and the sense of natural orders being disrupted is enhanced by the stream that falls 'like a downward smoke'. Again we encounter the distinctive vaporousness suggested by Berman in the 'smoke', the 'veils', the 'wavering lights' and the 'shadows', but this paradoxical distinctiveness is rendered indeterminate by the disruption of natural orders, namely in the 'downward smoke' just mentioned, and in the island being a 'land of streams'. In the end it seems impossible to impart any particularly substantial qualities to the island of the Lotos eaters, a feature that Tennyson draws attention to by describing the island in terms that suggest its lack of substance, yet also highlighting its permanent state of afternoon and envisaging it as 'A land where all things always seemed the same' (line 24). As a result the text oscillates between the transient and the unchanging in its use of contradictions.

The addicted islanders encountered by the exiled Ithacan sailors exhibit none of the ecstatic qualities that mark De Quincey's opium reveries, nor the emphatic accumulation and over-consumption of cultural tokens catalogued in 'The Palace of Art'. Nonetheless, their presence, in keeping with the dynamics of the island itself, is appropriately distanced from a clearly defined state of being:

> And round the keel with faces pale,
> Dark faces pale against that rosy flame,
> The mild-eyed melancholy Lotos-eaters came. (lines 25–27)

The collapse of a distinctive identity manifest in the discourse of addiction is represented here in the contradiction of the islanders being 'pale' then 'Dark' and then 'pale'; there is again the sense of a lack of a clear definition. Being neither one thing nor the other, they are as unlocated as the landscape that they inhabit and the spectres that have been encountered already. The sinister nature of their presence lies in their very passivity, their 'mild-eyed melancholy', which seems to mask the symptoms of the drug that they bear with them. The effects of consuming the Lotos flower as described by Tennyson are highly significant; he invests the narcotic with magical qualities, adding to its attraction and potential danger:

> Branches they bore of that enchanted stem,
> Laden with flower and fruit, whereof they gave
> To each, but whoso did receive of them,
> And taste, to him the gushing of the wave
> Far far away did seem to mourn and rave
> On alien shores; and if his fellow spake,
> His voice was thin, as voices from the grave;
> And deep asleep he seemed, yet all awake (lines 28–35)

Tennyson has previously described the sunset as 'charmed' (line 19); as a result the 'enchanted' Lotos flower becomes as liminal as the time that marks the threshold between day and night. Through consuming the Lotos flower the familiar world becomes displaced, rendered 'alien' and, ironically, it is this 'real' world – again the world of community – that seems to become spectral. The fellow sailors of the novice Lotos eaters speak 'as voices from the grave'. Balancing this, the Ithacan Lotos eater also enters an indeterminate state of being, 'deep-asleep ... yet all awake'. Again we are presented with an echoing text in that the intoxicated and sober subjects are as curiously liminal as each other; marginalization and alienation therefore occur on three counts, the immediate location becomes unfamiliar, friends become ghost-like and the Lotos eater himself enters a trance state that is neither sleeping nor waking. This accumulation of conditions of dislocation results in what Tennyson defines as a near-complete alienation from the supposedly familiar and rational hemispheres of nation, family and labour:

> They sat them down upon the yellow sand,
> Between the sun and moon upon the shore;
> And sweet it was to dream of Fatherland,
> Of child, and wife, and slave; but evermore
> Most weary seemed the sea, weary the oar,
> Weary the wandering fields of barren foam.
> Then some one said, 'We will return no more;'
> And all at once they sang, 'Our island home
> Is far beyond the wave; we will no longer roam.' (lines 37–45)

In keeping with the condition of the Lotos eaters themselves the consumption of the Lotos flower involves a pervasive weariness and lethargy. In addition the state of intoxication places them in a space that is again neither one thing nor the other. The Ithacan sailors are between 'the sun and moon' and on the 'shore' – in neither day nor night, on neither land nor sea – thus affirming their alienation from the supposedly stable and familiar worlds for the bourgeois Victorian identity of nation, home and work. Ithaca becomes a dream, and curiously the isle of the Lotos eaters becomes more real than the 'Fatherland'. However, in another instance of mirroring, the interplay between Ithaca and the island of the Lotos eaters becomes pronounced; both are after all islands, both seem to be part of an experience of dream states, and therefore both become in some way alienated and insubstantial. Just as in 'The Palace of Art', where the worlds of art and reality coincide and reflect each other, so here the worlds of languid intoxication and work (with all that that implies regarding nation and family) become concomitant. To the novice Lotos eater homeland seems as unreal and marginal as the magical island itself first seemed to be.

In the 'Choric Song', the monologue by the Ithacan Lotos eater that forms the main body of the poem, intoxication, which hypothetically should be a recreational pursuit in a land that 'seemed always afternoon', breeds discontent; to paraphrase the song, the question is asked, 'Why must we labour when everyone else has rest?' As in the works addressed previously, the speaker in the Choric Song veers alarmingly between assertions of a superior identity and a negation of self, claiming to be 'the first of things' (line 61) and 'the roof and crown of things' (line 69) but also seeking oblivion in dreams or death. As a result the song frequently becomes a hypochondriachal lament for the seeming injustices of life and labour; nonetheless, as with 'The Palace of Art', what is occurring is a radical reconfiguration of supposedly secure institutions, again indicative of the disintegrating self. As suggested in the prologue to the Choric Song, this fragmentation of the self involves and is even dependent upon, alienation from the areas of nation, home and work – the 'purpose, personality and culture' alluded to by Sinfield. Again we are presented with the contradictions that mark the discourse of addiction; intoxication shifts between languor and angry resentment, and the Song both laments the absence of home and provides an angry diatribe against the relentless labour that typifies the centralized world of Ithaca. It seems that to be marginalized here is to be intoxicated, at rest and content. Sinfield indicates the function of centres and margins in the poem by drawing attention to the significance of the location of the island: 'The combination of place and state of mind is the whole project of "The Lotos Eaters". The place is remote from the restless accumulation of the European system and its purposeful and compelled labour.'[12] For Sinfield therefore the poem involves the *alien*, the 'remote' island, and *alienation* from the prescriptive world of labour. What is alarming, he suggests, is not the possibility of intoxication, but the absence of purpose and by implication character. Identity for the bourgeois Victorian is only affirmed by hard work and its 'imperious desire to carry [its] head high', as Stevenson's Jekyll puts it. Sinfield's analysis of the poem is dependent upon the remote nature of the island; he argues that 'the state of mind which the island inspires in the mariners is ... remote from the European system'.[13] Like De Quincey's representation of incapacitating intoxication which can only take place in a mysterious Oriental location, so in Tennyson's verse the relinquishment of purpose has to take place in an environment that is emphatically not European. Despite the fact that we have a poem that expands upon an episode in the *Odyssey*, suggesting that 'The Lotos Eaters' adheres to the utilitarian marginalization of poetry as (uncannily echoing the theme of the poem itself) purposeless and fundamentally designed to avoid an intrusion 'on the real conditions of life', the marginalization ultimately tells us something about the centralized world of 'purposeful and compelled labour'. Ironically Sinfield also suggests: 'In Tennyson's practice, the marginalized activity of analysing states of mind occurs repeatedly within a move to a geographical periphery where he locates kinds of experience not valued in the centre.'[14] Certainly in 'The Palace of Art' we are presented with an 'experience not valued in the centre', for the crisis provoked by the inward contemplation of art is only rectified by returning to the central world of community and the domestic, suggesting that Tennyson is affirming the principles of the dominant Victorian hegemony. However, in 'The Lotos Eaters' we have an experience depicted that, as I have suggested in the introduction to this section, is in fact curiously central to Victorian society, albeit in an unacknowledged manner. As stated, opium, the dominant stimulus for intoxication for many in the nineteenth century, is freely and liberally consumed. As a result, although Tennyson and Sinfield suggest that the intoxicated state is part of a marginalized activity, we can see that, subversively, the activity also seeps into the centres to disrupt the stable norms of bourgeois convention.

Although Sinfield suggests that a possible way of reading the poems written by Tennyson in the 1830s and 40s is, due to the marginalization of poetry, as representations of individual states of mind divorced from the social, economic and cultural environment in which they were produced, it becomes increasingly apparent that there are alternative agendas being posited within them. Sinfield concurs that ultimately, despite his marginalization, Tennyson's verse adheres to dominant ideologies; however, it is Isobel Armstrong who emphasizes the topicality of the poems in terms of their critique of modernity: 'The poems are increasingly concerned with labour, appropriation and power, and with the forms in which culture perpetrates violence ... The movement is from an analysis in terms of individual psychology ... to a firmer cultural analysis ... even though, sometimes, it takes a cruder moral form.'[15] Armstrong labels the poem a 'modern myth' and explicitly draws attention to the correspondence between addiction and labour; it is the repudiation of labour by the Ithacan mariners that catalyzes the dislocation from home and nation, and it is consumption of the Lotos flower which distances the eater from work itself. Armstrong identifies the significance of this, claiming that '[i]t is no accident that the mariners' need for the Lotos is to allay the horrors of labour, for opium was taken by industrial workers for the same reason'.[16] Once again we are reminded of John Barton, that addicted and spectral industrial worker. Gaskell's Barton consumes opium to alleviate the pangs of hunger caused by unemployment, whereas Armstrong claims that opium consumption is used as a distraction from employment; nonetheless, there is a clear equation between the addicted industrial worker and the resentful mariners. In both Gaskell's and Tennyson's correlation between addiction and labour a process of forgetting is occurring; for the mariners it is the forgetting of endless toil, for Barton the forgetting of hunger – in both cases it highlights what Armstrong refers to as 'the cruelty of work, brute, mindless labour'.[17] Capital, as indicated in the discussion of Gothic *doppelgänger* novels, is inhuman, stripping the individual of a defined and autonomous identity through the machinations of production and consumption. Similarly the industrial bourgeoisie's advocation of the exchange value of capital and of self-interest devalues and parasitically exploits the role and function of its wage-labourers. As Tennyson's poem seems to demonstrate, the only way to assert identity and speak up against the brutality of work, indeed one of the few potent acts of social revolution, is paradoxically to embrace the forgetting state of Lotos eating.

As with the other addicts that we have encountered so far the result of Lotos consumption is that the mariners become spectre-like, and consequently move outside the parameters of time, location and community. The speaker in the Choric Song states:

> Let us alone. What is it that will last?
> All things are taken from us, and become
> Portions and parcels of the dreadful past. (lines 90–92)

Again we are presented with the possibility of impermanence; paradoxically enough in a land 'where all things always seemed the same', there is a sense that the Lotos-eating mariners are posthumous, part of the 'dreadful past'. The question is therefore effectively posited, 'Why work if everything is consigned to the past?' This shift outside present time is consolidated by the yearning for oblivion: 'Give us long rest or death, dark death, or dreamful ease' (line 98).[18] Addiction – the compulsion to eat 'the Lotos day by day' (line 105) – involves a contemplation of the transience of being and the subjects of familiarity, where 'those old faces of our infancy' are envisaged as 'Heaped over with a mound of grass, / Two handfuls of white dust, shut in an urn of brass' (lines 111–13). As a result the mariners, rejecting labour and embracing the forgetful state of Lotos consumption, envisage themselves as forgotten in their domestic world:

> Dear is the memory of our wedded lives,
> And dear the embraces of our wives
> And their warm tears: but all hath suffered change:
> For surely now our household hearths are cold:
> Our sons inherit us: our looks are strange:
> And we should come like ghosts to trouble joy. (lines 114–19)

The indeterminate status of the experience of addiction is stressed here, for in a land that 'always seemed the same' the possibility that in the domestic hemisphere 'all hath suffered change' is entertained. In effect the domestic world is emptied of life by the 'household hearths' becoming 'cold', just as the mariners become represented as spectral themselves. Familiar time schemes are disrupted by sons taking on the duties of their fathers before their deaths; consequently the addicted parent becomes defamiliarized – their 'looks are strange' – and if relocated in the domestic and national sphere they 'should come like ghosts to trouble joy', reaffirming the addict as social revenant. Again the spectre of that addicted parent and worker John Barton is evoked. In addition, disembodiment of the self is mirrored by dislocation within the social world, the relinquishing of responsibility by the addicted mariner results in a disruption at home, and the question is asked, 'Is there confusion in the little isle? / Let what is broken so remain/ ... 'Tis hard to settle order once again' (lines 124–27).

As seen in De Quincey's *Confessions* and 'The Palace of Art', mirroring and repetition become significant features of the representation of addiction in Tennyson's 'The Lotos Eaters'. Just as the addicted mariners become spectre-like, so too the household hearths are emptied of life; similarly with the dislocation of the mariners from their native world and their ensuing collapse into intoxication, a corresponding loss of order takes place at home in their absence. Armstrong draws attention to this use of repetition in her analysis of the poem. She suggests that the island of the Lotos eaters can be read as a colonial island, and that by using a distant location Tennyson 'makes strange the postulates underlying mechanised labour and exploitation', transferring his critique to an alien environment.[19] Drawing together the respective discourses of industrialism and colonization, Armstrong states:

> The contradictory terms of exploitation, in which natives offer resources which the intruders interpret as the magical release from toil, but which turn out to belong to the very conditions of labour, are disclosed by the simple move of allowing them to occur in another 'place', Homer's Greece. The colonial dream of magical consumption is located exactly in the mythological landscape from which its fantasies of obliterating the connection between labour and consumption derive, the untouched exotic island waiting for sailors to arrive.[20]

Sinfield has already suggested that colonization is in fact a compulsive activity in his assessment of Tennyson's 'Ulysses', arguing that the eponymous speaker in the poem 'is the colonizer who requires ever more remote margins to sustain the enterprise'.[21] For Armstrong the attraction of Lotos consumption, and the divorce from labour that it incorporates, is paradoxically mirrored by the suggestion that Lotos eating actually stems from the 'very conditions of labour'. She argues that Lotos consumption actually derives from the colonial project itself, that the suspension from labour is sited in the 'mythological landscape' of Homer's Greece and the 'untouched island' awaiting colonization. As a result it can be implied that colonization is as addictive an activity as Lotos consumption, and that the attraction of Lotos intoxication – with all that it implies regarding labour – stems itself from the colonial dream, a staple feature of Victorian bourgeois hegemony. This circular activity is emphasized, taking into account that the island of the Lotos eaters incorporates a projection of colonial desires, when the words of Marx and Engels are considered regarding the bourgeois project. In the *Communist Manifesto* they stress that the bourgeoisie 'compels all nations, on pain of extinction, to adopt the bourgeois mode of production; it compels them to introduce what it calls civilisation into their midst, i.e., to become bourgeois themselves. In one word, it creates a world after its own image'.[22]

Despite the fact that their description is emphatically not one word, what Marx and Engels suggest is that the bourgeois project revolves around repetition, creating colonized worlds in 'its own image', just as Armstrong suggests that the island of the Lotos eaters in Tennyson's poem is a projection of colonial fantasies. This mirroring therefore establishes a clearer connection between labour and addiction, whereby both reflect each other; indeed, as Armstrong argues, 'labour must be *the* consuming and destructive force' rather than addiction, as the Ithacan mariners consume the Lotos flower in response to labour itself.[23] It is repetition that is the key to the addictive experience here, just as it is to industrialized labour. One form of the action takes over from the other, explaining why the changing and the unchanging are features of both the alien and domestic hemispheres – expected order is destroyed in worlds where the 'broken ... remain[s]' or the sun and the moon shine simultaneously. This is why, as Armstrong suggests, 'the magical lethargy of the Lotos-Eaters is as uncomfortable and alienating as mechanical labour itself'.[24] Again we are presented with the sense that, despite its apparent marginalization and displacement by Tennyson via using distant locations and cultures as the site for representations of addiction, the experiences of addiction and intoxication are uncannily central to nineteenth-century modernity. The spectral mariner-addicts, here uneasily similar to that other dissatisfied labouring addict John Barton, do indeed come 'like ghosts to trouble joy'. Lotos consumption in Tennyson's poem finally gives the illusion of being 'like Gods' (line 155), rather than the pathetic, labouring individual; rest and dreaming are brought into opposition to labour, just as the debate in the poem seems to be about the illusory and the real. Nonetheless, the anxiety remains about what reality is, for labour itself seems to be as illusory a pursuit as Lotos eating, perhaps even more so, for it offers no clear material benefits. Man is 'an ill-used race' that fruitlessly 'cleave[s] the soil' (line 165), whom the Gods – the representatives of hegemonic authority – ultimately care little for.

10 Like honey to the throat but poison to the blood: Christina Rossetti's addictive market

> Please give my love to Lucy; and explain that I was on my way to say goodbye when the door at which I was presenting myself shut, and shut me out: I dare say she detects that I am sufficiently shy to lose heart under such a rebuff. The 'at home' seemed to me very successful, and I only regret not having had a glimpse of your library. What a beautiful stair carpet![1]

Much recent criticism of Christina Rossetti's poetry has tended to rely upon biographical material to support readings of her work. Her devotional verse in particular, with its themes of renunciation and self-sacrifice balanced by the articulation of frustration and inward tension, seems to lend itself to biographical interpretations. The details of her life – taking into consideration her association with the Pre-Raphaelite Brotherhood, her aborted engagements, and her acute, even masochistic religious faith, which seems to have accounted for her apparently frustrated love life – do indeed provide a provocative insight into her distinctive poetic practice.[2] In addition the internal conflicts between conceptions of the self as poet and woman (compounded by the nature of Rossetti's strict religious discipline) in the nineteenth century, has fuelled much feminist criticism of Victorian women's writing; paraphrasing much of this debate, Kathleen Jones, in her biography of Rossetti, states that feminist criticism views her craft as the 'articulation of the struggle for a voice within a creed which consistently denied it to her' and one where, in terms of this struggle, 'the existence of religious ritual, conformity and submission … won'.[3] I do not intend to enter into an analysis of either Rossetti's life with regard to her work, or of feminist critiques of her poetic achievements. That said, there is something particularly resonant in the letter that she wrote to her brother William and sister-in-law Lucy in 1891. In her correspondence of that date Rossetti presents herself, apologetically, as distanced from the realm of domestic security, finding that she is shut out from William and Lucy's home and unable to re-enter for reasons of shyness. The detail in itself is seemingly insignificant but it casts an intriguing light on a writer whose poem 'Goblin Market' – wherein two sisters, Laura and Lizzie, are seduced by the tempting fruits of strange goblin merchants, with Laura succumbing, consuming the fruit and sickening only to be saved by Lizzie heroically confronting the goblin men and finding an antidote to the poisonous fruit – deals so emphatically with threshold states, with the exclusion from the domestic, and with what can be read as a representation of addiction. Just as Rossetti's letter echoes John Barton's evaporation on the threshold of the domestic, her 'Goblin Market' anticipates the addicted dynamics of Stoker's *Dracula*.

'Goblin Market' is not the only poem by Rossetti to deal with threshold states; liminal areas or conditions of being occur in her writing with noticeable frequency. Indeed, ghosts and spectres, those emblems of dislocation, can be found in 'The Poor Ghost', 'The Ghost's Petition', and in less explicitly titled poems like 'At Home'. A Gothic element can therefore be detected in her work, and biographers have been fond of pointing out that her reading as a child included a number of Gothic romances.[4] This in itself is not unusual; Gothic influences and motifs within non-Gothic texts can be detected in much of the writing of the Victorian period, for example, in the work of Dickens, George Eliot and Henry James. However, Rossetti's connection with and utilization of the Gothic – particularly in 'Goblin Market', which is not a Gothic text *per se* – becomes increasingly resonant when the fact that Rossetti's maternal uncle was Dr. John Polidori is considered. The presence of Polidori, Lord Byron's physician for some time during the poet's self-imposed European exile, in Rossetti's family history provides a convenient catalyst for Gothic readings of 'Goblin Market'. Polidori was the author of *The Vampyre*, published in 1819, the first prose fiction vampire story in British writing. This sensational story, which tells of the aristocratic and infamous Lord Ruthven, who inhabits the salons of London society and other more exotic locations, was one of the products of a heavily mythologized 'wet, ungenial summer' spent near Lake Geneva by Polidori, Byron, Shelley and Mary Shelley, a period of time that also produced Mary Shelley's *Frankenstein*.[5] David F. Morrill highlights the apparent connections between 'Goblin Market' and the vampire story produced by Polidori, many features of which can be detected in subsequent vampire and Gothic fiction. He suggests:

> Christina Rossetti uses certain details of the vampire myth – acts of biting and sucking, enervation, and death without grace – in her own lurid tale of young maidens threatened by the sensual possibilities of an evil, seductive brotherhood. Such a threat rapes its victims, tears away masks of innocence, and drains lives as Rossetti's heroines experience the exotic yet fearful pleasures of a dark and mysterious Gothic landscape.[6]

Many of the features of Rossetti's poem fulfil the vampiric criteria suggested by Morrill, for example, the transgressive consumption of forbidden fruits and the explicit representation of intoxication. In addition such features correlate closely with nineteenth-century representations of addiction, bearing in mind that addiction, and the study of it by physicians, highlight the detrimental sensuality intrinsic to the condition, and – as Moseley pointed out in his *Eleven Chapters on Nervous and Mental Complaints* cited at the start of this section of the book – that, there is an equation between the mouth, the throat and intoxication, just as there is in the vampire myth. The 'enervation' of intoxication is fundamentally regarded as suspicious. In spite of the apparent connection between 'Goblin Market' and vampire texts, it is important to stress that the poem is not about vampires; however, it is possible to read it as representing processes and activities which we can regard as *vampiric*. Such a reading accentuates the issues that have shadowed the present discussion of addiction, issues that include otherness, nation, modernity, capital and consumerism. Ultimately the literary vampire myth can be interpreted as a cipher for addictive activities; in addition, it is possible to see that in the networks which draw together Christina Rossetti, Polidori's vampire text, Mary Shelley's *Frankenstein* and Bram Stoker's *Dracula*, the representation of addict as Gothic hybrid – traced in the accounts of Elizabeth Gaskell and William Booth – is mirrored.

It is not difficult to detect the addictive qualities represented in Rossetti's poem; Laura, the sister who is seduced by the fruits of the goblin men, is clearly intoxicated by her first taste of the alien fruit:

> She never tasted such before,
> How should it cloy with length of use?
> She sucked and sucked and sucked the more
> Fruits which that unknown orchard bore;
> She sucked until her lips were sore;

Then flung the emptied rinds away
But gathered up one kernel stone,
And knew not was it night or day.[7]

The compulsive, repetitive nature of the addict is present in Laura's reiterated act of sucking. In addition, just as the agents of intoxication in De Quincey's *Confessions* and Tennyson's 'The Lotos Eaters' are presented as having their source in an alien environment so too the goblin fruit is from a foreign, 'unknown orchard'; obviously there is something suspicious to be detected in both the fruit and the agents that bear it. Furthermore, as with other representations of addicted behaviour, the result is a trance-like state for the intoxicated consumer; Laura 'knew not was it night or day' and thus, echoing other conditions discussed previously, shifts outside the parameters of conventional time-schemes and into a threshold area. Also significant here is the suggestion that the ecstatic experience should involve pain, for Laura sucks 'until her lips were sore'. In previous depictions of the intoxicated state, the state is achieved in *response* to physical suffering; 'Goblin Market', however, again parallels the vampire text where ecstatic intoxication involves pain of some sort – it is possible to argue that this correspondence between agony and ecstasy evokes the subtle shift from oral consumption of narcotics to the increasing utilization of dermal applications, in particular the use of the hypodermic syringe.[8] In Laura's case consumption of the foreign goblin fruit triggers a condition that corresponds closely with classic definitions of opiate addiction; opiates, to paraphrase Berridge and Edwards, are drugs that the individual develops a high degree of tolerance to and which therefore require an increased dose to produce the desired state of intoxication, and Laura in 'Goblin Market' finds that 'I ate and ate my fill, / Yet my mouth waters still: / To-morrow night I will / Buy more' (lines 165–68). Addiction in Rossetti's text involves the increasing marginalization of the addict; just as the Ithacan mariners in 'The Lotos Eaters' shift outside the seemingly familiar world of the domestic and work, so Rossetti presents a comparison between Laura and her sister Lizzie going about their domestic chores:

Lizzie with an open heart,
Laura in an absent dream,
One content, one sick in part;
One warbling for the mere bright day's delight,
One longing for the night. (lines 210–14)

The increasing alienation of Laura, presented as in a 'dream', 'sick' and 'longing' for the anti-social time of night, results in a complete distancing from domestic responsibility, 'She no more swept the house ... But sat down listless in the chimney-nook/ And would not eat' (lines 293–98). More significantly, Rossetti represents Laura as suffering because she is unable to purchase further goblin fruit, becoming spectral during the day:

> when the noon waxed bright
> Her hair grew thin and grey;
> She dwindled, as the fair full moon doth turn
> To swift decay and burn
> Her fire away. (lines 276–80)

This daylight fading of the physical body is balanced by the nightly cravings for the goblin fruit:

> [She] crept to bed, and lay
> Silent till Lizzie slept;
> Then sat up in passionate yearning,
> And gnashed her teeth for baulked desire, and wept
> As if her heart would break. (lines 264–68)

Establishing connections between Laura's state of frustrated addiction and popular vampire conventions is straightforward; Morrill has identified one condition of the link between 'Goblin Market' and vampirism as orality, and here we can see it in Laura's gnashing teeth. Similarly, Laura becomes a passive, spectral body during the day and a violent and passionate entity at night. Indeed this oscillation between the passive daytime state and the aggravated night condition is the key to reading Laura in Rossetti's poem as addict and hypothetical vampire. Her position, in a series of mirroring occurrences that take place within the text, has its own precedent in the story of Jeanie; in a poetic anecdote that functions as both admonishment and premonition, Rossetti has Lizzie remind Laura, after her consumption of the goblin fruit, of what happened to the ill-fated Jeanie in similar circumstances:

> Dear, you should not stay so late,
> Twilight is not good for maidens;
> Should not loiter in the glen

In the haunts of goblin men.
Do you not remember Jeanie,
How she met them in the moonlight,
Took their gifts both choice and many,
Ate their fruits and wore their flowers
Plucked from bowers
Where summer ripens at all hours?
But ever in noonlight
She pined and pined away;
Sought them by night and day,
Found them no more, but dwindled and grew grey;
Then fell with the first snow,
While to this day no grass will grow
Where she lies low (lines 143–59)

Like Jeanie, Laura has been seduced by the tantalizing goblin fruit which, echoing the island of the Lotos Eaters, was grown in an environment that transcends natural order by remaining summer 'at all hours'. Similarly, like Jeanie, Laura dwindles, turns grey, and pines both for nightfall and the addictive forbidden fruit. The transgressive nature of Jeanie's actions – and therefore by implication Laura's – results in her grave becoming a site that is excluded from the processes of nature, 'no grass will grow' on it. In effect consumption of the goblin fruit excludes the consumer from natural processes and even poisons her resting place; the grave therefore becomes a place uneasily dislocated from the familiar and viewed as diseased.

Jeanie's function within the poem is cautionary, yet it also reveals certain other issues at stake in this discussion. Rossetti reintroduces the deceased character of Jeanie later in the poem as a stimulus for Lizzie to save Laura. Preparing to visit the goblin market in an effort to help the ailing, addicted Laura, Lizzie

thought of Jeanie in her grave,
Who should have been a bride;
But who for joys brides hope to have
Fell sick and died
In her gay prime,
In earliest Winter time (lines 312–19)

Rossetti's phrasing at this point in the text is significant; Jeanie, who 'should have been a bride', died 'for joys brides hope to have'. The normality of the domestic space plays a large part in the poem; indeed Laura's rehabilitation involves a return to the domestic hemisphere where she and Lizzie 'both [become] wives / With children of their own' (lines 544–45). However, Rossetti's wording is highly suggestive; Jeanie's demise as a result of the 'joys brides hope to have' hints at premarital consummation. D. M. R. Bentley speculates that, rather than being designed to be read by children, 'Goblin Market' was written to be read by the prostitutes of the St Mary Magdalen Home of Highgate where Rossetti worked as a voluntary helper during the 1860s.[9] Rossetti's intentions regarding the poem and its possible audience are not my concern here; however, the connotations manifest in Jeanie's demise and their association with prostitution in the late nineteenth century raise a number of significant issues resonant with the present discussion, including commodification, contamination and disease. It is possible to read the experience of the ill-fortuned Jeanie – who exchanged the 'joys brides hope to have' for the 'gifts both choice and many' of the goblin fraternity – as representing that of the prostitute. In her essay '"Eat Me, Drink Me, Love Me": The Consumable Female Body in Christina Rossetti's "Goblin Market"', Mary Wilson Carpenter draws attention to the commodification of the female body in the poem, pointing out that it is 'subject to "consumption" as a commodity'.[10] Carpenter locates Rossetti's poem within the capitalist, imperial and sexual economies of the 1860s, suggesting that all three are configured together in 'Goblin Market'. After all, the 1860s mark what Nancy Armstrong refers to as 'a new moment in the history of desire', where an expanding consumer culture, founded upon the British imperial project, redefines bourgeois English femininity.[11] To paraphrase complex arguments presented by both Armstrong and Wilson Carpenter, Victorian consumer culture produced objects of desire yet demanded that the feminine appetite be held in check; in short feminine desire must be controlled in contrast to the prostitute on the streets, that dark other of bourgeois femininity. It is easy to read 'Goblin Market' in the context of such structures: the lethal concoction of foreign fruit is purchased at a market where Laura exchanges a 'golden curl' (line 125) for the merchandise. The reiterated call of 'Come buy, come buy' (line 4) uttered by the goblins can be seen as an unsubtle advertising jingle, and, in the case of Laura, the female body is read by the male goblin's as both capital and commodity; when she claims to have no money with which to purchase their produce, they state '"You have much gold upon your head"' (line 123). The poem therefore, as Wilson Carpenter states, 'presents an explicitly articulated image of a marketplace in which female "appetite" is at stake'.[12] The poem warns of the perils of over-consumption and unrestrained appetites, with the spectral figure of Jeanie shadowing the main narrative. As a result we can see the notion of addiction reconfigured in a series of shifting formations, including vampirism, prostitution, contagion and purchasing power, which, considering the instances of doubling taking place, serve to problematize a unified sense of identity.

The correspondence between addict and prostitute has already been established in the discussion of De Quincey's *Confessions* where the prostitute Ann becomes the alter ego of the Opium Eater, who explicitly defines himself as a 'peripatetic, or a walker of the streets'. Also, in Elizabeth Gaskell's *Mary Barton*, the aunt of the eponymous heroine, Esther, is both prostitute and alcoholic. In 1861, in a sermon preached with Samuel Wilberforce the Bishop of Oxford at St Mary's Home, Wantage, Henry Parry Liddon suggested that the degeneration implicit in prostitution began with what he termed a woman's 'act of rebellion', one which was frequently followed by consecutive offences, to such an extent that 'you find yourself in the presence of a new and formidable force – the force of habit'.[13] The suggestion that the fall into prostitution involves the development of a compulsive 'act of rebellion', one that is defined as a 'habit', reinforces the connection between streetwalker and addict. The use of the word 'habit' is in itself curious, as it can be applied to religious practice and ritual – indeed Liddon suggests that the compulsive 'act of rebellion' can be challenged by 'a counter-habit of purity' – or to any form of repetitive behaviour, for example the vampire's nocturnal search for human blood or the *flâneur*'s perambulations.[14] The conflation of addict, prostitute and vampire in 'Goblin Market' becomes even more resonant when physiognomic details which typify the addict are taken into consideration. As late as 1928 C. E. Terry and M. Pellens state in *The Opium Problem* that 'a delicate female, having light blue eyes and flaxen hair' was the most likely addict, a description that loosely follows that of the golden–haired Laura in Rossetti's poem. Such formulations provide a point of significance considering that the practice of physiognomy is one of the more prominent of scientific methodologies utilized in *Dracula*, something that will be explored in greater detail in the ensuing discussion of Stoker's novel.[15] The apotheosis of this interaction arrives when the social context of the decade in which 'Goblin Market' appears is examined. The 1860s mark the passing by parliament of two acts, the Pharmacy Act of 1868, which limited the supply of drugs to professional pharmacists, and the Contagious Diseases Acts of 1864, 1868 and 1869, which allowed for medical and police inspections of prostitutes. The Contagious Diseases Acts, as Judith Walkowitz points out, indicated that prostitution was seen as an increasingly dangerous form of sexual activity, one which involved contamination and infection, and one 'whose boundaries had to be controlled and defined by the state'.[16] Similarly the Pharmacy Act coincided with medical concern at the possibility of a disease theory of addiction. Drawing attention to the perception of a morphine problem in the latter decades of the nineteenth century, Berridge and Edwards state:

> Morphine use and the problem, as medically defined, of hypodermic self-administration were closely connected with the medical elaboration of a disease view of addiction ... Disease entities were being established in definitely recognizable physical conditions such as typhoid and cholera. The belief in scientific progress encouraged medical intervention in less definable conditions. The post-Darwinian revolution in scientific thinking encouraged the reclassification of conditions with a large social or economic element in them on strictly biological lines. From one point of view, disease theories were part of late Victorian 'progress', a step forward from the moral condemnation of opium eating to the scientific elaboration of disease views. But such views were never, however, scientifically autonomous. Their putative objectivity disguised class and moral concerns which precluded a wider understanding of the social and cultural roots of opium use.[17]

The account by Berridge and Edwards indicates conditions uncannily similar to the principle behind the Contagious Diseases Act, mainly in the disease theory masking 'moral concerns'. In addition, addiction's medical status, involving 'less definable conditions', reaffirms the unlocated status of the category. Just as the reading of the prostitutes' 'act of rebellion' oscillates between disease theory and moral admonition, the condition of addiction veers between similar parameters. Berridge and Edwards point out that disease 'was generally defined in terms of deviation from the normal', suggesting the anti-social link between addict and prostitute, and go on to indicate the strangely inconsistent view of the condition:

> Addiction, clearly not simply a physical disease entity, was a 'disease of the will'. It was disease *and* vice. The moral weakness of the patient was an important element in causation; the disease was defined in terms of 'moral bankruptcy', 'a form of moral insanity', terms deriving from similar formulations in insanity.[18]

Like prostitution, therefore, addiction falls between the two areas of being 'disease *and* vice', an issue that Berridge and Edwards identify as, in fact, a retrogressive step in terms of medical thinking; they state that disease theories

> far from marking a step towards greater scientific awareness and analysis of the roots of dependence on narcotics, in many respects marked a closing of avenues, a narrower vision than before. The theories themselves were a hotch-potch of borrowings from developing medical science and established morality. The lack of definition of the term 'addiction' itself emphasized this.[19]

We can therefore identify a clear association between the addict and the prostitute in social thinking of the late nineteenth century, one that is conflated in the present reading of 'Goblin Market'. In addition, there is another significant association between the two positions; Mary Wilson Carpenter notes that, regarding the sermons given to the voluntary workers *and* prostitutes of the rescue homes attended by individuals such as Rossetti, 'ecclesiastical discourse constituted saving "sisters" and "fallen women" together, as if part of a unitary entity'.[20] The suggestion is that the sisters of the homes were potentially part of the body of women capable of acts of 'rebellion'. Regarding addiction, Dr J. St Thomas Clarke, the medical attendant at Mrs Theobald's Establishment for Ladies, noted in a letter to the *British Medical Journal* that the upper echelons of English society contributed to 'a considerable proportion' of morphine cases.[21] The implication is that the conditions for prostitution and addiction are not the preserve of the lower classes of Victorian society, a facet that in terms of cultural representation culminates in the vampirized Lucy Westenra of Bram Stoker's *Dracula*, a character who draws together addict, streetwalker and vampire in the ensuing discussion of Stoker's novel.[22] In fact the diseased and unstable grave of Jeanie which shadows Rossetti's 'Goblin Market' anticipates the home of the addicted, vampirized Lucy of *Dracula*.

'Goblin Market' is a poem that draws together a series of issues that revolve around or articulate notions of addiction. Such issues include the perils of consuming foreign fruit, the dangers of unrestrained appetites, anxieties about female sexuality and concern about disease in sexual or narcotic contexts. Shadowing these specific concerns are a series of broader issues, which have also emerged in an analysis of works by De Quincey and Tennyson, namely, ideas of nation, empire and capital – issues that are behind the main narratives of modernity. In these narratives a series of spectral figures emerge that inhabit shadowy and threshold spaces in cultural representation and social history; these figures, which shift across literary genres like phantoms, sometimes appearing at the centre of discourse, sometimes noticeably exiled to its margins, include the lunatic, the addict and the prostitute. To this list can be added the poor – as I have indicated earlier in this discussion, John Barton's addiction in Gaskell's novel stems from poverty – and the criminal. Berridge and Edwards point out that 'the development of disease theory [of addiction] was in general accompanied by a strong institutional trend, a desire to segregate the addict which had its parallel in custodial treatment of the insane, criminals and the poor'.[23] In addition, amongst its many other manifestations, what is the vampire representative of if not an addict-criminal, an individual compulsively driven to repeat an act of violation? All these figures possess an unlocated status in cultural representation, being presented more or less consistently as ghosts or spectres; they therefore have attributed to them the very '[f]luidity and vaporousness' that Marshall Berman suggests constitutes the aesthetic of modernity; indeed, they slot into that fact of modern life, noted in the *Communist Manifesto*, that 'all that is solid melts into air'. In Bram Stoker's *Dracula* all these issues are drawn together in a text that reveals the extent of the insecurities of modernity disguised as a Gothic novel. *Dracula* is a text that fundamentally thrives upon addictions, from the basic starting point of a blood-sucking ghoul to a compulsive need by the protagonists to tell the story from as many different points of view as possible and through as many different mediums. The result is a novel that revels in the tools and technologies of modernity while simultaneously unmasking its anxieties and instability.

Christina Rossetti's 'Goblin Market' also raises many of these issues, and, just as the urban Gothic in Stoker's *Dracula* masks them,

Rossetti's are concealed within a poem that has frequently been read as a fairy tale or children's narrative. However, just as De Quincey's *Confessions* seek refuge in the security of orthodox Christianity, so too Rossetti's poem retires to the sanctity of the domestic sphere at its conclusion, with Laura and Lizzie becoming wives and mothers. Nonetheless, there is still a significant point to iterate in this discussion of the text, namely, that it is one that, like De Quincey's, haunts itself. Attention has already been drawn to this feature in the story of the doomed Jeanie who shadows and echoes Laura's narrative. However, there are other instances of mirroring that are significant. Like Lewis Carroll's Alice stories, where the injunctions 'eat me' and 'drink me' are made, loosely repeating Lizzie's command to Laura to 'Eat me, drink me, love me; / Laura make much of me' (lines 471–72), Rossetti's poem inhabits a fantastical Wonderland populated by fantastical and sinister goblin men, and also a Looking Glass world.[24] Jeanie's experience echoes Laura's, yet Laura and Lizzie are also both equated with each other; Rossetti presents them as being

> Golden head by golden head,
> Like two pigeons in one nest
> Folded in one nest
> Folded in each other's wings,
> They lay down in their curtained bed:
> Like two blossoms on one stem,
> Like two flakes of new-fall'n snow,
> Like two wands of ivory (lines 184–90)[25]

This correspondence anticipates that between Lucy Westenra and Mina Harker in *Dracula*. However, where Laura and Lizzie both ultimately survive the lure of the otherworldly goblin men, Lucy and Mina's correlation is far more fatal for the former; like Laura, Lucy succumbs to the vamping process, but it is one that proves destructive for her. The most significant instance of repetition in 'Goblin Market' occurs when Lizzie, having faced the violation of the goblins, offers her fruit-smeared body to Laura as an antidote for her cravings. The effect of Laura's renewed consumption is startling, 'Shaking with aguish fear and pain, / She kissed and kissed her with a hungry mouth' (lines 491–92), resulting in a painful experience where 'Her lips began to scorch, / That juice was wormwood to her tongue, / She loathed the feast' (lines 493–95) and :

Swift fire spread through her veins, knocked at her heart,
Met the fire smouldering there
And overbore its lesser flame;
She gorged on bitterness without a name:
....
She fell at last;
Pleasure past and anguish past,
Is it death or is it life? (lines 507–23)

The ultimate result is that 'Life [comes] out of death' (line 524). What is significant here is that the consumption of the antidotal juices mirrors the primary consumption of the goblin fruit. Pain is intrinsic to both activities; where initially Laura 'sucked until her lips were sore', here 'Her lips began to scorch', again indicating the orality of the experience. The ecstasy of the initial ingestion is balanced by a corresponding agony which, taking into account the medical concern at morphine and hypodermic abuse, is explicitly intravenous. The antidotal consumption is ultimately effective; nonetheless, it involves a threshold state of being, where the boundaries of life and death are brought into question, just as the first experience questions the areas of night and day. In Christina Rossetti's 'Goblin Market', the addicted, degenerate and vamped Laura emerges from her trance state, from death into life and a return to the domestic world. In Bram Stoker's Gothic novel *Dracula* the boundaries between life and death are more fundamentally called into question.

11 The blood is the life: Bram Stoker's infected capital

> The habit was when a new batch arrived for whom there were no beds, to take those who were stupefied from opium and nearest death and remove them to make room for the new arrivals. Many were said to be buried alive. One man brought his wife to the hospital on his back and, she being in great agony, he tied a red neck handkerchief tightly round her waist to try and relieve the pain. When he came again to the hospital in the evening he heard that she was dead, and lying in the dead house. He sought her body to give it more decent burial than could be given there (the custom was to dig a large trench, put in forty or fifty corpses without coffins, throw lime on them and cover the grave). He saw the corner of his red handkerchief under several bodies which he removed, found his wife and saw that there was life in her.[1]

In a letter to her son, written around 1875, Charlotte Stoker provided a first-hand account of the cholera outbreak that took place in Sligo, Ireland, in 1832.[2] Taking into consideration the concentration upon contagious diseases from the 1860s onwards in British medical and social concerns, Stoker's mother's words draw together a series of issues that are intrinsic to this discussion, namely, the dangers of disease, opium treatment and the possibility that the supposed dead could still be animate. It is perhaps appropriate that, in a project that has been so firmly rooted in an attempt to address representations of the fragmentation of identity and disorientated consciousness in nineteenthcentury culture, this final chapter should be substantially located in the Victorian asylum. Indeed the 'immense lunatic asylum' that Dr John Seward has 'all under his own care' functions as the location for many of the incidents that provide the narrative drive in *Dracula*.[3] Locations are particularly significant in this text, and the fulcrum of Seward's asylum in London is important. It stands conveniently next to the Carfax estate in Purfleet that the vampire Dracula purchases and the business details of which catalyze the journey to Transylvania by Jonathan Harker at the start of the novel. Harker describes the estate to the vampire Count, stating that '[t]he house is very large and of all periods back ... It looks like part of a keep, and is close to an old chapel or church ... There are but few houses close at hand, one being a very large house only recently added to and formed into a private lunatic asylum'.[4] The proximity of chapel and asylum, a site that occupies much of the central space of the novel, indicates the tension between religion and science that informs much of the dynamic of vampire detection and containment in Stoker's novel. The rational empiricism of science and the symbols and structures of traditional faith seem to be equally employed in combating the alien force of the undead vampire count who effectively invades *fin de siècle* London. This polarization, where the Eucharistic host and crucifix are as appropriate as the phonograph, telegram and the practices of physiognomy and hypnosis in hunting the supernatural Dracula, provides just one of the significant paradoxes in the text.[5]

Reading the vampire as an addict in nineteenth-century Gothic texts is almost too obvious a connection to make. The simple fact that the vampire has a compulsive need to consume human blood on a regular basis in order to maintain its spectral existence alone indicates its addictive nature. De Quincey has already suggested that his addiction becomes as physiologically necessary to him as respiration and blood circulation; in effect addiction *is* existence, the 'blood *is* the life' (my emphasis).[6] The connection has been indicated by Judith Halberstam in her essay on Stoker's novel, 'Technologies of Monstrosity'; Halberstam compares the positions of Dracula and his acolyte, the 'zoophagous' lunatic Renfield, conveniently incarcerated in Seward's asylum, stating that '[t]he relation between Renfield and the vampire suggests that vampirism is itself a psychological disorder, an addictive activity'.[7] However, much of the vampire literature that was published prior to or roughly contemporaneous with Stoker's *Dracula* indicates the association. James Malcolm Rymer's *Varney the Vampire*, a huge penny dreadful published in 1847, presents an aristocratic English vampire who, in Christopher Frayling's words, has a 'vampiristic moon-madness [that] is more of an addiction than a built-in character trait'.[8] In addition, in the 1890s, just preceding Stoker's novel, two vampire stories were published, 'X. L.'s [Julian Osgood Field] 'A Kiss of Judas' and Mary Braddon's *Good Lady Ducayne*. In the former the vampiric 'kiss of Judas' – which suggests the perversion of orthodox

Christianity manifest in the vampire myth – is presented occurring 'as a mad dog who bites you and gives you hydrophobia ... sometimes as the breath of pestilence, cholera, or what not', suggesting the association between addiction, disease theories and vampirism; in Braddon's novel the aristocratic vampire Lady Adeline Ducayne makes the vampiric mark with a syringe, mirroring the concern amongst the medical profession about morphine and hypodermic abuse in the latter decades of the nineteenth century.[9] In *Dracula* itself there are numerous references to narcotics; Van Helsing administers a 'hypodermic injection of morphia', amongst other drug concoctions, to the increasingly vampirized Lucy Westenra on a number of occasions, balancing her escalating needs for addictive blood transfusions; the injection marks themselves echo the signs of vampirism that appear as 'little red points like pin-pricks'.[10] Dr Seward also claims '[i]f I don't sleep at once, chloral, the modern Morpheus ... I must be careful not to let it grow into a habit'; if Lucy's addicted transfusions are at least involuntarily induced, it seems as though there is at least one potential drug addict in the text.[11] Another significant narcotic presence in the novel occurs during one of the final attacks of Dracula upon Lucy, who leaves a memorandum stating that she found her mother's servants

> helpless on the floor, breathing heavily. The decanter of sherry was on the table half full, but there was a queer acrid smell about. I was suspicious, and examined the decanter. It smelt of laudanum, and looking on the sideboard, I found that the bottle which mother's doctor uses for her ... was empty.[12]

The implication is that Dracula has laced the sherry with laudanum; if narcotics are employed by the medical professions in the novel to combat the undead count, it is also possible to argue that narcotics are among the weapons of the vampire.

Dracula is, in itself, a fundamentally addictive text.[13] The seemingly endless cinematic remakes and reinterpretations of the novel alone indicate the perennial fascination of Stoker's text; it seems that popular culture has a compulsive desire to stake out the undead count, only to resurrect him consistently in another, slightly reconfigured incarnation. Paul O'Flinn, in an essay on *Frankenstein*, remarks of Mary Shelley's novel that '[t]here is no such thing as *Frankenstein*, there are only *Frankensteins*, as the text is ceaselessly rewritten, refined and redesigned'.[14] Ken Gelder, analyzing *Dracula*, suggests that 'it is tempting to go along with this view as far as critical readings of *Dracula* are concerned'.[15] Gelder's assessment is rather reticent; indeed it seems that *Dracula* holds a position unparalleled in terms of cultural reception – David Punter, in *The Literature of Terror*, emphatically states that '[t]he use of the term "myth" to describe a work of written literature is open to abuse, but if there is any modern work which fits the term adequately, it is *Dracula*, if on the grounds of reception alone'.[16] What is interesting about the two critical positions is that, although both Punter and Gelder draw attention in their respective analyses to the ephemeral and shifting qualities of the text, neither sees the need to demonstrate the points stated above to any great extent; it is as though *Dracula* holds a monolithic place in twentieth-century culture that needs no elaboration or demonstration. Although Gelder is hesitant in his affirmation of the status of the text, he nonetheless addresses the significant reasons that compel academia to return again and again to Stoker's work:

> Few other novels have been read so industriously as Bram Stoker's *Dracula*. Indeed, a veritable 'academic industry' has built itself around this novel, growing exponentially in recent years and, in effect, canonising a popular novel which might otherwise have been dismissed as merely 'sensationalist'. To enable its canonisation ... *Dracula* has become a highly productive piece of writing: or rather, it has become productive *through its consumption*. To read this novel is to consume the object itself, *Dracula*, and at the same time, to produce new knowledges, interpretations, different *Draculas*.[17]

Gelder's reference to *Dracula* having been 'read so industriously' and producing an 'academic industry' is appropriate when one considers that the text almost fetishistically celebrates the utilization of the burgeoning technological products of industrialization in combating the supernatural vampire; indeed, the actual recounting of the events *within* the text is frequently dependent upon technological development, for the typewriter, phonograph, telegram and shorthand are all employed. More significantly Gelder indicates that *Dracula* is fundamentally a text that is tied up in the mechanics of production and consumption. Reading and writing become addictive activities in relation to a novel that presents a variety of voices and readers and which, by implication, produces a variety of readings. Indeed Stoker's novel articulates the dynamic between consumption and production, no more so than in Dr Seward's account of Renfield's behaviour; Seward notes: 'He has evidently some deep problem in his mind, for he keeps a little notebook in which he is always jotting something down. Whole pages of it are filled with masses of figures ... as though he were "focussing" some account, as the auditors put it."[18] In Seward's account Renfield's production (writing) is fundamentally dependent upon consumption (the escalating devouring of his zoophagous behaviour), just in the same way that, for Gelder, the academic industry's interest in *Dracula*, and the subsequent work that it produces, is 'productive *through its consumption*'. In effect the process of reading (and writing about) the novel largely reproduces the activities that it represents; production and consumption are intertwined in writing *in Dracula* and readings *of Dracula*. Indeed the writing process within the text becomes almost pathologically compulsive: Seward indicates that Renfield 'has evidently some deep problem in his mind'; Seward himself notes in his diary '[e]bb-tide in appetite today. Cannot eat, cannot rest, so diary instead'.[19] In addition, the Transylvanian diary of Jonathan Harker which opens the text becomes obsessive, with his references to train timetables functioning as a talismanic symbol of the link with Western modernity in alien and seemingly backward Eastern Europe; the log of the *Demeter*, the ship that transports Dracula from Varna to Whitby, thoroughly and methodically documents the systematic decimation of its crew. All such examples indicate that writing is a retentive activity. As a result, what we have is a text that represents a multitude of voices resulting in multiple readings and interpretations; these compulsive, multiple readings render a monolithic text shadowy and inconclusive.

Gelder's analysis of Stoker's *Dracula*, as he points out, contributes to the canonization of the novel.[20] I do not pretend that this discussion does not also contribute to the already substantial 'academic industry' to which he refers; nonetheless, as befits a text that seems to inspire endless rereadings, there is something curiously resonant in Stoker's work regarding the discourse of addiction. In spite of the obvious correlation between addictive behaviour and vampirism there are less evident though more significant connections that can be established between the two. A particularly striking example of such connections can be found in the interaction between the origins of the vampire myth in cultural representation and its effect upon Stoker's *Dracula*, especially regarding nation, culture and the nineteenth-century drug trade. Just as the Malay (and by implication the Orient) is demonized in De Quincey's *Confessions*, in the vampire myth Turkey is demonized. In *Dracula* what we witness is a reversal of the colonial project that can be detected in Tennyson's 'The Lotos Eaters'; however, echoing the haunting words of the Ithacan Sailors in the 'Choric Song' of Tennyson's poem, Dracula really does come like a ghost to trouble joy. Like the addicted Malay of De Quincey, Dracula is involved in nomadic wandering and dislocated (and dislocating) activities; in effect both are represented as bringing infection to England from the mysterious and alien East.

As stated in the discussion of Christina Rossetti's 'Goblin Market' the origins of the literary vampire story are based within an historical narrative emphatically involving Turkey. John Polidori's 'The Vampyre', generally accepted as the progenitor of this Gothic subgenre, is substantially sited in Turkish-occupied Greece, so too is Byron's 'The Giaour', which is subtitled 'A Fragment of a Turkish Tale'. Byron's poem contains the memorable lines:

> But first, on earth as Vampire sent,
> Thy corse shall from its tomb be rent;
> Then ghostly haunt thy native place,
> And suck the blood of all thy race,
> There from thy daughter, sister, wife,
> At midnight drain the stream of life;
> Yet loathe the banquet which perforce
> Must feed thy livid living corse;
> Thy victims ere they yet expire
> Shall know the daemon for their sire,
> As cursing thee, thou cursing them,
> Thy flowers are wither'd on the stem.[21]

Gelder describes Byron's poem as 'a kind of revenge fantasy for Athens' occupation', suggesting that the poem can be identified with the political and cultural significance that Greece held for the radical Romantics.[22] For the purposes of this discussion, what is significant is that the hero of the poem is, nationally and culturally, an unlocated figure. *Giaour* itself is a derogatory Turkish phrase used to describe Christians. Nonetheless, the hero cannot be strictly identified as Christian; he is described as 'Apostate from his own vile faith' (line 616), suggesting that he was once a Muslim, yet is now 'only Christian in his face' (line 811), hinting at an ambivalent position. This unsituatedness – he is neither Turkish nor Greek – is compounded in his death where Byron states that 'He pass'd – nor of his name and race / Hath left a token or a trace' (lines 1329–30). The eponymous hero thus becomes a perplexingly nationless and creedless figure. In addition, the fact that he is isolated and exiled, though located within a resonant national narrative *and* turned into a vampire after death, suggests that the vampire is involved in a process of disturbing national identity. In early nineteenth-century literature the vampire therefore inhabits a fragmented nation-state (Greece) occupied by a foreign Eastern power (Turkey); in short a powerfully potent cultural figure, which is simultaneously spectral, emerges from a dislocated cultural space. In De Quincey's *Confessions* there is the articulation of an anxiety about points of origin for nation and culture which for him lie in the area between the Ganges and Euphrates, the '*officina gentium*'. For the British Romantics Greece performs a similar, if seemingly positive, function; however, Gelder points out the ambivalence of this position: 'Greece was identified as the origin of Europe itself, the most ancient of all European countries – and yet, under Turkish rule at the beginning of the nineteenth century and with an ethnically mixed population, its modern identity as a nation-state had not yet cohered.'[23] Gelder identifies an important contradiction, namely that Greece is authentic, 'the most ancient' country in Europe, and also a melting pot of nations with a national identity that is not coherent. National identity is effectively blurred in an area that has a talismanic status as a cultural point of origins. To consolidate this it can be observed that in Byron's notes to 'The Giaour', one of the original appellations for the Greek vampire is cited as the '*Vroucolochas*'.[24] We encounter this name again as *Vourkolakas* in Rennell Rodd's *The Customs and Lore of Modern Greece*, published in 1892.[25] Rodd claims that the 'genuine vampire is the *Vourkolakas*', yet paradoxically also argues that the 'word itself is undoubtedly of Slavonic origins'.[26] As a result what we are presented with is the authentic Greek vampire, yet one that is of Eastern European origins. Just as Byron's vampire-Giaour is culturally and nationally displaced, so too the indigenous Greek vampire has been imported from 'Slavonic origins'. There is a further blurring of national identities in a location where national identity is blurred already; in addition Eastern Europe is introduced within the Greek and Turkey axis. The eastern Turk and Slavonic vampire occupy Greece, in Romantic poem and folklore study, and the 'authentic' vampire is rendered nationally ambivalent in this fragmented 'authentic' point of European cultural origins. As Gelder points out, '[t]he more diverse a nation, the less claim it has to national identity; and this "weakening" of identity makes it more vulnerable to absorption by imperialistic nations elsewhere'.[27] In effect the unstable site of Greece – taking into account its position as the location for the earliest fictional and poetic vampires – is, due to the fragmentation of national identity, open to occupation by the colonizing Turk *and* the infected vampire.

In the first entry of his Transylvanian journal Jonathan Harker notes, regarding the population of that country, that

> there are four distinct nationalities: Saxons in the south, and mixed with them the Wallachs, who are the descendants of the Dacians; Magyars in the west, and Szekelys in the east and north. I am going among the latter, who claim to be descended from Attila and the Huns. This may be so, for when the Magyars conquered the country in the eleventh century they found the Huns settled in it. I read that every known superstition in the world is gathered into the horseshoe of the Carpathians, as if it were the centre of some sort of imaginative whirlpool; if so my stay may be very interesting. (*Mem*., I must ask the Count all about them).[28]

This quotation provides further evidence of the obsessive nature of Harker's memorandums; however, there are a number of other significant points at stake. Transylvania in Harker's account consists, as a nation-state, of a variety of nationalities: Saxons, Wallachs, Magyars and Szekelys. Blood, the dominant thematic motif of *Dracula*, is intermingled and inbred in the Transylvania of Stoker's novel. Transylvania therefore becomes as mongrel a nation as the Greece of Turkish occupation. Harker also notes that 'every superstition in the world is gathered' into the site to which he refers, rendering Transylvania a national and cultural melting pot – an 'imaginative whirlpool' in Harker's words – where story, history and nation are all drawn together. This notion of Transylvania as a national melting pot is supported by Dracula himself, who, in what purports to be a family history stretching back to the late ninth century and recounted to Harker, describes his homeland as 'the whirlpool of European races'.[29] Again the authentic site for European culture is shifted, from the space between the Euphrates and the Ganges in De Quincey's *Confessions* to Transylvania (and Eastern Europe) in Stoker's novel. In addition, just as the literary vampire story itself emerges from the varied ethnic site of Greece, so the most famous vampire comes from the national 'whirlpool' that is Transylvania; again it seems as though the vampire is both physically and nationally insubstantial. Like the notion of the 'undead' itself, labelled but indefinable, Dracula is given a clear national location and history – that of Transylvania – but what is Transylvania? As with Greece, Turkey is ever-present in this vampire history; Dracula describes a 'Dracula' who

> as Voivode crossed the Danube and beat the Turk on his own ground? This was a Dracula indeed! ... Was it not this Dracula, indeed, who inspired that other of his race who in later age again and again brought his forces over the great river into Turkeyland; who, when he was beaten back, came again, and again, and again.[30]

The battle for national identity and superiority in history proves as compulsive and repetitive for the 'historical' Dracula (and Dracula describes a number of Draculas) as the colonial project in the mid to late nineteenth century. The repetition of 'again and again' suggests that asserting nationality is an addictive activity, a notion that is itself both supported and mirrored by the narrative in *Dracula* itself, where vampirization becomes an act of colonisation indicated by Dracula's journey to England. Ultimately what we arrive at is an unlocated entity (the vampire) inhabiting a fragmented nation (Transylvania) which simultaneously seems to provide a fulcrum as a point of origins for European identity; this relationship uncannily echoes the pinpointing of Greece as the initial site for the literary vampire, and involves, as with Greece, the demonizing of Turkey.

To elaborate upon and consolidate the presence and significance of the Turkish axis in the vampire/addiction equation we can consider the possible historical prototype for Dracula in Stoker's text. It is possible that the search for the so-called 'real' origins of a fictional character is a tenuous and perhaps irrelevant critical practice. What does such literary detective work contribute to a reading of the novel? However, in the case of Stoker's *Dracula* it has to be remembered that Stoker had done a substantial amount of research into East European history and culture.[31] In addition, the hypotheses and conclusions manifest in reading a vampire text throw up interesting connections in keeping with the shape-shifting and colonizing spirit of the vampire.

After all the vampire, as myth, motif or metaphor, shifts across a variety of genres and discourse – as an assessment of the writing of Marx reveals – and, as Gelder points out, the vampire myth has a strange effect upon culture. He notes, with reference to Transylvania:

> One of the peculiarities of vampire fiction is that it has – with great success – turned a real place into a fantasy. It is impossible, now, to hear the name *without* thinking of vampires; the very word invokes an image of something unbelievable, something which inhabits an imaginary space rather than a real one.[32]

What Gelder indicates is that the vampire narrative, with its cultural resonance and longevity, has turned, in terms of cultural consciousness, Transylvania – the home of the most famous vampire – into a fantasy location. In fact, to reverse the original reservation, it can be argued that it is impossible to explore Dracula's historical antecedents without referring to the fictional vampire himself. The historical Dracula is generally identified as Vlad IV, also known as Vlad Tepes, Vlad the Impaler and Vlad Dracula (meaning 'son of the dragon'), a *Voivode* or prince of Wallachia in the mid-fifteenth century and a defender of Christianity against the Muslim Turks.[33] In spite of a certain historical and geographical flexibility in the account of family history that Stoker gives to his vampire, there are a number of things about Dracula, apart from the name, that are reminiscent of Vlad IV.[34] An obvious example is that the two figures – historical Prince and fictional Count – can be linked through an association with impaling, in Vlad IV's case his preferred method of dispatching his enemies, in Dracula's an effective way to destroy the vampire himself. More convincing is that Dracula himself refers to the hereditary title of his family as being 'Voivode', and Van Helsing, citing 'Arminius' (Vambery), Professor of Oriental Languages at the University of Budapest, states, echoing Dracula's own words, that '[h]e must, indeed, have been that Voivode Dracula who won his name against the Turk, over the great river on the very frontier of Turkey-land'.[35] There is a fundamental paradox in the identification of the fictional Dracula with the historical Vlad, one pointed out by David Punter, namely, that 'his [Dracula's] satanic aspects are all the more interesting if we remember that his real-life ancestor gained his reputation for cruelty because of his assiduity in defending the Christian faith against the marauding Turk'.[36] In fact the paradox of associating the 'Satanic'

Dracula with the Christian Vlad is actually in keeping with the inversions of Christianity manifest in Stoker's novel and identifiable in the vampiric process itself. Ken Gelder's observations regarding Vlad IV are more significant in terms of the debate about the blurring of national boundaries and cultural origins in vampire fiction; Gelder notes:

> As a Wallachian, Vlad Tepes was literally caught in the middle of a war between Hungary and Turkey. Captured by the Turks, he learnt their language and practices, returning to Wallachia both to 'cleanse' it and to defend it from an enemy he was now familiar with and for whom he was often mistaken. His Orientalisation ... no doubt contributed to his subsequent demonisation.[37]

What Gelder argues for is an historical figure who, as well as later being identified with a fictional vampire, is an East European who has been 'Orientalised'. Vlad IV (Tepes) is literally nationally dislocated by being caught between Hungary and Turkey – between West and East – and, after being captured by the Turks not only learns their cultural practices, but is frequently mistaken for one, leading, Gelder suggests, to his 'subsequent demonisation'. If Gelder's analysis of the 'historical' Dracula is accepted, particularly in the context of the present discussion, it becomes increasingly apparent that in cultural representation Turkey is not only demonized but also *demonic*. Vlad Dracula in Gelder's reading is effectively vamped by Turkey, infected by its customs and bringing strange habits back to his indigenous land; indeed, in Jonathan Harker's comically understated words, Dracula 'must be a very peculiar man!'[38] Once again, as with Greece, we see Vlad IV occupied by Turkey, alienated from national identity, and infected by the Orient. The hypothetically historical prototype for the vampire himself echoes (or anticipates) the conditions in the location for the original vampire tales. Both 'authentic' vampires (historical and literary) are caught up in a narrative that strongly involves Turkey and the Oriental.

The presence of Turkey in this discussion of the nineteenth–century vampire – taking into account its literary and historical origins – can ultimately be seen to intensify when the social origins of our modern conception of the vampire myth, stemming from the vampire scares of early to mid eighteenth-century Europe, are considered. The vampire scares and epidemics of this period reiterate the anxiety about

Turkish-occupied territories from whence the disease or infection of vampirism comes. The result of these scares was a public inquiry into vampires in Austria published in Belgrade in 1732; the report cites the case of one Arnold Paole who 'had told various people, in the course of previous years, that he had been bitten by a vampire, near Gossowa, in Turkish Serbia'.[39] Once again it seems as though the vampire myth, whether in its literary, historical or social manifestation, has its origins in a discourse that clearly involves the presence of Turkey. The connection between this and narcotic consumption reaches its apotheosis in the responses to this seeming epidemic. Frayling notes that a 'German philosopher blamed the whole thing on the effects of opium ... which could apparently cause collective nightmares, especially in Turkey'.[40]

It seems impossible to discuss vampirism, socially, culturally or historically, without referring to Turkey or the drug trade; both, after all, are represented as transporting disease and infection. It is again worth noting that Berridge and Edwards have indicated that the predominant source for the import of opium to Britain in the nineteenth century was Turkey. The actual process of transporting the opium from Turkey to Britain reveals further uncanny connections between the vampire and narcotic consumption. Berridge and Edwards note that the Turkish opium was taken to the port of Smyrna in 'oblong wicker baskets' and then shipped from Smyrna 'in hermetically sealed zinc-lined wooden cases'.[41] The correlation between these oblong containers and 'wooden cases' is echoed by Dracula's preferred mode of transportation; the *Demeter* which takes the Vampire from the Bulgarian port of Varna to England has a cargo that consists of 'great wooden boxes'.[42] Furthermore the log of the *Demeter* reveals that the ship sails via Turkey, for the Captain notes, 'On 11 July at dawn entered Bosphorus. Boarded by Turkish Customs officers. Backsheesh.'[43] To consolidate the connection between the vampire's migration to England and the import of opium, Mina notes, with probable reference to Dracula's previous incarnation as Prince Vlad, that Dracula's adventures in Turkey and England mirror each other:

> His past is a clue ... once before ... he went back to his own country from the land he had tried to invade, and thence, without losing purpose, prepared himself for a new effort. He came again, better equipped for his work; and won. So he came to London to invade a

> new land. He was beaten, and when all hope of success was lost, and his existence in danger, he fled back over the sea to his home; just as formerly he had fled back over the Danube from Turkey land.[44]

Mina's words indicate that Dracula invaded Turkey, returned to Transylvania, and then embarked upon the invasion of England. Taking into consideration all the configurations that Turkey plays in the vampire narrative it is possible to argue that Dracula transfers the vampiric disease from Transylvania to England via Turkey in wooden cases in much the same way that opium is transported in the nineteenth century. That Stoker should have Mina state that Dracula 'came to London to invade a new land' is significant in this context, for, as Gelder argues, '[v]ampirisation is colonisation'.[45] This position is emphasized in Harker's journal where he notes, upon observing the blood-satiated vampire in his coffin,

> This was the being I was helping to transfer to London, where, perhaps, for centuries to come he might, amongst its teeming millions, satiate his lust for blood, and create a new and ever-widening circle of semi-demons to batten on the helpless. The very thought drove me mad.[46]

What Harker indicates is a colonial process on the side of the vampire that involves both transformation and assimiliation: Dracula intends to 'create a new and ever-widening circle of semi-demons' in London, an activity that echoes the bourgeois project, as evaluated by Marx and Engels in the *Communist Manifesto*, which 'compels all nations, on pain of extinction, to adopt the bourgeois mode of production; it compels them to introduce what it calls civilisation into their midst, i.e., to become bourgeois themselves. In one word, it creates a world after its own image'.[47] In Stoker's *Dracula* what we are presented with is both a reflection and parody of this activity; as Harker points out Dracula intends to create a world – of 'semi-demons' – in his own image. Ironically, however, the action involves the 'pain of extinction'. Dracula's project would potentially be more bourgeois than the bourgeois project itself were it not for the fact that the bourgeois constituents of the novel view him as a savage, a monster and a degenerate. In effect the presence of Dracula in London potentially echoes the position of Greece at the start of the nineteenth century for the second generation Romantics, where a civilized, central site is occupied by an uncivilized, demonized Other. The result of all this is that the intertwined themes of vampirism and addiction – both regarded as diseases and both stemming in a variety of manifestations from Turkey – are intrinsically tied up in an imperial narrative that turns its focus from the notoriously blurred and mysterious East to the English capital. In *Dracula* the Oriental of De Quincey's *Confessions* enters English consciousness with greater vehemence; the servile Malay of De Quincey's nightmares is replaced by the aristocratic, though degenerate, vampire Count.

If the vampire and the vampiric process in Stoker's text (amongst others) is read as an addict/addiction it is possible to see that the text taps into the morphine debate in medical circles in the late nineteenth century. As I have already stated this period witnesses increasing concern about the possibility of addiction to the hypodermic administration of morphine, and an escalation in readings of addiction as a disease. In reality there was no real morphine epidemic of any great proportions; as Berridge and Edwards point out, oral opium consumption remained the most prevalently abused form of narcotic consumption in spite of the more immediate effect of intoxication produced by hypodermic injections:

> The new technology of morphine use – the hypodermic method – did indeed create new objective problems in the use of the drug. The drug effect was more immediate, and the smaller doses had a greater effect. But the profession showed a clear social bias in singling out this form of usage when there were still far larger numbers of consumers taking oral opium.[48]

What Berridge and Edwards indicate is that morphine abuse did not reach the escalated proportions that opium took earlier in the nineteenth century. Nonetheless, there are significant issues at stake in the medical perception of morphine abuse; the 'clear social bias' referred to indicates that concern about narcotic consumption is reserved for a new class of user. We have already seen that Dr J. St Thomas Clarke, in his letter to the *British Medical Journal*, noted that there was a susceptibility to morphine addiction amongst higher-class women, and Berridge and Edwards state that 'morphia was always the more expensive drug and opportunities for addiction more easily available to better-off patients'.[49] Whether there was an actual morphine epidemic or not, what we witness is a shift in the medical profession's conception of the typical addict; in cultural representation, therefore, particularly if we read the vampire as addict, the shift moves from the working-class man, represented by Gaskell's John Barton, to the middle/upper-class woman, epitomized in *Dracula* by Lucy Westenra. What is also significant is that if the late nineteenth century anticipates a morphine addiction scare, nonetheless, as Berridge and Edwards point out, oral opium consumption remains a significant form of intoxication. In effect *Dracula*, given the addictive dynamics of vampirism, encapsulates the morphine/opium debate of the late nineteenth century, blurring the boundaries of drug abuse. In Dracula's case the vampiric addiction is based upon oral consumption manifest in the sucking of blood, and in the case of the vamped Lucy her condition is based upon systematic dermal penetration and the subsequent addictive infection of the body. *Dracula* therefore effectively functions as a metaphor for both oral opium consumption (almost rendered uncannily literal in the transportation of opium to England from Turkey in wooden cases) and the 'new technology of morphine use' manifest in the dermal penetration of the infected vampire's bite. Old and new modes of addiction are thus conflated in the text.

The medical notion of a new type of addiction with its new type of addict is particularly relevant to a discussion of addiction in *Dracula*. St Thomas Clarke indicates that this addict is amongst the upper echelons of English women; in addition the *Lancet* also noted that '[g]iven a member of the weaker sex of the upper or middle class, enfeebled by a long illness, but selfishly fond of pleasure, and determined to purchase it at any cost, there are the syringe, the bottle, and the measure invitingly to hand'.[50] The medical profession therefore identifies the new addict as the middle- to upper-class woman. In Stoker's *Dracula* Lucy Westenra takes this role, and it is her position in the narrative that draws together a number of issues that have been manifest in this discussion about addiction. I have already argued that the vampire can be read as a metaphor for the addict; however, in Lucy's case we can detect a variety of facets to her post-vamping behaviour that are indicative of the compulsive features of addiction, involving criminality, disease, street walking and tabloidization.

The vamped Lucy appears in a fictional text (a newspaper report from the *Westminster Gazette* of 25 September entitled 'A Hampstead Mystery') within the text (*Dracula*) as the tabloidized 'Bloofer Lady', an incarnation that represents sensationalized serial attacks upon children.[51] In fact the vamping process regarding Lucy Westenra in Stoker's novel is significantly reminiscent of nineteenth-century discourse concerned with 'deviant' sexual behaviour. In the later stages of Lucy's vampiric infection Seward, in his diary, notes:

> Her breathing grew stertorous, the mouth opened, and the pale gums, drawn back, made the teeth look longer and sharper than ever. In a sort of sleep-walking, vague, unconscious way she opened her eyes which were dull and hard at once, and said in a soft, voluptuous voice, such as I had never heard from her lips:–
>
> 'Arthur! Oh, my love, I am so glad you have come! Kiss me!' Arthur bent eagerly over to kiss her; but at that instant Van Helsing ... dragged him back with a fury of strength ... I kept my eyes fixed on Lucy, as did Van Helsing, and we saw a spasm as of rage flit like a shadow over her face; the sharp teeth champed together.[52]

This concentration upon rage and the prominent emphasis upon the mouth and teeth in relation to sexual desire reoccur later in the text when the fully vamped Lucy is pursued back to her sepulchre and confronted by the all-male vampire hunters. Seward, in another of his diary entries, notes:

> She still advanced ... and with a languorous, voluptuous grace, said:–
>
> 'Come to me Arthur. Leave these others and come to me. My arms are hungry for you. Come, and we can rest together. Come, my husband, come!'
>
> There was something diabolically sweet in her tones ... when Van Helsing sprang forward and held between them his little golden crucifix. She recoiled from it, and, with a suddenly distorted face, full of rage, dashed past him as if to enter the tomb ... Never did I see such baffled malice on a face; and never, I trust, shall such be seen again by mortal eyes.[53]

The repetition of 'voluptuous[ness]' in both extracts indicates the sexual charge of the vampiric advances of Lucy. In addition, the concentration upon oral features, as well as indicative of similar qualities in the vampiric transaction, can be equated with the withdrawal symptoms of the addicted Laura, already equated with the vampiric Jeanie, in Rossetti's 'Goblin Market' who 'sat up in a passionate yearning, / And gnashed her teeth for baulked desire'.[54] In both texts desire, whether read as sexuality or addiction, is suggestive of aberrant passion, coinciding in an emphasis upon demonstrative oral behaviour. Significantly Lucy's behaviour corresponds with Henry Maudsley's definition of nymphomania in *Body and Mind*. Maudsley refers to 'the irritation of ovaries or uterus, which is sometimes the direct occasion of nymphomania – a disease by which the most chaste and modest woman is transformed into a raging fury of lust'.[55] Maudsley labels the condition a disease, establishing it as parallel with addiction and the infected prostitute's body, and indicates the transforming qualities of nymphomania; just as Lucy, in Seward's account, utters her sexual advance in a voice 'such as I had never heard from her lips' and experiences frustration with a 'spasm as of rage' and later 'with a suddenly distorted face, full of rage', so too the nymphomaniac in Maudsley's perception is a 'chaste and modest woman ... transformed into a raging fury of lust'. Such radical behavioural shifts are intrinsic to the pre- and post-vamped Lucy. In fact Lucy as the 'Bloofer Lady' engages in even more aberrant sexual behaviour; her attacks upon children are compulsively serial in their nature – the *Westminster Gazette* notes 'several cases' – and suggestive of molestation given the sexual undertones of the vampire attack.[56] The correlation between female vampire and the molestation of children is corroborated by the vampires encountered by Jonathan Harker in Dracula's castle; immediately after Dracula intervenes in an attack upon Harker by three seductive vampires, he notes in his journal:

> 'Are we to have nothing tonight?' said one of them, with a low laugh, as she pointed to the bag which he had thrown upon the floor, and which moved as though there were some living thing within it. For answer he nodded his head. One of the women jumped forward and opened it. If my ears did not deceive me there was a gasp and a low wail, as of a half-smothered child. The women closed round, whilst I was aghast with horror; but as I looked they disappeared, and with them the dreadful bag.[57]

In effect the vamped Lucy not only demonstrates the traits of nymphomania as represented in medical discourse, but, in terms of her tabloid incarnation, is a child abuser engaged in compulsive and repetitive serial attacks upon a specific type of victim. As the 'Bloofer Lady', Lucy, wandering Hampstead Heath in search of more child-victims, can be equated with that alter ego of the bourgeois *flâneur*, namely, the peripatetic or female streetwalker; however, the angelic Anne of De Quincey's *Confessions* becomes demonic in *Dracula's* Lucy. In addition the reading of the vamped Lucy as streetwalker conflates the equation, as discussed with reference to 'Goblin Market', between addiction and the prostitute's body as the site of disease and infection. Taking into account the fact that serial behaviour is an addiction, Lucy effectively becomes an infected and infecting body in three manifestations: as vampire, addict and street walker. This triple demonization becomes even more significant when we consider that it is encapsulated in the tabloidization of Lucy, where the sensational aspects of her supernatural transformation into the molesting 'Bloofer Lady' are themselves sensationalized within the text through newspaper accounts. The tabloidization of Lucy uncannily echoes the vampiric dynamic itself, leading to the commodification of the 'Bloofer Lady'; Jennifer Wicke notes that

> she is ... currency within mass culture, where she circulates in the mass blood stream with a delicious thrill ... Lucy becomes an object of the mass press simultaneously with her assimilation into the vampiric fold; the two phenomena are intertwined in the logic of this vampirism. Unless and until Lucy is commoditized out over an adoring, and titillated, public by virtue of her exciting vampiric identity, she cannot be said to have consummated that identity in the terms of the text. While her vamping by Count Dracula precedes her 'bloofer lady' role and indeed causes it, the un-dead Lucy is similarly vamped by the press, and vamps all those who come under her thrall by just reading about her in the morning newspaper.[58]

Wicke suggests that the rendering of Lucy as part of mass culture via the tabloid press establishes her as vampiric (after all the discovery of her posthumous condition by Van Helsing and Seward is dependent upon mass media reports) and is in itself vampiric; it determines the circulation of Lucy's condition by commodifying her *and* functions as a vehicle through which the media-Lucy can bewitch her readership. As a result we can detect a two-fold interaction between vampire and media; Dracula and the media vamp Lucy twice, and she herself vamps twice, namely, children and newspaper readers. In effect just as the serial attacks upon children by Lucy reveal an addictive tendency, so too the reportage and reading of these attacks become addictive. As

Wicke points out, Lucy 'circulates in the mass blood stream' transported by the media, just as vampiric infection, sexual disease and intoxicating intravenous drugs circulate in the human body.[59] Walter Benjamin notes, of the peripatetic's alter ego, the *flâneur*,

> The more conscious he becomes of his mode of existence, the mode imposed upon him by the system of production, the more he proletarianizes himself, the more he will be gripped by the chill of the commodity economy and the less he will feel like empathizing with commodities.[60]

Benjamin effectively renders the commodity economy sinister, possessing the bourgeois *flâneur* and transforming his nature, gripping him with its 'chill', features uneasily reminiscent of the undead and of the processes of mass media as discussed by Wicke. However, where the male *flâneur*, despite his possession by it, refuses to empathize with the commodity economy, the vamped female peripatetic, Lucy Westenra, is wholeheartedly embraced by and embraces her posthumous commodification. Ultimately *Dracula* itself, as a cultural artefact, reflects this process; the text is effectively vamped, rendered undead by mass culture and the 'academic industry', and simultaneously it vamps culture, producing compulsive and addictive readings of the novel.

This hall of mirrors of vampire and vamped, where commodity and mass culture to all intents take on the supernatural qualities and machinations of the Gothic icon, echoes the reflections and inversions intrinsic within the vampiric condition. In fact vampire lore within Stoker's narrative revolves around escalating cases of mirroring, an ironic position when one considers that the vampire possesses no reflection. This irony is heightened as we learn of Dracula's lack of a reflection; Harker, in his Transylvanian journal, shaving in front of a mirror, detects the presence of the vampire Count but can discern nothing in the mirror, Dracula disposes of the shaving glass, saying, 'It is a foul bauble of man's vanity.'[61] The nature of his comment echoes the critique of vanity manifest in the words of the Preacher in Ecclesiastes, suggesting a further inversion of Christianity, though one that strangely adheres to the tenor of the Old Testament. Dracula may not possess a reflection; nonetheless, he perversely creates himself as a mirror image of Harker. Watching the vampire embark upon his journey to colonize England, Harker notes:

> It was a new shock to me to find that he had on the suit of clothes which I had worn whilst travelling here ... This then is his new scheme of evil: that he will allow others to see me, as they think, so that he may both leave evidence that I have been seen in the towns or villages posting my own letters, and that any wickedness which he may do shall by the local people be attributed to me.[62]

With Dracula taking on Harker's appearance, and thereby creating his own idiosyncratic form of mirroring, fixed boundaries are further blurred and identity again becomes an insubstantial qualification. Like Berman's defining fluidity and vaporousness Dracula, the *fin de siècle* vampire, cannot be pinned down; indeed, the incarnations and reconfigurations utilized by popular culture in the twentieth century pay witness to the amorphous nature of the undead Count, himself a composite creation of historical anecdote and Gothic convention.

Attempts are made to fix Dracula within the text; for example, there is the clear typing advocated by Van Helsing. Citing the degeneration theorists Nordau and Lombroso, he states with reference to Dracula:

> The criminal always work at one crime – that is the true criminal who seems predestinate to crime, and who will of none other. This criminal has not full man-brain. He is clever and cunning and resourceful; but he is not of man-stature as to brain. He be of child-brain in much. Now this criminal of ours is predestinate to crime also; he too have child-brain, and it is of the child to do what he have done.[63]

This representation of Dracula, as unlikely as it might seem given the sophistication of vampiric strategies, corresponds with degeneracy theory and the correlation between the philosophy of crime and the study of the insane which suggests that both the criminal type and the lunatic have an absence of moral sensibility. Regarding the focus on particular abilities in the lunatic/criminal, Henry Maudsley noted that

> the insane temperament is compatible with, and indeed it not seldom coexists with considerable genius. Even those who have it in a more marked form often exhibit remarkable special talents and aptitudes ... when they may be little better than imbecile in other things.[64]

He goes on to suggest that 'if there be a class of persons who are without the moral sense, who are true moral imbeciles, it is the class of habitual criminals', adding:

> there is a class of criminals formed of beings of defective physical and mental organization; one result of the defect, which really determines their destiny in life, being an extreme deficiency or complete absence of moral sense ... Though born in good circumstances of life, and having every advantage of education ... they are inherently vicious ... everything that their vicious nature prompts them to desire is for them right, and they exhibit a remarkable cunning in gratifying their evil propensities.[65]

In many ways Maudsley's definition coincides with Foucault's critique of nineteenth-century psychiatry, with its invention of that 'entirely fictitious entity': the crime that is nothing but insanity and the insanity that is nothing but crime encapsulated in the 'homicidal maniac'. Indeed Maudsley's emphasis upon an imbecile/criminal categorized by an absence of 'moral sense' indicates the limitations of his analysis with regard to empirical thinking; the classification effectively becomes a convenient way of containing both crime and insanity as reflections of each other as Foucault suggests. Ironically Maudsley's category does become more appropriately applicable to a 'fictitious entity'; the clear demarcation of 'evil', the cunning strategies that lead to gratification, the compulsive nature of the 'habitual' criminal, even the possibility of being well bred are all relevant to an assessment of the criminal yet aristocratic Count. Nonetheless, in spite of Van Helsing's intentions and the medical support of that most eminent of late nineteenth-century mental doctors Maudsley, the aristocratic but shape-shifting vampire evades any such reductive typing. He is represented as a refined and sophisticated character, yet Harker notes in his journal that Dracula's hands 'had seemed rather fine and white; but seeing them close to me, I could not but notice that they were rather coarse – broad, with squat fingers. As the Count leaned over me and his hands touched me, I could not repress a shudder.'[66] Appearances are apparently deceptive as the previously sensitive hands of Dracula become, on closer inspection, 'coarse'. This equivocality regarding physical appearance is even more noticeable when one of the main criteria of typing, physiognomy, is applied; Harker first observes Dracula as 'a tall, old man, clean shaven save for a long white moustache', yet in the course of the narrative he is rejuvenated, appearing as 'a tall, thin man, with a beaky nose and black moustache and pointed beard'.[67] Clearly typing based upon physical details is a practice fraught with contradictions. Dracula has clear and consistent features – his height, thinness, lips, teeth and pallor are all emphasized – yet any stable assessment based upon these characteristics is impossible considering the reversal in ageing and the very fact that he is a protean character who appears as or is likened to bats, wolves and lizards. In effect Dracula is a vaporous entity, beyond defined categorisation, encapsulated with no greater clarity than in his disappearance after assaulting Mina Harker, when Seward observes that 'we saw nothing but a faint vapour'.[68] Appropriately enough one of Dracula's main strengths in his putative colonization of England's capital is his ability to blend into the London smog. In mapping that most modern of mid-nineteenth-century cities, Baudelaire's Paris, Benjamin, citing those other chroniclers of the modern metropolis, Charles Dickens, Robert Louis Stevenson and Edgar Allan Poe, discusses the significance and decline of the gaslight within the arcades that defined the modern city and which provided the location for the perambulations of the *flâneur*.[69] In Benjamin's study the gaslight holds a rather ambivalent position, both a defining feature of the modern city in the nineteenth century yet also being supplanted by the new technology of electric lighting, an event elegized by Stevenson. He also draws attention to the peculiar shades that the gaslight provides within the metropolis; quoting Poe's short story 'The Man of the Crowd' he states: 'There can hardly be a weirder description of this light: "The rays of the gas-lamps, feeble at first in their struggle with the dying day, had now at length gained ascendancy, and threw over every thing a fitful and garish lustre. All was dark yet splendid.'[70] In isolating this section of Poe's text Benjamin draws attention to the uncanny nature of the gaslight, particularly in identifying its weirdness. Poe himself describes the insubstantiality of the light, referring to it as 'feeble at first' and then, even at its ascendancy, 'fitful and garish', concluding with the apparent contradiction that all 'was dark yet splendid'. It is in such an insubstantial environment, modern yet lit by the anachronistic and flickering gaslight, and one which therefore problematizes the notion of modernity within the nineteenth-century city, that the vaporous and shape-shifting vampire Count enters and exits.

Ultimately *Dracula* is a text which, despite its utilization of relatively conventional Gothic motifs, the mysterious castle, for example, is crammed with the symbols and symptoms of modernity and technology – the presence of typewriters, phonographs and shorthand cited earlier are obvious indications of this. Nonetheless modernity, as demonstrated in Benjamin's reading of Baudelaire and Poe's representation of the nineteenth-century modern city, with its flickering gaslights, and in Marshall Berman's discussion of the fluid and vaporous modern aesthetic, is ambivalent and unsettling in essence. Jennifer Wicke, in her analysis of the modern in Stoker's novel, refers to

> the work that the text can do as a liminal modernist artefact, an exemplary text that then lies hauntingly behind the uncanny creations of modernism, at the borders of what is accepted as 'high modernism', the high art tradition of its literature. The vampirism this text articulates is crucial to the dynamics of modernity ... *Dracula* is not a coherent text; it refracts hysterical images of modernity. One could call it a chaotic reaction-formation in advance of modernism, wildly taking on the imprintings of mass culture.[71]

In drawing attention to *Dracula* as a 'liminal ... artefact', referring to its haunting qualities, its lack of coherence and its position *vis-à-vis* mass culture, Wicke verifies the ambivalence of the novel's position and of the shifting nature of modernity. *Dracula* hysterically generates the images of modernity, yet, by comparison, is uncomfortably 'in advance of modernism' as a literary and cultural classification. It is the paradoxes within a text that emerges in a liminal period between the nineteenth and twentieth centuries that contribute to its fascination within academic discourse. Ken Gelder indicates the curiously unbalanced nature of the vampire in his conclusion to *Reading the Vampire*, arguing that the Gothic icon is

> far from exhausted as far as contemporary cultural production is concerned. The vampire's *nature* is fundamentally conservative – it never stops doing what it does; but *culturally*, this creature may be highly adaptable. Thus it can be made to appeal to or generate fundamental urges located somehow 'beyond' culture (desire, anxiety, fear), while simultaneously, it can stand for a range of meanings and positions *in* culture. The simultaneity at work here, it seems to me, explains why the vampire has lived so long.[72]

Jennifer Wicke argues for Stoker's novel as a precursor for the strategies that lie behind 'high modernism' and for vampirism as a condition 'crucial to the dynamics of modernity', suggesting that to some extent, and I use the term with some reservation, *Dracula* can be read as a radical text. Gelder's position in his conclusion, particularly in terms of his interpretation of the 'conservative' nature of the vampire, seems to contradict Wicke. Nonetheless, Gelder identifies the adaptability and flexibility of the vampire within cultural representation, compounding the liminal area occupied by the vampire that both critics address. In short, and to quote Gelder, it is the 'simultaneity' in *Dracula*, its shift between past and future, its oscillation between representations of identity and epoch, its blending of narrative techniques, that 'explains why the vampire has lived so long'. The mass production, circulation and consumption of a myth (the vampire) and of a text (*Dracula*) indicates the apparent status of both as commodities; to utilize Wicke's argument about the tabloidization of Lucy as the 'Bloofer Lady', they circulate 'in the mass blood stream with a delicious thrill'. Yet this commodification of *Dracula* and the vampire reiterates a concern about excess and overconsumption, the overconsumption of and unrestrained appetite for a text that is precisely about the perils of these very things. *Dracula* is blatantly a text that represents an addict who creates addicts *within* the text – the 'ever-widening circle of semi-demons' described by Harker – and in its *readership*, as popular culture so succinctly demonstrates. In effect the respective identities of monster, bourgeois character, reader and critic are all tied up with and in the dynamics of addiction.

I have suggested in the course of this chapter that opium use and addiction has an unlocated position within the nineteenth century; frequently demonized in cultural representation opium nonetheless remained for much of the century a credible medical treatment for a variety of maladies despite the fact that medical and legal discourse engaged with disease theories regarding narcotic abuse. If vampirism is read as a metaphor for addiction in the nineteenth century, the insubstantial, apparently contradictory or at least inconsistent nature of the vampire maintains the shadowy and ephemeral qualities that addiction possesses for the nineteenth century. In addition, as much of this discussion has been concerned with modernity in the nineteenth century, the conflation of addiction with the vampire, particularly in the light of the critical positions offered by Walter Benjamin, Marshall Berman and Jennifer Wicke, reveals that a conception of modernity is as 'vaporous' and insubstantial in definition as the vampire and addiction themselves.

In terms of an analysis of modernity, much of this debate has been underpinned by the figure of Marx, who has made his presence felt in the studies of Benjamin, Berman, Wicke, Gelder *et al.* As stated in the introduction to this section, Marx, in Chapter 10 of *Capital*, employs a Gothic metaphor in his analysis of the nature of capital, referring to it as 'dead labour which, vampire-like, lives only by sucking living labour, and lives the more, the more labour it sucks'.[73] In this celebrated statement, certainly for Marxist readings of Stoker's text, Marx indicates the compulsive qualities of capital and, through the utilization of the Gothic image, the vampire itself; the statement efficiently conflates both capital and vampire as parasitic, inhuman and addicted. Ken Gelder elaborates upon this, arguing that 'capitalism is by nature driven to consume *excessively*' and suggesting that it 'would not be an exaggeration to say that this representation mobilised vampire fiction at this time, to produce a striking figure defined by *excess* and unrestrained appetite – whose strength increased, the more victims he consumed'.[74] Gelder's assessment compounds the conjunction of vampire with capital and proffers the convincing suggestion that Marx's critique of capital acts as a catalyst for vampire literature, defined as it is by excessive and unrestrained appetite. Judith Halberstam emphasizes the Gothic-Marxian equation stating that '[t]he modern world for Marx is peopled with the undead; it is, indeed, a Gothic world haunted by specters [*sic*] and ruled by the mystical nature of capital', suggesting, in a near-reversal of Gelder's position, that rather than Marx's representation of capital infecting Gothic literature, Marx's vision of the modern world is invaded and haunted by Gothic 'specters'.[75] Jennifer Wicke compounds this association to an even greater extent:

> Shorthand may seem to fall innocently outside the sphere of mass cultural media, but in fact it participates in one of the most thoroughgoing transformations of cultural labour of the twentieth century, the rationalization ... of the procedures of bureaucracy and business, the feminization of the clerical work force, the standardization of mass business writing. The modern office is very far afield from Transylvania, the doomed castle, and the ghostly doings Jonathan experiences there, but shorthand is utterly material to the ramifications of vampirism.[76]

Wicke effectively shifts the debate, arguing that the rationalizing and standardizing procedures manifest in the 'transformations of cultural labour' are as guilty of possessing vampiric traits as vampirism itself. As rational and justifiable as it might seem, the shifting reconfiguration of labour by, to use Wicke's example, shorthand, that tool of the capital-oriented institutions of bureaucracy and business, is as culpable as the criminal and parasitic properties of the vampire. In fact the redesignation of labour is intrinsically 'material to the ramifications of vampirism'; it is in such conjunctions between the old world of Gothic superstition and the new world of capital-oriented manipulation that modernity achieves its slippery status.

In his chapter 'The Working Day' Marx chooses to compare the evolution of the English factory and the 'voracious appetite for surplus labour' of capital with the economic relationship between peasant and feudal lord, using for one of his examples the 'Wallachian boyar'.[77] Dracula, the Transylvanian aristocrat who is located within the 'whirlpool of European races', asserts his feudal dominance by stating, 'I am *boyar*; the common people know me, and I am master.'[78] It can be suggested therefore that, in terms of the connection between vampirism and capital, Dracula epitomizes the Wallachian boyar. As tenuous as this connection might seem, given that *Capital* was first published in its English translation in 1887 and *Dracula* a decade later, Christopher Frayling notes that Marx's point of reference for the Wallachian boyar was Elias Regnault's *Histoire Politique et Sociale des Principautes Danubiennes* of 1855.[79] Frayling, citing Regnault, argues that the Wallachian boyar 'was none other than Vlad the Impaler, Vlad Dracula', the supposed historical antecedent of Stoker's fictional vampire, and therefore that the boyar was 'the first reference to Dracula [for symbolic purposes] in the English language'.[80] Again it seems that the vampire transcends and transgresses cultural, national, chronological and discursive boundaries, infecting and disseminating cultural discourse and circulation, while simultaneously consolidating metaphors that operate outside the apparently strict dividing lines of social and cultural practice. In many ways it seems impossible to refer to Marx's critique of capital without citing vampiric tropes manifest in cultural representation and vice versa. David Punter, in justifying why his critical paradigm for *The Literature of Terror* privileges Freud over Marx, writes: 'It is ... perhaps worth pointing out the obvious, that Marx had little to say about literature in general, and nothing whatever about Gothic fictions, whereas Freud's theory both contains an implicit aesthetic dimension and centres upon an analysis of fear.'[81] This may be true; certainly Freud's essay 'The Uncanny' has become a staple model for approaches to Gothic writing.[82] Nonetheless Marx's writing, as Halberstam identifies, explicitly utilized Gothic metaphors and similes in its analysis of modern social and economic structures. Terry Eagleton, discussing Marx in *The Ideology of the Aesthetic*, emphasizes this point by observing, 'Capital is a phantasmal body, a monstrous *Doppelgänger* which stalks abroad while its master sleeps, mechanically consuming the pleasures he austerely forgoes ... Both capitalist and capital are images of the living dead.'[83] Eagleton conflates a series of Gothic motifs in his reading of Marx, suggesting that capital (in a manner reminiscent of the analogies detected in Elizabeth Gaskell's opium addict, John Barton, which opened this discussion) evokes both the vampiric ('the living dead') and the Frankensteinian automaton (here 'mechanical'). More significantly Eagleton identifies capital as a 'monstrous *Doppelgänger*', evoking the vampire–capital equation of Marx, the vampiric processes manifest in the transformation of labour suggested by Wicke, and the mirroring of the bourgeois Harker by Dracula himself in Stoker's text. In fact the notion of capital as Gothic is reciprocated within Stoker's narrative by Dracula himself; confronted in his house at Piccadilly by the vampire hunters and their old world symbols of the crucifix and communion host, Dracula is struck with Jonathan Harker's Kukri knife. Seward notes in his diary entry:

> The blow was a powerful one; only the diabolical quickness of the Count's leap back saved him. A second less and the trenchant blade had shorne through his heart. As it was, the point just cut the cloth of his coat, making a wide gap whence a bundle of bank-notes and a stream of gold fell out.[84]

Metaphorically impaled by Harker's blade the vampire bleeds 'a stream of gold', suggesting that the inhuman Dracula is made up of capital in a way that echoes Inspector Newcomen's comment that 'money's life to the man' for the equally monstrous Hyde. Where Marx argues that capital is a vampire, in Stoker's *Dracula* the vampire is capital. Indeed, when exploring Dracula's castle Harker notes in his Transylvanian journal, 'The only thing I found was a great heap of gold in one corner – gold of all kinds, Roman, and British, and Austrian, and Hungarian, and Greek and Turkish money.'[85] Significantly in a discussion that involves a Greek/Turkey axis regarding vampirism and addiction, the vampire gold that Harker finds incorporates these two nations. In addition the presence of such a variety of currency indicates that the vampire can circulate within a multitude of economies, suggesting a particularly modern sense of business interests. As with Stevenson's Hyde, it is ironic yet significant that this capital-constituted creature should operate within the *capital* for much of the text, revealing and revelling in the anxieties of modernity. Capital and *the* capital are after all the source of and locus for technological development bound up in the notion of modernity. As Jennifer Wicke points out, Dracula's compulsion is not, in the end, for blood, but

> for a kind of knowledge and power he has become aware of as the attributes of modern, consumer capitalist culture. His 'desire is keen' surely not just to enlarge the vampire dominions, but to transform vampiredom, to take it to the heart of the metropolis, where it feeds on the forces already set in motion by technological development.[86]

As a creation bound up symbolically and metaphorically in the discourse of capital, exaggerated appetites and overconsumption, addiction for Dracula ultimately manifests itself in Stoker's liminal text as an obsession with the technology of modernity, and the unstable nature of modernity is distilled in the fascination that it holds for the vaporous vampire Count.

Conclusion
Ghost-script

> Unreal City
> Under the brown fog of a winter dawn,
> A crowd flowed over London, so many,
> I had not thought death had undone so many.
> Sighs, short and infrequent, were exhaled,
> And each man fixed his eyes before his feet.[1]

It is somehow appropriate that this book should close with a discussion of the vampire, for its shadowy, vaporous and shifting presence draws together and metaphorises many of the issues which have been significant throughout it. If my initial premise has been to explore the nature of identity for the individual within nineteenth-century modernity through its representation in a variety of different cultural texts and intertexts, what then *can* be said about the state of identity in the nineteenth century? As should be clear by now, identity, certainly in terms of its representation in the works scrutinized here, can be seen to be in a state of flux, crisis and transition in all sorts of different configurations. Marx and Engels's claim that modernity for the nineteenth-century bourgeoisie consists of constant and destabilizing revolution and reinvention – encapsulated in the all too familiar phrase '[a]ll that is solid melts into air' so usefully interrogated by Marshall Berman – goes some way to explain why identity should have such unstable qualities during the period. The reasons for this dislocation, subsumed within the broad spectrum of analysis offered in the *Communist Manifesto*, are manifold. Marx and Engels are of course assessing the emergence and social dominance of the industrial bourgeoisie, and it is the relative novelty of this social grouping that perhaps initially explains the instability of identity represented in many of the texts discussed above. David Punter has assessed the significance of this phenomenon, suggesting that in many ways 'the Industrial Revolution constituted some kind of birth trauma' and that the 'bourgeoisie is itself the child of a curious miscegenation of class, and can be seen as still engaged in a series of attempts to come to grips with the problems of its conception and its emergence into the world'. Punter's description, couched as it is in terms that evoke birth, family origins and uncertain heritage, goes some way to explain the role of blighted family relations and the emphasis upon inheritance that haunt the texts discussed in the first section of this work. In a wider context his assessment that the bourgeoisie of the nineteenth century struggles to get to grips with 'the problems of its conception and its emergence into the world' proffers another possible reason for a destabilized identity – in effect identity is not fully formed, it is still learning to know itself and the world around it. The impact of the Industrial Revolution upon British social, cultural and economic structures cannot be underestimated; as Punter points out, its effect, frequently read as part of a nineteenth-century master-narrative of progress, can be interpreted as traumatic, particularly where notions of collective or individual identity are concerned. We witness ambivalent responses to it by members of the literati in British Romanticism, exemplified in this discussion by Wordsworth's *The Prelude*, and in what Isobel Armstrong defines as the post-Romantic in Victorian writing. This ambivalence perhaps reaches its apotheosis in the Great Exhibition of 1851, where examples of British and European industrial and economic pre-eminence are housed within Crystal Palace, itself representative of the architectural avant-garde and transient in nature – a feature that echoes Marx and Engels's maxim cited above.

However, the advent and consolidation of the Industrial Revolution in nineteenth-century Britain is not the only significant phenomenon to implement a disorientating effect upon identity in modernity. Indeed profound commentaries upon identity for the purposes of this discussion have their origins in the early modern, and in particular in René Descartes' *Discourse on Method* and the *Meditations*. As well as his assessment of body/mind divisions, Descartes' work, as analyzed by Francis Barker in *The Culture of Violence*, describes the emergence of the cohesive and autonomous individual which implicitly brings with it 'the dispersed and fragmented disidentical' self. The result is a sense of fragmentation and division within the self. Descartes puts the division in terms of 'extended' and 'non-extended things', body and mind; Barker takes this tension further stating that 'the Cartesian subject is already deeply divided in and from itself'. This fragmentation of the subject finds traces in Shelley's sonnet 'Ozymandias'; however, the sense of inner division, as well as being powerfully evoked in Gothic *doppelgänger* novels by Hogg, Stevenson and Wilde, is also present in 'High' cultural discourse, particularly in the work of Hallam and Arnold. Throughout the nineteenth century, in a cultural and socio-economic climate where identity can be read as fragile, the question of authenticity with regard to selfhood emerges. What or who is the real self? The question is asked in a variety of different contexts from representations of disorientation experienced by the individual lost in the crowded metropolis, through Arnold's meditation upon authenticity in 'The Buried Life', to the posturing narcissism of the *fin de siècle* dandy.

Francis Barker's definition of disidentity has been particularly helpful in terms of the concerns of this book, for each text assessed posits the possibility that individuals possess no cohesive sense of identity, or at least do not belong to themselves. However, the condition of disidentity in nineteenth-century modernity differs considerably from that defined by Barker. Where disidentity for him involves a fragmentation of the self that 'dislocates it from any conceivable historical burden of responsibility either for the past or the future', the disidentical self in the nineteenth century is very much aware of history – past, present and future – though it is not necessarily able to formulate its place within history with certainty. As noted above, David Punter draws attention to the fact that the bourgeois individual, disorientated by the 'birth trauma' of the Industrial Revolution, is forced to come to terms with the 'problems of its conception and its emergence into the world'; in short to become aware of its origins and its surroundings. We have seen instances of the profound effect that this consciousness instigates on identity in the alienation depicted by Matthew Arnold in 'Dover Beach'; we can also detect elements of it in the rejection by Tennyson's Lotos Eaters of the imperatives of labour and the compulsion towards intoxicated oblivion. Marshall Berman takes Punter's discussion further by suggesting that to be modern in the nineteenth century is to be governed by 'inner dichotomies' arising from a sense of living in two worlds at once, one aware of the changes and transformations surrounding the individual and one which is conscious of a past that was not modern. Again the possibility occurs that inner division, here constituted by an awareness of historical placement, contributes to the instances of disidentity evoked in the texts discussed above. Whatever the case, it would certainly seem that the condition of disidentity for the nineteenth century individual is one that involves a clear awareness of history.

I use the term 'condition' of disidentity advisedly, for the nineteenth century posits a series of 'conditions' that attempt to define and control the lack of cohesion manifest in instances of disidentity. Such categorizations range from the 'city condition' discussed by William Greenslade in *Degeneration, Culture and the Novel*, through the various definitions of insanity posited by medical practitioners during the period, to degeneration theory itself with its attempt to bunch an amorphous series of examples of 'deviancy' under the single term 'degeneration'. In this context the frequent intrusion of the Gothic genre and Gothic motifs into this study has been hardly surprising, for the Gothic simultaneously contains apparent abnormality through its generation of monstrosity only to reveal that monstrosity itself defies fixed interpretative categorization. As Judith Halberstam puts it:

> The pleasure of monsters lies in their ability to mean and to appear to crystallize meaning and give form to the meaning of fear. The danger of monsters lies in their tendency to stabilize bias into bodily form and pass monstrosity off as the obverse of the natural and the human. But monsters are always in motion and they resist the interpretative strategies that attempt to put them in place.[2]

It is evident that the variety of different readings of, for example, Hyde in Stevenson's novel and Dracula in Stoker's, indicate the fluidity of monstrosity with regard to interpretation, and furthermore suggest that the attempts to stabilize human identity through defining it in relation to monstrosity, deviancy or otherness is at best a tenuous one. The Oriental nightmares that so trouble the opium eater in Thomas De Quincey's *Confessions* also suggest the fragility of attempts to assert identity through contrast and opposition; demonizing the antiquity of the Orient merely reveals the relative juvenility and fragility of the Western bourgeois identity.

In the course of this project I have examined three key examples of conditions in nineteenth-century modernity where the fragility and subsequent fragmentation of identity are powerfully evoked. Of course the chosen areas themselves do not exhaust possible avenues of interpretation with regard to a possible crisis of identity in the nineteenth century. I have not, for example, explored gender or sexuality in any great detail. Nonetheless the three sites that I have examined do subsume within them a number of issues that overlap and traverse the boundaries established in immediate areas of study. Part I addressed the idea of self-division and inner-conflict by looking in detail at the three novels by James Hogg, Robert Louis Stevenson and Oscar Wilde. Descartes' theory of the division of the human subject, espoused in the *Meditations* and addressed by Barker in *The Culture of Violence*, provided a significant and convenient starting point for such a discussion, particularly as Descartes explores the possibility that the body might be a basic technology, an automaton, and that the idea of an integrated and cohesive self might prove to be illusory. What is particularly noticeable is that the concept of inner division can be found not only in the 'shilling shockers' of the Gothic novelists, but in a variety of different and even unusual contexts, such as Matthew Arnold's cultural criticism and the embryonic sociological discourse of the degeneration theorists Max Nordau and Cesare Lombroso. In this light, Arnold's lyric 'The Buried Life', as much as it explores the search for a genuine self, proffers significant moments that uncannily echo the preoccupation of the Gothic with the unspeakable, taboo, guilt and secret selves. It is also noteworthy that in each text scrutinized, basic Cartesian duality is troubled in such a way that, rather than evoking a series of oppositions or binaries – Jekyll versus Hyde for instance – the boundaries between self and other, normal and abnormal, human and inhuman are blurred. The result is that rather than evoking a nineteenth-century split personality, the novels, to use Karl Miller's terms, suggest a transition from dipsychism to polypsychism. Identity therefore becomes a fluid thing, yet also something that is forced, in the ever-changing milieu of modernity, to change itself consistently and compulsively. As well as covering the influence of capital in the problematic relation between identity and the marketplace, the role of inheritance, anti-social criminal activity, social conditioning, and the areas of authenticity and inauthenticity with regard to the self, it can be observed that these texts, which posit a variety of egos and alter egos, ultimately suggest the inability of the subject to speak itself. As Jekyll puts it in Stevenson's novel with regard to Hyde and more significantly himself, '[h]e, I say – I cannot say, I'. What we witness is a disintegration and collapse of the self.

Part II assessed the impact of religion in crisis upon poetry and the poetic persona by considering poems by Alfred Tennyson, James 'B.V.' Thomson and Gerard Manley Hopkins. In many ways the effects that new scientific thought, European-influenced studies of

Christian scripture and political radicalism in the nineteenth century had upon traditional Christianity coincide with Marshall Berman's assessment of the 'internal dichotomies' facing the individual in modernity. It is possible to argue that, as far as the religiously inclined individual is concerned, perception of the present demonstrates the increasing social and cultural marginalisation of religion, yet simultaneously there is a consciousness that the sacred had a resonance in the past which is now lost, or, as Arnold eloquently puts it in 'Dover Beach', 'The Sea of Faith / Was once, too, at the full and round earth's sure ... But now I only hear / Its melancholy, long, withdrawing roar'. In this context identity is troubled hypothetically because it is deprived of value. The possibility that the experience of modernity in the nineteenth century becomes a valueless one is explored by Arnold in this lyric and in his prose writing, and it is one which can, perhaps surprisingly, be traced in Marx and Engels's descriptions of the bourgeoisie stripping the halo from the priest and rendering 'all that is holy' profane found in the *Communist Manifesto*. However, the poems under scrutiny are not conventional laments for the passing of religious centrality in an increasingly secular and materialist world. Instead they are a complex concatenation of works that articulate various manifestations of the sometimes awful effect that religion has upon identity and the individual. Religious lunacy and extreme self-obsession, in the form of a dramatic monologue from the perspective of a dying anchorite, was addressed and contextualized in terms of nineteenth-century medical writing on morbid fanaticism. The paradox at the heart of anchorite activity is that self-denial becomes acute self-consciousness, and thus a perverse form of narcissistic delusion – identity is troubled by being simultaneously negated and over-stated. In Tennyson's elegy, *In Memoriam*, the doubts and anxieties instigated by the premature death of Hallam result in an apparent crisis of faith where the human subject, in the face of scientific materialism and the apparent indifference of Nature to individual existence, becomes a 'discord' – identity is seemingly meaningless in a world where God does not or cannot confirm His existence. Thomson and Hopkins represent the possibility that God is absent or does not even exist in strikingly different ways. Thomson's avowedly atheistic perspective incorporates the possibility that, as life in the modern metropolis is so relentlessly miserable and void of meaning, the nonexistence of God is a reassuring thing; ultimately there is no divine being determining behaviour or existence. As a consequence the negation of identity is a relatively unproblematic occurrence as life is meaningless anyway. By contrast Hopkins's 'Terrible Sonnets' pay witness to the apparently devastating sense that God may be absent, and without God identity becomes meaningless. However, for the poetic persona this does not erase the self, but rather throws identity in upon itself, resulting in a series of poems that are solipsistic in the extreme but fail to reassure the speaker that identity is in any way an integrated thing. In fact the absence of God only makes Hopkins' poetic persona more conscious of its own disintegration.

In the discussion of addiction many of the themes considered in this project start to come together. Just as the notion of self-division is significant in the nineteenth century due to the work on clinical duality by Alfred Wigan amongst others, and religion possesses an obvious currency in many discussions of the nineteenth century, so too addiction has a certain resonance, not least because of the ubiquity of opium and other narcotics during the period, but also because of the disease theories applied to it during the period. In addition, where traces of each theme addressed can be detected in other chapters – for example, religious lunacy in James Hogg's *Private Memoirs* and doubling in De Quincey's *Confessions* – addiction, appropriately enough given the unlocated and shifting qualities that it possesses, haunts many of texts discussed outside Part III. Indeed, much of this project deals with addicts and the connotations of addiction; Arnold talks of the 'strange disease of modern life' in 'The Scholar Gypsy', a phrase that has an added resonance when Berman's analysis of bourgeois identity as compulsively addicted to self-transformation is considered. More literally we can find addicts in Stevenson's *Jekyll and Hyde*, where Jekyll is both addicted to the strange compound that he discovers and to his transformation into Hyde, and in Wilde's novel where Dorian Gray visits the opium dens of the London Docklands and is addicted to a book that poisons him; addiction can also be detected in Simeon Stylites's morbid and helpless obsession with self-denial and in the opium-haunted inhabitants of Thomson's 'The City of Dreadful Night'. At the heart of addiction is the notion that individuals no longer belong to themselves but to some extraneous power that sustains them, a feature that defines the automaton and the Faustian pact as discussed in Part I. In this context addiction takes many different forms and appears in many different guises, some literal and some metaphorical. It certainly contributes to destabilizing identity; intoxication after all consists of a shift in consciousness as De

Quincey's opium eater aptly demonstrates. It also incorporates a number of themes that render identity even more tentative; the discourse of addiction reveals anxieties for the bourgeois individual about nation, empire, capital, gender, culture, even modernity itself, as Jennifer Wicke points out in her discussion of *Dracula*.

One of the other areas that has haunted this project all along has been the presence of the urban metropolis, which, along with the emergence of the nineteenth-century bourgeoisie, is the other progeny of the Industrial Revolution. We can detect traces of its fluid, crowded and foggy qualities in the work of Wordsworth, De Quincey, Arnold, James Thomson, Charles Dickens and the urban Gothic writers; it can also be found in Walter Benjamin's work on Baudelaire and the *flâneur* who loses himself in the crowd. In this environment, perhaps more than anywhere else, identity becomes a difficult thing to establish or ascertain; it is either concealed behind public masks, as Arnold indicates in 'The Buried Life', or it is reduced to a meaningless uniformity in the chaos of the crowd, as Wordsworth suggests in *The Prelude*. It is in such an environment, shadowy and vaporous, that homicidal criminals can conceal themselves and their activities. Such instances have been observed in Stevenson's *Jekyll and Hyde*, Wilde's *Dorian Gray*, and Stoker's *Dracula*, to name but a few examples of the criminal disappearing into the night. As I stated earlier, it is appropriate that this project should conclude with a discussion of the vampire, for the vampire, as well as being homicidal criminal, metaphorizes and torments a number of significant anxieties which trouble and haunt the stability of bourgeois identity in the nineteenth century – anxieties about things that predominantly concern the bourgeoisie, for example class, nation, capital, technology and work. In addition, the resonance of Stoker's *fin de siècle* vampire lies in the fact that, aristocratic and Other as he is, in Stoker's text he is very much tied up with the dynamics of modernity. As Jennifer Wicke points out, Stoker's vampire 'highlight[s] the banal terrors of modern life' which 'we are still living today', and therefore for Wicke *Dracula* remains 'the first great *modern* novel in British literature'.[3] Wicke's assertion is arguably overdemonstrative; however, it is worth considering that Dracula – the shadowy, fluid and protean figure who uncannily reflects or parodies many of the imperatives of late nineteenth-century bourgeois individualism – remains one of the most potent popular culture symbols of the nineteenth century to be successfully and consistently resurrected throughout the twentieth century, and no doubt into the twenty-first. Indeed the vampire, as popular culture icon and in terms of what it represents, haunts modernity today.

This book started with, amongst other things, an analysis of fragmentation in modernity. As well as other notable texts that deal with this theme, I addressed Eliot's *The Waste Land*, and it is to *The Waste Land* that I finally wish to return. In the fragment from 'The Burial of the Dead' deployed as an epigraph for this conclusion Eliot posits a vision of the modern metropolis as an 'Unreal City', one that evokes Baudelaire's Paris of *Les Fleurs Du Mal* with its mixture of dream and reality. Like the images of the city encountered in nineteenth-century writing, it is seen through fog and crowded. In addition, like Wordsworth's description of the city in *The Prelude*, identity is reduced to a uniform mass where 'each man fixed his eyes before his feet'.[4] Eliot's poem is fragmented – it utilizes a wide variety of cultural reference points, it does not possess a linear narrative, it gives the illusion of consisting of a plethora of perspectives and voices – nonetheless it is possible to argue that it possesses a certain thematic consistency that echoes Arnold's lament for religion and culture in 'Dover Beach'. However, like Wicke's description of *Dracula*, it is not a 'coherent text' and, through its varied ventriloquisms, it 'refracts hysterical images of modernity'. It is no surprise then that Eliot's London Bridge is passed over by spectral presences 'undone' by death, and that the metropolitan vampire is reborn, even revamped, in the 'bats with baby faces' (line 379) of 'What the Thunder Said'.

Notes

Introduction

1 Alfred Tennyson, 'OI REONTES', *Poems, Chiefly Lyrical* (1830), in *The Poems of Tennyson*, ed. Christopher Ricks (London: Longman, 1987), p. 436.
2 Karl Marx and Friedrich Engels, *The Communist Manifesto*, trans. Samuel Moore (Harmondsworth: Penguin, [1888] 1985), p. 83.
3 Matthew Arnold, 'The Scholar Gypsy', *Poems, 1853*, in *Selected Poems and Prose*, ed. Miriam Allott (London: Everyman, 1993), p. 99.
4 Isobel Armstrong, *Victorian Poetry: Poetry, Poetics and Politics* (London: Routledge, 1993), p. 3.
5 David Punter, *The Literature of Terror*, vol. 2, *The Modern Gothic* (London: Longman, 1996), p. 193.
6 Armstrong, *Victorian Poetry*, p. 3.
7 William Wordsworth, *The Prelude (Text of 1805)*, ed. E. de Selincourt (London: Oxford University Press, 1933), 7, p.
8 Punter, *The Literature of Terror*, vol. 2, p. 193.
9 I am indebted to Francis Barker's challenging study of identity, tragedy, modernity and postmodernity, *The Culture of Violence: Essays on Tragedy and History* (Manchester: Manchester University Press, 1993), for the construction of a notion of disidentity; however, my use of the term does differ in significant ways to that of Barker. Barker, in his reading of Friedrich Nietzsche's essay 'On the Uses and Disadvantages of History for Life' (1874), argues that the experience of the Western individual in modernity involves either 'a certain reinstallation of the self, as in a sense self-invented, imaged, styled, even replicated', or a 'bucolic pastoral of disidentity, the forms of fragmentation and dispersal of the self which defuse both its centrality and its centredness, and thus dislocates it from any conceivable burden of responsibility either for the past or the future' (p. 93). The first option, an attempt to present an identity that is coherent if not necessarily authentic (or indeed *more* authentic for the very reason that it is invented, even replicated) has a useful resonance considering the plurality of invented selves and masked identities in nineteenth-century culture, from Mary Shelley's composite creature in *Frankenstein* (1818) to the stylized and superficial dandy in Oscar Wilde's *The Picture of Dorian Gray* (1891). However, it is the second condition, that of disidentity – with its emphasis on fragmentation, the dispersal of the self, dislocation and decentring – which proves apposite in terms of the themes of this study. That said, in Barker's definition disidentity is a happy 'pastoral' that relieves the individual of 'the historical burden of responsibility either for the past or the future'. Obviously

representations of disidentity, by which I mean a fragmentation of the self and consciousness that echoes Cartesian dualism, in the nineteenth century are most often located in an urban environment; Wordsworth's *The Prelude*, in spite of the fact that it suggests a reducing of identity, indicates this. In addition, where Barker places disidentity outside past and future, we can see that in the nineteenth-century, fragmentation of the self stems from a repeated dichotomy between a consciousness of past and future. As we will see, Marshall Berman, in his assessment of the experience of modernity, argues that it is from this sense of temporal uncertainty and dislocation that nineteenth-century modernism – with all its fissures and fragmentary manifestations – emerges. Although Barker's conception of disidentity rises from historical conditions, notably the emergence of the individual in Western modernity, it reveals itself as a 'bucolic' idyll bereft of historical responsibility. By the nineteenth century, disidentity can be equated explicitly with the 'condition of crisis' described by Armstrong. In my discussion of 'Dover Beach' I will demonstrate that Matthew Arnold's apprehension of the fragmentation and decentring of self derives emphatically from an acute and painful consciousness of past and future.

10 Peter Stallybrass and Alan White, *The Politics and Poetics of Transgression* (London: Methuen, 1986), p. 123.

11 Marshall Berman, *All That is Solid Melts into Air: The Experience of Modernity* (London: Verso, 1982), p. 17.

12 William Greenslade, *Degeneration, Culture and the Novel 1880–1940* (Cambridge: Cambridge University Press, 1994), p. 17.

13 Greenslade, *Culture and the Novel*, p. 17.

14 Greenslade, *Culture and the Novel*, p. 18.

15 Armstrong, *Victorian Poetry*, p. 6.

16 For the dating of Arnold's lyric see S. O. A. Ullmann, 'Dating through Calligraphy: The Example of "Dover Beach"', *Studies in Bibliography*, 26 (1973), pp. 19–36.

17 Percy Bysshe Shelley, 'Ozymandias', in *The Complete Works of Percy Bysshe Shelley*, ed. Neville Rogers, vol. 2 (Oxford: Oxford University Press, 1975), pp. 319–20.

18 The phrase 'terminal beach' is used by David Punter in *The Literature of Terror*, vol. 2, p. 213. Punter lifts it from the title of a collection of short stories by the writer J. G. Ballard, whom he compares to Shelley, claiming that 'what is shared is a preoccupation with a terminal breakdown of power, and also an imagistic concentration on petrification'; see David Punter, *The Hidden Script: Writing and the Unconscious* (London: Routledge, 1985), pp. 175–76, and J. G. Ballard, *The Terminal Beach* (London: Gollancz, [1964] 1997). In *The Literature of Terror* Punter uses the phrase with reference to William Gibson's seminal 'cyber-punk' science-fiction novel *Neuromancer*. This text, which has echoes of Romanticism in the title itself, is set in a post- technological, millenial world and reconfigures many of the concerns of Romanticism, such as the problems facing human identity in a mechanized world, the search for the source of creative agency – whether theological, biological, ethical or aesthetic – body/machine interfaces, and duality. As Gibson's novel also deals with decaying dynasties and the fragmentation of identity, the use of the phrase 'terminal beach', used by Punter with regard to Ballard

and Gibson, seems appropriate when applied to Shelley's sandscape scenario in 'Ozymandias'. Interestingly, Francis Barker's assessment of disidentity as a response to what he calls the 'post-historical condition' involves the idea that 'history has been traduced as one of the meta-narratives towards which, now, nothing but a famous incredulity is due; or, substantively, as the *fin de siècle*, if not millenarian theme of the end of history gathers force, the real process itself is adjudged to have come to an end'; see Barker, *The Culture of Violence*, p. 93. Barker's references to an 'incredulity to meta-narratives' and the 'end of history' allude to J.-F. Lyotard's *The Postmodern Condition: A Report on Knowledge*, trans. G. Bennington and B. Massumi (Manchester: Manchester University Press, 1984), and Francis Fukuyama's *The End of History and the Last Man* (Harmondsworth: Penguin, 1992) respectively; see Barker's note in *The Culture of Violence*, p. 116. In its title Fukuyama's text reveals again how indebted postmodern theory and fiction is, via Nietzsche, to Romanticism; 'last man' images and motifs abound in Romantic writing, indeed 'Ozymandias', with its solitary figure in the midst of a wilderness, can be read as such a narrative. For other contemporary writings on the subject see Mary Shelley, *The Last Man*, ed. Anne McWhir (Ontario: Broadview Press, [1826] 1996), this novel covers the theme at length and also provides appendices that list further examples of such narratives in Romantic writing; see pp. 369–81 in particular. As we have seen, Barker's conception of disidentity involves an abdication of responsibility for past or future; in his complex reading of history and historicity, 'Nietzsche's Cattle', Barker dismisses the theories of history advocated by Lyotard and Fukuyama as involving 'singular and banal formulations' such as the ones cited above; see *The Culture of Violence*, p. 109. However, the suggestion of a late twentieth/early twenty first-century *fin de siècle* and a 'millenarian ... end of history' demonstrates the strange resonance of Shelley's poem, a resonance which David Punter picks up on. Disidentity in Shelley's poem, which is ultimately millenial in its apocalyptic themes, proves more sophisticated and contradictory than the formulations criticized by Barker, for as much as the 'terminal beach' of 'Ozymandias' obliterates (and effectively ends) history (and the history of the disidentified subject), it also offers a lesson *in* history, as David Punter goes on to suggest. This exercise in archaeology uses the past to inform the future, particularly in the haunting words inscribed upon the pedestal.

19 David Punter, *The Literature of Terror*, vol. 1, *The Gothic Tradition* (London: Longman, 1996), p. 97, and *The Hidden Script*, p. 12.

20 Matthew Arnold, 'Dover Beach' (1867); this and all further quotations from the poem can be found in Matthew Arnold, *Selected Poems and Prose*, ed. Miriam Allott, (London: Everyman, 1993), pp. 76–77.

21 Karl Marx, 'Speech at the Anniversary of the *People's Paper*', in *The Marx– Engels Reader*, ed. Robert C. Tucker (New York: Norton, 1978), pp. 577–78.

22 Berman, *All That Is Solid*, p. 17.

23 W. B. Yeats, 'The Second Coming' (1920), in *W. B. Yeats: The Poems*, ed. Richard J. Finneran (London: Macmillan, 1984), p. 187.

24 For *Spiritus Mundi* see Finneran's explanatory notes, *W. B. Yeats*, pp. 643–45.

25 T. S. Eliot, *The Waste Land* (1922), in *The Complete Poems and Plays of T. S. Eliot* (London: Faber & Faber, 1975), pp. 61–75.

26 Berman, *All That Is Solid*, p. 237.
27 Berman, *All That Is Solid*, p. 237.
28 Berman, *All That Is Solid*, p. 238
29 Berman, *All That Is Solid*, p. 238
30 W. J. Fox, *Monthly Repository*, 6 (January 1832), pp. 1–4.
31 Marx and Engels, *The Communist Manifesto*, p. 83.
32 Berman, *All ThatIis Solid*, pp. 95–96.
33 Charles Dickens, *Bleak House* (Harmondsworth: Penguin, [1853] 1985), p. 148.
34 Dickens, *Bleak House*, pp. 327, 420, 440.
35 Dickens, *Bleak House*, p. 339.
36 Marx and Engels, *The Communist Manifesto*, p. 92.
37 Dickens, *Bleak House*, p. 319.
38 Dickens, *Bleak House*, p. 199.
39 It is interesting to note that Jo, particularly in terms of the brevity of his name, is not merely a caricatured and symbolic figure. Edwin Chadwick, citing the words of a Scottish superintendent of Police, claimed that the horrors of London contained 'a thousand children who have no names whatever, or only nicknames, like dogs'; see Edwin Chadwick, *Report on an Enquiry into the Sanitary Conditions of the Labouring Population of Great Britain* (London: W. Clowes, 1842), p. 133.
40 Dickens, *Bleak House*, pp. 272–73.
41 Dickens, *Bleak House*, pp. 49–50.
42 Dickens, *Bleak House*, pp. 179, 279.
43 Berman, *All That Is Solid*, p. 144. Interestingly the fluidity, both of environment and identity, discussed here can also be traced to a fragment of an early draft of 'Ozymandias', where Shelley writes that the traveller sees the ruined statue 'Quiver through sultry mist'; see Shelley, *The Complete Works of Percy Bysshe Shelley*, vol 2, p. 320.
44 Judith Walkowitz, in her study of late-Victorian London, *The City of Dreadful Delight* (London: Virago, 1992), describes Jack the Ripper as a 'disappearing shadow' (p. 1). This assessment is appropriately tautological, emphasizing the shadowy and insubstantial nature of the figure. Indeed, for Walkowitz Jack the Ripper has a deeply unlocated nature, he is a central figure in twentieth- century representations of *fin de siècle* London – no 'single criminal has appeared so tirelessly in literature, drama, opera, television, and motion pictures' (p. 3) – yet this appeal seems to be founded largely in a comprehensive failure to establish his identity, in spite of a variety of plausible and not so plausible speculative theories. One of the significant features in Walkowitz's analysis of Jack the Ripper is her assessment of the manner in which he operates within the metropolis. She states that '[o]ften imagined as a seasoned urban traveller, the Ripper could move effortlessly and invisibly through the spaces of London, transgressing all boundaries' (p. 3); his invisibility, his ability to melt into air, is stressed again, as is the way in which boundaries, limits, *containment* within the spaces of the city, are all transgressed. These features can all be detected in the behaviour of the Gothic villains Hyde and Dracula, and echo the topography of the city itself as represented by Dickens; in effect Gothic villain and urban environment are reflections of each other.
45 Dickens, *Bleak House*, pp. 511–12.

Part I: (De)Generating doubles

Introduction

1 Alfred L. Wigan, *The Duality of the Mind* (London: Longman, 1844), p. 26.
2 Oscar Wilde, *The Picture of Dorian Gray* (Harmondsworth: Penguin, [1891] 1985), p. 22.
3 Wigan, *Duality of the Mind*, p. 26.
4 Anne Harrington, *Medicine, Mind and the Double Brain: A Study in Nineteenth Century Thought* (New Jersey: Princeton University Press, 1987), p. 22.
5 Harrington, *Medicine, Mind*, p. 29.
6 John Elliotson, 'On the Joint Operation of the Two Halves of the Brain: With a Notice of Dr Wigan's Work Entitled The Duality of the Mind, etc.', *The Zoist*, 15 (1847), p. 359.
7 Barker, *The Culture of Violence*, p. 94.
8 Barker, *The Culture of Violence*, p. 95.
9 For the '*cogito*' equation, see René Descartes, *Discourse on Method and the Meditations*, trans. F. E. Sutcliffe (Harmondsworth: Penguin, [1637] 1968), p. 53.
10 René Descartes, *Meditations on First Philosophy, with Selections from the Objections and Replies*, trans. John Cottingham (Cambridge: Cambridge University Press, [1641] 1986), p. 12.
11 Descartes, *Meditations on First Philosophy*, p. 54.
12 Descartes, *Meditations on First Philosophy*, p. 58.
13 Punter, *The Literature of Terror*, vol. 2, p. 193.
14 For comprehensive analyses of instances of doubling in nineteenth-century literature see Masao Miyoshi, *The Divided Self: A Perspective on the Literature of the Victorians* (New York: New York University Press, 1969), and Karl Miller, *Doubles: Studies in Literary History* (Oxford: Oxford University Press, 1985).
15 See Armstrong, *Victorian Poetry*, p. 31.
16 Arthur Henry Hallam, 'On Some of the Characteristics of Modern Poetry', *Englishman's Magazine*, August 1831, pp. 616–28; cited Isobel Armstrong, *Victorian Scrutinies: Reviews of Poetry 1830–1870* (London: Athlone, 1972), p. 91.
17 Armstrong, *Victorian Poetry*, p. 492.
18 Matthew Arnold, 'Preface' to *Poems 1853*, in *Selected Poems and Prose*, p. 115.
19 Berman, *All That Is Solid*, p. 39.
20 Greenslade, *Degeneration*, p. 122.
21 Max Nordau, *Degeneration* (London: Heinemann, [1895] 1898), p. 560.
22 Cesare Lombroso, *The Man of Genius* (London: Walter Scott, 1891), pp. 5–6.
23 Greenslade, *Degeration*, p. 21.
24 Robert Nye, *Crime, Madness and Politics in Modern France: The Medical Concept of National Decline* (Princeton: Princeton University Press, 1984), p. 47.
25 Greenslade, *Degeneration*, p. 2.
26 Nye, *Crime, Madness and Politics*, pp. 47–48.
27 See Michel Foucault, *The Archaeology of Knowledge*, trans. A. M. Sheridan-Smith (London: Tavistock Publications, [1969] 1972), in particular part 2, chaps. 1–7, and *The History of Sexuality*, trans. R. Hurley, vol. 1 (Harmondsworth: Penguin, [1976] 1981), in particular part 2, chap. 1, and part 4, chap. 2.
28 Greenslade, *Degeneration*, p. 2.

29 Greenslade, *Degeneration*, p. 3.
30 Nye, *Crime, Madness and Politics*, p. 48.
31 Greenslade, *Degeneration*, p. 3.
32 Greenslade, *Degeneration*, p. 18.
33 Greenslade, *Degeneration*, p. 16.
34 Jon Stratton, 'Serial Killing and the Transformation of the Social', *Theory, Culture and Society*, 13 (1996), , pp. 77–98 (92).
35 Michel Foucault, 'The Dangerous Individual', in *Michel Foucault: Politics, Philosophy, Culture; Interviews and Other Writings 1977–1984*, ed. Lawrence Kritzman (London: Routledge, 1988), p. 132.
36 Judith Halberstam, *Skin Shows: Gothic Horror and the Technology of Monsters* (Durham and London: Duke University Press, 1995), pp. 1, 179.
37 See Miller, *Doubles*, p. 330.
38 Halberstam, *Skin Shows*, p. 23.
39 Halberstam, *Skin Shows*, pp. 56–57, 193–94.
40 Matthew Arnold, *Culture and Anarchy*, in *Selected Poems and Prose*, pp. 201–08.
41 John Storey, *An Introductory Guide to Cultural Theory and Popular Culture* (London: Harvester Wheatsheaf, 1993), p. 22.
42 Arnold, *Culture and Anarchy*, in *Selected Poems and Prose*, pp. 197–201.
43 Arnold, 'The Buried Life' from *Empedocles on Etna and Other Poems*, in *Selected Poems and Prose*, pp. 84–86. All further quotations from the poem can be found on these pages.
44 Halberstam, *Skin Shows*, p. 20.
45 James Hogg, *The Private Memoirs and Confessions of a Justified Sinner* (Harmondsworth: Penguin, [1824] 1983), p. 240.
46 See Robert Louis Stevenson, *The Strange Case of Dr Jekyll and Mr Hyde*, in *Dr Jekyll and Mr Hyde and Other Stories* (Harmondsworth: Penguin, [1886] 1979), pp. 58–59, 72, and Wilde, *Dorian Gray*, p. 147.
47 Stevenson, *Jekyll and Hyde*, pp. 40, 58.

1 Speaking and answering in the character of another

1 Hogg, *Private Memoirs*, p. 177.
2 Wigan, *Duality of the Mind*, p. 126.
3 Punter, *The Literature of Terror*, vol. 1, p. 130.
4 Punter, *The Literature of Terror*, vol. 1, p. 130.
5 Punter, *The Literature of Terror*, vol. 1, p. 136
6 For details of the letter, see John Wain's editorial introduction to Hogg's *Private Memoirs*, pp. 7–8.
7 For the letter see *Private Memoirs*, pp. 230–34, and p. 241 for the manipulation of the title.
8 Hogg, *Private Memoirs*, pp. 43–44.
9 Note that later in the editor's first narrative, Robert utterly rejects the Colwan association, saying to George that 'henceforth I disclaim the name' to which George replies '[m]y mother's son you may be, – but *not a Colwan*' (Hogg, *Private Memoirs*, p. 48). This troubles Robert's sense of authentic identity further.
10 Hogg, *Private Memoirs*, p. 109.
11 Hogg, *Private Memoirs*, p. 106.

12 Magdalene Redekop, 'Beyond Closure: Buried Alive with Hogg's *Justified Sinner*', *English Literary History*, 52 (1985), pp. 159–84 (164).
13 Fred Botting, *Gothic* (London: Routledge, 1996), p. 112.
14 Hogg, *Private Memoirs*, p. 234.
15 Mark L. Schoenfield, 'Butchering James Hogg: Romantic Identity in the Magazine Market', in *At the Limits of Romanticism: Essays in Cultural, Feminist and Materialist Criticism*, ed. Mary A. Favret and Nicola J. Watson (Bloomington and Indianapolis: Indiana University Press, 1994), pp. 207–24 (210).
16 Schoenfield, 'Butchering James Hogg', p. 208.
17 Schoenfield, 'Butchering James Hogg', p. 209.
18 Schoenfield, 'Butchering James Hogg', p. 209.
19 Hogg, *Private Memoirs*, p. 125.
20 Botting, *Gothic*, p. 131.
21 Hogg, *Private Memoirs*, p. 173.
22 Hogg, *Private Memoirs*, p. 175.
23 Hogg, *Hogg, Private Memoirs*, p. 176.
24 Hogg, *Private Memoirs*, p. 177.
25 Hogg, *Private Memoirs*, p. 177.
26 Hogg, *Private Memoirs*, p. 173.
27 Miyoshi, *The Divided Self*, p. 95.
28 Hogg, *Private Memoirs*, p. 135.
29 Wigan, *Duality of the Mind*, p. 126.
30 Hogg, *Private Memoirs*, p. 157.
31 Hogg, *Private Memoirs*, p. 220.
32 Hogg, *Private Memoirs*, p. 167.
33 Hogg, *Private Memoirs*, p. 91.
34 Hogg, *Private Memoirs*, p. 95.
35 Hogg, *Private Memoirs*, p. 181.
36 Hogg, *Private Memoirs*, pp. 182, 187.
37 Hogg, *Private Memoirs*, p. 183.
38 Hogg, *Private Memoirs*, p. 190.
39 Wringhim can be read as deviant for a number of reasons: he is apparently a murderer, a debauchee, arguably insane and certainly a fanatic. This representation of himself in a figurative sado-masochistic relationship with his mentor merely confirms his deviancy. In psychoanalytical terms this monstrous depiction of Gil-Martin establishes Wringhim as a paranoiac. Judith Halberstam notes that paranoia is the 'clinical term for the transformation of desire into fear and of the desired / feared object into monster' (*Skin Shows*, p. 9).
40 Hogg, *Private Memoirs*, p. 214.
41 Hogg, *Private Memoirs*, p. 219.
42 Hogg, *Private Memoirs*, pp. 231-32.
43 Hogg, *Private Memoirs*, p. 230.

2 He, I say – I cannot say, I

1 Marx and Engels, *The Communist Manifesto*, pp. 85–86.
2 James (B. V.) Thomson, 'The City of Dreadful Night' (1874), IV, lines 70–72, from *The City of Dreadful Night and Other Poems* (London: Watts & Co., 1932), pp.

1–46. All further references to Thomson's poem are from this edition.
3 Robert Louis Stevenson, *Weir of Hermiston* (London: Heinemann, [1896] 1924), p. 64.
4 Stevenson, *Jekyll and Hyde*, p. 48.
5 Halberstam, *Skin Shows*, pp. 21–22.
6 Botting, *Gothic*, p. 136.
7 Punter, *The Literature of Terror*, vol. 2, p. 3.
8 Alan Sandison, *Robert Louis Stevenson and the Appearance of Modernism: A Future Feeling* (London: Macmillan, 1996), p. 255.
9 Halberstam, *Skin Shows*, p. 80.
10 For the latter two readings of Hyde, namely degenerate throwback and androgynous deviant, see Greenslade, *Degeneration*, pp. 83–85, and Janice Doane and Devon Hodges's essay 'Demonic Disturbances of Sexual Identity: The Strange Case of Dr. Jekyll and Mr/s Hyde', *Novel: A Forum on Fictions*, 23 (1989), pp. 63–74.
11 Stevenson, *Jekyll and Hyde*, p. 40.
12 Stevenson, *Jekyll and Hyde*, pp. 83–84.
13 Sandison, *Robert Louis Stevenson*, pp. 224–25.
14 Punter, *The Literature of Terror*, vol. 2, p. 2.
15 Stevenson, *Jekyll and Hyde*, p. 31.
16 Punter, *The Literature of Terror*, vol. 2, p. 4.
17 Stephen Heath, 'Psychopathia Sexualis: Stevenson's *Strange Case*', *Critical Quarterly*, 28 (1986), pp. 93–108 (93).
18 Miller, *Doubles*, p. 211.
19 Stevenson, *Jekyll and Hyde*, p. 47.
20 Martin Tropp, *Images of Fear: How Horror Stories Helped Shape Modern Culture (1818–1918)* (Jefferson, NC: McFarland & Co., 1990), p. 130.
21 Halberstam, *Skin Shows*, p. 56.
22 Stevenson, *Jekyll and Hyde*, p. 81.
23 Wigan, *The Duality of the Mind*, p. 80.
24 Stevenson, *Jekyll and Hyde*, pp. 81–82.
25 Stevenson, *Jekyll and Hyde*, p. 82.
26 Stevenson, *Jekyll and Hyde*, p. 82.
27 Stevenson, *Jekyll and Hyde*, pp. 37–38, 80.
28 Stevenson, *Jekyll and Hyde*, p. 86.
29 Stevenson, *Jekyll and Hyde*, pp. 53–54.
30 Walter Benjamin, *Charles Baudelaire: A Lyric Poet in the Era of High Capitalism*, trans. Harry Zohn (London: Verso, 1983), p. 66.
31 Benjamin, *Charles Baudelaire*, p. 171.
32 Marx and Engels, *The Communist Manifesto*, p. 82.
33 Stevenson, *Jekyll and Hyde*, p. 85.
34 Stevenson, *Jekyll and Hyde*, p. 71.
35 Havelock Ellis, *The New Spirit* (London: Constable & Co., [1890] 1926), p. 7.
36 Greenslade, *Degeneration*, p. 16.
37 Berman, *All That Is Solid*, p. 115.
38 Halberstam, *Skin Shows*, p. 67.
39 Stevenson, *Jekyll and Hyde*, p. 89.

40 Richard Dellamora, *Masculine Desire: The Sexual Politics of Victorian Aestheticism* (Chapel Hill and London: University of North Carolina Press, 1990), pp. 198–99.
41 The 'dark side of progress' alludes to J. Chamberlain and Sander L. Gilman's collection *Degeneration: The Dark Side of Progress* (New York: Columbia University Press, 1985).
42 Halberstam, *Skin Shows*, p. 3.
43 Stevenson, *Jekyll and Hyde*, p. 86.
44 Stevenson, *Jekyll and Hyde*, p. 73.
45 Stevenson, *Jekyll and Hyde*, p. 49.
46 Stevenson, *Jekyll and Hyde*, p. 50.
47 Stevenson, *Jekyll and Hyde*, p. 48.
48 Terry Eagleton, *The Ideology of the Aesthetic* (Oxford: Blackwell, 1990), p. 201.
49 Stevenson, *Jekyll and Hyde*, p. 32.
50 Stevenson, *Jekyll and Hyde*, pp. 95–96.
51 Stevenson, *Jekyll and Hyde*, p. 89.
52 Punter, *The Literature of Terror*, vol. 2, p. 205.

3 The psychopathology of everyday narcissism

1 Wilde, *Dorian Gray*, p. 214.
2 Henry Maudsley, *The Pathology of the Mind: A Study of Its Distempers, Deformities and Disorders* (London: Macmillan, 1895), p. 314.
3 Benjamin, *Charles Baudelaire*, p. 96.
4 Wilde, *Dorian Gray*, p. 117.
5 Herein lies one of Wilde's many slippery contradictions and echoes, for the intoxicating effect of the flowers of Covent Garden reflects the effects of Dorian's use of opium in the Docklands of the east of London. This employing of a west–east axis as the paradigm for anxieties about intoxication and addiction reaches its apotheosis in the discussion of addiction in Part III of this book.
6 Wilde, *Dorian Gray*, p. 118.
7 Wilde, *Dorian Gray*, pp. 159–60.
8 Wilde, *Dorian Gray*, p. 57.
9 Wilde, *Dorian Gray*, pp. 182, 184–85.
10 Wilde, *Dorian Gray*, pp. 50, 57.
11 Wilde, *Dorian Gray*, p. 173.
12 Wilde, *Dorian Gray*, pp. 48, 49.
13 Wilde, *Dorian Gray*, p. 81.
14 Wilde, *Dorian Gray*, p. 14.
15 Miller, *Doubles*, p. 227.
16 Wilde, *Dorian Gray*, p. 49.
17 Wilde, *Dorian Gray*, p. 27
18 Wilde, *Dorian Gray*, p. 50.
19 Wilde, *Dorian Gray*, p. 83.
20 Wilde, *Dorian Gray*, p. 226.
21 The representation of the devil as an heroic figure can be traced from Milton, through the work of many of the Romantic and Gothic writers of the late eighteenth and early nineteenth century, and into the work of the French symbolist poets who influenced Wilde. Mario Praz's discussion of the changes in the char-

acter of Satan from Milton onwards is perhaps the seminal one; see the chapter 'The Metamorphosis of Satan', in *The Romantic Agony*, trans. Angus Davidson (Oxford: Oxford University Press, [1933] 1970), pp. 53–94.

22 Wilde, *Dorian Gray*, p. 254.
23 Wilde, *Dorian Gray*, pp. 174, 175.
24 Wilde, *Dorian Gray*, pp. 41–42.
25 Wilde, *Dorian Gray*, pp. 43, 65.
26 Wilde, *Dorian Gray*, pp. 83–84.
27 Miyoshi, *The Divided Self*, p. 319.
28 Wilde, *Dorian Gray*, pp. 225, 190.
29 Wilde, *Dorian Gray*, p. 172.
30 Miyoshi, *The Divided Self*, p. 311.
31 Wilde, *Dorian Gray*, p. 160.
32 Wilde, *Dorian Gray*, p. 160.
33 For Dorian's obsession with different art forms and Wilde's sumptuous description of them, see chap. 12 in *Dorian Gray* in particular.
34 Wilde, *Dorian Gray*, p. 156.
35 Wilde, *Dorian Gray*, pp. 177, 179.
36 Wilde, *Dorian Gray*, pp. 218, 221.
37 Wilde, *Dorian Gray*, pp. 179, 222.
38 Wilde, *Dorian Gray*, p. 173.
39 Punter, *The Literature of Terror*, vol. 2, p. 8.
40 Wilde, *Dorian Gray*, p. 180.
41 Wilde, *Dorian Gray*, p. 192.
42 Wilde, *Dorian Gray*, p. 199.
43 Wilde, *Dorian Gray*, pp. 202–03.
44 Wilde, *Dorian Gray*, p. 220.
45 Wilde, *Dorian Gray*, p. 220.
46 Wilde, *Dorian Gray*, p. 229.
47 Wilde, *Dorian Gray*, p. 261.
48 Wilde, *Dorian Gray*, p. 261.
49 Wilde, *Dorian Gray*, p. 262.
50 Wilde, *Dorian Gray*, p. 263.

Part II: The stripping of the halo

Introduction

1 Marx and Engels, *The Communist Manifesto*, p. 82.
2 Andrew Scull, *Social Order/Mental Disorder: Anglo-American Psychiatry in Historical Perspective* (London: Routledge, 1989), p. 235.
3 The figures can be found in Black's *Dissertation on Insanity* (London: Ridgeway, 1810); they are also collated in Richard Hunter and Ida Macalpine's *Three Hundred Years of Insanity: 1535–1860* (London: Oxford University Press, 1963), p. 646. See also Roy Porter, *Mind Forg'd Manacles: A History of Madness in England from the Restoration to the Regency* (Harmondsworth: Penguin, 1990), pp. 33–34 for Black's report and pp. 121–29 for a history and account of Bethlem

Hospital.

4 For an account of early philosophical and theological testimonies of religious madness, including discussions of St Paul and Erasmus, see M. A. Screech, 'Good Madness in Christendom', in *The Anatomy of Madness: Essays in the History of Psychiatry*, vol. 1, *People and Ideas*, ed. W. F. Bynum, Roy Porter and Michael Shepherd (London: Tavistock Publications, 1985), pp. 25–39. For St Paul's views see 1 Cor. 1:25 and 2 Cor. 5:13.

5 For a brief discussion of 'Religious Melancholy' from Burton to the early nineteenth century see Porter, *Mind Forg'd Manacles*, pp. 62–81.

6 Thomas Arnold, *Observations on the Nature, Kinds, Causes and Prevention of Insanity* (London: Phillips & Macmillan, [1782–86] 1806), p. 203.

7 George Man Burrows, *Commentaries on the Causes, Forms, Symptoms and Testament, Moral and Medical, of Insanity* (London: Underwood, 1828), p. 33.

8 W. A. F. Browne, *What Asylums Were, Are and Ought to Be* (Edinburgh: Adam & Charles Black, 1837), p. 33.

9 For an account of the Oxford Movement and Tractarianism see Elizabeth Jay, *Faith and Doubt in Victorian Britain* (London: Macmillan, 1986), p. 24; for its effect on the major Victorian poets see Bernard Richards, *English Poetry of the Victorian Period: 1830–1890* (London: Longman, 1988), p. 219. For a study of the National Secular Society and its aims see Tom Leonard, *Places of the Mind: the Life and Work of James Thomson (B.V.)* (London: Jonathan Cape, 1993), pp. 128–29.

4 A life of death

1 Henry Maudsley, *Natural Causes and Supernatural Seemings* (London: Kegan Paul, Trench & Co., 1887), pp. 250–51.

2 For the origins of 'St Simeon Stylites' (1842) see *Tennyson: A Selected Edition*, ed. Christopher Ricks (London: Longman, 1989), pp. 124–25.

3 Leigh Hunt, *Church of England Quarterly Review*, 12 (October 1842), pp. 361–76. See also *Tennyson: A Selected Edition*, p. 125.

4 Maudsley, *Natural Causes*, p. 249.

5 Maudsley's choice of simile is interesting when we consider that Tennyson includes apes within the poem itself; they are the form taken the devils that apparently appear and torment Simeon: 'I smote them with the cross; they swarmed again. / In bed like monstrous apes they crushed my chest.' See Tennyson, 'St Simeon Stylites', in *The Poems of Tennyson*, ed. Christopher Ricks, 2 vols. (London: Longman, 1987), vol. 1, lines 170–71. This and all further quotes from the poem can be found in *Tennyson: A Selected Edition*, pp. 124–35.

6 Ann C. Colley, *Tennyson and Madness* (Athens: University of Georgia Press, 1983), pp. 106–07.

7 James R. Kincaid, *Tennyson's Major Poems: The Comic and Ironic Patterns* (New Haven: Yale University Press, 1975), pp. 47–48.

8 Kincaid, *Tennyson's Major Poems*, p. 47.

9 Kincaid, *Tennyson's Major Poems*, p. 48.

10 Roger S. Platizky, *A Blueprint of His Dissent: Madness and Method in Tennyson's Poetry* (London and Toronto: Associated University Presses, 1989), p. 46.

11 W. A. F. Browne, *What Asylums Were, Are, and Ought to Be* (Edinburgh: Adam & Charles Black, 1837), p. 33.

12 Platizky, *A Blueprint of His Dissent*, p. 32.
13 Platizky, *A Blueprint of His Dissent*, p. 35.
14 Platizky, *A Blueprint of His Dissent*, p. 41.
15 Platizky, *A Blueprint of His Dissent*, p. 39.
16 Maudsley, *Natural Causes*, pp. 182–83.
17 Dr Hawdon, 'The Religious Sentiment in Epileptics', *Journal of Mental Science*, January 1873. Maudsley, who was joint-editor of the journal from 1863, cites this in *Natural Causes*, p. 175.

5 But what am I?

1 From a letter by Henry Sidgwick written to Hallam Tennyson when the latter, Tennyson's son, was preparing *Alfred Tennyson: A Memoir*, 2 vols. (London: Macmillan & Co. Ltd, 1897). Sidgwick, Cambridge philosopher and author of *Methods of Ethics* (1874), gave up orthodox Christianity as intellectually untenable, marked by his resignation as a Fellow of Trinity College in 1869. He remained a lecturer and eventually became Knightbridge Professor in moral philosophy at Trinity. For an account of Sidgwick's work and his correspondence with Hallam Tennyson see Bernard M. G. Reardon, *From Coleridge to Gore: A Century of Religious Thought in Britain* (London: Longman, 1971), pp. 303–05, 367.
2 For the genesis and development of *In Memoriam*, and for an account of Hallam's death and its effect upon his contemporaries, see Ricks's notes in *Tennyson: A Selected Edition*, pp. 331–36.
3 Reardon, *From Coleridge to Gore*, p. 366.
4 See Owen Charwick, *The Victorian Church*, vol. 1 (Kent: Mackay, 1966), pp. 167–232, and Bernard Richards, *English Poetry*, p. 219, for this aspect of Tractarianism and the Oxford Movement.
5 Tennyson read Lyell's *Principles of Geology* in 1836 and 1837; see Tennyson's correspondence dated 1 November 1836 in *The Letters of Alfred Tennyson*, ed. Cecil Y. Lang and Edgar F. Shannon, 2 vols (Oxford: Clarendon Press, 1982), vols. 1, p. 145. For a brief account of Tennyson's reading of evolutionary texts see Ricks's notes in *Tennyson: A Selected Edition*, pp. 341, 396–99. For critical examinations of evolutionary theory in Tennyson's poetry see William R. Rutland, 'Tennyson and the Theory of Evolution', *Essays and Studies by the Members of the English Association*, 26 (1940), pp. 7–29, George Hough, 'The Natural Theology of *In Memoriam*', *Review of English Studies*, 33 (1947), pp. 244–56, and Walker Gibson, 'Behind the Veil: A Distinction between Poetic and Scientific Language in Tennyson, Lyell and Darwin', *Victorian Studies*, 11 (1958), pp. 60–68.
6 Ricks's note, in *Tennyson: A Selected Edition*, pp. 338–39, is a condensed but quite comprehensive survey of the structure of the poem.
7 Alfred Tennyson, *In Memoriam* (1850), XVI, lines 1–3. All further quotations from *In Memoriam* can be found in *Tennyson: A Selected Edition*, pp. 341–484.
8 Maudsley, *Pathology of the Mind*, pp. 314, 383.
9 Apart from some political poems written prior to the death of Hallam, the ABBA rhyme scheme was used exclusively by Tennyson for the poems that addressed Hallam's death; see Ricks's note in *Tennyson: A Selected Edition*, p. 338, for his

comments on the subject.
10 Jay, *Faith and Doubt*, p. 30.
11 Eric Griffiths, *The Printed Voice of Victorian Poetry* (Oxford: Clarendon Press, 1989), p. 98.
12 Colley, *Tennyson and Madness*, pp. 80–81.
13 Tennyson, *Alfred Tennyson: A Memoir*, vol. 1, p. 304.
14 George Moore, *The Power of the Soul over the Body, Considered in Relation to Health and Morals* (London: Longman, 1845), p. 4.
15 Griffiths, *The Printed Voice*, p. 152–53.
16 Miyoshi, *The Divided Self*, p. 205.
17 Arnold, 'Preface', *Poems* (1854), in *Selected Poems and Prose*, p. 129.
18 Colley, *Tennyson and Madness*, p. 132.

6 All is vanity and nothingness

1 James Thomson, *Poems, Essays and Fragments*, ed. John M. Robertson (London: A. & H. B. Bonner, 1892), p. 262.
2 See Leonard, *Places of the Mind*, p. 192, for the publishing history of the poem.
3 See Leonard, *Places of the Mind*, pp. 83–84 for the launching of the *National Reformer*. The words of the advertisement are Bradlaugh's, quoted from Hypatia Bradlaugh Bonner, *Charles Bradlaugh: A Record of His Life and Work*, 2 vols. (London: Fisher Unwin, 1898), vol. 1, p. 120–21.
4 For the structure of the poem see Leonard, *Places of the Mind*, p. 191.
5 James Thomson, 'The City of Dreadful Night', I, lines 36–42.
6 Benjamin, *Charles Baudelaire*, p. 36.
7 Benjamin, *Charles Baudelaire*, pp. 48–53. I will discuss the *flâneur* in greater detail in Part III of this book.
8 James Thomson, 'William Blake', *National Reformer*, 14 January–4 February, 1866. Quoted in *Poems, Essays and Fragments*, pp. 142–43.
9 Arnold, *Observations*, p. xx.
10 Maudsley, *Natural Causes*, p. 158.
11 For an account of Maudsley's philosophy, see Vieda Skultans (ed.), *English Madness: Ideas on Insanity, 1580-1890* (London: Routledge & Kegan Paul, 1979), pp. 131–35.
12 Henry Maudsley, *Responsibility in Mental Disease* (London: Henry S. King & Co., 1874), p. 273.
13 Maudsley, *Natural Causes*, p. 86.
14 Maudsley, *Natural Causes*, p. 85.
15 Moore, *The Power of the Soul*, p. 4.
16 Moore, *The Power of the Soul*, p. 9.
17 Henry Maudsley, *Body and Mind* (London: Macmillan, 1873), p. 76.
18 Maudsley, *Responsibility in Mental Disease*, p. 272.
19 Leonard, *Places of the Mind*, p. 144.

7 Dead letters

1 From a letter to Robert Bridges (poet and Hopkins's correspondent and literary executor) written on 1 September 1885. Included in *The Letters of Gerard Manley Hopkins to Robert Bridges*, ed. C. C. Abbott (Oxford: Oxford University Press,

1935), p. 221. See also *Poems and Prose of Gerard Manley Hopkins*, ed. W. H. Gardner (Harmondsworth: Penguin, 1985), pp. 239–40.

2 Platizky, *A Blueprint of His Dissent*, p. 13. Platizky's interpretation of the poem, in terms of the relationship between the speaker and audience, is Lacanian. He identifies Simeon's words as an attempt to appropriate aspects of the self that exist in the other (i.e. the audience); it is this narcissistic action, intended to integrate and complete a sense of self, that Platizky claims corresponds with Lacan's 'mirror' stage. For Platizky the angel represents Simeon's idealized self, and it is the playful withholding of the crown at the climax of the poem that indicates or is symptomatic of Simeon's fluctuating self-esteem and feelings of alienation. See Platizky, *A Blueprint of His Dissent*, pp. 13–14 for this reading of the poem. For Lacan's definition of the 'mirror' stage see Jacques Lacan, *Ecrits: A Selection*, trans. A. Sheridan (London: Tavistock, 1977), especially pp. 1–29, and *The Four Fundamental Concepts of Psycho-Analysis*, trans. A. Sheridan, ed. J. A. Miller (Harmondsworth: Penguin, 1986).

3 See *The Poetical Works of Gerard Manley Hopkins*, ed. Norman H. Mackenzie (Oxford: Clarendon Press, 1990), pp. 443–45, for comprehensive notes on the selection and ordering of the so-called 'terrible sonnets'. The six poems are named after their respective opening words except for 'Carrion Comfort', which was given its title by Robert Bridges in the first edition of Hopkins's collected works; see Mackenzie's note, p. 455. It was Bridges who gave the poems the title 'terrible sonnets': in the 'Preface to Notes' for *Poems of Gerard Manley Hopkins*, ed. Robert Bridges (London: Humphrey Milford, 1918), p. 101, Bridges expresses 'high admiration and respect' for the 'terrible posthumous sonnets'. Other critics have preferred to name them the 'sonnets of desolation' or the 'dark sonnets' – see Mackenzie, p. 443. I have chosen the title given by Bridges, it is also the one used by Daniel A. Harris in *Inspirations Unbidden: The 'Terrible Sonnets' of Gerard Manley Hopkins* (Berkeley and Los Angeles: University of California, 1982), to which I will refer. Harris identifies the six sonnets in manuscript form in folios 29, 31, 33 and 35 found in the Bodleian Library, Oxford. It is these folios that Harris refers to in his work, and which are reproduced in facsimile in his appendices; see Harris, *Inspirations Unbidden*, pp. 147–63.

4 In this sense the poems by Hopkins are the most devastating articulation of personal despair and self-fragmentation encountered in this section so far. Tennyson's 'St Simeon Stylites', in spite of its cultural topicality, remains ostensibly a dramatic work and Simeon a grotesque and pitiful figure. In *In Memoriam* the poetic voice resolves itself and dispels doubt by evading the schism between reason and belief that it creates for itself, resulting in a return to the assurance offered by orthodox faith and poetic genre and convention. In Thomson's 'The City of Dreadful Night' we encounter a poetic voice that is at times confident, assertive, even empowered by the knowledge of its own despair. In Hopkins's sonnets the poetic voice really does seem to evoke abandonment and desolation.

5 J. H. Miller, *The Disappearance of God: Five Nineteenth Century Writers* (New York: Schoken, [1963] 1965), pp. 352–53.

6 Richards, *English Poetry*, p. 219.

7 See Patricia A. Wolfe, 'The Paradox of Self: A Study of Gerard Manley Hopkins's Spiritual Conflict in the "Terrible Sonnets"', *Victorian Poetry*, 6 (1968), pp. 80–91.

Wolfe claims that '[t]he sonnets represent successive stages in the poet's progression towards a resolution' and '[a]s the redeemed he finally establishes a relationship with God [by] surrendering his mortal selfhood to the immortal selfhood of God' (p. 85). See also W. H. Gardner, *Gerard Manley Hopkins: A Study of Poetic Idiosyncrasy in Relation to Poetic Tradition*, 2 vols. (Oxford: Oxford University Press, [1949] 1966), vol. 2, pp. 339, 345, 360.

8 Harris, *Inspirations Unbidden*, p. 7. Harris questions the ordering of the poems both in Hopkins's manuscripts and Bridges's editing of the first edition, thereby challenging positivist, sequential readings of the poems; see pp. 7–8.

9 Harris, *Inspirations Unbidden*, p. 8.

10 Harris, *Inspirations Unbidden*, p. 10.

11 Harris, *Inspirations Unbidden*, pp. 11–12.

12 From 'I Wake and Feel', lines 12–14, *Poems* (1918). All further citations from the 'terrible sonnets' can be found in *The Poems of Gerard Manley Hopkins*, ed. W. H. Gardner and N. H. Mackenzie (Oxford: Oxford University Press, 1967), pp. 99–103.

13 See Harris's note on the loss of natural imagery and the change in poetic method in Hopkins's writing, *Inspirations Unbidden*, p. 3.

14 W. David Shaw, *The Lucid Veil: Poetic Truth in the Victorian Age* (London: Athlone Press, 1987), p. 151.

15 Harris, *Inspirations Unbidden*, p. 77.

16 See Harris's discussion of this in chap. 4 of *Inspirations Unbidden*, titled 'Poetry and the Ministry', pp. 129–44. Harris summarizes Hopkins's own perception of the antagonism between his priestly and poetic vocations on pp. 130–31.

17 Yvor Winters, *The Function of Criticism* (Denver: Alan Swallow, 1957), suggests that Hopkins 'is a poet of fragments for the most part, and it is only if one can enjoy a chaos of details afloat in vague emotion that one can approve the greater part of his work (p. 145). In the 'terrible sonnets' the fragmentation of the poems and of the vocal self is intrinsic to the experience of chaos and abandonment depicted within them.

18 Howard W. Fulweiler, *Letters From the Darkling Plain: Language and the Grounds of Knowledge in the Poetry of Arnold and Hopkins* (Columbia: University of Missouri Press, 1972), p. 137.

19 Harris defines the colloquy within the Ignatian meditations as 'the central and climactic occasion towards which the entire meditative exercise should move' (*Inspirations Unbidden*, p. 80). The exercises are analyzed structurally and discussed in terms of function, progress and achievement by the same writer, pp. 80–88. They can be found in Ignatius Loyola, *The Spiritual Exercises*, trans. Thomas Corbishley (Westminster: Christian Classics, 1973).

20 Arnold, *Observations*, p. 203. What is interesting about Arnold's account is that it contains an oscillation between 'intoxication' and 'depression'; such a motion is balanced, albeit in terms of the positive and negative icons of religious culture, by Fulweiler's depiction of the change in Hopkins's poetic personality.

21 Maudsley, *Natural Causes*, p. 234.

22 See Tennyson, 'St Simeon Stylites', line 2.

23 See Tennyson, *In Memoriam*, II, line 4.

24 Thomson, 'The City of Dreadful Night', I, lines 1–2.

25 In the land of Sheol 'the light is as darkness' and in Thomson's City 'The sun has never visited that city, / For it dissolveth in the daylight fair' ('The City of Dreadful Night', I, lines 6–7).

26 I will not list the references systematically, just offer examples. God, at the start of chap. 38, speaks to Job 'out of the whirlwind' (Job 38:1) and see Job's last words to his three friends, 'let thistles grow instead of wheat, and cockle instead of barley' (Job 31:40).

27 Thus allowing the poet the opportunity to give the prophet in his poem the ironic words 'Good tidings of great joy for you, for all: / There is no God'.

28 Ignatius Loyola, *Spiritual Exercises*, p. 109.

29 From 'The Leaden Echo and the Golden Echo', first published in *Poems* (1918). See *The Poems of Gerard Manley Hopkins* (1967), pp. 91–93.

30 See *In Memoriam*, XXXV, lines 3–4, and 'The City of Dreadful Night', XIV, lines 52–53.

31 'Spelt From Sibyl's Leaves', line 2; first published *Poems* (1918). See *The Poems of Gerard Manley Hopkins* (1967), pp. 97–98.

32 'That Nature is a Heraclitean Fire', *Poems* (1918). See *The Poems of Gerard Manley Hopkins* (1967), pp. 105–06.

33 Tennyson, *In Memoriam*, XXXIV, lines 1–4.

34 Again it is significant that the primary cause of admission into Bedlam, tabulated by William Black and referred to at the start of this section, is 'Disappointments, Grief'.

35 It is interesting to note that desolation or an appropriate experiential synonym is applied to many of the religious delusions of the insane, Arnold referring to it as the 'horrors of despair' and Maudsley as the feeling of being 'forsaken by God'. See Arnold, *Observations*, p. 203, and Maudsley, *Natural Causes*, p. 234.

36 Harris, *Inspirations Unbidden*, p. 106.

37 Harris, in *Inspirations Unbidden*, notes the extraordinarily explosive experience that Hopkins strives to represent: 'Turned against itself, converting God's creation into a mirror of the natural self, the mind distorts normal categories of space, scale, relation: in a metaphor of extraordinary emotive force, the skull bursts to encompass images of the earth's giant formations. As imagination becomes fearfully and destructively measureless ... structure dissolves, interchanges between perceiver and object become blurred, the perceiver loses grasp of his own modes of sensory perception' (pp. 51–52). For Harris, Hopkins's use of natural imagery at this point in the poem takes on an hallucinatory aspect, with the mind itself possessing a disturbing and overwhelmingly interiorized topography. Ironically, what Harris suggests can be read as a parody of orthodox Christian beliefs; by stating that Hopkins converts 'God's creation into a mirror of the natural self', there is a hint that what the poet is doing is trying to transform nature into his own image – a fundamentally blasphemous practice. The significance of Harris's statement lies in his emphasis on the distortion of 'normal categories of space [and] scale' and the 'images of the earth's gigantic formations'; once again we are reminded, through Harris's reading of 'No Worst', of the evolutionary section of *In Memoriam*, where Tennyson evokes an immense geological/theological landscape of 'scarped cliff and quarried stone' and of 'the great world's altar stairs', and of the vast time-scheme of 'Infinite Aeons' in Thomson's 'The City of Dreadful Night'. What is

also significant is that Harris states that 'fantasy dominates' (p. 51) in Hopkins's poem. In *Natural Causes*, Henry Maudsley argues that '[w]hen imagination withdraws entirely from the domain of the supernatural, and ceases to fashion the absolute into form, then prayer and worship must cease to have meaning for mankind; and when that comes to pass, if it ever comes to pass, man may be a wiser, but not perhaps happier, being than he is now' (p. 147). What Maudsley anticipates is the thorough secularization of a society, so much so that it can no longer collectively imagine the 'absolute'. In many ways this prediction parallels the experience that Harris reads in Hopkins's poem. There the divine is no longer incarnate in creation, rather the poet rereads creation in his own form; similarly poetic imagination, rather than entering into a colloquy with the absolute through prayer or meditation, reconfigures itself in a union with an overwhelming natural landscape where 'interchanges between perceiver and object become blurred'. With the failure of the imagination to encapsulate the absolute, the imagination (the mind) becomes a thing to fear, as do the immediate surroundings (the landscape) that it perceives. In such a psychic environment prayer ceases to have any meaning, as Hopkins's 'terrible sonnets' demonstrate.

38 See Maudsley, *Natural Causes*, p. 234.

39 Harris, *Inspirations Unbidden*, p. 113.

Part III: Infected ecstasy

Introduction

1 Daniel Noble, *Elements of Psychological Medicine* (London: John Churchill, 1853), p. 238. Also cited in Vieda Skultans, *Madness and Morals: Ideas on Insanity in the Nineteenth Century*, (London: Routledge, 1975), p. 55.

2 Benjamin, p. 55.

3 The last example is an interesting if unusual instance of addiction which, due to its taboo qualities, can be viewed as akin to sexual trangression rather than more conventional acts of consuming to excess. A link can, of course, be suggested between the cannibal and the vampire in nineteenth-century Gothic fiction. For an informed discussion of the cannibal in the nineteenth century see H. L. Malchou, *Gothic Images of Race in Nineteenth-Century Britain* (Stanford: Stanford University Press, 1996), especially pp. 100–01.

4 William Black, *Dissertation on Insanity*; cited in Hunter and Macalpine, *Insanity*, p. 646.

5 Victoria Berridge and Griffith Edwards, *Opium and the People: Opiate Use in Nineteenth Century England* (London: Allen Lane, 1981), p. 278, state that '*addiction* is the word which is popularly in use to describe compulsive drug taking'. They go on to indicate that 'opiates are drugs of addiction' (p. 278), and offer a useful description of the process of opiate addiction: 'Opiates are drugs to which the individual's central nervous system will, on repeated exposure, develop a high degree of tolerance – a much bigger dose of the drug is then required to produce the same and desired effect in the tolerant than in the naive subject. There is therefore in the drug's intrinsic properties a ready and in-built invitation to escalate the dose (p. 278).

6 Berridge and Edwards, *Opium and the People*, p. 24. Berridge and Edwards go on to state, without hyperbole, that '[e]veryone had laudanum at home' and comment that '[t]he extent of such sales (i.e. of laudanum) was barely realised in mid-Victorian Britain' (p. 29).

7 Berridge and Edwards, *Opium and the People*, p. 21.

8 Such sedatives are cited by Althea Hayter in *Opium and the Romantic Imagination* (London: Faber and Faber, 1968), p. 31.

9 See Berridge and Edwards, *Opium and the People*, p. 65.

10 Burrows, *Commentaries*, pp. 21–23.

11 William Willis Moseley, *Eleven Chapters on Nervous and Mental Complaints* (London: Simpkin & Marshall, 1838), cited in Skultans, *Madness and Morals*, p. 45.

12 Moseley, *Eleven Chapters*, cited in Skultans, *Madness and Morals*, p. 46.

13 Berridge and Edwards, *Opium and the People*, p. 33.

14 Berridge and Edwards note that in 1863 the rate of fatal overdose per 1,000,000 of the populace was 6.1 (*Opium and the People*, p. 34).

15 Porter, *Mind Forg'd Manacles*, p. 132. See also J. V. Pickstone, *Medicine and Industrial Society: A History of Hospital Development in Manchester and Its Region, 1752–1946* (Manchester: Manchester University Press, 1985), pp. 14–15.

16 Porter, *Mind Forg'd Manacles*, p. 185.

17 Berridge and Edwards, *Opium and the People*, p. 36. They cite the cotton famine in Lancashire in the 1860s as a time when supplies of opium were drastically limited; purchases of even a pennyworth were difficult.

18 Berridge and Edwards, *Opium and the People*, p. 281.

19 Elizabeth Gaskell, *Mary Barton* (Harmondsworth: Penguin, [1848] 1970), p. 219.

20 Elizabeth Gaskell, *Mary Barton*, pp. 412–13.

21 Gaskell refers explicitly to the industrial labouring classes as a Frankenstein's monster in *Mary Barton*: 'The actions of the uneducated seem to me typified in those of Frankenstein, that monster [*sic*] of many human qualities, ungifted with a soul, a knowledge of the difference between good and evil … Why have we made them what they are; a powerful monster, yet without the inner means for peace and happiness' (pp. 219–20). Gaskell's comparing of the proletariat with Gothic fantasy is also utilized by Marx in *Capital*, as I will demonstrate later in this section of the book. However, it is again noteworthy that Gothic devices lend themselves to discussions of class, fears of class division and the social and cultural significance of capital. As Franco Moretti points out in his essay 'Dialectic of Fear: Towards a Sociology of the Modern Monster', '[t]he literature of terror is born precisely *out of the terror of a split society*' (Moretti's emphasis); see his *Signs Taken for Wonders: Essays in the Sociology of Literary Forms*, trans. Susan Fischer, David Forgacs and David Miller (London: Verso, [1983] 1988), p. 83. Moretti's basic premise is that Dracula and Frankenstein's monster represent capital and the worker respectively, a notion that I will refer to in my discussion of *Dracula*, and one that again stems fundamentally from Marx. In Gaskell's *Mary Barton*, John Barton is linked emphatically with the mindless proletariat automaton that can be equated with Frankenstein's invention, yet he can also be associated with the addict-criminal whom we encounter as the vampire Count of Stoker's *Dracula*. As a supplement to this discussion, it is interesting that William Booth, founder of the Salvation Army, observed in 1890 that 'some men of science hold that persistence

in habits tends to convert a man from a being with freedom of action and will into a mere automaton. There are some cases within our knowledge which seem to confirm the somewhat dreadful verdict by which a man appears to be a lost soul on this side of the grave' (see *In Darkest England and the Way Out* [London: Salvation Army, 1890], pp. 204–05). It would appear that the correlation between addict (for which read Booth's 'persistence in habits') and automaton and spectre is not just manifest in fictional writing or political economy. It is also significant that at this point in his discussion Booth is assessing the role of asylums for what he refers to as the 'morally demented' (p. 204). What I am indicating is that Gothic metaphors for addiction appear in a variety of different texts throughout the nineteenth century.

22 See Karl Marx, *Capital*, trans. Ben Fowkes, vol. 1 (Harmondsworth: Penguin, [1867] 1990), chap. 10,'The Working Day', pp. 340–416. This is the chapter where most of Marx's significant analogies can be found; subsections in this chapter include 'The Voracious Appetite for Surplus Labour' (p. 344), indicating Marx's concern with the rampant overconsumption of capitalism. I will explore Marx's use of Gothic metaphor at a later point in this section, in a discussion of the relationship between addiction, capital and the spectre in the work of the writers under scrutiny. However, it is significant that Gaskell chooses to represent the addicted proletariat as spectral in *Mary Barton*.

8 A change in physical economy

1 Thomas De Quincey, *Confessions of an English Opium Eater* (Harmondsworth: Penguin, [1821] 1986), p. 88.

2 At one point De Quincey claims to be consuming 320 grains of opium or 8,000 drops of laudanum on a daily basis (*Confessions*, p. 89). Althea Hayter, in her introduction to the Penguin edition of the *Confessions*, suggests that this is impossible and an exaggeration by the author, a significant factor in this discussion of De Quincey's writing; see *Confessions*, p. 14.

3 De Quincey, *Confessions*, p. 89.

4 De Quincey, *Confessions*, p. 102. 'These patterns seen when the eyes are closed are now known as hypnagogic vision', Hayter's note, *Confessions*, p. 222.

5 De Quincey, *Confessions*, p. 29.

6 Hayter makes this observation, and notes that De Quincey's mother was converted by the dissenting sect known as the Clapham Saints (*Confessions*, p. 17).

7 De Quincey, *Confessions*, pp. 99–100.

8 De Quincey, *Confessions*, p. 101.

9 De Quincey, *Confessions*, p. 71.

10 De Quincey, *Confessions*, p. 43.

11 De Quincey, *Confessions*, p. 45.

12 De Quincey, *Confessions*, p. 46.

13 V. A. De Luca, *Thomas De Quincey: The Prose of Vision* (Toronto: University of Toronto Press, 1980), p. 12.

14 De Luca, *Thomas De Quincey*, pp. 12–13. Hayter notes that '[t]he privations he then suffered were the cause of the painful gastric disease for which he began to take opium as a regular anodyne ten years later', see De Quincey, *Confessions*, p. 10.

15 De Luca, *Thomas De Quincey*, p. 13.

16 De Quincey, *Confessions*, p. 55. The name concealed by the dash is that of De Quincey's father, Thomas Quincey [*sic*]. It seems ironic that in a text so concerned with attempts to assert identity, De Quincey should use concealing dashes to maintain his anonymity.

17 De Quincey, *Confessions*, pp. 80–81.

18 Benjamin, *Charles Baudelaire*, pp. 36–37. Benjamin's study of Baudelaire and Paris frequently echoes the direction taken by De Quincey's narrative; both writers oscillate between indulgence and guilt, De Quincey between the pleasures of opium and the inability to write under its influence, Benjamin between being drawn aesthetically to Baudelaire's city and its attractions and yet seeing it as hollow and oppressive. Both are ambivalent about renouncing their vices.

19 In fact Benjamin identifies the earliest literary *flâneur* as Edgar Allan Poe's protagonist in the story 'The Man of the Crowd', first published in *Burton's Gentleman's Magazine* (1840) and revised for *Tales of the Grotesque and Arabesque* (1845); see Benjamin, *Charles Baudelaire*, p. 54.

20 Benjamin, *Charles Baudelaire*, p. 55.

21 De Quincey, *Confessions*, pp. 81–82.

22 Berman, *All That Is Solid*, p. 132. This is a notion that Benjamin concurs with in his discussion of Baudelaire; see the section on 'modernity' in Benjamin, *Charles Baudelaire*, pp. 67–101.

23 De Quincey's contribution to the discourse of modernity can be problematized when one considers Berman's definition of the symbols of modern life in art cited earlier in this project. To reiterate: Berman states that '[f]luidity and vaporousness will become primary qualities in the self-consciously modern painting, architecture and design, music and literature, that will emerge at the end of the nineteenth century'. This statement is significant when one considers that the *Confessions* frequently involve a representation of the fluidity of De Quincey's literary identity that oscillates between manifestations such as street urchin, proto-*flâneur* and political economist. It is interesting that De Quincey's relationship with modernity should be so problematic, particularly considering the way in which he distances himself from Rousseau by drawing attention to a specifically 'English' response to the expression of emotions. Berman argues that Rousseau 'is the first to use the word *moderniste* in the ways in which the nineteenth and twentieth centuries will use it (Berman, *All That Is Solid*, p. 17), further alienating De Quincey's relationship with modernity. As stated already, the title of Berman's book refers to Marx and Engels's comment on the dissolution of stability in modernity from the *Communist Manifesto*, where '[a]ll that is solid melts into air, all that is holy is profane, and man is at last compelled to face with sober senses, his real conditions of life, and his relations with his kind'. It is possible to see that in De Quincey's *Confessions* the first clause of Marx and Engels's maxim rings true, certainly in terms of the extreme moments of De Quincey's opium addiction; however, the emphasis upon sobriety and community is at odds with the sense of alienation represented in the *Confessions*. The association between De Quincey and Marx will be made clearer as this discussion develops. To return briefly to the opening discussion in this section of the book, it is also significant that the oscillating and unlocated nature of opium in the nineteenth century

echoes the 'fluidity and vaporousness' that Berman ascribes to modernity, perhaps suggesting that opium is one of the first tools of nineteenth century, post-industrial modernity – anodyne for the working classes and commodity for the bourgeoisie.

24 De Quincey, *Confessions*, p. 50.

25 De Quincey, *Confessions*, p. 52.

26 Deborah Epstein Nord, 'The Urban Peripatetic: Spectator, Streetwalker, Woman Writer', *Nineteenth Century Literature*, 26:3 (December 1991), pp. 351–75 (351).

27 Nord, 'The Urban Peripatetic', pp. 353–55.

28 De Quincey, *Confessions*, p. 81.

29 De Quincey, *Confessions*, pp. 105–06.

30 De Quincey, *Confessions*, p. 106.

31 It is opportune to note that the other addict in Gaskell's text is also a streetwalker – the prostitute Esther, Mary Barton's aunt, who is, along with her other 'vice', an alcoholic.

32 De Quincey, *Confessions*, p. 71.

33 Again Berman's notion of the vaporous in modern culture seems to be evoked; what is the druggist in De Quincey's terms if not a vaporous being? The disappearance itself is reminiscent of Krook's spontaneous combustion in *Bleak House*.

34 De Quincey, *Confessions*, p. 82.

35 De Quincey, *Confessions*, p. 78.

36 'The opium sold and used in England for most of the century came not from India or China, but from Turkey' (Berridge and Edwards, *Opium and the People*, p. 3). One of their reference points is the text by 'W. B. E.', *A Short History of Drugs and Other Commodities, the Produce and Manufactory of the East Indies* (London, eighteenth century, exact date uncertain), which states that opium came 'chiefly ... from Turkey, where they prepare it much better than what comes from India' (p. 47).

37 De Quincey, *Confessions*, p. 90.

38 De Quincey, *Confessions*, p. 90.

39 De Quincey, *Confessions*, p. 91.

40 De Quincey, *Confessions*, p. 91.

41 De Quincey, *Confessions*, p. 91.

42 De Quincey, *Confessions*, p. 92.

43 De Quincey, *Confessions*, p. 97.

44 De Quincey, *Confessions*, pp. 103–04.

45 De Quincey, *Confessions*, pp. 102, 107.

46 It is possible that De Quincey's representation of this shift outside a sense of temporality and history can be read as an instance of Francis Barker's conception of disidentity, that 'bucolic pastoral' where identity relinquishes 'any conceivable burden of responsibility either for the past or the future'. In many ways, out of all the conditions analyzed in this project, De Quincey's might conceivably lend itself to Barker's reading of the condition. Two things contradict such a conclusion, however: firstly, the state as represented by De Quincey is hardly an idyll, secondly, the account provided is obviously too self-conscious to concur with Barker's definition.

47 De Quincey, *Confessions*, p. 108.

48 De Quincey, *Confessions*, p. 108.

49 In his seminal survey of European construction of the east, Edward Said notes that '[t]he Orient was overvalued for its pantheism, its spirituality, its stability, its longevity, its primitivity, and so forth'; certainly De Quincey's representation of the Orient fits in with Said's model, drawing attention to facets of Eastern religion and its historical longevity. Said goes on to comment that 'the Orient [also] appeared lamentably under-humanized, antidemocratic, backward, barbaric and so forth', again De Quincey's 'antediluvian' Chinese and the 'mystic sublimity of *castes*' perhaps concurs with Said; see Edward Said, *Orientalism* (London: Routledge, 1978), p. 150. Said notes that Orientalism depends upon constructing a series of relationships between West and East 'without [the Westerner] ever losing ... the upper hand' (p. 7); De Quincey does seem to focus upon his own individuality confronted with a collective conception of the Orient, nonetheless at this point in his account the Opium Eater seems to be in awe, fearful of and overwhelmed by the East rather than demonstrating intrinsic superiority, drawing further attention to the instability of identity.

50 Alan Sinfield, in his study of Tennyson, suggests that early nineteenth-century writing negotiates a relationship between centres and margins, with British utilitarian society representing the centre, and both poetry and the East representing the margins, a notion that will be examined in more detail in the next chapter of this section. However, at this point in De Quincey's text it can be argued that De Quincey has become marginalized, in spite of being English, as he explores the space between the Ganges and the Euphrates where civilization seems to have its origins. The hypothetically central location of England is therefore displaced as the East becomes the point of generation for nations.

51 De Quincey, *Confessions*, p. 114.

52 De Quincey, *Confessions*., p. 109.

53 De Quincey, *Confessions*, p. 109.

54 De Quincey, *Confessions*, p. 110.

55 De Quincey, *Confessions*, p. 109.

56 De Quincey, *Confessions*, pp. 111–12.

57 The city of Jerusalem replaces the space between the Ganges and the Euphrates as the centre for civilization; it is, however, an antiquated location, having its origins as the centre of the world in medieval thinking.

58 See De Luca, *Thomas De Quincey*, p. xi, and De Quincey, *Confessions*, p. 75.

59 Marx and Engels, *The Communist Manifesto*, pp. 113–14.

9 Coming like ghosts to trouble joy

1 De Quincey, *Confessions*, p. 107.

2 Alfred Tennyson, 'The Lotos Eaters', *Poems* (1833; revised 1842). All citations can be found in *Tennyson: A Selected Edition*, pp. 70–79.

3 The comments by Hallam can be found in Armstrong, *Victorian Scrutinies*, pp. 92–93.

4 For further details see Alan Sinfield, *Alfred Tennyson* (Oxford: Blackwell, 1986), 'The Politics of Poetry', pp. 11–56.

5 Alan Sinfield, *Alfred Tennyson*, p. 19.

6 Alan Sinfield, *Alfred Tennyson*, p. ix.

7 Sinfield argues that Tennyson is involved ultimately in 'metaphorically … a kind of colonisation and trade: the poet throws his imagination out to the periphery, plants himself as securely as he can there, adapting all that he finds to his project, and brings back to the mother country a rich hoard' (p. 50). The correlation between colonization, addiction and culture is a significant factor in the present discussion.
8 Sinfield, *Alfred Tennyson*, p. 44.
9 Tennyson, 'The Palace of Art', *Poems* (1833; revised 1842). See *Tennyson: A Selected Edition*, pp. 50–70.
10 Armstrong, *Victorian Poetry*, pp. 78–79.
11 Armstrong, *Victorian Poetry*, p. 79. The commodification of art is significant in the poem if we consider that in an early draft of 'The Palace of Art' Tennyson wrote, in depicting one of the tapestries on display, that it 'seemed a place of mart. The seller held / The buyer's hand, and winked and smiled, / And pointed to his wares.' See *Tennyson: A Selected Edition*, p. 59–60.
12 Sinfield, *Alfred Tennyson*, p. 39.
13 Sinfield, *Alfred Tennyson*, p. 40.
14 Sinfield, *Alfred Tennyson*, p. 39.
15 Armstrong, *Victorian Poetry*, p. 77.
16 Armstrong, *Victorian Poetry*, p. 87.
17 Armstrong, *Victorian Poetry*, p. 87.
18 Again it might be possible, as with the collapse of linear temporality in De Quincey's *Confessions*, to read the condition depicted by Tennyson as concurring with Francis Barker's definition of disidentity. However, what the mariners *seek* is such a state of consciousness (i.e. to be oblivious of past and future); here they, like so many of the other examples provided in this project, are profoundly conscious of past, future (in their yearning for the oblivion offered by the Lotos) and in particular of the conditions defining the present.
19 Armstrong, *Victorian Poetry*, p. 87.
20 Armstrong, *Victorian Poetry*, p. 87.
21 Sinfield, *Alfred Tennyson*, p. 53. 'Ulysses' was first published in *Poems* (1842); see *Tennyson: A Selected Edition*, pp. 138–45.
22 Marx and Engels, *The Communist Manifesto*, p. 84.
23 Armstrong, *Victorian Poetry*, p. 88.
24 Armstrong, *Victorian Poetry*, p. 90.

10 Like honey to the throat but poison to the blood

1 Christina Rossetti, 23 April 1891; cited Kathleen Jones, *Learning Not to Be First: The Life of Christina Rossetti* (Oxford: Oxford University Press, 1992), p. 215.
2 Biographies include Lona Mosk Packer's *Christina Rossetti* (Cambridge: Cambridge University Press, 1963), and Georgina Battiscombe, *Christina Rossetti: A Divided Life* (London: Constable, 1981).
3 Jones, *Not to Be First*, p. 232.
4 Kathleen Jones cites Mrs Radcliffe, 'Monk' Lewis and Charles Maturin as examples of Rossetti's juvenile reading predilections; see Jones, *Not to Be First*, p. 12.
5 Mary Shelley's *Frankenstein* was first published in 1818. For her subjective and rather unreliable account of the genesis of both *Frankenstein* and *The Vampyre*, see

her introduction to the edition of 1831 – the words 'wet ungenial summer' are hers – which is included in *Frankenstein*, ed. Maurice Hindle (Harmondsworth: Penguin, 1986), pp. 6–10. This edition also contains Polidori's *The Vampyre* in its appendices; see pp. 233–55. For recent discussions of *The Vampyre* see James Twitchell, *The Living Dead: A Study of the Vampire in Romantic Literature* (Durham: Duke University Press, 1981), pp. 103–15, and Ken Gelder's *Reading the Vampire* (London: Routledge, 1994), pp. 26–34. Gelder draws attention to the fact that early literary representations of vampires were located in Greece – also citing Byron's poem 'The Giaour: A Fragment of a Turkish Tale' of 1813 – at an historical moment when Greece was under Turkish rule; see Gelder, *Reading the Vampire*, p. 26. The tension between Greece and Turkey is significant in terms of representations of addiction and the literary vampire, features that have already been established in De Quincey's *Confessions* and Tennyson's 'The Lotos Eaters', and which reach an interesting pitch in my discussion of Bram Stoker's *Dracula*.

6 David F. Morrill, '"Twilight is Not Good for Maidens": Uncle Polidori and the Psychodynamics of Vampirism in "Goblin Market"', *Victorian Poetry*, 28.1XXVIII:1 (Spring 1990), pp. 1–16 (1).

7 Christina Rossetti, 'Goblin Market', *Goblin Market and Other Poems* (1862), lines 132–39. All further citations are from *The Complete Poems of Christina Rossetti*, ed. R. W. Crump (Baton Rouge and London: Louisiana State University Press, 1979), pp. 11–26.

8 Concern about the hypodermic use of morphine only really started to develop amongst the medical professions in the last quarter of the nineteenth century, a period of time which also saw the emergence of the addict as a medical identity. Indeed, it is possible to view the final decades of the century as involving a conflict in medical opinion between the dangers of opium and morphine abuse, a conflict that echoes the tension between oral consumption and dermal penetration in *Dracula*. For an assessment of morphine use and the hypodermic needle at the close of the nineteenth century see Berridge and Edwards, *Opium and the People*, p. 135–49.

9 See D. M. R. Bentley, 'The Meretricious and the Meritorious in "Goblin Market": A Conjecture and an Analysis', in *The Achievement of Christina Rossetti*, ed. David A. Kent (Ithaca and London: Cornell University Press, 1987), pp. 57–81 (58).

10 Mary Wilson Carpenter, '"Eat Me, Drink Me, Love Me": The Consumable Female Body in Christina Rossetti's "Goblin Market"', *Victorian Poetry*, 29.4 (Winter 1991), pp. 415–34 (416).

11 Nancy Armstrong, 'The Occidental Alice', *Differences*, 2 (Summer 1990), pp. 3–40 (17). See also Wilson Carpenter, 'Eat Me, Drink Me', p. 415, for an analysis of the correlation between consumer capitalism, imperialist culture and 'Goblin Market'.

12 Wilson Carpenter, 'Eat Me, Drink Me', p. 415.

13 *On Penitentiary Work ... Two Sermons Preached at the Opening of the Chapel of St Mary's Home, Wantage, July 30, 1861, by Samuel [Wilberforce], Lord Bishop of Oxford, and Henry Parry Liddon, M. A., with a Short Preface on Sisterhoods by W. J. Butler, M. A., Vicar of Wantage* (Oxford and London, 1861), p. 19.

14 *On Penitentiary Work*, p. 20.

15 C. E. Terry and M. Pellens, *The Opium Problem* (New York: Bureau of Social

Hygiene, 1928), p. 470. It is also possible to note that Joseph Sheridan Le Fanu, in his short story 'Carmilla' – an erotically charged lesbian vampire story - presents the vampire Carmilla as having 'golden hair and blue eyes'; see Joseph Sheridan Le Fanu, 'Carmilla', from *In a Glass Darkly* (1872), collected in *The Penguin Book of Vampire Stories*, ed. Alan Ryan (Harmondsworth: Penguin, 1988), p. 86. Bram Stoker knew Le Fanu's short story well and it influenced his own vampire narrative considerably, originally siting *Dracula* in Styria from whence Carmilla comes; for an account of this influence see Clive Leatherdale, *Dracula: The Novel and the Legend. A Study of Bram Stoker's Gothic Masterpiece* (Wellingborough: Aquarian Press, 1985), pp. 59, 88.

16 Judith R. Walkowitz, *Prostitution and Victorian Society: Women, Class and the State* (Cambridge: Cambridge University Press, 1980), p. 3. For further associations between the female body, sexuality and disease in cultural representation, see Charles Bernheimer, *Figures of Ill Repute: Representing Prostitution in Nineteenth Century France* (Cambridge, MA: Harvard University Press, 1989), p. 2, where Bernheimer states that the fear of contamination – given medical validation by 'theories of degenerate heredity and syphilitic infection' – resulted in representations of the female body as the site of 'animality, disease, castration, excrement, and decay'.

17 Berridge and Edwards, *Opium and the People*, p. 150. They go on to note that it 'was indeed a medical "growth area" in the last decades of the century. No textbook was complete without its section on the "morphia habit", "morphinism" or "acute and chronic poisoning by opium"', p. 152.

18 See Berridge and Edwards, *Opium and the People*, pp. 152, 155. Berridge and Edwards state that medical thinking, despite applying the 'formulations of insanity', frequently chose to view addiction as slightly different to insanity. Addicts were regarded as abnormal or neurotic rather than insane (p. 157). However, as they point out, the structure of discourse is markedly similar.

19 Berridge and Edwards, *Opium and the People*, pp. 159–60.

20 Wilson Carpenter, 'Eat Me, Drink Me', p. 422.

21 J. St Thomas Clarke, letter to the *British Medical Journal*, 2 (1882), p. 540.

22 This association between class and addiction can also be detected in Marshall Berman's suggestion that the modern individual must actively and compulsively 'yearn for change' in a way that corresponds with the social changes operating around them, and in Richard Dellamora's description of the middle-class dandy who 'consumes to excess'. Both notions are conflated in Stevenson's *Jekyll and Hyde*, where the bourgeois Jekyll is ultimately unable to control his transformation into the parasitic Hyde.

23 Berridge and Edwards, *Opium and the People*, p. 164.

24 See Lewis Carroll, *Alice's Adventures in Wonderland* (1865), in *The Annotated Alice*, ed. Martin Gardener (Harmondsworth: Penguin, 1965), pp. 31, 33. Wilson Carpenter addresses the correspondence between 'Goblin Market' and the Alice stories, pointing to the similar themes in terms of consumer culture with reference to Nancy Armstrong's essay 'The Occidental Alice' (see Wilson Carpenter, 'Eat Me, Drink Me', 415).

25 The bird imagery is significant when it is considered that Judith Walkowitz, in *City of Dreadful Delight*, p. 22, refers to groups of prostitutes as 'soiled doves'.

Frequently there seems to be an element in the poem that can be regarded as homoerotic, Laura and Lizzie share the same bed and the injunction to 'Eat me, drink me, love me' is erotically charged; that said, the two characters are clearly represented as sisters and the poem affirms that 'there is no friend like a sister (line 562). Wilson Carpenter dismisses the hint of an implicit sexual element in the relationship between Laura and Lizzie, stating that 'the poem excludes difference between the two girls or women in order to focus on women's common plight as commodities in the linked capitalist and sexual economies' (p. 426); she argues that the poem deals with the tension between desire and repression where '[t]he sisters represent women's double plight in the Victorian sexual economy: either risk becoming a commodity yourself, or never tasting desire' (p. 428). For the purposes of the present argument, therefore, the commodification of women and its correlation with prostitution is at stake rather than any homoerotic undertones.

11 The blood is the life: Bram Stoker's infected capital

1 From Charlotte Stoker's account of 'The Cholera Horror' in a letter to Bram Stoker (*c.* 1875), cited in Harry Ludlum, *A Biography of Dracula: The Life Story of Bram Stoker* (Slough: W. Foulsham, 1962), pp. 25–31.

2 For the context and reasons behind Charlotte Stoker's letter, see Maurice Hindle's editorial notes in the Penguin edition of Bram Stoker's *Dracula* (Harmondsworth: Penguin, 1993), p. 498. Stoker's novel was first published in 1897; all further citations are from the Penguin edition.

3 Stoker, *Dracula*, p. 76.

4 Stoker, *Dracula*, p. 35.

5 Ken Gelder, *Reading the Vampire*, indicates such a paradox in his discussion of the vampire hunter Van Helsing's advocating of the practice of hypnosis, stating that it 'is consistent with his tendency to believe in the unbelieveable, to maintain an "open mind": his claim that hypnosis "would have been deemed unholy" ... by less up-to-date scientists provides an interesting auto-critique of his own view of the "unholy" vampire (is Van Helsing, then, not up-to-date with Dracula?)'; for Van Helsing's comments see Stoker, *Dracula*, p. 247. Such paradoxes, whether conscious or not on Stoker's behalf, occur with noticeable frequency in the text; for example, Van Helsing refers to his medical bag as containing 'the ghastly paraphernalia of our beneficial trade' (p. 157), unfortunately labelling the tools that are designed to detect and destroy the vampire with as sinister an adjective as those applied to the undead Count himself.

6 Stoker gives this phrase to the addicted lunatic Renfield who issues the injunction repetitively: 'over and over again' (see Stoker, *Dracula*, pp. 184, 301). The words probably stem from the Old Testament Book of Deuteronomy: 'Only be sure that thou eat not the blood: for the blood *is* the life; and thou mayest not eat the life with the flesh' (12:23), indicating again the ambivalent status that orthodox religion possesses in the text.

7 Halberstam, *Skin Shows*, p. 99. Seward diagnoses Renfield as 'zoophagous', stating that '[m]y homicidal maniac is of a peculiar kind. I shall have to invent a new classification for him, and call him a zoophagous (life-eating) maniac; what he desires is to absorb as many lives as he can, and he has laid himself out to achieve it in a

cumulative way. He gave many flies to one spider and many spiders to one bird, and then wanted a cat to eat the many birds' (Stoker, *Dracula*, pp. 95–96). This condition, with its compulsive 'cumulative' shift along the food chain, is just one of the connections that can be established between lunatic, addict and vampire in Stoker's text. The equation is given greater resonance when Van Helsing's single reference to his wife is considered. He refers to her as 'dead to me , but alive by Church's law, though with no wits' (p. 227), effectively giving her the same qualities as the undead *and* linking her to Renfield as the other lunatic in the text, who in his own right is associated emphatically with Dracula. If this is not enough evidence for the hypothesis, at the point in the narrative that these words are uttered, Van Helsing suggests that his blood transfusion, given to the vamped Lucy, has made him a 'bigamist' (p. 227), suggesting another correlation between the conditions under scrutiny.

8 Christopher Frayling, *Vampyres: Lord Byron to Count Dracula* (London: Faber & Faber, 1991), p. 39. Rymer's *Varney the Vampire, or, The Feast of Blood* can be found in an edition edited by Devendra P. Varma (New York: Arno Press, 1970). Gelder states that 'Varney was so huge … that it might have seemed as if Rymer himself was driven by "irresistible forces" he could not control' (*Reading the Vampire*, p. 21), suggesting that the writing of vampire texts is also a compulsive activity in itself, a feature that will become increasingly significant in this discussion.

9 Field's 'A Kiss of Judas' was first published in the *Pall Mall Magazine* (1894) and reprinted in his collection of stories *Aut Diabolus Aut Nihil* in the same year. It is reprinted by Frayling, *Vampyres*, from which the quotation is taken, p. 230. Mary Braddon's *Good Lady Ducayne* was first published in 1896; Frayling, *Vampyres*, provides a brief analysis, pp. 58–59.

10 Stoker, *Dracula*, pp. 123, 167. For further narcotic administration see p. 160; the addictive propensity of the blood transfusions is highlighted when Van Helsing baldly states '[s]he want blood, and blood she must have or die' – uneasily reminiscent of the vampiric transaction itself.

11 Stoker, *Dracula*, p. 134.

12 Stoker, *Dracula*, pp. 186–87.

13 Indeed, Stoker himself, paradoxically given the intoxicating dynamics and strategies employed within his text, referred to popular novels as 'noxious drugs' and 'intoxicants' in his essay 'The Censorship of Fiction', *Nineteenth Century*, 64 (1908), pp. 479–87 (483, 485).

14 Paul O'Flinn, 'Production and Reproduction: The Case of *Frankenstein*', in *Popular Fictions: Essays in Literature and History*, ed. Paul Humm, Paul Stigant and Peter Widdowson (London: Methuen, 1986), pp. 167–219 (197).

15 Gelder, *Reading the Vampire*, p. 65.

16 Punter, *The Literature of Terror*, vol. 2, p. 16.

17 Gelder, *Reading the Vampire*, p. 65.

18 Stoker, *Dracula*, p. 93.

19 Stoker, *Dracula*, p. 82.

20 See Gelder, *Reading the Vampire*, p. 65.

21 Byron, 'The Giaour: A Fragment of a Turkish Tale' (1813), lines 755–68; cited in *Byron*, ed. Jerome J. McGann (Oxford: Oxford University Press, 1986), pp. 207–

47; all further references to the poem are from this edition.

22 Gelder, *Reading the Vampire*, p. 27. For an account of the political and historical context of 'The Giaour' see Daniel P. Watkins, *Social Relations in Byron's Eastern Tales* (Cranbury: Associated University Presses, 1987).

23 Gelder, *Reading the Vampire*, p. 36.

24 Note on line 755 of 'The Giaour', *Byron*, p. 245.

25 See Rennell Rodd, *The Customs and Lore of Modern Greece* (Chicago: Argonaut, [1892] 1968), p. 188. Gelder describes the text as 'partly a late Victorian travelogue, and partly an ethnographic work with scientific pretensions (*Reading the Vampire*, p. 38), a definition which is loosely applicable to Stoker's *Dracula* itself.

26 Rodd, *Modern Greece*, p. 188.

27 Gelder, *Reading the Vampire*, p. 12.

28 Stoker, *Dracula*, p. 8.

29 Stoker, *Dracula*, p. 42.

30 Stoker, *Dracula*, p. 43.

31 See for example Stoker's working papers for *Dracula*, reproduced by Frayling, *Vampyres*, pp. 303–47.

32 Gelder, *Reading the Vampire*, p. 1.

33 For further details about Vlad IV see Frayling's account, *Vampyres*, pp. 77–79.

34 An example of Stoker's selective and partial treatment of Eastern European history is that Dracula has the family tree of a Szekely, yet the Szekelys were Hungarian rather than Transylvanian.

35 Stoker, *Dracula*, p. 309.

36 Punter, *The Literature of Terror*, vol. 2, p. 22.

37 Gelder, *Reading the Vampire*, p. 25.

38 Stoker, *Dracula*, p. 39.

39 Cited by Frayling, *Vampyres*, p. 20; pp. 19–23 deal with the extent of the vampire epidemics in some detail.

40 Frayling, *Vampyres*, p. 24.

41 Berridge and Edwards, *Opium and the People*, pp. 6–7. In the context of a discussion presenting a correlation between the opium trade and vampirism, Berridge and Edwards' phrasing is strangely ambivalent; the 'hermetically sealed' cases suggest airtight containers, but also ones that have been sealed by occult means.

42 Stoker, *Dracula*, p. 108.

43 Stoker, *Dracula*, p. 109.

44 Stoker, *Dracula*, pp. 439–40.

45 Gelder, *Reading the Vampire*, p. 12. Indeed the process is one of reverse colonization as Stephen Arata argues; Arata suggests that *Dracula* reveals the anxiety of a seemingly stable imperialist nation that it can be invaded and absorbed by something more imperial than itself – colonization is effectively brought back to the colonizers. See Stephen D. Arata, 'The Occidental Tourist: Dracula and the Anxiety of Reverse Colonisation', *Victorian Studies*, 33 (1990), pp. 621–46.

46 Stoker, *Dracula*, p. 71.

47 Marx and Engels, *The Communist Manifesto*, p. 84.

48 Berridge and Edwards, *Opium and the People*, p. 149.

49 Berridge and Edwards, *Opium and the People*, p. 149.

50 Cited Berridge and Edwards, *Opium and the People*, p. 145.

51 See Stoker, *Dracula*, pp. 228–30.
52 Stoker, *Dracula*, pp. 208–09.
53 Stoker, *Dracula*, p. 272.
54 Rossetti, 'Goblin Market', lines 266–27. The 'baulked desire' of the poem effectively mirrors the frustrated 'baffled malice' of Lucy's cravings in Stoker's novel.
55 Maudsley, *Body and Mind*, pp. 82–83.
56 Stoker, *Dracula*, p. 229.
57 Stoker, *Dracula*, p. 55.
58 Jennifer Wicke, 'Vampiric Typewriting: *Dracula* and its Media', *English Literary History*, 59 (1992), pp. 467–93 (474).
59 Lucy's vampiric activity provides an interesting point of comparison with Stevenson's Hyde, who, as bourgeois dandy, consumes to excess, is equated with and dependent upon capital, and circulates through the arteries of the city.
60 Benjamin, *Charles Baudelaire*, p. 58.
61 Stoker, *Dracula*, p. 38.
62 Stoker, *Dracula*, p. 62.
63 Stoker, *Dracula*, pp. 438–39.
64 Maudsley, *Body and Mind*, pp. 63–64.
65 Maudsley, *Body and Mind*, pp. 129–30, 249.
66 Stoker, *Dracula*, p. 28.
67 Stoker, *Dracula*, pp. 25, 222–23.
68 Stoker, *Dracula*, p. 363.
69 See Benjamin, *Charles Baudelaire*, pp. 50–52. His reference points are Dickens's letters of the 1840s, Stevenson's essay 'A Plea for Gas Lamps' and Poe's short story 'The Man of the Crowd'.
70 Benjamin, *Charles Baudelaire*, p. 51.
71 Wicke, 'Vampiric Typewriting', p. 469.
72 Gelder, *Reading the Vampire*, p. 141.
73 Karl Marx, *Capital*, trans. Ben Fowkes, vol. 1 (Harmondsworth: Penguin , 1990), p. 342.
74 Gelder, *Reading the Vampire*, pp. 21–22.
75 Halberstam, *Skin Shows*, p. 102.
76 Wicke, 'Vampiric Typewriting', p. 471.
77 Marx, *Capital*, p. 344.
78 Stoker, *Dracula*, p. 31.
79 See Marx's footnote in *Capital*, p. 348, and Frayling, *Vampyres*, p. 84.
80 Frayling, *Vampyres*, p. 84.
81 Punter, *The Literature of Terror*, vol. 1, p. viii.
82 Freud's essay of 1919 can be found in the *Standard Edition of the Complete Psychological Works*, trans. James Strachey, vol. 17 (London: Hogarth Press, 1955), pp. 218–56.
83 Eagleton, *Ideology of the Aesthetic*, p. 200.
84 Stoker, *Dracula*, pp. 393–94.
85 Stoker, *Dracula*, p. 66.
86 Wicke, 'Vampiric Typewriting', p. 490.

Conclusion

1 T. S. Eliot, 'The Burial of the Dead', *The Waste Land*, lines 60–65.
2 Halberstam, *Skin Shows*, p. 85.
3 Wicke, 'Vampiric Typewriting', pp. 467–68.
4 Eliot, 'The Burial of the Dead', *The Waste Land*, line 65.

Bibliography

Arata, Stephen D., 'The Occidental Tourist: *Dracula* and the Anxiety of Reverse Colonization', *Victorian Studies*, 33 (1990), pp. 621–46.

Armstrong, Isobel, *Victorian Poetry: Poetry, Poetics and Politics* (London: Routledge, 1993).

——, *Victorian Scrutinies: Reviews of Poetry 1830–1870* (London: Athlone Press, 1972).

Armstrong, Nancy, 'The Occidental Alice', *Differences*, 2 (Summer 1990), pp. 3–40.

Arnold, Matthew, *Selected Poems and Prose*, ed. Miriam Allott (London: Everyman, 1993).

Arnold, Thomas, *Observations on the Nature, Kinds, Causes and Prevention of Insanity*, 2 vols. (London: Phillips & Macmillan, [1782–86] 1806).

Ballard, J. G., *The Terminal Beach* (London: Victor Gollancz, [1964] 1997).

Barker, Francis, *The Culture of Violence: Essays on Tragedy and History* (Manchester: Manchester University Press, 1993).

Battiscombe, Georgina, *Christina Rossetti: A Divided Life* (London: Constable, 1981).

Benjamin, Walter, *Charles Baudelaire: A Lyric Poet in the Era of High Capitalism*, trans. Harry Zohn (London: Verso, 1983).

Bentley, D. M. R., 'The Meretricious and the Meritorious in "Goblin Market": A Conjecture and an Analysis', in *The Achievement of Christina Rossetti*, ed. David Kent (Ithaca and London: Cornell University Press, 1987), pp. 57–81.

Berman, Marshall, *All That Is Solid Melts into Air: The Experience of Modernity* (London: Verso, 1983).

Bernheimer, Charles, *Figures of Ill Repute: Representing Prostitution in Nineteenth Century France* (Cambridge, MA: Harvard University Press, 1989).

Berridge, Victoria, and Griffith Edwards, *Opium and the People: Opiate Use in Nineteenth Century England* (London: Allen Lane, 1981).

Black, William, *Dissertation on Insanity* (London: Ridgeway, 1810).

Bonner, Hypatia Bradlaugh, *Charles Bradlaugh: A Record of His Life and Work (With an Account of His Parliamentary Struggle, Politics and Teaching by John M. Robertson)*, 2 vols. (London: Fisher Unwin, 1898).

Booth, William, *In Darkest England and the Way Out* (London: Salvation Army, 1890).

Botting, Fred, *Gothic* (London: Routledge, 1996).

Browne, W. A. F, *What Asylums Were, Are, and Ought to Be* (Edinburgh: Adam & Charles Black, 1837).

Burrows, George Man, *Commentaries on the Causes, Forms, Symptoms and Testament, Moral and Medical, of Insanity* (London: Underwood, 1828).

Bynum, W. F., Roy Porter and Michael Shepherd (eds.), *The Anatomy of Madness*, 3 vols. (London: Tavistock, 1984).

Byron, Gordon Noel, *Byron*, ed. Jerome J. McGann (Oxford: Oxford University Press, 1986).

Carpenter, Mary Wilson, '"Eat Me, Drink Me, Love Me": The Consumable Female Body in Christina Rossetti's "Goblin Market"', *Victorian Poetry*, 29.4 (Winter 1991), pp. 415–34.

Carroll, Lewis, *Alice's Adventures in Wonderland* (1865), in *TheAnnotated Alice*, ed. Martin Gardener (Harmondsworth: Penguin, 1960).

Chadwick, Edwin, *Report on an Enquiry into the Sanitary Conditions of the Labouring Population of Great Britain* (London: W. Clowes, 1842).

Chamberlain, J. Edward, and Sander L. Gilman, *Degeneration: The Dark Side of Progress* (New York: Colombia University Press, 1985).

Charwick, Owen, *The Victorian Church*, 2 vols. (Kent: Mackay, 1966).

Clarke, J. St Thomas, 'Letter', *British Medical Journal*, 2 (1882).

Colley, Ann C., *Tennyson and Madness* (Athens: University of Georgia Press, 1983).

Dellamora, Richard, *Masculine Desire: The Sexual Politics of Victorian Aestheticism* (Chapel Hill and London: University of North Carolina Press, 1990).

De Luca, V. A., *Thomas De Quincey: The Prose of Vision* (Toronto: University of Toronto Press, 1980).

De Quincey, Thomas, *Confessions of an English Opium Eater* (Harmondsworth: Penguin, [1821] 1986).

Descartes, René, *Discourse on Method and the Meditations*, trans. F. E. Sutcliffe (Harmondsworth: Penguin, [1637] 1968).

———, *Meditations on First Philosophy, with Selections from the Objections and Replies*, trans. John Cottingham (Cambridge: Cambridge University Press, [1641] 1986).

Dickens, Charles, *Bleak House* (Harmondsworth: Penguin, [1853] 1985).

Doane, Janice, and Devon Hodges, 'Demonic Disturbances of Sexual Identity: The

Strange Case of Dr Jekyll and Mr/s Hyde', *Novel: A Forum on Fictions*, 23 (1989), pp. 63–74.

Eagleton, Terry, *The Ideology of the Aesthetic* (Oxford: Blackwell, 1990).

Eliot, T. S., *The Complete Poems and Plays of T. S. Eliot* (London: Faber & Faber, 1975).

Elliotson, John, 'On the Joint Operation of the Two Halves of the Brain: With a Notice of Dr Wigan's Work Entitled *The Duality of the Mind*, etc.', *The Zoist*, 15 (1847).

Ellis, Havelock, *The New Spirit* (London: Constable & Co., [1896] 1926).

Favret, Mary A., and Nicola J. Watson (eds.), *At the Limits of Romanticism: Essays in Cultural, Feminist, and Materialist Criticism* (Bloomington and Indianapolis: Indiana University Press, 1994).

Foucault, Michel, *The Archaeology of Knowledge*, trans. A. M. Sheridan-Shaw (London: Tavistock Publications, [1969] 1972).

———, 'The Dangerous Individual', in *Michel Foucault: Politics, Philosophy, Culture; Interviews and Other Writings 1977–1984*, ed. Lawrence Kritzman (London: Routledge, 1988).

———, *The History of Sexuality*, trans. R. Hurley, vol. 1 (Harmondsworth: Penguin, [1976] 1981).

Fox, W. J., *Monthly Repository*, 6 (January 1832), pp. 1–4.

Frayling, Christopher, *Vampyres: Lord Byron to Count Dracula* (London: Faber & Faber, 1991).

Freud, Sigmund, 'The Uncanny', in *Standard Edition of the Complete Psychological Works*, trans. James Strachey, vol. 17 (London: Hogarth Press, 1955).

Fukuyama, Francis, *The End of History and the Last Man* (Harmondsworth: Penguin, 1992).

Fulweiler, Howard W., *Letters from the Darkling Plain: Language and the Grounds of Knowledge in the Poetry of Arnold and Hopkins* (Columbia: University of Missouri Press, 1972).

Gardner, W. H., *Gerard Manley Hopkins: A Study of Poetic Idiosyncrasy in Relation to Poetic Tradition*, 2 vols. (London: Oxford University Press, [1949] 1966).

Gaskell, Elizabeth, *Mary Barton* (Harmondsworth: Penguin, [1848] 1970).

Gelder, Ken, *Reading the Vampire* (London: Routledge, 1994).

Gibson, William, *Neuromancer* (London: Voyager, [1986] 1995).

Gibson, Walker, 'Behind the Veil: A Distinction between Poetic and Scientific Language in Tennyson, Lyell and Darwin', *Victorian Studies*, 11 (1958), pp. 60–68.

Graves, Robert, and Raphael Patai, *Hebrew Myths: The Book of Genesis* (London: Arena, [1964] 1989).

Greenslade, William, *Degeneration, Culture and the Novel 1880–1940* (Cambridge: Cambridge University Press, 1994).

Griffiths, Eric, *The Printed Voice of Victorian Poetry* (Oxford: Clarendon Press, 1989).

Halberstam, Judith, *Skin Shows: Gothic Horror and the Technology of Monsters* (Durham and London: Duke University Press, 1995).

Hallam, Arthur Henry, 'On Some of the Characteristics of Modern Poetry', *Englishman's Magazine*, August 1831.

Harrington, Anne, *Medicine, Mind and the Double Brain: A Study in Nineteenth Century Thought* (New Jersey: Princeton University Press, 1987).

Harris, Daniel A., *Inspirations Unbidden: The 'Terrible Sonnets' of Gerard Manley Hopkins* (Berkeley and Los Angeles, University of California, 1982).

Hawdon, Dr R., 'The Religious Sentiment in Epileptics', *Journal of Medical Science*, January 1873.

Hayter, Althea, *Opium and the Romantic Imagination* (London: Faber & Faber, 1968).

Heath, Stephen, 'Psychopathia Sexualis: Stevenson's *Strange Case*', *Critical Quarterly*, 28 (1986), pp. 93–108.

Hogg, James, *The Private Memoirs and Confessions of a Justified Sinner* (Harmondsworth: Penguin, [1824] 1983).

Hopkins, Gerard Manley, *Poems and Prose of Gerard Manley Hopkins*, ed. W. H. Gardner (Harmondsworth: Penguin, 1985).

———, *Poems of Gerard Manley Hopkins*, ed. Robert Bridges (London: Humphrey Milford, 1918).

———, *The Letters of Gerard Manley Hopkins to Robert Bridges*, ed. C. C. Abbott (Oxford: Oxford University Press, 1935).

———, *The Poems of Gerard Manley Hopkins*, ed. W. H. Gardner and Norman H. Mackenzie (Oxford: Oxford University Press, 1967).

———, *The Poetical Works of Gerard Manley Hopkins*, ed. Norman H. Mackenzie (Oxford: Clarendon Press, 1990).

Hough, Graham, 'The Natural Theology of *In Memoriam*', *Review of English Studies*, 33 (1947), pp. 244–56.

Humm, Paul, Paul Stigant and Peter Widdowson (eds.), *Popular Fictions: Essays in Literature and History* (London: Methuen, 1986).

Hunt, Leigh, *Church of England Quarterly Review*, 12 (October 1842), pp. 361–76.

Hunter, Richard, and Ida Macalpine, *Three Hundred Years of Insanity: 1535–1860* (London: Oxford University Press, 1963).

Jay, Elizabeth, *Faith and Doubt in Victorian Britain* (London: Macmillan, 1986).

Jones, Kathleen, *Learning Not to Be First: The Life of Christina Rossetti* (Oxford: Oxford University Press, 1992).

Kent, David (ed.), *The Achievement of Christina Rossetti* (Ithaca and London: Cornell University Press, 1987).

Kincaid, James R., *Tennyson's Major Poems: The Comic and Ironic Patterns* (New Haven: Yale University Press, 1975).

Lacan, Jacques, *Écrits: A Selection*, trans. A. Sheridan (London: Tavistock, 1977).

———, *The Four Fundamental Concepts of Psycho-Analysis*, ed. J. A. Miller, trans. A. Sheridan (Harmondsworth: Penguin, 1986).

Leatherdale, Clive, *Dracula: The Novel and the Legend. A Study of Bram*

Stoker's Gothic Masterpiece (Wellingborough: Aquarian Press, 1985).

Leonard, Tom, *Places of the Mind: The Life and Works of James Thomson ('B. V.')* (London: Jonathan Cape, 1993).

Lombroso, Cesare, *The Man of Genius* (London: Walter Scott, 1891).

Loyola, Ignatius, *The Spiritual Exercises*, trans. Thomas Corbishley (Westminster: Christian Classics, 1973).

Ludlum, Harry, *A Biography of Dracula: The Life Story of Bram Stoker* (Slough: W. Foulsham, 1962).

Lyotard, Jean-Francois, *The Postmodern Condition: A Report on Knowledge*, trans. G. Bennington and B. Massumi (Manchester: Manchester University Press, 1984).

Malchou, H. L., *Gothic Images of Race in Nineteenth-Century Britain* (Stanford, CA: Stanford University Press, 1996).

Marx, Karl, *Capital*, trans. Ben Fowkes, vol. 1 (Harmondsworth: Penguin, 1990).

———, and Friedrich Engels, *The Communist Manifesto*, trans. Samuel Moore (Harmondsworth: Penguin, [1888] 1985).

———, *The Marx–Engels Reader*, ed. Robert C. Tucker (New York: Norton, 1978).

Maudsley, Henry, *Body and Mind* (London: Macmillan, 1873).

———, *Natural Causes and Supernatural Seemings* (London: Kegan Paul & Co., 1887).

———, *Responsibility in Mental Disease* (London: Henry S. King & Co., 1874).

———, *The Pathology of the Mind: A Study of Its Distempers, Deformities and Disorders* (London: Macmillan, 1895).

Miller, J. Hillis, *The Disappearance of God: Five Nineteenth Century Writers* (New York: Schoken, [1963] 1965).

Miller, Karl, *Doubles: A Study in Literary History* (Oxford: Oxford University Press, 1985).

Miyoshi, Masao, *The Divided Self: A Perspective on the Literature of the Victorians* (New York: New York University Press, 1969).

Moore, George, *The Power of the Soul over the Body, Considered in Relation to Health and Morals* (London: Longman, 1845).

Morretti, Franco, *Signs Taken for Wonders: Essays in the Sociology of Literary Forms*, trans. Susan Fischer, David Forgacs and David Miller (London: Verso, [1983] 1988).

Morrill, David F. '"Twilight Is Not Good for Maidens": Uncle Polidori and the Psychodynamics of Vampirism in "Goblin Market"', *Victorian Poetry*, 28.1 (1990), pp. 1–16.

Moseley, William Willis, *Eleven Chapters on Nervous and Mental Complaints* (London: Simpkin & Marshall, 1838).

Noble, Daniel, *Elements of Psychological Medicine* (London: John Churchill, 1853).

Nord, Deborah Epstein, 'The Urban Peripatetic: Spectator, Streetwalker, Woman Writer', *Nineteenth Century Literature*, 46.3 (1991), pp. 351–75.

Nordau, Max, *Degeneration* (London: Heinemann, [1895] 1898).

Nye, Robert, *Crime, Madness and Politics in Modern France: The Medical Concept of National Decline* (Princeton: Princeton University Press, 1984).

O'Flinn, Paul, 'Production and Reproduction: The Case of *Frankenstein*', in Humm, Stigant and Widdowson (eds.), *Popular Fictions*, pp. 167–219.

Packer, Lona Mosk, *Christina Rossetti* (Cambridge: Cambridge University Press, 1963).

Pickstone, J. V., *Medicine and Industrial Society: A History of Hospital Development in Manchester and Its Region 1752–1946* (Manchester: Manchester University Press, 1985).

Platizky, Roger S., *A Blueprint of His Dissent: Madness and Method in Tennyson's Poetry* (London and Toronto: Associated University Presses, 1989).

Porter, Roy, *Mind Forg'd Manacles: A History of Madness in England from the Restoration to the Regency* (Harmondsworth: Penguin, 1990).

Praz, Mario, *The Romantic Agony*, trans. Angus Davidson (Oxford: Oxford University Press, [1933] 1970).

Punter, David, *The Hidden Script: Writing and the Unconscious* (London: Routledge, 1985).

———, *The Literature of Terror: A History of Gothic Fictions from 1765 to the Present Day*, 2 vols. (London: Longman, 1996).

Reardon, Bernard M. G., *From Coleridge to Gore: A Century of Religious Thought in Britain* (London: Longman, 1971).

Redekop, Magdalene, 'Beyond Closure: Buried Alive with Hogg's *Justified Sinner*', *English Literary History*, 52 (1985), pp. 159–84.

Richards, Bernard, *English Poetry in the Victorian Period: 1830–1890* (London: Longman, 1988).

Rodd, Rennell, *The Customs and Lore of Modern Greece* (Chicago: Argonaut, [1892] 1968).

Rossetti, Christina, *The Complete Poems of Christina Rossetti*, ed. R. W. Crump (Baton Rouge and London: Lousiana State University Press, 1979).

Rutland, William R., 'Tennyson and the Theory of Evolution', *Essays and Studies by Members of the English Association*, 26 (1940), pp. 7–29.

Ryan, Alan (ed.), *The Penguin Book of Vampire Stories* (Harmondsworth: Penguin, 1988).

Rymer, James Malcom, *Varney the Vampire, or, The Feast of Blood*, ed. Devendra P. Varma (New York: Arno Press, [1847] 1970).

Said, Edward, *Orientalism* (London: Routledge, 1978).

Sandison, Alan, *Robert Louis Stevenson and the Appearance of Modernism: A Future Feeling* (London: Macmillan, 1996).

Schoenfield, Mark L., 'Butchering James Hogg: Romantic Identity in the Magazine Market', in Favret and Watson, *At the Limits of Romanticism*, pp. 201–24.

Screech, M. A., 'Good Madness in Christendom', in Bynum, Porter and Shepherd, *The Anatomy of Madness*, vol. 1, pp. 25–39.

Scull, Andrew, *Social Order/Mental Disorder: Anglo-American Psychiatry in Historical Perspective* (London: Routledge, 1989).

Seltzer, Mark, 'Serial Killers', *Differences: A Journal of Feminist Cultural Studies*, 5.1 (1993), pp. 92–128.

Shaw, W. David, *The Lucid Veil: Poetic Truth in the Victorian Age* (London: Athlone, 1987).

Shelley, Mary, *Frankenstein* (Harmondsworth: Penguin, [1818] 1986).

———, *The Last Man*, ed. Anne McWhir (Ontario: Broadview Press, [1826] 1996).

Shelley, Percy Bysshe, *The Complete Works of Percy Bysshe Shelley*, ed. Neville Rogers, vol. 2 (Oxford: Oxford University Press, 1975).

Sinfield, Alan, *Alfred Tennyson* (Oxford: Blackwell, 1986).

Skultans, Vieda (ed.), *English Madness: Ideas on Insanity, 1580–1890* (London: Routledge & Kegan Paul, 1979).

———, *Madness and Morals: Ideas on Insanity in the Nineteenth Century* (London: Routledge, 1975).

Stallybrass, Peter, and Alan White, *The Politics and Poetics of Transgression* (London: Methuen, 1986)

Stevenson, Robert Louis, *Dr Jekyll and Mr Hyde and Other Stories* (Harmondsworth: Penguin, [1886] 1979).

———, *Weir of Hermiston* (London: Heinemann, [1896] 1924).

Stoker, Bram, *Dracula* (Harmondsworth: Penguin, [1897] 1993).

———, 'The Censorship of Fiction', *Nineteenth Century*, 64 (1908), pp. 479–87.

Storey, John, *An Introductory Guide to Cultural Theory and Popular Culture* (London: Harvester Wheatsheaf, 1993).

Stratton, Jon, 'Serial Killing and the Transformation of the Social', *Theory, Culture and Society*, 13 (1996), pp. 77–98.

Sykes, Egerton, *Everyman's Dictionary of Non-Classical Mythology* (London: Dent, 1952).

Tennyson, Alfred, *Tennyson: A Selected Edition*, ed. Cristopher Ricks (London: Longman, 1989).

———, *The Letters of Alfred Lord Tennyson*, ed. Cecil Y. Lang and Edgar F. Shannon, 2 vols. (Oxford: Clarendon Press, 1982).

———, *The Poems of Tennyson*, ed. Christopher Ricks (London: Longman, 1987).

Tennyson, Hallam, *Alfred Tennyson: A Memoir*, 2 vols. (London: Macmillan & Co. Ltd, 1897).

Terry, C. E., and M. Pellens, *The Opium Problem* (New York: Bureau of

Social Hygiene, 1928).

Thomson, James (B. V.), *Poems, Essays and Fragments*, ed. John M. Robertson (London: A. & H. B. Bonner, 1892).

———, *The City of Dreadful Night and Other Poems* (London: Watts & Co., [1874] 1932).

Tropp, Martin, *Images of Fear: How Horror Stories Helped Shape Modern Culture (1818–1918)* (Jefferson, NC: McFarland & Co., 1990).

Twitchell, James, *The Living Dead: A Study of the Vampire in Romantic Literature* (Durham: Duke University Press, 1981).

Ullmann, S. O. A., 'Dating through Calligraphy: The Example of "Dover Beach"', *Studies in Bibliography*, 26 (1973), pp. 19–36.

Walkowitz, Judith R., *Prostitution and Victorian Society: Women, Class and the State* (Cambridge: Cambridge University Press, 1980).

———, *The City of Dreadful Delight* (London: Virago, 1992).

Watkins, Daniel P., *Social Relations in Byron's Eastern Tales* (Cranbury, NJ: Associated University Presses, 1987).

Wicke, Jennifer, 'Vampiric Typewriting: *Dracula* and Its Media', *English Literary History*, 59 (1992), pp. 467–93.

Wigan, Alfred, *The Duality of the Mind* (London: Longman, 1844).

Wilde, Oscar, *The Picture of Dorian Gray* (Harmondsworth: Penguin, [1891]1985).

Wilberforce, Samuel and Henry Parry Liddon, *On Penitentiary Work ... Two Sermons Preached at the Opening of the Chapel of St Mary's Home, Wantage, July 30 1861, by Samuel [Wilberforce], Lord Bishop of Oxford, and Henry Parry Liddon, M. A., with a Short Preface on Sisterhoods, by W. J. Butler, M. A., Vicar of Wantage* (Oxford and London, 1861).

Winters, Yvor, *The Function of Criticism* (Denver: Alan Swallow, 1957).

Wolfe, Patricia A., 'The Paradox of Self: A Study of Gerard Manley Hopkins' Spiritual Conflict in the "Terrible Sonnets"', *Victorian Poetry*, 6 (1968), pp. 80–91.

Wordsworth, William, *The Prelude (Text of 1805)*, ed. E. De Selincourt (London: Oxford University Press, 1933).

Yeats, W. B., *W. B. Yeats: The Poems*, ed. Richard J. Finneran (London: Macmillan, 1984).

Index